The Translated World

DEBRA A. CASTILLO

The
Translated
World

A POSTMODERN TOUR OF
LIBRARIES IN LITERATURE

Florida State University Press/Tallahassee

UNIVERSITY PRESSES OF FLORIDA

UNIVERSITY PRESSES OF FLORIDA is the central agency for
scholarly publishing of the State of Florida's university
system, producing books selected for publication by the
faculty editorial committees of Florida's nine public
universities: Florida A & M University (Tallahassee),
Florida Atlantic University (Boca Raton), Florida Inter-
national University (Miami), Florida State University
(Tallahassee), University of Central Florida (Orlando),
University of Florida (Gainesville), University of North
Florida (Jacksonville), University of South Florida
(Tampa), University of West Florida (Pensacola).
ORDERS for books published by all member presses of
University Presses of Florida should be addressed to
University Presses of Florida, 15 NW 15th Street,
Gainesville, FL 32603.

Permissions to quote from copyrighted material on p. 357.

Library of Congress Cataloging in Publication Data

Castillo, Debra A.
    The translated world.

    Bibliography: p.
    Includes index.
    1. Libraries in literature.   I. Title.
PN 56.L48C37   1985   809'. 93355   84-17200
ISBN 0−8130−0792−5 (alk. paper)

Printed in the U.S.A. on acid-free paper

CONTENTS

for Carlos

PREFACE

"LITERATURE BEGINS," SAYS Michel Foucault, "when the book is no longer the space where speech adopts a form . . . but the site where books are all recaptured and consumed."[1] Analogously, the library, a concrete visible structure, begins when the scattered documents housed under its roof are recaptured and organized according to a dream of unity imposed by a rigidly ordered catalogue and are consumed in silence and in solitude. Gradually, as the ever-larger masses of documents threaten to expand beyond human control, the librarian counters with ever more rigid structuring systems. Yet, eventually the place that was to serve as a repository of all knowledge, by the very fact of its existence comes to proclaim the inevitable failure of attempts to gather and organize the scattered documents of human production. The rigid orders intimate a brutal usurpation of power as the captive books overwhelm the captors. As the library becomes less accessible, it also becomes more fear-provoking, and that which was an essential part of the sociopolitical structure becomes a threat to structure. One kind of consumption suggests another; the library is burned.

But the myth is not destroyed. From the smouldering ruins, the librarian emerges unscathed, determined to gather once again the scattered bits of knowledge, to submit them to a new and more powerful system. Another opaque, windowless structure is built, the masses of documents begin to gather again, the librarian blindly submits himself to the delirium of a catalogue that proliferates toward infinity. The student, the librarian, turns his back on the outward visible forms, searching in books, in that mediated realm, for the unmediated truth, the secrets of being itself.

The library, then, represents a basis for spiritual communion among men and a denial of both spirituality and community. It represents a power structure and a menace to that structure. The study of the library and of the librarians who inhabit it involves, therefore, a close examination of this "site where books are all recaptured and consumed," a space of hierarchical constructions, which, because secularized, are constantly open to question as artificial and meaningless but whose orders are no less rigid or powerful because of this recognized artificiality. The study involves a history spatialized, like the library stacks and like the catalogue itself, in overlapping layers, in unlikely juxtapositions of scattered bits and pieces. It involves as well a questioning of the process by which reality is constituted, problems of mythic, metaphysical proportions, of naming, and of the relation between language and being.

The structure of the library itself suggests broadly political concerns, a history institutionalized, documents metamorphosed through juxtapositions that are far from haphazard. The library stands for a mode of knowledge that is both rational and mystical: time-laden yet timeless, free from the dismal onward movement of history. In the tight, windowless enclosure of the library walls, history is negated, parodied, and apotheosized at the same time.

For the librarian the issue is largely psychological and reflects how the human being identifies with the inhuman creation in his search for immortality (or death). Thus, the central point is not basically a question of illusion versus reality, but of illusion opposed to/joined with illumination in a willed blindness, in an inward-turning quest that is moral (sacrilegious) and, ultimately, erotic (perverse). The librarian mimics the enclosure of the library by closing the windows and doors of his body, by choosing inward visions over outside reality. He chooses, thus, the historical form of the sacred (the mystic's or the gnostic's path) without committing himself to the sacred per se; he imposes a secular law on a reality that seems too fluid, too changeable, too fatal. This adoption of a religious form, without religious substance, gives rise to a metaphysical dilemma in the librarian that forces him to exercise his waning control over reality by excluding all apparent contradictions to the monumental form he has chosen. Eventually, the library becomes the world, as the librarian cannot allow even the smallest hint of life outside the structure to remain. To do so would be to reveal a fatal flaw, to place the entire structure in danger of collapse, of burning down, and it would force him to face his own bodily existence, which is not monumental or likely to be.

In exploring the scope and significance of these political, psychological constructions, it is not my intention to praise or condemn. Rather, I wish to recognize and lay bare the workings of a structure in which I find myself deeply implicated. At the same time, I realize that my catalogue is also incomplete and flawed, marked by texts chosen for personal reasons, marred by arbitrary exclusions: a historical analysis with no similarity to a traditional literary history. In adopting this course, I have been influenced by a method whose precedents are found in the work of Erich Auerbach (*Mimesis*) and André Malraux (*The Voices of Silence*), and like them I have chosen to follow a few vital, basic motifs in a series of texts and watch as they converge in a more general conclusion. This study, like that of Auerbach, proposes no model for the discovery of the absolute; like the work of Malraux, it suggests no finality but that of death, of a death deferred through blindness and psychological defense mechanisms: the imperfect librarian ill at ease, burdened with a sense of betrayal by the world in which he must live, groping toward a new language, a new form by which to free himself from bondage. This literary, pseudomystical "lying against time" (Harold Bloom's phrase) brings about other evasions, other falsifications, other saving lies. Bloom himself contrasts a formula from Blake with one from Emerson, a folk maxim with the taboo of cannibalism, displaying the divergent workings of two forms of wisdom—or two myths, transforming "you are what you eat" to "you are what you read."

The first transformation, from bodily to spiritual food, implicates Bloom, as he recognizes, in the workings of the library, in the cataloguing and hierarchizing processes of canon formation. The canon (religious, secular) permits the transformation of food into spiritual

essence, into a text—a falsification or dream vision. The first transformation licenses a second: "let us compare two formulae: 'You
are or become what you read' and 'That which you are, that only
can you read.' The first formula gives priority to every text over
every reader; the second makes of each reader his own text."[2] The
divergent formulas—"You are what you eat" and "You eat what
you are"—not only converge in their literary transformations, but
become necessary to each other. The reader becomes the text and
the text is given priority over the reader, over every reader, over
every potential reader who accepts the canon. Canon, text, reader:
all are cannibalized, all are consumed in this lying against time. The
world is still a library, still a monument (tombstone) that houses
(buries) and preserves (transforms) the documents of Auerbach, of
Malraux, of Bloom.

What is lost in this deliberate decorporalization, in this willed
turning of the self into a book? People die, but books do not,
though they may be discarded, defaced, misunderstood, burned.
Perhaps, as Ihab Hassan suggests, "Transhumanization in a time of
torture and terrorism, of poverty, pollution, and exponential popu-
lation, may seem criminally utopian."[3] Yet, this formula too is a falsification, lying against time. I uneasily recognize that any revolution against these outrages will (must) evolve into a resumption of
the old orders in a disguised form and that, furthermore, I, as a librarian and as a character in a book, have a stake in this being so.

CHAPTER I

Introduction:
Founding the Library

BEFORE MAN'S FALL from grace in the Garden of
Eden, books were unnecessary—Adam and Eve spoke with God directly or read his will in the *abecedarium naturae* of their surroundings. With the Fall, this unmediated communication was disrupted,
and the first book—the Holy Scriptures—was required to mediate
God's word and interpret his will to a people whose vision had
clouded. Perfect understanding was lost forever, and effortless communication gave way to flawed expression. Man, when he emerged
from Eden, became conscious of his vulnerability and was consumed by the desire to cover himself. With his clothing and his
dwellings, he sheltered himself from the inclemencies of weather
and protected himself from the aggressions of man and beast. The
psychic impact of these protective devices is important: symbolically, man hides his imperfect self from others of his own kind in an
original masking that is the precursor of the Apollonian veil described by Nietzsche. Nevertheless, despite the imperfections of this
painful new existence, man was still comforted by his sense of belonging to one family with a single shared tongue. The language of
Eden, which man retained after his Fall from the paradisiacal garden, was an unclouded language free from distortion and illusion, a
language of potentially great power. The wrenching loss of Eden

was followed by a second catastrophe that further aggravated the disunity of man and changed human nature:

> And they said, Go to, let us build us a city and a tower, whose top *may reach* unto heaven; and let us make us a name lest we be scattered abroad upon the face of the whole earth. And the Lord came down to see the city and the tower, which the children of men builded. And the Lord said, Behold, the people *is* one, and they have all one language; and this they begin to do: and now nothing will be restrained from them, which they have imagined to do. Go to, let us go down, and there confound their language, that they may not understand one another's speech. So the Lord scattered them abroad from thence upon the face of all the earth: and they left off to build the city. Therefore is the name of it called Babel. (Gen. 11 : 4–9)

The men of what came to be called Babel were, in their original state, a powerful unity—what they imagined, they could achieve. They sought to further intensify this unity in the construction of a city that to them represented an ideal society, a rational order that held the potentiality for perfection. With their science they were building themselves the name of God. This threat was not allowed to go unpunished. The unity was shattered by the confusion of tongues; the tower and the city were left to fall into decay. The name sought by the men of earth was denied them, and instead of an earthly unity, the human effort was disbanded into an infernal disunity. They were allowed no name they could give themselves— instead an outside force applied to the place of their defeat an appellation of shame: "the name of it [was] called Babel." Imagination, language, name—all these are denied man by this mystic wound to the pre-Babel world of order and significance.

Thus, the first fall—from Eden—is followed by a second—from Babel. The single mediated vision gave way to a multiplicity of points of view; the Holy Book of God's unique will was lost in the welter of conflicting interpretations (the Koran, the Talmud, the Vedas, etc.) in mutually unintelligible tongues: the first library. Language passes beyond its function as a cloaking device to become an almost impenetrable barrier. As George Steiner says, with the second fall, "Men were harried . . . out of the single family of man. And they were exiled from the assurance of being able to grasp and communicate reality."[1] Inside the reconstructed tower, books gather dust upon the shelves.

This study begins with a myth, as all stories of origins must: the vast, disastrous breach with perfection can be described in no other way, as only myth has the power and overdetermination of significance to encompass such metaphysical pain. To question the origin of the poisoning of language is essentially naive, though probably unavoidable, since the problematic wound thus opened has such a strong and significant effect on man's subsequent efforts at expression. "Man today," says Nietzsche, "stripped of myth, stands famished among all his pasts and must dig frantically for roots. . . . What does our great historical hunger signify, our clutching about us of countless other cultures, our consuming desire for knowledge, if not the loss of myth, of a mythic home, the mythic womb?"[2] The search for a name continues, allied with the search for a new universal language, and the library has become the locus of this quest and symbol of its inevitable failure. From the myth of the Fall arises a new myth—that of Library Science.

The objects of myth are absolute: absolutely real, absolutely concrete, absolutely free of metaphor. Myth serves to maintain a stable relationship between the things of the world and the things of men. We do not "regress to myth" if we forget that fictions are fictive as Frank Kermode would have us believe;[3] myth is always with us in one form or another. Yesterday's myths become today's fictions when they lose their compelling numinous power, but new myths always take their place. Science is an example of such a myth that only recently has begun to reveal its fictiveness. Conversely, what we reject as part of a naive mythic past is never completely lost. Though myth loses actuality through the operations of fiction and metaphor, it remains psychologically compelling.

So we return briefly to the original myth. The Sacred Scripture represents for many the myth of an absolute text, yet the fall from Eden guaranteed its corruption and the fall from Babel, its unintelligibility. How can it be absolute when it exists in various forms and is subject to the errors of chance that befall human texts? Can

these sacred texts be considered in any way infinite, or only susceptible to infinite imperfect interpretations? Sacred Scripture also falls
subject to the penalties of Babel; it has no one name, no one language. The words that compose it are doubly, triply metaphorical.
The word of God is mediated through a human word, translated
into human languages, further mediated by the distance separating
man from a direct relationship to the things of the world. Translated from one language to another, always with a slippage of
meaning. Which, if any, language was the original word of God?

Science serves as a refuge from this confusion of meaning, from
this plethora of ancient myth. The myth of science and rational order allows man to rethink these myths of origins and supplant them
with a new collective myth, a myth of a return to pre-Babel times
when man can once again, brick by brick, rebuild the city and the
tower of earthly unity and perfection to reach an apotheosis in the
scientific heaven being prepared for us. Thus, Werner Heisenberg,
one of the foremost scientists of our time, can say that "technology
. . . fundamentally interferes with the relation of nature to man, in
that it transforms his environment in large measure and thereby incessantly and inescapably holds the scientific aspect of the world
before his eyes."[4] As in primitive myth, reality is reshaped in an-
thropomorphic form: "The conception of the objective reality of
the elementary particles has thus evaporated in a curious way, not
into the fog of some new, obscure, or not yet understood reality
concept, but into the transparent clarity of . . . mathematics."[5]
Through science and mathematics, Heisenberg indicates the creation of a second, verifiable form of knowledge in which the immediate data of experience encounter coherence through the filter of one
of man's most prized creations—the perceived mathematical substructure of all phenomena.

There is, of course, a snake in this delightful mathematical Garden
of Eden. Heisenberg recognizes it when he recalls that for many,
"electricity has something uncanny about it."[6] Kenneth Burke
points to another aspect of the same problem when he wryly observes that man is "goaded by the spirit of hierarchy (or moved by
the sense of order) and rotten with perfection."[7] The search for an
immense and perfected cyclic table that contains and coordinates
all the varied data of the universe is only a Linnean dream. Perfec-

tion is inevitably accompanied by the taste of ripe-rottenness recognized and saluted by Baudelaire in his own table of human/inhuman "correspondences."

Heisenberg's observation points to the irrational at the heart of the most abstract and rational of sciences; perfect clarity of formulas does not cancel the awe of the unknown. Man's language, even at its most mathematically precise and abstract, cannot counteract primitive instinctual responses to a natural manifestation of such power and magnitude as a lightning bolt. Burke's observation addresses another aspect of this desire for order through the perfectionist impulse, which he sees as a central motivating factor in the nature of language. Man is subject to the post-Babel longing "to name something by its 'proper' name,"[8] despite the fact that the language of the builders of the city has been irrevocably lost. The lesson of Babel reminds us that there is no one "proper" name, just as there is no possible manner of ascertaining the true nature of the observed natural object.

This urge to give each thing its proper name harks back to the biblical myth of Genesis once again. Adam's mastery over the other created beings resided in his unique ability to give them names: "Whatsoever Adam called every living creature, that *was* the name thereof" (Gen. 2:19). Similarly, the people of what was to be called Babel sought to extend this privilege to themselves by giving themselves a name, thus confirming their existence and conferring a unified identity upon their efforts. This attempt at self-identification represents a step beyond the naming powers conferred on Adam by God. Adam named only the lesser beings (including his wife), but his own identity was confirmed from above by the source of all identity and all meaning. By taking responsibility for making their own name, the people of Babel involved themselves in a power struggle with the Creator.

The punishment for such presumption was cruelly appropriate. Not only was their self-awarded name lost, but the only name recorded by history is posterior to their building efforts. It is a name that reflects their confusion and dispersal, but it is not *their* name. The real name, the "proper" name of these people is absent from the biblical account—surely a significant omission by the biblical historian! The name left them, that of Babel, does not confer identity. It is the name of their defeat, a heavenly curse that breaks up identity and starts man on his historical search to recover it. Secular history since Babel could be mythically or metaphorically described as man's effort to reduce the differences of society into a single, coherent form, to recover the unity of Babel, to rebuild the city and the tower. Foucault describes the process thus: "History, in its traditional form, undertook to 'memorize' the *monuments* of the past, transform them into *documents*. . . . In our time, history is that which transforms *documents* into *monuments*. . . . in our time history aspires to the condition of archaeology." [9] That is, history seeks to uncover the ruins of Babel, to recuperate the lost identity of its people.

On another level, however, the twin gods of identity and universality were fundamentally incompatible from the start, so that the proud enterprise was doomed to failure by human agencies as well as divine ones. To act in such a manner, to map out and create a city, is intrinsically limiting. Such an action can only be accompanied by a certain renunciation, in the case of the builders of Babel, the renunciation of universality in favor of an inside/outside dichotomy. Even without divine intervention, their dream of unity would have slowly slipped away, their monumental tower would have dissolved like a dream-castle, and gradually they would have discovered that they no longer understood one another's language. Wallace Stevens's poem "An Ordinary Evening in New Haven" evokes a city dissolving in the mist when a too-strenuous effort has been made to define it and endow it with human identity:

> Suppose these houses are composed of ourselves,
> So that they become an impalpable town full of
> Impalpable bells, transparencies of sound,
> Sounding in transparent dwellings of the self.
>
> .   .   .   .
>
> A great town hanging pendant in a shade,
> An enormous nation happy in a style,
> Everything as unreal as real can be. [10]

To choose a name or a style is to play a role, and to force others to play roles they did not request, that is, to contaminate them with unreality. The imposition of a name is a quantification of human conduct, the signaling of an act in which the action becomes unique, untransferable, irrecuperable. Adopting an identity is static and exclusive. Universality is dynamic and inclusive. The building of Babel was dynamic and exclusive, thus doomed to failure. Division need not have been imposed from above it; it could easily have resulted from man's division of earth into city and field.

The scandal of Babel is an occurrence of multiple values and multiple effects. It demonstrates that there is no language in and of itself, nor any universality of language. This loss of the universal language brings about a paradoxical result—the obsession with language in all its multiple forms. It is this obsession that is institutionalized on one level in histories with, as Foucault reminds us, their tendency to move from monuments to documents to monuments, and on another level in the library, which houses the documents and is itself a monument.

The relation of history/identity to the collection of documents has not gone unnoticed by writers past and present. Aaron, the villainous Moor of Shakespeare's *Titus Andronicus*, has assembled his own curious library of documents that combines para-archaeological excavations and the confrontation with identities that slip away in the corruptions of death. As he tells Lucius:

> Oft have I digg'd up dead men from their graves,
> And set them upright at their dear friends' doors,
> Even when their sorrows almost were forgot;
> And on their skins, as on the bark of trees,
> Have with my knife carved. . . . (V.i.135–39)

This gruesome conversion of men into documents is repeated again and again literally and metaphorically in other of Shakespeare's plays. In more recent times, the prisoner in Kafka's penal colony is subjected to a similar procedure. His crime, which is also his identity, is written on his flesh. When the writing is done, fixing his identity in its permanent, static form, he expires. Similarly, Joyce chooses his own eschatological version of this body writing in *Finnegans Wake*. In this novel, Shem the Penman used his own excrement as ink and "wrote over every square inch of the only foolscap available, his own body, till by its corrosive sublimation one continuous present tense integument slowly unfolded all marryvoising moodmoulded cyclewheeling history."[11] Defecation is related to creation; the substance that gives fertility to the soil also reveals the mind's fertility.

These human documents are horrible (or disgusting) and the identities they define are equally so. But the libraries, without losing their horror, can also be places of refuge from an unbearable reality. The withdrawal into documents can be related to the motivation of Beckett's narrator in *How It Is*, though the extremity of the conditions described therein go beyond a normal library-universe. In a world where mud, sacks, and tins of food seem to compose the sole elements of a hideous reality, the narrator takes refuge in literature. He prods Pim to sing (poetry) and requires him to tell stories of a former life in the light (narration). In his desperate necessity, the character himself becomes an author, carving his work with his fingernails upon the only surface available—the living back of his companion, combining in a sense the motivations of Kafka and Joyce: "with the nail then of the right index I carve and when it breaks or falls until it grows again with another on Pim's back intact at the outset from left to right and top to bottom as in our civilization."[12] The ever-present slime of *How It Is* belongs to a world in which even the library of Babel has been blown away, but the memory of it remains in the nearly uninhabitable vacuum left by its disappearance.

The posited eternal oscillations in the relationship of the couple point to another problem. Bom and Pim are not names, but stages in a cycle of victimization that is insistently and eternally replayed. Bom is merely a convenient label for what is essentially a nameless entity that embodies both author and text at different stages. His attempt at mastery through the power of the written word is a transient one, and as Pim's back heals and Bom replaces him as the victim, his individuality is effaced in the mud. Perhaps then, the library has not completely disappeared—Pim, Bom, and the others (if they exist) are themselves authorless texts, smoothly blended into this corporeal library, and like the texts of more conventional libraries, they speak with the same voice that erases the figure of the physical author standing behind the text. As Roland Barthes reminds us,

"This 'I' which approaches the text [as Bom approaches Pim] is already itself a plurality of other texts, of codes which are infinite or, more precisely, lost (whose origin is lost)." Barthes continues with a remark that is strongly reminiscent of the scratching of nails on helpless backs: "The meanings I find are established not by 'me' or by others, but by their *systematic* mark."[13]

Borges's terrifying Library of Babel does not differ in essence from Beckett's apparently library-less void. In both, humanity is stripped away by something that is eternal, emotionless, and deadening to the spirit. In Borges's library, the labyrinthine structure is adamant to all human endeavor to pierce its mysteries; in Beckett, the endless sea of mud functions in a like manner. Both worlds are ruled by an order that the inhabitants are able to discern but cannot control, and thus the uncovering of the ordering principle brings no relief from tension. In Borges's library, infinite mathematical conjunctions frustrate the librarian's pursuit of the key texts; in Beckett's world the perpetual conjunctions and disjunctions of the crawling bodies serve a similar dehumanizing and demoralizing end. A description John Updike applies to Borges is strikingly fitting for Beckett's work as well: "We move . . . beyond psychology, beyond the human, and confront, in his work, the world atomized and vacant. Perhaps not since Lucretius has a poet so definitely felt men as incidents in space."[14] The implications of this desperate situation are far-reaching. That the library is a labyrinth and that the mud has no landmarks for the weary librarian/traveler are perhaps consequences of the characters' inability to distinguish the coordinates that would meaningfully orient them. If meaning remains inert and all objects are relegated to the same level of significance in space, no meaning can possibly be derived; the world is out of sympathy with the body. Our world, a world in which the library and the slime appear only tangentially, is a world *incarnate* with meaning. We partake of a symbiotic relationship, a symbolic pregnancy that is lost in the inhuman universe of Borges and Beckett.

The abstract vacuum conjured by Borges and Beckett forces the reader to experience the discomfort common to aphasiacs in their ordinary relation to self and space. Foucault agrees: "The uneasiness that makes us laugh when we read Borges is certainly related to the profound distress of those whose language has been destroyed:

loss of what is 'common' to place and name. Atopia, aphasia."[15]
The loss of a sense of place: a disorientation so obvious in these
texts as to require no further comment. Loss of name: the librarian
has no name, only his function. The Immortal, in another of Borges's
stories, has used so many names that he no longer knows (or cares)
which, if any, is his own true name. Beckett's narrator shares this
amnesia. If he ever had a name and a human identity it has long
since been lost in the mud; now he merely calls himself by a congenial syllable, unnecessary but convenient for identification purposes.

Roland Barthes reports that this loss of the sense of self is also
common to the aphasic condition: "'I' cannot be defined lexically
. . . yet it participates in a lexicon . . . ; in it, the message 'straddles'
the code, it is a shifter, a translator; of all the signs it is the most
difficult to use, since the child acquires it last of all and the aphasiac
loses it first."[16] The writer, he concludes, is also and always in the
same situation as the aphasiac in respect to the "I," and the works
of these two authors bear out his conclusion. The narrators of these
works clutch at momentary resemblances and devise theories based
on nameless fragmentary forms. As their efforts at organization dissolve and slip through their fingers, so too does the ego that frantically tried to hold to the slippery remnants of logical thought. It is
fascinating and appropriate that an appeal to the abstract universe
of numbers is the result of the search for meaning in both *How It Is*
and "The Library of Babel," and the reader is reminded once again
of the comforts of science and the clear orders of mathematics. But
mathematics, in these texts, is a prelude to transgression, and Ionesco recognizes explicitly the link that both Borges and Beckett describe implicitly in their narratives: "Now didn't I warn you, just a
little while ago: arithmetic leads to philology and philology leads to
crime."[17]

Yet this sense of horror before the wounded name is not universal—Babel teaches us that universality of motive or appreciation is
impossible—and many writers find the plurality of tongues a joyous experience. The fall from unity into multiplicity represents a
fortunate fall, a curse that reveals itself as a blessing. The recognition of the imperfections of human languages can be joined to cele-
bration: the "Glory be to God for dappled things" of Gerard Man-
ley Hopkins, the nimble-footed dancing of James Joyce through the

gamut of Western culture, the easy meanderings of Borges in libraries of actual and invented worlds. Stéphane Mallarmé speaks of the very human paradox involved in the acceptance of the imperfection and imperfectibility of human languages: "The diversity of languages on earth means that no one can utter words which would bear the miraculous stamp of Truth Herself Incarnate. . . . *But*, let us remember that if our dream were fulfilled, *verse would not exist*—verse which, in all its wisdom, atones for the sins of language."[18] Ronald Barthes takes an even more radical stance. Rather than speaking in terms of the atonement derived from a poetic composition, he celebrates the perverse pleasures of an illicit relationship, "the cohabitation of languages" whose friction conduces to bliss. For Barthes, "the text of pleasure is a sanctioned Babel."[19] The philosophical stances in Mallarmé and Barthes are quite different, yet there can be discerned an underlying similarity in the impulse that provokes these statements. Both are confronting a metaphysical lack with the hopeless desire for some kind of order, although it may be an arbitrary or incomprehensible one, or one that bears the mark of man's inept machinations. Both are confronting an excess of language that is also a dearth of signification; both recognize the inadequacy of each and every attempt to order experience; both testify to man's mania for constructing systems that justify themselves and literature.

One reaction, when confronted with this impossible situation, is to yield to the blandishments of invented systems. There is a propensity to relax into a preference for works constructed according to a rigorous and symmetrical order, with clear beginnings and denouements, that give the impression of completeness and mastery. Foucault refers to this as man's "perpetual tendency to constitute a *metaphysics* of life, labour, and language."[20] Confronting this tendency is another, equally powerful one that deliberately fixes on the indeterminate, on that which is still vague and in process of formulation, on the incommensurable flux. This tendency combats the former as claustrophobic and "denounces metaphysics as a veil of illusion."[21] Most of us settle for some more or less comprehensive ordering system to which we remain faithful though we may deplore its deficiencies. It is, perhaps, a mark of genius to reject order and disorder both (or to accept both, which comes to nearly the same thing), to recognize the boundaries of an object or the limitations of an art form and then go beyond this recognition and gradually free them from rigid forms as the bottle unbottled in the library fire of William Carlos Williams's *Paterson*, or the glass of water in Wallace Stevens's poem of that title. In these poems a meticulous order is disrupted and flows away into an absence of order that is not disorder. "To create," says Mallarmé, "is to conceive an object in its fleeting moment, in its absence." In order to do so, in order to "conjure up a scene of lovely, evanescent, intersecting forms,"[22] the writer must do violence to the mind's tendency to stabilize and define things. He must reject the orderly existence of the library without rejecting the variousness of its contents.

No one illustrates better than Joyce the manner in which the word becomes words, the Book becomes the library, man becomes language. While all of history and all of culture are resumed in Shem's excremental texts, in order to comprehend the smallest portion of this new Scripture the reader is tempted into the labyrinth of libraries where he invariably loses his way. It is not surprising that Joyce's chaotic world is represented in a comic rather than a tragic form, since the underlying ontological assumption of the character-writer seems to be that this chaotic world can be completely textualized through the intervention of human beings. It is an assumption that bears theological implications as well, for the writing of Shem (the *Wake* itself?) obviates the necessity for other books, though it harks back to them, and to libraries, constantly. The *Wake* is an antiscripture, the inverse of the medieval Book of Nature that reveals God's will in the "broken and illuminated letters"[23] of earthly creatures. It is, however, a book of nature to which a modern scientific component has been added.

Man's mythic insertion into the language game is not completely a fortunate fall even for encyclopedic writers like Joyce, as the difficulties and distastefulness of reading a noisome excremental text may well testify. We avoid direct contact, seeking mediated gratification and accepting partial answers to questions raised. Similarly, modern science makes no pretense of reading nature directly. The instruments of science inject men into a perceptual game in which reality comes to resemble a prewritten Shemian text that the scientist can barely understand despite the fact that he himself wrote the outline. The ordering is imperfect, incomplete. Despite its apparent logic, the systematization of nature and of the encyclopedic text is an arrangement which does not cease to allow incongruous juxtapositions, and which invites the user to dream of other possible systems. This discontinuity of scientific thought is reflected in the discontinuity of the library, which, likewise organized by the most modern principles of library science into LC or Dewey Decimal configurations, is nevertheless quite ruthless in its fetishization of the ordering process itself. We can easily comprehend Foucault's interest in the archive, which not only establishes customary procedures for the disposition of texts, but prescribes and proscribes individual elements of a linguistic system according to its own internal laws. The archive represents an economy and a politics of expression:

> The archive is first the law of what can be said, the system that governs the appearance of statements as unique events. But the archive is also that which determines that all these things said do not accumulate endlessly in an amorphous mass, nor are they inscribed in unbroken linearity, nor do they disappear at the mercy of chance external accidents; but they are grouped together in distinct figures, composed together in accordance with multiple relations, maintained or blurred in accordance with specific regularities.[24]

Inside the walls of the archive, or library, the human nostalgia for a cosmic unity finds its most perfect expression; inside the library the fascination with plurality also manifests itself. It is, furthermore, an alien presence. Foucault continues: "The analysis of the archive, then, involves a privileged region: at once close to us, and different from our present existence, it is the border of time that surrounds our presence, . . . it is that which, outside ourselves, delimits us."[25] The Foucaultian archive is more than an ordinary human library; it is a Borgesian library of Babel, an infinite, eternal (though not unchanging) presence. By imposing its amoral artificiality on the recalcitrant mass of human thought, the peculiar system of the archive attracts admiration and repels human emotion. The library in general, then, pursues a politics of isolationism in that it is separate from man even as it encloses his possibilities.

In the library that has solidified and closed around us, classificatory systems serve as a kind of map to keep the confusion at bay. The catalogue is open, connected, susceptible to constant additions and modifications. It provides multiple entrances to and exits from the library-labyrinth. Unlike the books on the shelves, which are for the most part read from beginning to end and then reinterred in the stacks, the catalogue is in constant motion; one selects a card here, a card there. The catalogue is always complete with respect to the library it orders; the library never is. The library catalogue resumes the work of Adam and names (renames) all the objects in its world; it becomes a *systema culturae* that corresponds on a second metalinguistic level to the *systema naturae* of Linnaeus. Modern man, recognizing his separation from nature, attempts to heal the breach resulting from the Babelic fall from linguistic simplicity by substituting abbreviations, keys, ciphers, and initials for the names of things and by accepting the resultant deformations of the maternal tongue as a necessary sacrifice to the gods of technology. But in this very comprehensiveness is summarized the madness—or perhaps the intolerable sanity—of the institution. Linnaeus failed in his attempt to display the order of nature; his logical and very sane system was based on the mad premise that nature's order was recuperable by man. The library catalogue is another such attempt at completeness and comprehension, and it too leads to the most logical madness.

The properties of the catalogue as map and as madness have been recognized and exploited extensively in narrative. A catalogue of the books contained in a character's library is a traditional shorthand indication of crucial facets of his character; thus the early chapter in *Don Quixote* detailing the contents of his library, the revelation by Ionesco of the half-dozen books preserved by his protagonist in *The Hermit*, and the reference in Malraux's *The Walnut Trees of Altenburg* to the three books that "hold their own against prison life": *Robinson Crusoe, Don Quixote*, and *The Idiot*. ("And the Bible," said someone. "No. . . .")[26] It is a tradition that is so well recognized as to be subjected to repeated parody; by Voltaire, for example, when in *Candide* the catalogue of the books in Pococurante's library reveals that character's personality only through inversion and in Flann O'Brien's *At Swim-Two-Birds*, where the bedridden novelist's exclusive interest in books with green covers leads to a hilarious catalogue of his lopsided library. These parodies reveal but do not break out of the tradition, and it is only with J. K. Huysmans's *Against the Grain* that the fiction of the catalogue is given a new twist. If Joyce's work, with its encyclopedic all-inclusiveness, could appropriately be described as a fiction of the library, Huysmans's novel is a fiction of the catalogue. In this book no longer is the catalogue a mere narrative device that reveals the nature of a fictional character. In *Against the Grain*, the book to a large extent *is* a catalogue; that is, the catalogue becomes an end in itself, independent of its relation to the protagonist whose peculiar likes and dislikes it reveals. Catalogues abound in this book—of flowers, scents, music, paintings, and so forth, but most of all, of books. Nearly a third of the length of Huysmans's text is taken up with a catalogue and a description of the contents of Des Esseintes's library. Here, the catalogue has its own intrinsic interest and importance for the reader.

This valorization of the catalogue is taken still one step further in certain postmodernist texts. In John Barth's *Letters* or Gilbert Sorrentino's *Mulligan Stew*, Huysmans's technique becomes a novelistic gambit. The catalogue is not only of interest in and of itself; it becomes practically the whole of the narrative and the only subject of interest. These books seem to attempt to fuse the two traditions of the all-inclusive text and of the textual catalogue in a text that is an all-inclusive catalogue. The madness of extreme order has never been more apparent.

Such works of fiction can become, at their worst, little more than inventories of literature without further transcendence, and all effort is exhausted in the building up of a body of documents and their division into different groups and subgroups for an analysis that does not take place. The gathering and classification of ideas takes the place of real thought. As Marthe Robert realizes, while "the vagaries of mysticism were supposed to be dissipated by the meticulously drafted catalogue,"[27] the abstract repository satisfies nothing but man's rational interests and ignores his emotional and psychological needs. This is a situation that Shakespeare was aware of well before the advent of Linnaeus and an amelioristic approach to science as pure reason. In his response to the assertion of the hired killers of Banquo that they are men, Macbeth says:

> Ay, in the catalogue ye go for men;
> As hounds, and greyhounds, mongrels, spaniels, curs,
> Shoughs, water-rugs, and demi-wolves, are clept
> All by the name of dogs . . . (*Macbeth*, 3.i. 93−96)

The classificatory system describes the genus, but does not reveal the peculiar characteristics of the individual, and thus is found greatly lacking. Books go through a similar alienation on being forced into catalogues, and for this reason the fiction of the catalogue is often amusing, but, like the hired killers, frequently found lacking in some critical element.

The children of technology, the keepers of the catalogue, accompany us everywhere in the library. They are the librarians, the caretakers of the books. They have not built the tower, but dwell within its walls, alternately enchanted and nauseated by the library space. But their realm, for all its technological implications, is not dehumanized or inhuman. Like modern science, it is doubly human because the library and its contents are human creations. The library is, however, a transgressive space despite its nature as lawgiver to language, a modern Babel of Babels; and the librarians, who would seem by tradition and custom the most staid, least transgressive of beings, are actually deeply implicated in one of the most revolutionary modes of existence conceivable. In the library are preserved all the most potentially disruptive forms, all the most potentially explosive energies as yet unharnessed by society. The librarian stands at the place where transgression provides a gap for entry and possible dissolution. He always operates at the linguistic extreme since he is by association integrative to writing through his choice of career, and transgressive to society by his isolation from it. Thus the librarian, who seemingly functions in an innocuous world of illusory word-myths, in some sense partakes of the relationships of power in their pure, unharnessed state. It is he who provides the key to the "open sesame" described by Nietzsche that reminds men "what their existence really is—an imperfect tense that never becomes a present."[28] The truths the librarian utters are lost in the babble of tongues, adding but one more name to a series that is long since overdetermined, one more interpretation to an overburdened history:

> We are sown with ideas . . . ; we suffer from the malady of words, and have no trust in any feeling that is not stamped with its special word. And being such a dead fabric of words and ideas that yet has an uncanny movement in it, I have still perhaps the right to say *cogito ergo sum*, though not *vivo ergo cogito*. I am permitted the empty *esse*, not the full green *vivere*.[29]

Further: the historical linking to the *cogito* is such that the librarian can barely even say "*cogito ergo sum*"; instead, his existence in the imperfect tense forces him to look always backward to an uncanny death-in-life that is neither "green" nor permanently sealed: not "I am," but "I have been." In consequence, the extreme meticulousness of thought of the typical librarian cannot bear fruit in life, but must disgorge itself in the ceaseless cataloguing of his surroundings. The overdetermination on the formal level is paralleled by a dearth of meaning and by an incomprehension of the physical sphere. The only witness to his existence is the uncanny movement of thought, the ghostly shaking of the dead fabric of words.

The existence, present and imperfect, of the library itself is central, so much so that the librarian may seem to fade in and out of the shelves, becoming one with the books that line the walls or meshing into the texture of the book that is being written. If the library can be said to embody anything, it would be the rational impulse itself. The ethics/aesthetics of its operation imply not so much an assumption as a resumption of knowledge, a refinement of abstraction that presumes to embrace and index the whole of human thought. In the process, the sensuality of the literary experience is somewhere mislaid or lost, as the sensuality of the old physics was lost in the new science purified and indexed by mathematics. There is more to comprehend in the modern physics of subatomic particles, and less to apprehend.

Two well-known phrases confirm this contrast in a more specifically literary setting. The first is from the *Odyssey*: "The Gods did this, and spun the destruction / of peoples, for the sake of the singing of men hereafter,"[30] and the second is from Mallarmé: "The world exists in order to become a Book."[31] Both contain the germ of the same idea, that is, that man is made for art, for literature, but the difference in the manner of expressing this concept could not be more clear. Homer speaks of generations that *sing*: a human, sensual, social act. Mallarmé speaks more abstractly of an object, a thing among other things, a product of writing from which the sensual aspect of music has been, willy-nilly, removed. Furthermore, the *Odyssey* inscribes (or sings) itself in an order where words and things coincide, where every song is a version of divine will: "The Gods did this." These gods are not the abstract God of the Christians, but the personified Fates who spin out the thread of a man's life like their human counterpart, Penelope, whose constant weaving becomes an emblem in the epic. In Mallarmé's world, by contrast, things become words in the abstract realm of the deified "Book." Words, in his world, are the only meeting point of the worlds. When Michael Foucault is asked what a book is for him, he replies that it is a "box of tools,"[32] following directly in the spirit of Mallarmé's observation. A book is like a wrench or a screwdriver; if it fits the nut to be removed it is useful, if not it can be easily discarded among other useless objects. Here there is no representation of the world, no enchanted beings to be awakened with a song, but a small machine made of twenty-six interchangeable parts and a few conventions of punctuation, a tool that, like the abstract language of the mathematics, provides a voiceless written text. Homeric aesthetics becomes an economics of use-value.

Since Walter Benjamin's essay entitled "Work of Art in the Age of Mechanical Reproduction" (1936), it has become commonplace to refer this devaluation of the written text to a process of mechanization that has trivialized the unique work of art. The oral recitation of the Homeric text gave way to a handwritten manuscript, which in turn gave way to an easily accessible printed text, which is, finally, made even more available to the interested individual through the advent of cheap, readily available photocopying services. It is no wonder that writing can be associated with nonbeing, with an objectified box of tools. Complete accessibility, absolute knowledge, drives away shadows, subjecting literature to the blinding light of science and killing off the old gods and enchanters that once resided within the covers of books.

A medieval anecdote illustrates the contrast between the ancient and modern perceptions of books. Saint Augustine relates that in the course of his travels through his diocese he stopped at the church of his old teacher, Saint Ambrose. He surprised his friend sight-reading from a book without articulating the words, a fact that astonished the bishop.[33] Since at the time of Saint Augustine manuscripts were rare, precious books were invariably shared with the public in opening readings. They were not read silently, but declaimed aloud. Thus, the work was known only by ear and associated in the listener's mind with the presence of the reader and the audience in a specific configuration that involved all the senses. A reading that made no use of the voice was so extraordinary as to throw the observer off balance. Such a reading represented in the words of Gérard Genette, the birth of "a new idea of the book and of its *use*."[34]

From this, we can easily comprehend the transformation of monuments to documents intuited by Foucault. The monument, a shared form of artistic expression, is changed by an alteration of perception into a document, an art form that is now perceived as proper for solitary enjoyment. As new conditions are created for the enjoyment of art, old ones fall into disuse. If we were to find someone alone in a room, without an audience, we would expect him to read silently. (Does not the library, with its SILENCE signs, reenforce this practice?) If we found someone reading aloud, it would throw us off balance, and we would tend to think he was slightly crazy, like a person who talks to himself.

In their physical dimension as well, mass-produced texts are denied the participation of the body that would erase their inhumanity. Printed books are recalcitrant to the historian because their nature is antithetical to the historian's spirit. Deprived of body, they are also in a certain sense deprived of history, if history can be conceived of as a series of changes. For the manuscripts and autographs so beloved by historian-librarians, there is no continuity between texts, only rupture. Each book was an original; no two books, even if they shared the same text, were identical. Time is allowed to conquer the individual manuscript gracefully, but there is no past or present for the printed book. Before printing, each book was a unique treasure, each bore the mark of the scribe's peculiar style. With printing came the repeatability of books and the deadening aspects of an inhuman library existence that are eventually transferred to the historian, putting his humanity to the doubt. Even the unique, original manuscript is subject to this outrage with the development of ever more advanced photocopying techniques that make the manuscript available in facsimile editions. There is a tendency to forget that verbal signs can also be sensual and that the act of narration can negate the inhumanity of the printing press.[35]

It is, then, perfectly appropriate that the first novel, Cervantes's *Don Quixote*, should recount, near its close, the adventure of the mad knight's introduction to the economics of publishing and bookselling through his visit to a printing shop in Barcelona. The printing press is a precondition for many of Don Quixote's adventures, though in Cervantes's novel the economics of printing is closely conjoined to the belief in the enchanters residing in books. He has, therefore, the best of both the Homeric and the Mallarméan worlds; the economic factors ruling the beginning of the age of mechanical reproduction allow books to fall into the hands of an impoverished landowner, and the felt sensuality of the books permits them to come to life in the actions of the mad knight.

It will be argued that Cervantes's age was one of transition, when printing was still a novelty, and large book collections had not yet found their way into the public domain. Flaubert's feminized Don Quixote, Emma Bovary, lives in a much more prosaic world, as did Flaubert himself. Nineteenth-century mechanistic science had already killed off the old gods in Flaubert's thinking, and he dedicated himself to a vigorous scientific search for the ideal fiction. In modern times, Joyce carried the Flaubertian precision even further. "You have been seeking the *mot juste?*" Frank Budgen asked him after a day's work. "No," replied Joyce, "I have the words already. What I am seeking is the perfect order of the words in the sentence. There is an order in every way appropriate. I think I have it."[36]

It is a grandiose and richly revealing assertion. Joyce claims nothing less than absolute beauty, rationally conceptualized and painstakingly achieved. The notion of such perfection of form and content is itself a fiction, is founded on fiction, and is conveyed to an audience through fiction. There is, nevertheless, an unnerving political implication in this clear assumption of an absolute value standard based on Joyce's background and culture, an implicit claim of aesthetic superiority over other cultures. It represents, in a sense, the tacit colonialization of the world of print, subjecting the word to a history of increasing rigor and control. These political tensions become increasingly apparent as opposition to the library grows and Joyce's tightly controlled encyclopedic space comes under attack through parody and through the confrontation with belligerently conflictive ideological systems such as Burroughs's recipes for cut-up and fold-in texts. When the aesthetic becomes transformed into an anti-aesthetic through the actions of these literary counterrevolutionaries, the existence of the library is itself endangered.

This transformation of the repository of knowledge into a potential threat is not new or unique to modern times and modern literature, but the problematic has been more insistently foregrounded than in the past, and the implications of such a revolutionary stance have been more clearly focused. The problem, essentially, lies in nature (or man's conception of it) and its relation to/against scientific thought. Modern scientific thought, with its emphasis on mathematical models, has moved away from a mimesis of nature without ceasing to search for an underlying order and pattern that would reduce natural phenomena to human models. But nature, and man's own models, escape this implicit thrust toward closure; nature refuses to be encompassed. Similarly, the library by definition cannot be closed since it is always open to the future through the addition of new elements. The source of difficulty is similar to that discussed by Geoffrey Hartman in reference to "anti-representational theories—which try to free rhetoric from representational ends. The problem is that they are more referential than they know: they have secretly declared what the *bad* magic is, even if they consistently and rigorously doubt that it can be remedied by the *good* word, or any word-cure whatsoever."[37]

One cannot help but note the contamination of Hartman's own analysis by metaphors derived from a mythic past (that is, "good" and "bad" magic) prior to representability itself. Hartman bypasses both mechanistic (representational) and modern (nonrepresentational) science for an appeal to a primitive life source: the power of the magic word, which, when spoken, drives directly to the essence of the theory in question, breaking apart all the brittle, unfinished human models. Language is both disease and cure, and the commitment to its magical components reflects dynamic, life-preserving psychological factors. That Hartman doubts the efficacy of such word-cures is a sign of the times. He is, after all, a modern man, and the nostalgia for past simplicities can only be expressed through metaphor.

Language is life preserving—or death dealing—since such is the ambiguity of magic: good or bad, depending on its uses. The opposition between the two types of magic is rooted in the differing use of language, in oppositions that could be described in terms of radically differing metaphysics, or as two opposing styles of presentation. Villiers de l'Isle-Adam's *Axel* poses this problematic concretely; for while the protagonists in the nearly unrepresentable play live almost totally in the world of ideas, still in the unfolding of the drama the interplay of metaphysical essences becomes visible and takes on a sensuous, sensual quality. The hero, Count Axel of Auersperg, a "*fin de siècle* 'Faust',"[38] lives in isolation in a Gothic castle, studying alchemy (the forerunner of modern science) and practicing magic, a way of life and a course of study befitting his desire to detach himself from the world of matter. The heroine, a well-born convent novice named Sara, also seems destined for a spiritual life through her approaching dedication to God. But Sara, "a darkly mysterious orphan" has immersed herself in the convent library; she has been "tempted and captivated by so many books!"[39] Through the books she studies, Sara has learned much of spiritual matters, but she has also learned to yearn for the forbidden pleasures of a life lived physically, a yearning which is expressed in her refusal to take her final vows, in her rejection of "the Light, the Hope, and the Life" (p. 28) for the darkness of the crypt, the hope of discovering Axel's hidden treasure, and for a life that would express itself in a human relationship with a kindred soul. Where Sara suffers a lapse from her religiously inculcated spirituality, Axel experiences a similar renunciation of the values of Master Janus, his tutor into the recondite realms of scientific spiritualism. He decides to use his carefully nurtured magic powers to seek the same treasure of which Sara, through her extensive reading, has already discovered the location. In a climactic moment, Axel discovers both the treasure and the escaped novice. Sara immediately shoots the young man, sight unseen, and then profers him a bitter apology: "I must have wounded you with my guns: I'm sorry. I wanted only to kill you" (pp. 164–65). Axel stays his own murderous attack with a dagger "at the sight of the girl's sublime face" (p. 162), falls violently in love (as does Sara), and narrowly avoids succumbing to the temptation to return to reality with her at his side. Passionate love gives way before impassioned speech and the passionate embrace of death in a double suicide that seems aimed at preserving their reawakened spirituality from the taint of corporeal lusts. Says Axel: "How wearisome and fruitless, Sara! [to return to the world] and not a worthy sequel to this miraculous wedding night, when, though still virgins, we possessed each other forever!" (pp. 183–84).

In Axel and Sara, science meets the library, magic confronts recalcitrant nature, spiritual essence comes into contact with earthly contamination. The confrontation seems inevitable. Axel's studies of alchemy separate things and spiritual essences, but his pursuit of magic follows a conflicting course by its implicit assumption that words (signs, unreal essences) *are* things. The decision to use magic to seek the treasure leads back to a confrontation with the bodily text, the objectified beloved, with eroticism, and with death.

The magic that brings together Sara and the treasure is of a different sort. The magic practiced by Axel is, implicitly, a Faustian black magic. The storyteller's magic that relates Sara and the treasure is more closely allied to what Vladimir Nabokov, in his novel *Pale Fire*, calls the "blue magic" of imitation.[40] Sara is drawn to the treasure because she, as the epitome of sublime womanhood, is herself a treasure, and her "coldly flawless" (p. 10) physical, intellectual, and spiritual beauty is mirrored in the coldly flawless perfection of the sparkling gems. Sara is mimetic of the treasure she discovers; she is, further, transformed by Axel's passion into the embodiment of the priceless philosopher's stone sought by alchemists.

This transformation is perverse, of course, and it represents the perversion of the library that can only result in other parallel perversions in a world where economics, politics, language, and sexuality have all gone wrong. Thus Jacques Derrida points out that "the relationship between reason, madness, and death is an economy, a structure of deferral whose irreducible originality must be respected."[41] It goes without saying that this economy advanced by Derrida is a perverse economy, one ruled by the demonic. The economic equation reason→madness→death (deferred) reveals one aspect of the perversion of the library that results in its transformation.

But Sara and Axel also parlay sexual desire into the death wish, and the library incorporated in the body is killed with the body. Muteness is achieved through mutilation, their unfulfilled sexual desires perverted into a radical and symbolic castration that takes their lives. Another perverse idea is joined to the economy adduced above, that of physical sexuality reduced to a verbal and spiritual ideal. Primitive corporeal language symbolized by magic gives way to an erotics of mathematics, the perversion intimated by Ionesco in his association of arithmetic and crime. Because "Love has pitched his mansion in / The place of excrement,"[42] Axel and Sara must remain chaste. Derrida's equation holds—if the body is removed from the library, then the mind can also be. One perversion leads to another, extracting the mind leads to insanity (or holy furor) and intimates fatal consequences.

The leveling implied by reason→madness→death has a deep political component as well. Foucault reminds us that "knowledge of man . . . is always linked, even in its vaguest form, to ethics or politics; more fundamentally, modern thought is advancing towards that region where man's Other must become the Same as himself."[43] The perversion of such a process on the level of the library has clear and inevitable consequences. The book as tool box becomes book as tool of the state, a tiny machine that enforces the Same through insistence on conformity and consistency. On the level of the critic, this enforcement of the Same becomes a kind of fascism that engenders and ruthlessly applies a system to a text. The fascism of the library does not recognize metaphor; its precepts must be taken literally. Or rather, the metaphor is so pervasive, so overriding that it can no longer be perceived at all. Axel and Sara do not act out roles; they behave as only the total ritualization of their beliefs could force them to behave. This transformation is expressed in what becomes, eventually, purely formulaic existential terms.

They must DO nothing, only BE, and their destiny is tied up in the perfection of this art of being ideal Rosicrucians. If Sara and Axel faltered in their devotion to the word, then they must be punished. Treason is punishable by death, and so they die. The protagonists of the drama must be satisfied to *be* in an ultimate timeless, static existence. The slightest motion, the smallest attempt at being in the world, constitutes rebellion against the fascism of the letter that rules their lives.

This insight into the existential perversions of the library has not escaped other writers. Sartre's Roquentin, staring at the statue of Impétraz, experiences the "delicate touch of horror"[44] that goes with any recognition of unchanging being, and he associates this static being with a magical presence. He explains, "When they cast this scholar in bronze they also turned out a sorcerer. . . . A mute power emanates from him."[45] This repugnance in the presence of scholarly magic is felt intensely by Roquentin in relation to this bronze, but as Maurice Blanchot affirms, all literature contains at least a germ of this evil: "The experience of literature is, perhaps, fundamentally close to the paradoxes and sophisms which Hegel, to ward it off, called the evil infinity."[46] It is evil because it is inhuman, because it is perverse, because it is bewitching, because it is dangerously attractive. After their long, unsatisfactory wanderings, Bouvard and Pécuchet also succumb to the delicious seduction of the library's magic. No longer do they perform; instead they return to the simplicity of their former existence: "they will occupy themselves copying books, copying their own books, copying every book; and unquestionably they will copy *Bouvard et Pécuchet*. Because to copy is *to do* nothing; it is *to be* the books being copied."[47] If it is permissible, after Borges, to disrupt chronology, one might add that *Don Quixote* goes even further than *Bouvard et Pécuchet* in this direction, and Cervantes extends Flaubert's discoveries in relation to the magic horrors of books. Don Quixote *is* the chivalric romance he reads, literally, with no intervention of metaphor. His madness is that he recognizes the work of the enchanters, comments on it, and cannot find (nor does he wish to find) the counter-enchantment to free himself. The tension between the Other and the Same has been dissolved in the library's magic space, and being has been reduced to its most minute zero point.

Yet, strangely enough, at this zero point of greatest apparent repression, the perversion is doubled back on itself once again to give a free space. Though Don Quixote, Bouvard and Pécuchet *are* the books they read, their insertion into the library space changes forever the nature of these books. The books of chivalry are forever affected by Don Quixote's too-literal reading of them, and Bouvard and Pécuchet's encyclopedic endeavor finds fruit in the clearly transgressive *Dictionary of Received Ideas*, which was to have been incorporated into the completed work. Such literalism bears its own metaphoric children as Don Quixote becomes more than just another in a long line of knights-errant and Bouvard and Pécuchet become judges rather than mere exempla of the encyclopedic mania they represent. Transgression exists and grows in the context of the most severe repression, in a movement of liberation that is at least partially due to the deceptions and duplicities of memory.

The library in itself mirrors no one temporal or spatial model; it would perhaps be fair to say that it reflects back on the perceiver his hypotheses about temporal succession. In this, the library is similar to nature as conceived of by modern science, a nature that is ultimately unknown, a nature that reproduces the image of man. The temporal/spatial dimension of the library is closely allied to the reigning philosophy of history. In an older, rationalistic model, time is conceived of as a spatial continuum. One moment follows the other in an eternal succession, the singular event is dissolved into an ideal, circular, recurring continuity. This is the model strikingly illustrated by Vico, an epistemological system dependent on a continuum of presence, a delicate but stable and orderly progression. Past and future frame the present; the general thrust is teleological; the metaphysics is coherent and hierarchical. It is not difficult to see how this temporal model can be fitted to the library space. In the library, past and present are concrete presences, in the form of the books that line the shelves. Past prepares the way for present, and present lays the building stones of the future, all in neat, orderly rows, each work fitting into a continuous succession, yet each retaining its uniqueness and identity. The individual event merges into a discrete, perfect order. Temporal succession is obviated in spatial juxtaposition that can be illustrated in a series of discrete moments, not a temporal flux; a rigid, spatial, authoritarian order.

There is a potential tension, however, in this eternal library. Relations do not stop with the orderly progression from past to present and into the future. Relations cross lines, move backwards, reinfect, revitalize, change the past. The past remembered is not the unique, unchangeable moment, but the past as present: the work removes itself from *that* time into this. Progression, evolution, the temporal and spatial succession of presences toward an unknown future, is interrupted by these profoundly antigenealogical cross-fertilizations. The time and space of the library, then, enclose another, mythical order of perpetual presence. Time no longer occurs or manifests itself cyclically; it is a ritual presence that consumes itself day by day in the hope of a magical participation. In mechanistic, circular time there is a formal rigor that stratifies and hardens successions and hierarchies. In the mythic vision time is annulled, each work of art repeats the other in an ahistorical ritual. Movement is not progressive, but peripatetic. Time does not pass; it is eternally present. The mythic mode liberates the works from historical constraints and frees them to argue with each other in a space free from chronology—an insight Swift implemented in "The Battle of the Books" where the author, as historian, recounts the story of a war in which Paracelsus strikes Galen, Aristotle narrowly misses his aim at Bacon only to wound Descartes, and Virgil carries out an exchange of armour with Dryden. Swift reveals the failure of the library in its appointed task of making visible the order and succession of human thought and demonstrates the pretensions upon which such an order was built, tumbling the mechanistic Babel long before the advent of modern science. Through satire, Swift reveals the power struggles taking place within the community of scholars without standing either inside or outside the battlefield thus generated. He suggests what Nietzsche, in *The Use and Abuse of History*, describes as the manner by which "an excess of history seems to be an enemy to the life of a time." Among the dangers detailed by Nietzsche is precisely this averted "contrast of *inner* and *outer*," which in the excess of history becomes overly emphasized to the detriment of personality.[48] Swift, as a critical presence, stands beside the system he discusses, neither a combatant nor a counterforce to the war he describes. Swift, after all, appears in the text as a mock historian, and he adds a further twist to these ahistorical differences of opinion by the fact of recording them. He sets out to prove the differences of opinion by the detailing of irreconcilable difference. He attempts to prove the impossibility of history in the confusion of the library; then, typically, he writes the history of that impossibility. He does not, therefore, install himself in the mythic world, but neither does he accept the implications of the historical outlook of his contemporaries.

The tension between the mythic and mechanistic-historical ontologies of the library was not resolved, although it was at least held in abeyance, with the addition of a third problematic feature in contemporary cognitive models, a revisionary humanism foreseen by Swift and Nietzsche but given currency by modern science. Thus, Freud, though he proceeded to draw rather mechanistic conclusions about the function of the unconscious mental processes, was generally correct when he reflected that "we are today in a position to embark on a discussion of the Kantian theorem that time and space are 'necessary forms of thought.'"[49] Temporal succession is one of these insubstantial "forms," an illusion that is tenuously preserved to maintain sanity, though its illusiveness is recognized. In this manner, the impenetrable individuality of the seasonal man penetrates the incorporeal timeless (mythic) or circular (mechanistic) eternity of the library. This amounts to a new humanism that is fully endorsed by modern relational theories of science. Werner Heisenberg comments:

> When we speak of a picture of nature provided by contemporary exact science, we do not actually mean any longer a picture of nature, but rather a picture of our relation to nature. The old compartmentalization of the world into an objective process in space and time, on the one hand, and the soul in which this process is mirrored, on the other . . . is no longer suitable as the starting point for the understanding of modern science.[50]

With the loss of the solid, encompassable object of cognition comes a parallel loss of objectivity in the conception of space and time. Heisenberg centers modern conceptions of temporality and spatiality firmly in the observing subject. Man, through the language of mathematics and with the aid of instruments he has created, creates himself and an intersubjective universe. From the perspective of this mental universe, Heisenberg goes on to hypothesize the unthinkable—a discontinuous space and time.

Maurice Merleau-Ponty, harking back to the old metaphor of time as a river, has discussed at length the implications of this concept in terms of a man-centered fabrication:

> We say that time passes or flows by. We speak of the course of time. The water that I see rolling by was made ready a few days ago in the mountains, with the melting of the glacier; it is now in front of me and makes its way towards the sea into which it will finally discharge itself. If time is similar to the river, it flows from the past towards the present and future. The present is the consequence of the past, and the future of the present. But this often repeated metaphor is in reality extremely confused. For, looking at the things themselves, the melting of the snows and what results from this are not successive events, or rather, the very notion of event has no place in the objective world. When I say that the day before yesterday, the glacier produced the water which is passing at this very moment, I am tacitly assuming the existence of a witness tied to a certain spot in the world, and I am comparing his successive views: he was there when the snows melted and followed the water down, or else, from the edge of the river and having waited two days, he sees the pieces of wood that he threw into the river at its source. The "events" are shapes cut out by the finite observer from the spatio-temporal totality of the objective world. But on the other hand, if I consider the world itself, there is simply one indivisible and changeless being in it. Change presupposes a certain position which I take up and from which I see things in procession before me: there are no events without someone to whom they happen and whose finite perspective is the basis of their individuality.[51]

For Merleau-Ponty, as for Heisenberg, the entire notion of change and development is a purely human one. Human thought requires the use of such notions, but they are untenable from the objective viewpoint of the world itself (the world we can imagine intellectually but are prohibited from seeing by the aforestated subjective pressures). Without an observer to perceive change, time does not exist.

For Kenner, a book such as *Finnegans Wake* imitates and explores these temporal/spatial discontinuities: "And still more than *Ulysses* it [*Finnegans Wake*] dispenses with narrative in time. Time-ridden according to its own proclamation, time-obsessed because it distills voices that search forward in time, it yet inhabits typographic space, drawing . . . towards its own last page, . . . and then circling forward to do the only thing the reader can do who has reached the end of a book and has no other book: begin again."[52] This circumvention of chronology and approximation of discontinuity does not, as Kenner concedes, take place in a timeless void. Indeed, the absence of traditional, clear temporal markers makes the desire for a time scheme even more urgent as the reader searches for information to fill in the gaps, to create the illusion of chronology. Joyce makes our temporal and spatial alienation all too clear, but he cannot dispense with those necessary forms of thought.

Hartman, with Derrida, makes an even more radical point in reference to the micro-level of the word: "Writing destabilizes words, in the sense that it makes us aware at one and the same time of their alien frame of reference . . . and of the active power of forgetfulness . . . which it enables and which, in turn, enables us to write."[53] The word is alien, belonging to another, overdetermined by a set of discontinuous "representamens" (the word is Hartman's), made yet more radically discontinuous by active forgetting, which selectively removes accrued values from words so that they can be used again in an illusion of creativity. This theory would seem to be similar to that advanced by Harold Bloom in his discussion of the strong poet and the authoritative father-precursor, but I believe that Bloom is more strongly genealogical along the lines of Freud's *Totem and Taboo*, while Hartman and Derrida espouse a deeply antigenealogical point of view that focuses not on the father, but on the Other (or the others) who breed like ideas in a library, fertilizing and polluting across the branches and up and down the trunk of the genealogical tree. For Hartman, art is strange, since it "point[s] to historical otherness, to assumptions or conventions we have difficulty appreciating." Hartman goes on to differentiate between strangeness, which "involves a sense that the strange is really the familiar, estranged," and otherness, which "precludes any assumption about this matter,"[54] but leaves the issue undecided, the dilemma intact, thus approaching the limits of the unthinkable intimated by Heisenberg.

Otherness, or alterity, recalls the situation of the animal who exists ahistorically, in oblivion to its past, whereas man exists historically, forgetting and unable to forget, estranged, yet on the point of total recall. Nietzsche speaks of the cure to this "malady of history" in terms of two other, equally potent poisons: the "unhistorical"— or the power of active forgetting, which induces the self-limitation that allows man to write—and the "superhistorical"—"which turns the eyes from the process of becoming to that which gives existence an eternal and stable character,"[55] that is, to the apparently antagonistic myths of art, religion, and science.

Even the modern physicist, so different from the nineteenth-century scientist scorned by Nietzsche, is unable to accept the destabilizing influence of the unhistorical cure, a perspective that would enable him to encompass the concept of discontinuity. The observations of P. W. Bridgman are apposite. After a discussion of possible manners of conceiving discontinuity in space, he concludes: "We cannot admit a discontinuous space, simply because it is unthinkable," and after an examination of the ontology of discontinuous time, he admits, "I find it much more difficult to imagine circumstances under which I would want to say that time is discontinuous than circumstances for a discontinuous space."[56] He appeals to the continuity of mathematics, a man-made abstraction, to preserve his belief in the necessary forms of thought that have ruled our relation to nature and to history.

In Bridgman, as in Heisenberg, the scientist turns back from the frontier of the unthinkable into the most precise orders of thought, into mathematics, held up as a talisman to ward off the evils of that which is beyond human comprehension. Yet, Ionesco's warning is never more to the point: "arithmetic [the study of mathematics applied to the new laws of physics] leads to philology [the exposition of these laws and their philosophical import in nonmathematical terms] and philology leads to crime."[57] What crime? Frances A. Yates reminds us and points to a historical precedent:

When in 1550, in the reign of Edward VI, the government commissioners visited Oxford, bonfires were made of the contents of the libraries, and, according to Wood [How appropriate the name of this historian!], particular suspicion was attached to works containing mathematical diagrams.

> Sure I am that such books wherein appeared Angles or Mathematical Diagrams, were thought sufficient to be destroyed because accounted Popish, or diabolical, or both.

The humanist dislike of metaphysical and mathematical studies has turned into a Reformation hatred of the past and fear of its magic.[58]

Mathematical diagrams, then, were seen as hieroglyphs hiding demonic secrets, secrets that would incline the student to black magic, to popish heresy, and ultimately, to treason. Yet, in the burning of the mathematical texts, the commissioners were not able to free the university from the magic they represented, nor were they able to break the hold of the popish past and remake history in the Anglican image. The burned books, perversely sacralized, have retained a hold on the imagination and a place in history, inciting other commissioners and other students to other crimes.

In Freud, the conflict is recast in terms of an unremitting tension between the demands of man's primitive instincts and the requirements of civilization. Thus, in discussing sublimation of the instinctual impulses, Freud refers the reader to artists and scientists who displace libido through a heightened emphasis on intellectual pleasures. He finds that "the energies available for 'cultural' development are thus in great part won through suppression of the so-called perverse elements of sexual excitation."[59] The quotation marks around the word "cultural" and Freud's addition of the "so-called" before the word "perverse" indicate his own ambivalent stance toward the fruits of civilization. Culture, he implies, is not necessarily a boon, and the animal instincts have their role to play in stable human development. There are at least two implicit problems with these intellectual displacements. The first is that mental stimulation provides only a partial outlet for animal instincts; the pleasure derived from intellectual work is great, "but their intensity is mild as compared with that derived from the sating of crude and primary instinctual impulses, it does not convulse our physical being."[60] The pleasure of creative work resides in the artist's ability to give body to his fantasies,[61] but this intellectual or spiritual birth process cannot compare to the pain and the satisfaction of physical sex and actual childbirth. Second, while the link of civilization and reality is securely maintained through an emphasis on work, if this emphasis is lost, the satisfaction obtained through the creation of fantasies and illusion is perverted into madness. With this severing of the reality link, "one can try to re-create the world, to build up in its stead another world in which its most unbearable features are eliminated."[62] As the artist slips into madness, writing becomes an antisocial, anticivilizing act. As the artist gives body to his fantasies, he also makes reality into a phantom, effacing the world and setting on pieces of paper the outlines of a spurious reality. The madman exchanges the rigidities of the "culture" deplored by Freud for rigidities of his own making.

Furthermore, the antisocial tendencies of the artist's work can pervert in another sense, since such isolation and alienation preclude normal human relationships. Rather than choosing another human being as the object of his sublimated sexual instincts, the artist, and the librarian, indulge in a narcissistic self-love; the artist chooses himself in the guise of his works, the librarian chooses himself in the fantasies of others most congenial to his own imaginative impulses. But in this objectifying of and grasping for fantasies of the self, alienation is intensified, since this self is a shadow identity, an imaginary construct that binds the artist further into an intrasubjectivity. It represents what Nietzsche refers to as accepting the empty *cogito ergo sum* over the plenitude of *vivo ergo cogito*. The process of replacing reality by a phantom presence whose only movement is uncanny and unalive proceeds apace for the librarian, until dead language and dead literature are the only field open to his imagination. The therapeutic value of artistic closure is evaporated in this claustrophobic sealing off.

But the negative closure of a dead (or deadened) literature is not the end; the burial of the phantom presence gives rise, not to a phoenixlike rebirth, but rather to a ghostly haunting of the cemetery. Thus, the library, the mausoleum of dead books, becomes the eerie locus of a comprehensive haunting by the ghosts of a phantom presence. It is easier in this context to understand the preoccupations of T. S. Eliot, who in "Tradition and the Individual Talent" discusses the relation of the modern artist to the dead poets and their still-living works, and Bloom, who in the *Anxiety of Influence* raises the question of the contemporary artist's haunting by the ghosts of his mighty precursors. The library can never be that *heimlich* place described by Freud, "withdrawn from the eyes of others" yet "free from ghostly influences."[63] Prisoners in a Freudian dream-fantasy, the librarians withdraw themselves from the eyes of others, eyes half-closed to the ghosts that haunt their abode, half-opened to the Anguish of seeing nothing but the faintest narcissistic projection in the mirror of the self. According to Mallarmé:

> She [Anguish], defunct nude in the mirror, still
> While, in the oblivion closed by the frame, settles down
> Of scintillations so soon the septet.[64]

The extension of *heimlich* into *unheimlich*, of homey into uncanny, takes into account a similar anxiety born of animism and narcissism: "for this uncanny is in reality nothing new or foreign, but something familiar and old-established in the mind that has been estranged only by the process of sublimation."[65] In the library, the uncanny is reality, a reality that has been estranged through a too-severe attenuation of the self in the reduplicating shadow worlds of books, and in a resurrected animism that finds a living human spirit in things long dead. The uncanniness of the library results from the derangements of the imagination that substitute Unreal for Real, not through unreason, but through a super-plus of the reasoning faculty. Reason meets the oneiric without recognition; the points of contact refer only to transgression. It is a paradox ably resumed by Yeats in his discussion of the importance of the figure of Leda in his philosophy. In Leda the transgression (rape) of human laws results in the birth of two physical/spiritual children—Love and War: desire and violent death—that represent the positive and negative poles of the primitive imaginative impulse. The imaginative impulses, in turn, come into contact with the dark abstractions of unimaginative reason: "and when in my ignorance I try to imagine what older civilization that annunciation rejected, I can but see bird and woman blotting out some corner of the Babylonian mathematical starlight."[66] The primitive instincts meet the scientific impulse without comprehension, but the surcharge of the uncanny is evident in the point of contact. In Leda, the subject is displaced, in anxiety or in ecstasy: an anxiety that is not lost in the confines of civilization, an ecstasy that is continually resurrected in the annals of Babel. To comprehend the significance of Leda, Yeats must also understand himself and engage in a process of encoding and decoding that is as interminable as the interminable dream analyses of Freud—and for the same reason.

Equally interminable is the quest undertaken by Robert Browning's Childe Roland. He begins the poem at what is nearly the end of the tale, turning onto a road indicated by a "hoary cripple" with "neither pride / Nor hope rekindling at the end descried, / So much as gladness that some end might be."[67] His hope, he admits, is merely a ghost, his spirit like that of a man so near death that he is already treated as beyond the grave by his acquaintances. The tired knight no longer seeks fame or victory; even failure would be welcome if it were to bring about an end to his wanderings. The poem is so eerie precisely because this desired end does not, cannot, occur. The knight has, at some undeterminable moment, already passed into the ghostly fantasy life, and he could come upon the Dark Tower (of Babel?) at any moment if only he would recognize this fact. The constructed meanings of reason again touch the discovered meanings of dream with the recognition that the order and coherence to be derived from the desired end cannot be forced. The only possible order for Childe Roland is his initiation into the ghostly company of watchers that provides not so much an end as a transition into another order of being; one consonant with the aims and goals of the library:

> There they stood, ranged along the hill-sides, met
> > To view the last of me, a living frame
> > For one more picture! in a sheet of flame
> I saw them and I knew them all. And yet
> Dauntless the slug-horn to my lips I set.
> > And blew. "Childe Roland to the Dark Tower came."[68]

The knight succeeds in his quest when he accepts the dictates of his logical faculty that he cannot succeed, but he fails in the most essential aspect—he cannot achieve death. He will become another picture, another work of art to be framed and hung. Yet the frame is a *living* frame, and he will join the ghostly company in their living sheet of flame like the sages of Yeats's Byzantium or the strong poets of the past tortured by the depredations of their successors in Bloom's world of misprision. Browning points to the interminability of the written word that permanently defers the possibility of a satisfactory end and threatens the sanity of discourse itself. Yeats discovers the anxiety of a world bifurcated into rational and irrational elements, each with their antithetical doubles, and he gives voice to his confused incomprehension. Childe Roland finds a peculiar, uncanny world where the demands of the rational and irrational faculties are reversed, finally to be reintegrated into one devouring flame and one sustaining image: the portrait of the knight, horn to lips, blowing his defiance before the portals of the mysterious tower. The lone seeker, like the alienated artist or the isolated librarian, exists within the oneiric shadow world he has constructed of his own wishes and longings, recognizing the tower as an uncanny enemy, refusing to see that it was built from the same derangements of imagination that sent him away from civilization on his lonely quest.

The knight's quest is, finally, a metaphysical one. Yet, as the two realms of rational and irrational do not serve to subsume all possibilities of human behavior, so too calling the knight's journey an essentially metaphysical quest does not exhaust its nature or importance. His goal, the metaphysical/physical tower, is not achieved, indicating that at the end of the more extensive and wearying search, there is still something to be sought, that the squat tower conceals some essence impenetrable to metaphysics or any other form of thought.

This painful discovery of the insufficiency of human thought in general and of metaphysics in particular makes Childe Roland's quest a profoundly modern one. As Foucault recognizes, "There had formerly been a correlation between a *metaphysics* of representation and of the infinite and an *analysis* of living beings, of man's desires, and of the words of his language." Such is not the case following the modern inversion of the classic conception of knowledge, and as a result, "Modern thought . . . will contest even its own metaphysical impulses, and show that reflections upon life, labour, and language, in so far as they have value as analytics of finitude, express the end of metaphysics: the philosophy of life denounces metaphysics as a veil of illusion, that of labour denounces it as an alienated form of thought and an ideology, that of language as a cultural episode."[69] Such denunciations do not spell the disappearance of metaphysics from the sphere of human knowledge. As Foucault realizes, the metaphysical impulses are still present, if in an inverted form, though vilified, contested, or even denied. Still, such considerations return to haunt us like ghostly presences and fill us with an uncanny chill—what Borges calls "an indefinite fear imbued with science, which is the best clarity of metaphysics."[70] Metaphysical distinctions remain even when the field of their operation has been reversed, when the hierarchy of idea and form has been annulled.

Such reversals could be called by many names, but Nietzsche, in his redefinition of tragedy, envisions them in the form of the Apollonian/Dionysian dichotomy, and Walter Pater, writing at nearly the same time, also worked out an Apollo/Dionysus model. Both note the subjective, feminine-perverse affiliations of Dionysus as opposed to the objective, masculine-rational nature of Apollo. Of the two writers, however, Nietzsche's formulation is more widely known and influential.

Nietzsche sees the role of Apollo as that of the order-giver, the rationalizing force that throws a veil of illusion over the numinous Dionysian presence. The Apollonian man is the man of theory, worshiping at the altar of cognitive power. He is, Nietzsche tells us, dissatisfied in his cold and empty knowledge: "He remains eternally hungry, the critic [Beckett would say, "Crritic!"] without strength or joy, the Alexandrian man who is at bottom a librarian and a scholiast, blinding himself miserably over dusty books and typographical errors."[71] The Apollonian man is a powerless voyeur of life, a metaphysician who cannot tolerate the full force of the Dionysian life-giving impulse and thus congeals his quasicadaverous existence into an impossible Ideal, until the Ideal too becomes living-dead, uncanny and fear provoking. Nietzsche notes: "philosophizing was always a kind of vampirism. Looking at these figures, even Spinoza, don't you have a sense of something profoundly enigmatic and uncanny?"[72] Such men stretch their cognitive abilities to the utmost, yet remain willingly captive to the enchantments of dead books, searching, as Nietzsche informs us, to name all the periods and styles of world literature as Adam named all the beasts in the Garden of Eden.[73]

This is the same impulse that seduced Linnaeus into believing that he could achieve a perfect representation of nature through a continuity ordering its component parts. One form of representation becomes another; instead of a word bridging the gap between the natural object and its name, scientific classifications, a new set of names in a dead tongue, attempt to link names in a purely linguistic representation. But the results of such classification are peculiar; temporally and spatially removed, the names persist in a void, linked only by a doubly metaphorical displacement to that which they represent. The attempt at continuity reveals a discontinuous undercurrent; the veil of illusion is ripped away revealing the Dionysian core of Apollo. Thus science instigates its own reversals that are more apparent the more the men of theory strain to keep them hidden. No wonder the scholiasts described by Nietzsche are so miserable; struggling to keep their cadavers in order and their metaphysics stable, they are constantly threatened by the uncanny Dionysian twitchings under the veil.

For the Dionysian man, in contrast, the names and identities so carefully built up in the Apollonian visionary Ideal are completely destroyed, even to the proper name—the identity—of the person who profers the Dionysian alternative. The Dionysian man privileges the night vision, the delightful and recognized illusions of dream. The Dionysian artist, as opposed to the Apollonian scholar, turns away from the dazzlements of the sun, suppressing the sunborn visions of reason for the secret luminous afterimage of darkest night. The night vision may be more than man can easily bear; it holds out the dazzling freedom of a discordant reality. It is discordant, however, only to the lingering Apollonian doubts that fear the night and Dionysus's intolerable music. The Dionysian music, and the Dionysian sensibility in general, are radically different from the Apollonian, though the two are interdependent. It is impossible to speak of a Dionysian identity since the Dionysian spirit is totally opposed to the giving of names and the stabilization of identity. Apollonian identity and name-giving are based on the reiteration of the Same; recurring rhymes and tonalities in music and poetry, repetition of similar objects and acts, a concretization of being. In the Dionysian night, recurrence can only be understood in relation to the dissolution of the self, the Dionysian identity is a fantasmal structure, a field of difference that never degenerates into stasis. In this interplay, paradoxically, day stands revealed as a superficial structure of appearances; night is lauded as the profoundest truth of being. In the brightest daytime sunlight of noon, there are no shadows; in the fantasmal Dionysian night the dark glow of shadows overwhelms. The Dionysian is demonic and transgressive, but such transgression is not necessarily negative, as Foucault reminds us: "Transgression opens onto a scintillating and constantly affirmed world, a world without shadow or twilight, without that serpentine 'no' that bites into fruits and lodges their contradictions at their core. It is the solar inversion of satanic denial."[74] But this solar inversion is already inverted—inverted from the shifting daylight of reason that Nietzsche rejected as the province of the scholiast and the critic.

The freedom of the Dionysian spirit gives birth to a new kind of laughter that intensifies the nauseating, the disgusting, the ugly, and the terrible. This too is part of the transgressive affirmation described by Foucault. It is the cleansing laughter that undoes contradictions, affirming the transmutative powers of Dionysus, confounding the petty rationalistic codes and freeing the subject from the narcissistic anxiety of Apollo. It is the deafening, maddening, liberating laughter of the true artist—or the true revolutionary.

Nietzsche's Apollo/Dionysus metaphor relates to and reveals the metaphoricity of the library in which the frozen identity of "a life of . . ." confronts the metamorphic transpositions of living. The scholiast and the critic deplored by Nietzsche see only the former, the parceling out of the continuum of living into discrete packages: Dionysus dismembered. The true Dionysian philosopher would take a step beyond; to the remembering of the god, to the reconstitution of a primordial unity that is accompanied by the remembrance of the discontinuous body. This second step is unnatural or supernatural; the resurrection of a phantom presence. The resurrected god is not the same as the dismembered body. Solid natural animality is lost in a spiritualized presence just as metaphor itself is (cf. Ernst Cassirer, *The Philosophy of Symbolic Forms*, 1955) intimately associated with the loss of primordial, immediate responses to the natural world and their replacement by conceptualized representations. As Derrida observes in "White Mythology":

> To avoid ending up with an empiricist reduction of knowledge and a fantastic ideology of truth, we should no doubt have to substitute for the classical opposition (maintained or eliminated) between metaphor and concept, another articulation. This articulation, without bringing in the whole metaphysics of the classical opposition, would also have to account for the specific gaps which epistemology cannot ignore between what it calls metaphorical and scientific effects. Undoubtedly the need for this new articulation is already announced in Nietzsche's discourse.[75]

In the Apollo/Dionysus dichotomy, however, Nietzsche remains bound to the closure of metaphysics in his generalization of this metaphor to unnatural versus proper, natural states of being. Throwing back the veil of Apollo does not free the Dionysian impulse as long as it is constrained by Nietzschean discourse to a definable field of operations. Dionysus masquerades in the cloak of Apollo—granted, the cloak is a veil of illusion laid upon him by others—but it is a cloak nevertheless which has been accepted and worn, obscurely addressing itself to the hidden nature of things, an unnatural (resurrected) nature, one that is known only in absence and forgetting. The mythic impulse is celebrated and prolonged, if inverted, by a Dionysian oracle that ejects the Oracle of Delphi. Apollonian radiance is replaced by Dionysian subterranean obscurity, superficiality and exteriority become profundity and interiority, but the myth, the metaphor, is not deconstructed. The library, the metaphysical realm of operations, is not destroyed by the inverting of Dionysus within its walls. A further metamorphosis is necessary, one which Derrida hints that Nietzsche has also already foreseen.

Nietzsche's privileging of philology as a key to the rigorous science of reading well is important. His goal, through philology, is to strip the veil of falsifying beliefs, "to translate man back into nature; to become master of the many vain and overly enthusiastic interpretations and connotations that have so far been scrawled and painted over that eternal basic text of *homo natura*."[76] Nietzsche recognizes the logophiliac impulses of interpretation, and in his return to Dionysus he also, paradoxically, seeks a return to the granite substratum common to humanity. He sees and despises the palimpsest, looking for the purity of the original text, the original body that has not yet been tortured out of recognition by human scrawlings on its back. Nietzsche calls for a new science unlike the old, odd scratchings of scholiasts and critics, seeing in the library that strange hell where man reads on palimpsests the phantom of the original, hidden discourse. The logic of the scholiast's delirium (and ours) is subsumed in the etiology of semiotics, in the link established and maintained between logophilia and the science of language. Nietzsche's madness cancels the other madness and permits us to think anew of the time before Babel and, perhaps, to begin again the cycle of a new Eternal Return.

Logophilia begets logorrhea, begetting in its turn taxonomies, an Apollonian endeavor carried into the world of language by the subtilization to the nth degree of the figures of speech and style of classical rhetoric. Like other mechanistic sciences, this classificatory system only superficially attempted to find a common ground among the different figures; it was both positive and positivistic in its goals and methods. Verbal equations were elevated to a preeminent structural level. Nietzsche's new rhetoric is based on different premises; its valorization is negative, in that it postulates the destruction of traditional stylistic modes, of traditional lines of interpretation. Out of the remaining primitive chaos of language comes the resurgence of the vital, necessary figures of the world. But clearing accrued palimpsestic adherences from the body of the text is an active and ongoing process, not one that can be set aside after the first cleansing. The interpretations resettle and again cloak the body with a veil of appearances: "If we could imagine an incarnation of dissonance—and what is man if not that?—that dissonance in order to endure life, would need a marvelous illusion to cover it with a veil of beauty."[77]

The old, original fall from the simplicity of language conditions every moment in this cyclical pattern. In its simplest form, it asserts that man is discontinuous with language, and the structures of language are likewise discontinuous. The basic, eternal text of *Homo natura* exists only in the form of a fragmented, dismembered body. Here is the essence of how logophilia becomes logorrhea—or how it can shift into logophobia or into logo-folly (a madness of letters that can also take many forms). Thus Don Quixote's madness consists in his attempt to protect the purity of his basic text from the tainting of vulgar incrustations through the creation of a mythic existence that denies the contamination inscribed in all language. Yet these quixotic adventures become for us an affair of surfaces, a palimpsest of languages, dialects, customs, usages. The psychological complexity that overdetermines man and keeps him from his pure, original past also results in the overdetermination of linguistic codes, an overcoding that is linked to the death sentence passed on man in the Garden of Eden.

From this thanatography written by God to close the circle of man's existence derives the human straining against death. Don Quixote's is a mad logophilia, but in this schizophrenic (Apollo/Dionysus) life there exists another logophilic madness that seeks to avert death by endorsing infinite flow. Don Quixote represents the static and turgid immorality of the academician who attempts to interrupt linguistic motion in the rigid categories of traditional rhetoric. Beckett would, perhaps, indicate a possibility for another type of madness; that of logophilia disguised as logophobia, the apotheosis of language in the infinite repetition of the same. Cervantes's love of words stands against Beckett's disgust for them; Don Quixote's poised and perfect enunciations, his varied adventures, contrast with the Beckettian babble of nothing to say, nothing to be done. The Cervantean language stays death in its seizure of a single moment of narrative time and space; Beckett's timeless, spaceless dramas are poised against the wish for, and hope of, a death infinitely deferred. In Cervantes, death must be forestalled; in Beckett the characters long for the foreclosure of infinitude. The Beckettian endeavor embodies another kind of rhetoric described by Paul de Man, the rhetoric that "radically suspends logic and opens up vertiginous possibilities of referential aberration."[78] De Man, with

Nietzsche, does not point to a rhetorical structure, but to a practice of rhetoric, a radical activity that subverts structures; that unmakes, deletes, or redistributes codes. It is a revolutionary praxis that signals the failure of nominalization and traditional rhetorical signification to sustain a stable system.

But is the quixotic purely an Apollonian furor? Is not madness itself a sign of the surreptitious entry of Dionysus into the library? And how, in the library space, is the classic confrontation between these two metaphorical forces finally resolved?

CHAPTER 2

Librarians and Madness: Cervantes, Nabokov, O'Brien

IN HIS HISTORY of insanity, Michel Foucault identi-
fies the first true recognition of madness and the subsequent separation of madmen from society with the decline of Gothic forms: "as
if that world, whose network of spiritual meanings was so close-
knit, had begun to unravel, showing faces whose meaning was no
longer clear except in the forms of madness."[1] While the forms still
persist, he continues, soon they cease to have anything to say; they
become *mere* forms that have lost their latent content; that is to say,
they are emptied of the spiritual essences that once gave them life
and meaning. With the weakening of the theological knot that held
together being and meaning, the recognized ambiguity as to the relation between figure and language forces an even deeper scission, a
more rapid unraveling of the knot that now barely holds the two
terms in stable conjunction. No longer is there any linguistic reality
to be discovered behind the forms, the colors, the words that inspire
the Gothic impulse. Paradoxically, says Foucault:

> This liberation derives from a proliferation of meaning, from a
> self-multiplication of significance, weaving relationships so nu-
> merous, so intertwined, so rich, that they can no longer be de-
> ciphered except in the esoterism of knowledge. Things them-

selves become so burdened with attributes, signs, allusions that they finally lose their own form. Meaning is no longer read in an immediate perception, the figure no longer speaks for itself; between the knowledge which animates it and the form into which it is transposed, a gap widens. It is free for the dream.[2]

Henceforth, madness cannot be translated into the language of knowledge and knowledge has no foothold in the world of madness. The world of madness institutes the reign of appearances and the dissolution of forms; the world of knowledge attaches itself to science and the establishment of new forms. Yet both knowledge and madness derive from the same source, and both come together in their captivation with the same chaotic maelstrom. As Foucault notes, though it does not *fascinate* the scientist, madness still attracts him. And in the attraction by madness, the world of reason and stilled forms becomes involved in a continual metamorphosis; the scientific space unfolds, breaks into fragments, and is dispersed:

No doubt, madness has something to do with the strange paths of knowledge. . . . But if knowledge is so important in madness, it is not because the latter can control the secrets of knowledge; on the contrary, madness is the punishment of a disorderly and useless science. If madness is the truth of knowledge, it is because knowledge is absurd, and instead of addressing itself to the great book of experience, loses its way in the dust of books and in idle debate; learning becomes madness through the very excess of false learning.[3]

It is this multiplication of meaning, this excess of false learning (or its mirage) that becomes a weight bearing down on the librarian, catapulting him from knowledge into dream and madness. The presence of books acts as a catalyst in this transformation. The librarian, who has lived so long in the midst of books, finds that the project of saying is foreclosed before he can start. The pressure of forms ensures his silence and initiates his descent into madness. This weight of dead texts bears down upon Foucault as well, and in his "Discourse on Language," he begins with an evocation of

Beckett's Unnamable, who achieves a heroic stature by acknowledging that weight, by saying that he can't say, and going on from there:

> I would really like to have slipped imperceptibly into this lecture, as into all the others I shall be delivering, perhaps over the years ahead. I would have preferred to be enveloped in words, borne way beyond all possible beginnings. At the moment of speaking, I would like to have perceived a nameless voice, long preceding me, leaving me merely to enmesh myself in it, taking up its cadence, and to lodge myself, when no one was looking, into its interstices. . . .
>
> Behind me, I should like to have heard . . . the voice of Molloy, beginning to speak thus: "I must go on; I can't go on; I must say words as long as there are words, I must say them until they find me, until they say me—heavy burden, heavy sin; I must go on; maybe it's been done already; maybe they've already said me."[4]

Foucault not only says that he can't say, but he says it in another's words. He admits that beginning is a torture—and so begins with another beginning selected from the "dust of books" in the library. With the Unnamable, Foucault indicates that what he is about to say may already have been said, but that his burden, like that of Beckett's character, is to say it (or to be said) again. The forlorn hope that words might someday find him is the hope that makes the world of forms human and inhabitable. Faced with the progressive disintegration of the Christian, Gothic myth, Foucault, and Beckett's unnamed voice, find no recourse other than to embrace their "sin," their "burden," their joy, in the full recognition that in so doing they are inventing another myth, a personal myth, which has grown out of the contact with the library, out of stray bits and pieces of philosophies and religions.

This project of saying approaches the madness of a Don Quixote, who is also ruled by the already said and by his need to find the words that say his existence. It is a peculiar madness, best described not by formlessness, but by the formalistic excesses of a false learning—a literary, library-based madness. Foucault and the Unnamable approach this madness, but stand apart from it. Unlike Don Quixote, who steadfastly attaches his "mad" identity to a name, Foucault expresses his desire to merge himself with the maelstrom, to blend his words with those of a "nameless voice," thus avoiding imprisonment in a fixed identity. One of the major features of the insane mind, as contrasted with the Beckettian voice imagined by Foucault, consists of the way it knows. The madman, the Don Quixote, is imprisoned by the insanity of a name; and thus he seeks to assimilate whatever he encounters into his frame of reference, without ever truly recognizing or acknowledging any new fact. In this sense, "to know" has no relation to the increment of knowledge; it consists in the subjugation of new facts to an old framework, in the perpetration of a cognitive rape as a means of asserting control over the environment. It is only in this sense that the mad librarian can be said to know at all, and only in the recognition of this special sense of knowledge can the Foucaultian claim that "madness is the truth of knowledge" be accepted and understood.

The bars of the madman's prison, constructed of the chimerical speculations of history and psychology, are unreal; imprisonment by the name in a fixed identity is a far more substantial form of incarceration. Says Foucault: "In madness equilibrium is established, but it masks that equilibrium beneath the cloud of illusion, beneath feigned disorder; the rigor of the architecture is concealed beneath the cunning arrangement of these disordered violences."[5] The disorders and irrationalities of madness are easily construed, but it is the solid formalist underpinnings that provide a more fruitful basis for analysis.

In a work of art, form provides solidity and the illusion of reality. "Form *is* reality in the writing of critics," says Georg Lukács. "It is the voice with which they address their questions to life."[6] The echoes and correspondences between elements that make up the work become for the critics (other Don Quixotes buried in libraries and subject to their theoretical biases) the basis for deriving a visible, coherent configuration: a presence, a form, a reality. But the architecture of this form is unstable; the building is constructed over the abyss of madness. Foucault recognizes the abyss and longs for the words that would fill the void, "beyond all possible beginnings," words pronounced by a nameless voice. Thus, what Foucault proposes is not the triumph of one form, one voice, one reality, but the linking of two or of an infinite number of realities, filling the abyss of formalistic madness with an onslaught of difference. The words come to him from beyond the origin, from behind him, from a *there* which is also *here*.

The void of the origin and the abyss of madness always say the same thing, and while it would be presumptuous to assume that the nameless voice holds out the hope of a magic word that, once spoken, would break apart the brittle formalism of reality with its usurped knowledge, the desire for its existence keeps alive the oscillation between the spoken rigid identities of knowledge and the silent rigidities of madness. It is an oscillation that can be figured, once again, in the movement from a traditional historical sense (which "undertook to 'memorize' the *monuments* of the past, transform them into *documents*, and lend speech to those traces which, in themselves are not verbal") to a contemporary deployment of historical researches ("which transforms *documents* into *monuments*");[7] that is, in the shift from history to a Foucaultian archaeology or a Nietzschean genealogy.

The same oscillation obtains in the critic's relationship to an individual work. Werner Hamacher finds that "Script is [said to be] a stone that resists the transformation into the subjective totality which represents itself in it," and further:

> A similar experience holds for reading. All reading is mournful, since it has to work through the experience of the non-unifiability of the body of the script—in which the thought is ossified into an exterior form—with its subjective animation in the act of understanding. Reading is the labor of mourning over the loss of this union of objectification and subjectivity, which loss the act of reading itself causes. Thus it is potentially endless—melancholy—since it itself repeats the tear [*Riss*] which it labors to close.[8]

Endless and without origin, melancholy and sinful; says Derrida, "The sign, monument-of-life-in-death, monument-of-death-in-life, ... the hard text of stones covered with inscriptions is *the pyramid*."[9] But the pyramids now stand empty, mournful monuments to a lost past, symbols now of the absent origin, their inscriptions testifying more clearly to the murmur of a nameless voice than to the preservation of an identity fixed for all time in death.

In his concept of archaeology, Foucault combines the science of the archive (library science) with the study of the *archè* (the monuments left by the ancients), in an attempted disengagement from the either/or of historical studies. Yet Foucault's reading of madness, like Hamacher's reading of Hegel, is endless and endlessly melancholy since the opening premise is the scission (Hamacher says "the tear") which allowed it to come into being. This point is related to that made by Derrida is his review of Foucault's history of madness: "A history, that is, an archaeology against reason doubtless cannot be written, for, despite all appearances to the contrary, the concept of history has always been a rational one."[10] While Foucault sometimes rejects this language of reason and order, a complete disengagement is theoretically and practically impossible.[11] Like the Unnamable, Foucault breaks the chains of silence ("I can't go on") with the determination to say ("I must go on"). Two processes coexist in the Foucaultian library of madness. In the first, a group of contradictory signifiers resists the efforts of the historian or archaeologist to impose signifieds; in the second, a system of signifiers combine to dissolve their precarious connection with their significations. "The impossibility of history" confronts "the necessity of madness."

The cloven text, that which is exemplified in the scission between subjective and objective, madness and reason, archaeology and history, is necessarily an ironic text; recognition of the cleavage compels it to self-consciousness, reading itself at the same time as it is written. But if the text is spatially determined by scission, it is temporally defined by scission's near opposite—allegory. For Derrida, texts are "always already," a distinction that Foucault would seem to accept in his adoption of another's words (behind him) as his words, in the acceptance of words already said that refer the reader to what has (perhaps) "been done already." The ironic text is diachronic, maintaining a distance between the two terms involved. The allegorical text is synchronic; it operates as a function of metaphor, serviceable only as texts can be mediated by correspondence. The cloven text is, obviously, a possible/impossible text, always verging on its own destruction, typified by the cleavage of irony and the mediation of analogy. Says Octavio Paz:

> Irony and analogy are irreconcilable. The former is a product of linear time, successive and unrepeatable; the latter is the manifestation of cyclical time: the future is in the past and both are in the present. Analogy inserts itself into mythic time, and further: it is myth's foundation; irony belongs to historical time, it is the consequence (and the conscience) of history.[12]

On the one hand, Paz points to a massive monumental concept of time, to an analogical time without cleavage, to an inescapable cycle. On the other hand, and as Paz intimates, perhaps as a consequence of the weight of this very inescapability, analogy's irreconcilable double breaks apart the cycle to operate in a cursive time, a time that flows. Mythic time is replaced by the conscience of history. Not without loss, however; for in his opposition of the two terms, Paz uncritically verbalizes what is essentially an ideological (or a theological) problem. As myth is replaced by a historical conscience, what takes the place of the gods, of the numinous power of the sacred word? Driven by a desire for spiritualized content, the author or the librarian seeks to merge irony and analogy. Says Sartre: "I confused things with their names: that amounts to believing."[13] The ethical consequences of Sartre's antihistorical appeal to a systematized transcendence are clear; to be historical is to be mortal; thus Sartre chooses "as my future the past of a great immortal and I tried to live backwards. I become completely posthumous."[14]

Still, Sartre could not escape from the exigencies of his time; the totalizing mind takes the conscience of history and makes of it an ahistorical self-consciousness by leaving unacknowledged (but not absent) the disparity between statement and reality. Confusing things with names is a belief, a myth, not a fact. Living backwards so as to ignore mortality is a lie that does not make death any less real. Sartre refuses to resign himself to loss. As an immortal he can insert himself into the mythic hush of the library and remain sublimely unmoved by historical man's mourning over the fact of his mortality and the absence of spiritual consolation. An imagined tangible presence (words as things) allows Sartre to remain oblivious to his own present and to his own material presence. The confusion of word as thing is a self-conscious forgetfulness that remembers itself and then ignores the consequences of that remembrance through a false analogy. The word is the thing only in an impossibly material/spiritual presence.

These impossible monuments, these imagined material presences, are indestructible precisely because they are also presumed to be spiritual. Yet, as Sartre shows, as material presences, they can still be classified, reproduced, or burned in response to shifting inner needs. It is the mindful forgetfulness, the knowing choice of the lie that most fully distinguishes the ironic consciousness from the unconscious formalizations of myth. Sartre *chooses* the library, the company of immortals, as a faith to cling to, as a reaction against the discovery of the cursiveness of historical existence. He attempts to collapse the categories into a synchronic history, an ironic myth, an enterprise which, if taken un-ironically, would inevitably cause madness by merging rational thought into the nonrational, antirational reaches of myth. We can classify myths and deny myth, we can classify books or destroy books, yet myth remains an indestructible monument and history does not crumble under the challenges to its epistemological authority.

Foucault's text, *Madness and Civilization*, exemplifies the reasoning mind's approach to madness. Further, its approach can be applied without significant modifications to the fictional treatment of madmen (mad librarians) by sane, reasoning, author-librarians. Specifically, Foucault avoids the traps set by irony and analogy, by metonymy and metaphor, by diachrony and synchrony, by standing, as it were, alongside such formulations. It is indicative of Derrida's critical acuteness that he gives prominence to Foucault's use of the word "alongside" in his review of the Cartesian discussion of madness and dream.[15] It is a concept that Foucault uses frequently. In *The Order of Things*, Foucault refers to the "unthought" as the Other: "the Other that is not only a brother but a twin, born, not of man, nor in man, but *beside* him and at the same time, in an identical newness, in an unavoidable duality" (emphasis mine).[16] Similarly, in *Madness and Civilization*, Foucault describes madness—a version of the unthought—not as an alienated state, but as a mirror image of reason, an asymmetrical reproduction of man from the inside out. He discusses the circumstances under which "the soul of desiring man has become a prisoner of the beast," and indicates that it is this nightmare figure of the beast within "which fascinates the gaze of the ascetic—both are prisoners of a kind of mirror interrogation." Finally, by an ironic return, Foucault concludes that the "impossible animals issuing from a demented imagination, become the secret nature of man." [17]

It is the mirror interrogation, madness alongside reason, that provides the key to these transformations. Foucault's metaphor of the beast-become-essence as man's nature is turned inside out would seem at first to postulate a relationship of identity between man and beast. It is the mirror interrogation that reveals the ambiguity of this facile identification; the beast is the Other and it is the Same as opposition disappears in mirror likenesses—disappears only to re-surface in the same instant. Still, the impossible animals, products of madness, are not mere unreal reflections; they "become the secret nature of man." That which is other exists alongside the self, and the fearful beastly presence is at least partially incarnated (incarcerated) in the self. Beast and man change places; the animal looks at man and converts man into its reflection. The desiring man is concentrated in madness (the beast), concentrated and hardened in the crystal surface of the mirror, in cold stone worked by man and inscribed with his silent words. And the reverse. The silent words are spoken, they come to life and decry the madness in the coldness of reason and the warmth of desire. In Cervantes, Nabokov, and Flann O'Brien, this traversal by madness (by reason) is figured in the form of novels that describe the madness of books coming to life in the hands of their caretakers.

Don Quixote is, in a large measure, the product of his own library, and he can be defined through his relationship to books. Not only is he a being created out of language in the obvious sense that he is a character in a novel, but his nature within the novel is intimately related to an interplay with other books; that is, the reading of the romances of chivalry that line the library walls and that the country squire avidly devours in his moments of leisure. As Foucault describes him in *The Order of Things*, even his physical presence evokes "a long, thin graphism, a letter that has just escaped from the open pages of a book." [18] Though many of his books are destroyed by the curate and his willing assistants, Don Quixote is never alienated from the essence of his library. He becomes, in fact, a traveling library of sorts, carrying with him the characters, mannerisms, and customs of the tales he has read. The literary frame provided by the country squire's library of mouldering romances establishes the limits of investigation. Outside the squire's study and the books contained in it, reality and madness both crumble away at the edge of the abyss. Only within the frame set by Don Quixote's love of books can the reader pursue his archaeological researches.

But *Don Quixote* represents not merely the relation between a system of fictional signs and a world converted into another verbal system, but an interplay among several levels of verbal signs: the authentic and the apocryphal histories, the real and fictional worlds, and so forth. Entering into this situation and complicating it still further is the possible (probable) duplicity of the narrator/author/ translator in the production of this tale that we are asked to accept as authentic. The narrator of *Don Quixote* speaks at several removes from the original text, which, he tells us, he encountered by chance in Alcaná de Toledo. These papers, originally bound for a silk merchant's shop to be recycled into fresh writing material, were discovered to be the Arabic text of the story of Don Quixote written by the "historian" Cide Hamete Benengeli. Immediately following this fortuitous encounter, the narrator reflects upon the question of the reliability of the text, given the proposition that all Moors are liars by nature. Thus, this first novel departs radically from the tradition of literature as monument, as sacred text. In Marthe Robert's words: "It was manipulated, truncated, adulterated at random. It was lost, sought, found, bought, translated and finally resold according to a law of order or disorder that Cervantes is committed to articulate. . . . its text is doubtful, riddled, one suspects, with gaps, interpolations, errors, perhaps even deliberate lies." The result, she finds, is "a composite melange of novel and scholarly gloss."[19] Without physically destroying the manuscript, the narrator of Don Quixote has managed to undermine its credibility, to pulverize its language. The subject is lost, the reason for its inscription is unknown; history must be remade. The novelty of this fiction resides not in its exposure to corruption, but in its wholehearted acceptance of the contamination inscribed in all language. Cervantes already knows that all literature is written over an abyss.

The narrator of *Don Quixote*, like the protagonist of the "true history" he has discovered, recovers the scattered elements of an episodic text and rearranges them in new sequential chains, thus corroding the surface of ordinary language and quotidian reality as surely as the mad knight who sees in his surroundings only the configurations that correspond to the rigorous caprice of his obsession. The full word is emptied out into a surface representation; the plenitude of reason becomes the mirror of the vertiginous abyss of madness. Says Robert Alter: "In primitive culture, the word is magical, exerting power over the physical world; in biblical tradition it is sacred, instinct with unfathomable divine meaning. For Cervantes, the word simultaneously resonates with its old magical quality and turns back on itself, exposing its own emptiness as an arbitrary or conventional construct."[20] Don Quixote's heroism resides in his effort to create forms from life. His tragedy is that he wants to live these empty forms as if they were life rather than fictional constructs. Perhaps life and form can only be tolerated in their dissonant juxtaposition, in the transcription of a true history written by a liar.

Don Quixote, in his madness, stands at the furthest extreme of literature, but he is framed and controlled by his text as if imprisoned. Says Foucault, "*Where there is a work of art, there is no madness*; and yet madness is contemporary with the work of art, since it inaugurates the time of its truth."[21] The mad knight is so immersed in the magic of his verbal world that he is unable to construe its arbitrariness. He is beyond (or outside of) metaphor and metonymy; in his madness he is no longer either an archaeologist or a historian. His chosen literature and adopted language become for him a chaos of atomized forms from which his desire resolves the figures of this world.

Kinbote, the mad scholar of Nabokov's *Pale Fire*, is also involved in a shattered "true history," as he recounts the travails of King Charles the Beloved: an unreliable Don Quixote telling his own story. As is the case with *Don Quixote*, Kinbote's story is literature built out of literature, the pale fire of criticism reflecting the pale fire of a derivative academic poem. It involves, as does *Don Quixote*, a combinatory play of surface features. Thus, Kinbote (or Charles) alludes to his lost homeland as "that crystal land" and indicates that his beginnings as a scholar were devoted to the study of "the Zemblan variants, collected in 1798 by Hodinski, of the *Kong-skugg-sio (The Royal Mirror)*."[22] The royal mirrors and the crystal land become recurring motifs in the novel as Kinbote, the prisoner of his own linguistic combinations, is imaged in the form of a figure captured in ice, in crystal, in the surface of a mirror. An avid reader of other literature, Kinbote reads in each new work the ghostly presence of his own story. "For we are most artistically caged," says Kinbote's mirror image, Shade, in a line of the poem that the scholar does not choose for exegesis (p. 26).

A lonely man, imprisoned by the crystal cage of his own artistry, Kinbote finds a way to consecrate his solitude, to make his loneliness and isolation from others the crucial element in an uncommunicated subtext to Shade's poem. In his commentary on that poem, Kinbote imagines that he has escaped the imprisoning crystal—in actuality, he has merely transferred himself from one cage into another. He remains imprisoned by his game of linguistic surfaces, waiting expectantly (and dreading) the arrival of Gradus, another asymmetrical mirror image of himself as familiar to him as his own body.

Yet, while the scholarly Kinbote is comfortable in the tortuous mirror-labyrinth of his linguistic madness, Gradus, no scholar, becomes lost in its concrete representation. Thus, the hapless villain is often led astray in his search for the King by unfamiliar linguistic geography: "in the vicinity of Lex he lost his way among steep tortuous lanes" (p. 141). Gradus eventually finds his way out of Lex only to lose himself once again as he nears the hiding place of the exiled king, this time in the university library. Every incursion into the realm of words and books has the same result: "Not being a mariner or a fugitive king, he promptly got lost . . . in a labyrinth of stacks" (p. 98). After escaping this labyrinth, his continuing peregrinations lead him into similar troubles with another "among the bewitched hush of Rare Books" (p. 199).

The problems encountered by Gradus in his exposure to the silent linguistic systematization of the library call to mind similar difficulties experienced by one of Beckett's characters, the protagonist of *How It Is*. He, like Gradus, started out from Zembla only to lose himself in alien surroundings. But where Gradus loses himself in a physical-linguistic geography, Beckett's character loses his way in a tangle of verbs: "to listen as though having set out the previous evening from Nova Zembla I had just come back to my senses in a subtrophical subprefecture that's how I was has become or always was it's one or the other geography I had."[23] For the librarian, language is viewed conceptually as a map of the universe, a map which at best is only partially comprehensible. But this partially assimilated map is also a labyrinth, the most inhuman simulacrum of a map devised by man, because the labyrinth perverts the cartographer's enterprise of representing a chaotic multiplicity ordered by human intelligence. This order is, however, an order ruled by apparent disorder, the key to which is necessarily of limited access. Nevertheless, the little that librarians like Kinbote and Don Quixote understand about the linguistic manipulations of the literary world is still more than the minuscule amount the nonlibrarians are able to comprehend. Gradus and his fellow antilinguists inevitably lose themselves in the stacks of the labyrinthine library.

Still, despite his confusions, Gradus does manage to infiltrate the library by the fact of his presence, an unlikely infiltration into the land of Lex that is paralleled by Kinbote's insertion of his own hallucinated life into the text of Shade's poem. The forcing of unlikely elements into the straightforward text of the academic poem becomes, by incorporation, part of the decorum of the text itself. The text is violated, but its structure remains rigid, logical, and controlled.

It is this combination of control and designed infiltration that exemplifies Flann O'Brien's comic masterpiece, *At Swim-Two-Birds*. Like the scholar-author of *Pale Fire*, the student-author of *At Swim-Two-Birds* has created a model of a rigidly structured, despotic world, a world that is logical, coordinated, impeccably designed— but nevertheless a world that seems liable to fall apart in his hands at any moment. "The novel," pontificates the student-author, "in the hands of an unscrupulous writer, could be despotic. In reply to an inquiry, it was explained that a satisfactory novel should be a self-evident sham to which the reader could regulate at will the degree of credulity."[24] To test this theory, the opinionated student creates his own despotic novelist within the novel. This fictional author, Dermot Trellis, is doubly unbending in his relationship to his work, for not only does he force the reader to participate in a tightly structured reality, but he also exerts a tyrannic control over his characters. Both characters and readers rebel against their un-democratic treatment. Despite his assumption of rigid control, plot, character, and readers all escape his grasp:

> He has been in bed for the last twenty years, I said.
> You are writing a novel of course? said Byrne.
> He is, said Brinsley, and the plot has him well in hand.
> Trellis' domination over his characters, I explained, is im-paired by his addiction to sleep. There is a moral in that.
> (p. 139)

Soon the contrived novel escapes from its artificial plot, the charac-ters defy Trellis's orders and lead independent lives, and the reader applauds them in their rebellion. Despite these various initiatives, the structure of the novel as a whole is not so much chaotic as laby-rinthine. Trellis's dreams, like Don Quixote's and Kinbote's halluci-nations, are framed by the story in which they appear, retained and domesticated by the transparent forms of the novel in which they are contained. The basic text (the romances of chivalry, Shade's poem, Trellis's novel) is structurally disordered on a primary level, but it immediately accommodates itself to the secondary fixations and classifications of madness.

The whole of these complex machinations and distortions of the basic text is much to the point. The dispersion of the original, pre-sumably sacred (or in this case, at least more accurate) account is a distinctly Babelic procedure. This original document, hypothesized in the text by a madman, cannot become a monument; the vagaries of its historical existence put its truth value to the question. It is only the found document, present to the reader and to the mad li-brarian alike, about which a history can be construed. The func-tions of the narrator of *At Swim-Two-Birds*, the literary critic of *Pale Fire*, and the "editor" of *Don Quixote* are similar to that of all historians and librarians: to accept the found artifact and try to re-construct a history (Foucault would say an archaeology) devised through the selection and interpretation of material at hand. In the marketplace, the document has a real value—it is worth whatever the reader or the silk merchant has contracted to pay. For the librarian, who commits himself morally and professionally to the authenticity of its contents, the document becomes very nearly priceless.

The hypothesized original, authentic document stands outside the proliferating documents of the library and represents an opaque, unassimilated (unassimilable) object; in the eyes of madness the missing document is the archetypal monument, now present only in the vague, imprecise memories that collect around a ruin. Immobile, monstrous (beastly), the mental monument of madness already foretells its preordained end. Within the frame of the text, this unavailable monument is inscribed with a human name, and thus named, it can be fixed and classified in the structures of madness— and those of reason.

The importance given the proper name in these three novels is a significant index to this monumentalizing impetus. The Spanish landowner and the Russian professor doff their work-a-day identities with the change of a name, becoming Don Quixote, knight errant, and Charles the Beloved, exiled king of Zembla. *At Swim-Two-Birds* begins with three unrelated openings as the student-author tests out three different alter egos before eventually deciding in favor of a fourth figure, the hallucinatory dreamer and prescient author, Dermot Trellis. In each case, the scholar-protagonist rejects his own given name for a name he gives himself, one dense with meaning and monstrous in its application. Yet, the existence of the frame serves as a constant reminder that these new and more exact proper names are artificial, the temporary products of a hallucinatory (or at least disordered) imagination. Indeed, the "proper" name undergoes considerable slippage. Don Quixote at various times adopts alternative sobriquets: the Knight of the Rueful Figure, the Knight of the Lions, and finally, as his knightly monomania self-destructs under the pressure of severe disappointment, the equally literary "shepherd Quixotiz." The narrator of *Pale Fire* has an equally impressive list of variations on his proper name: the "Index" to his critical study lists V. Botkin, Charles II (Charles Xavier Vseslav), K, and Dr. Charles Kinbote. Finally, Trellis's tight control over the identities of his characters—his brainchildren—is eroded by the student-author's insistence that "characters should be interchangeable as between one book and another" (p. 33). Thus, while Trellis strives for autonomous creations, the student recirculates old characters derived from the storehouses of literature and folktale. The importance of exactitude in naming is lost in this second theory of character invention, a theory that gives no importance whatsoever to Name and explodes the myth of a subject-object unification.

Like Kinbote and Don Quixote, Dermot Trellis is a monomaniac; in this case, the obsession is not only literary but chromatic. The narrator of the novel informs the reader that "it is important to remember that he reads and writes only green books." And then he repeats, "That is an important point" (p. 139). Further elaboration follows:

> All colours except green he regarded as symbols of evil and he confined his reading to books attired in green covers. Although a man of wide learning and culture, this arbitrary rule caused serious chasms in his erudition. The Bible, for instance, was unknown to him. . . . For many years he experienced a difficulty in obtaining a sufficiency of books to satisfy his active and inquiring mind, for the green colour was not favoured by the publishers of London, excluding those who issued textbooks and treatises on such subjects as fretwork, cookery and parabolics. The publishers of Dublin, however, deemed the colour a fitting one for their many works on the subject of Irish history and antiquities and it is not surprising that Trellis came to be regarded as an authority thereon and was frequently consulted by persons engaged in research, including members of the religious orders, the enclosed class. (pp. 139–40)

Trellis's obsession, like that of Kinbote and Don Quixote, nicely juggles the extremes of compulsive orderliness and uncontrollable chaos. Each of these characters, in their selection of a scholarly area of investigation, has exercised extreme care in limiting his field, and each has made his position in this area of expertise comically unassailable. Don Quixote has so identified himself with the romances of chivalry that he is absorbed into their world, Kinbote has isolated himself in a motor lodge to transpose Zembla onto Appalachia, and Trellis, the reader of green books, has made himself a specialist in the area of Irish history, and parabolics, and fretwork. His knowledge as gleaned from green books is so comprehensive and so valuable, that he is even consulted by the religious orders, that "enclosed class," despite his ignorance of their primary text—the Bible.

In each case, the conjunction of extreme order and proliferating chaos gives rise to a most unstable balance, one that is easily overset—especially by a madman. But these novels are not yet mad; more precisely, they approach the edge of madness, recognizing its necessity but denying its controlling structures by recourse to a literature already written. The novelists play at the limits of convention and structure, speaking of a Golden Age, but writing in an ironic mode. The controlling structures of madness are destructive or self-destructive—violently so. Don Quixote is defeated in battle and dies in his bed of the psychic wounds. Kinbote's nemesis, Gradus, murders his double, Shade. In his "Conclusion of the book, ultimate," the author of *At Swim-Two-Birds* asks, "Was Hamlet mad? Was Trellis mad? It is extremely hard to say. . . . Even experts do not agree on these vital points" (p. 314). And the novel closes with the anecdote of the "poor German who was very fond of three." This unfortunate obsessive "went home one evening and drank three cups of tea with three lumps of sugar in each cup, cut his jugular with a razor three times and scrawled with a dying hand on a picture of his wife good-bye, good-bye, good-bye" (p. 316). The character self-destructs, but the novel does not.

Nevertheless, as Kinbote's commentary on Shade's poem reveals, the structures of madness are tremendously potent. In his preface to the poem, Kinbote clearly indicates the dominant role his notes are to play in this volume: "Although those notes, in conformity with custom, come after the poem, the reader is advised to consult them first and then study the poem with their help, rereading them of course as he goes through its text, and perhaps, after having done with the poem, consulting them a third time so as to complete the picture" (p. 18). While Kinbote demonstrates no self-consciousness or self-awareness about the parodic nature of this undertaking, the reader sees in Nabokov's novel an uncomfortable approximation, a pale fire of the truth. But this approximate form gradually assumes validity as the only appropriate form—a perfect antidote to Shade's academic art. If the reader follows the commentary according to the critic's recommendations, Shade's poem loses interest under the impact of Kinbote's. There is, in fact, no Shade's poem as such; the lines of verse serve as a point of departure for the mad king's weavings of fantasy. And we, his readers, by following his instructions, become accomplices in this incessant reading of the self into a preexisting text.

It is not surprising that Shade, the academic author of this vanishing poem, is haunted by thoughts of death and the loss of self-identity; his existence is obliterated both physically and literarily in Kinbote's text. In fact, Kinbote garners his strength from Shade's obliteration. Radically isolated within himself by the alienating force of his fantasies, Kinbote forges an artistic life for himself in the to-and-fro movements of his commentary, sucking the sparse hints of life from the poem to feed his own hallucinatory existence. Kinbote reenters the human community, the community of literati, through his imagined friendship with the great man and through his painstakingly exact parody of a critical text. Says Robert Alter: "Kinbote's mad Commentary represents an extreme instance, at once moving and farcical, of the general difficulty of decoding such artful texts."[25] The poem that prefixes Kinbote's commentary is based on many of the conventions of artistic creation: Shade ascribes to a Keatsian lyric standard of beauty and delight, he enjoys the combinations of sounds in a poetic language that is enveloped in a web of taste and good sense, he is motivated by one of mankind's most enduring illusions—the quest for immortality. Yet this artful poem disintegrates in the process of Kinbote's meditation on it, as the loneliness and despair of his madness overwhelm the sterile beauty of the unfinished poem.

Shade's art is a very limited one; limited by the parochialism of his concerns and the pettiness of his dreams. Kinbote, on the other hand, dreams too wildly, too grandly, and is full of dark imaginings that can be put on paper only when subjected to the perceived restrictions of a critical edition. There is a curious balance implicit in this recognition of restriction, a balance that Kinbote feels is threatened by the menacing presence of the professional assassin, Gradus, an unacknowledged side of his personality. Lost in language, lost in the library, Gradus nevertheless manages to emerge from the university to give the deathblow to academic artistic pretensions. Kinbote's melodramatic reconstruction of Shade's assassination need not be accurate to be poetically true. The poet's artistic death is more certain than this physical death that parallels and precedes it, since the artistic death occurs before the reader's eyes as the poem is infected by Kinbote's revisionary zeal and slowly dies: "*Botkin. V.*, American scholar of Russian descent, 894; kingbot, maggot of extinct fly that once bred in mammoths and is thought to have hastened their phylogenetic end, 247; bottekinmaker, 72; *bot*, plop, *boteliy*, big-bellied (Russ.); botkin or bodkin, a Danish stiletto" (p. 216).

In his implicit recognition of the terrible risks of death and annihilation that accompany the "blue magic" of literary imitation, Charles Kinbote enters into the illustrious company established by Don Quixote. Like Don Quixote, who must die as Quijano to be resurrected as the knight errant, Kinbote the scholar must fade into insignificance and Shade the poet die a violent death in order that the exiled king might spring to life. In her book, *The Old and the New*, Marthe Robert offers an elegant description of this constructive-destructive magic as a footnote to this comment by Kafka: "His reasoning goes hand in hand with sorcery. One can escape from reasoning by taking refuge in magic and from sorcery by taking refuge in logic; but one can also eliminate them both at once in such a way that they become a third thing, living magic, or destruction of the world that does not destruct but constructs." Marthe Robert writes that "this aphorism . . . defines the quixotic word (*la verbe donquichotesque*), which is invocation and critique, conjuration and radical probing, both one and the other with their risks and perils."[26] If the individual word is no longer, after Babel, divine, it still retains some kind of magic potency that can be released in the gesture of madness. With his blue magic, Kinbote gives life to a fantastic king, builds a crystal palace for him to inhabit, and peoples a country from which he must flee. But in the process of his labor of construction, there is a parallel and undeniable risk of destruction: the death of Shade and the emptying out of the words/ worlds of his poem, the immortalization of the empty shell of Kinbote in the crystal cage of his madness, the loss of a homeland and its replacement by the isolation and mobility of "this wretched motor lodge, with that carrousel inside and outside my head, miles away from New Wye" (p. 18).

But the gesture—what depths of attraction it still holds! To use words to express life, to construct real worlds from insubstantial dreams; the gesture is perfect in and of itself, a movement from ambiguity to clarity. Kinbote's King Charles, like Cervantes's Don Quixote, is full of splendidly heroic life purchased at the cost of another life, a turning away from reason to self-delusion and death. Says Foucault: "In Shakespeare or Cervantes, madness still occupies an extreme place, in that it is beyond appeal. Nothing ever restores it to truth or reason. It leads only to laceration and thence to death. . . . But death itself does not bring peace; madness will still triumph—a truth mockingly eternal, beyond the end of a life which yet had been delivered from madness by this very end."[27] The impossible becomes the necessary and remains so, immutably; the gesture toward madness is captured in a rigidly permanent form: the document that is always to be found once again, the silent inscribed stone of the monument inhabited by a ghostly Shade. "What is a ghost?" Stephen Dedalus asks the assembled company in the library in the ninth chapter of Joyce's *Ulysses*. And he answers his own question: "One who had faded into impalpability through death, through absence, through change of manners."[28] The word, the Cervantean and Nabokovian word, tingles with the energy of its old magical resonances, and, simultaneously, reveals its absence, its emptiness, its pure conventionality.

Don Quixote, of course, sees only the magical energy of the word, not its conventionality as part of a system of arbitrary signs. Because his faith in the magic power of words is so strong, he is willing to make the gesture that we interpret as madness, the leap from staid fact to impossible reality. In Foucault's terms, Don Quixote's function is nothing less than to reestablish the relationship between knowledge and the "divinatio," and thus his philosophical importance is closely related to the nature of a post-Babel world. Says Foucault, "Its task [that of divinatio] was to uncover a language which God had previously distributed across the face of the earth; it is in this sense that it was the divination of an essential implication, and that the object of its divination was *divine*."[29] Don Quixote is indeed mad if he hopes to reunite the scattered children of Babel under his banner through his espousal of the chivalric cause, but madmen and fools are traditionally the harbingers of divine revelation.

Through the magic of Don Quixote's madness, through his divination of the secret resemblances between the world of fiction and his own world, there arises a paradox that puts to the doubt all preconceived notions of reality. Because a madman sees resemblances where there are supposedly none, all resemblances become suspect and words are wrenched apart from the things they represent. Since Don Quixote's system is patently false, the question arises as to whether all philosophical systems are not equally so. Don Quixote's system, Kinbote's system, Trellis's system, no less than other "nonfictional" systems, impose a perceptual order on the banal events of daily life so that the insignificant appears resplendent with transcendental significance. If no systematic approach to life is available, we are menaced by the fragmentary impressions of aphasia. But adherence to system can trap man into the belief that he is freeing himself from the atrocious aspects of an infinite and chaotic reality, while he is actually only reducing it to the false security of his interpretation. Don Quixote is different from such sane system-builders only because his system does not share the sanction of his society; he is mad because he is unaware of the disjunction he has perpetrated. Foucault calls him "the hero of the Same,"[30] undermining in this definition all similitude: "This being so, the written word ceases to be included among the signs and forms of truth; language is no longer one of the figurations of the world, or a signature stamped upon things since the beginning of time."[31] Don Quixote insists on setting the stamp of permanence on a world that is characterized by transience; in this he reveals his nature as the quintessential librarian who tries to stop the passage of time through an appeal to the timeless aspect of literature. In his invented world, all lack of correspondence is a sign of deceit by the evil enchanters, who divide rather than join together. These malicious enchanters are the sworn enemies of the diviners who, like Don Quixote, seek to affirm the holistic and eternal nature of reality. On another level, the readers of *Don Quixote* are themselves in complicity with this scheme. We can accept Don Quixote's inspiration and join the forces of the librarians, or we are thrust into the opposite camp of the evil enchanters who persist in maintaining difference in the face of the madman's "homosemanticism."[32]

Significantly, *Don Quixote* opens with a description of the protagonist's library and details the course of an obsession that cost the country squire land, health, and sanity. From this beginning, the book pursues an argument in which books play a major role. Books of the past confront contemporary books, and "true" books are contrasted with "false" books. Cervantes's novel is, as Marthe Robert finds, similarly split: "Split in two from its first pages, the novel is a theater where the ideal book it wanted to be, messenger of order and truth, continually collides with what it is perforce: a black book of the lessons life scribbles every day with a child's clumsiness or the malevolence of a demon."[33] The simpleminded recommendation of the niece that "all those excommunicated books . . . deserve to be burned as heretics"[34] and the housekeeper's fear that "one of the many enchanters from those books" (p. 85) might cast an evil spell on them as well are equally rejected by the more broadminded curate. But it must be noted that the curate approves the burning of the false books in the library. The auto-da-fé that symbolically destroys these false books from Alonso Quijano's collection does not do away with their pernicious influence. Similarly, as book burners often fail to realize, many books that are acclaimed as valuable and true can do great harm when misused. William Carlos Williams recognizes and salutes this dangerous ambiguity:

> A cool of books
> will sometime lead the mind to libraries
> of a hot afternoon, if books can be found
> cool to the sense to lead the mind away.[35]

Books that are "cool to the sense" can be as potentially dangerous as the disproportionate ravings of books that heat the brain and drive away sanity. By implication, "true" books (the ones saved from the burning of Don Quixote's library) can also be brought under pressure and forced to reveal their dubious claims to validity, and as the dividing line between "true" and "false" books is blurred, the reader rapidly enters a Borgesian library world where reality is contingent and truth is secondary. Signification only exists in reference to the system from which it is derived.

Nowhere is this distinction made more clearly than in the conversation between Don Quixote and the bachelor Sansón Carrasco in the opening pages of Book II. The knight errant (or errant knight) is puzzled and gratified to find his adventures already in print, but he is concerned about the book's accuracy. "If, however, it were true that such history was in existence," he muses, "seeing that it was about a knight-errant, it must of necessity be grandiloquent, lofty, distinguished, and true. . . . but he was worried to think that its author was a Moor, as the name Cide suggested, for he could expect no truth from the Moors, since they were all imposters, forgers, and schemers" (pp. 544–45). Sansón consoles Don Quixote with the observation that "it is one thing to write as a poet, and another as a historian" (p. 547)—an ambiguous statement that Don Quixote is left to interpret as he wills. The chronicle of Don Quixote's adventures can be true to life without being true to fact; even though the author be a lying imposter and a roguish Moor, the lesson of Don Quixote's adventures is not invalidated. The reader can accept or discount Cide Hamete Benengeli's claims to historical accuracy. If not a historian, the Moor is a poet, and a poet also achieves truth in his artful saying of things "not as they were, but as they ought to have been" (p. 547). Truth is not an absolute value that can only be associated with historical fact; the fictional constructs of madness subvert history without falling into lie.

Cervantes's concept of the nature of historical reconstruction is, then, a surprisingly modern and relativistic one. Rather than conceiving of history as a continuum, a kind of biblical genealogy, *Don Quixote*'s narrator recognizes the role of chance, and, in the acceptance of the Arabic account as historically accurate, the function of will and interpretive license. It is a notion of history radically distinct from the teleological Christian concept. For Cervantes, the library is a fundamental figure of human knowledge; furthermore, it is a post-Babel figure. Unlike the unchanging order of divine history, the library has no teleology: its order is defined by adjacency rather than progression.

The parallel between poetry and history can be extended to an analogous parallel between madness and reason. The sane tend to consider themselves the guardians of truth and light against the onslaught of unreason, a distanciation and disengagement from madness that are necessary partially in order to separate reasoning historical man from the slightly attractive, at least marginally poetic, corruption of unreason. The madman erases rational structure through his actions and in this manner poses a threat to the continued maintenance of a stable society. There is in man, therefore, a double pull toward freedom and toward submission to repression. We are library-builders who resist the imposition of the structure we have developed to protect and console ourselves. Part of the attraction and the suggestiveness of *Don Quixote* resides in these convolutions of desire and reason. From such impossible confluences of history and poetry, of reason and madness, of the library as fluid enterprise and fixed structure, it is easy to discern at least one aspect of the force of the "desdoblamiento" (which translates as "unfolding" but retains a hint of "doubleness") of Don Quixote as the "loco/cuerdo" (the man who becomes mad through an excess of sanity, and remains sane even when most afflicted by madness), as well as the doubling of the author (the narrator and Cide Hamete Benengeli), and the doubling of the protagonist (Don Quixote and Sancho Panza). The madman and the Janus-faced author escape the dialectic of freedom/repression, and though they do not escape from the library ("the dust of books"), they are more free than most to project their fantasies on a contingent world. The "loco/cuerdo" belongs neither to the world of the sane nor to the chains of madness, but to the gap between them and to the frictions that occur when one field meets another that is discontinuous with it.

Don Quixote is not the only character so afflicted by literature. Near the end of the novel, Altisidora recounts to Don Quixote an amazing dream in which she dies and arrives at the gate of a most literary hell:

> "A dozen devils were playing tennis. . . . In their hands they had rackets of fire, and what surprised me was that, instead of balls, they used what looked like books stuffed with wind and fluff, an astonishing sight! . . . after the first volley, there wasn't a ball left whole or fit to be used a second time, so they whirled away books, old and new, which was a wonderful sight. To one

of these volumes, brand new and smartly bound, they gave such a whack, that they knocked its guts out and scattered all the leaves about. The one devil said to another: 'Look, what book is that?'

"And the other devil replied: 'This is the second part of *The History of Don Quixote of La Mancha*, not composed by Cide Hamete, its original author, but by an Aragonese who calls himself a native of Tordesillas.'

"'Away with it out of here,' answered the other devil, 'and plunge it into the pit of hell and never let me set eyes on it again.'" (pp. 1024–25)

In her dream, Altisidora reminds the reader once again of the involuted literariness of the novel. The opening pages of *Don Quixote* indicate that this is a book that is incessantly referred back to other books, and in one of the early chapters the curate conducts an extended critical scrutiny of the country squire's library, condemning bad books to a well-deserved hell. Altisidora's devils repeat this critical survey, no longer on the level of reason and conscious moral judgment, but through the agency of the unconscious hallucinations of dream. Like the curate, their double and opposite, the devils condemn bad books to the fiery hell of oblivion. Don Quixote is contented in the retelling of this dream, apparently oblivious to the deeper question of the reliability of his sources. Devils are not particularly trustworthy critics in the best of cases; trusting their judgment on a book is akin to accepting the word of a lying Moor as true history. Furthermore, while devils in general are not to be trusted, dream devils are even less trustworthy. Don Quixote ignores these difficulties and expresses his joy that the spurious text has been fittingly condemned to hell for its sins of falsehood and bad taste. The novel as a whole is framed by these two episodes of literary criticism and condemnation followed by destruction of the offending texts. The first, seen through the eyes of reason and inspired by the example of the Holy Office, results in a massive auto-da-fé. The second, envisioned in a dream and inspired by the spirit of unholy fun, has a similar outcome. The two incidents stand facing each other at the opposite ends of the novel, mirroring the whole of Don Quixote's strange adventures in between.

Kinbote would have us see the two halves of *Pale Fire*, poem and commentary, standing in a similar position as framing mirrors that reflect the convolutions of his friendship with the poet, John Shade. Instead, both poem and commentary become isolated pale fires, reflecting the fears and frustrations (death, exile) of their authors. Yet, these twinned literary exercises are only pale fires (of their authors, of each other) to the degree that they are perceived historically or biographically. As is the case with *Don Quixote*, the true illumination deriving from this doubled text resides in its appeal to the "blue magic" of the poetic enchanters who turn artifacts into art. Says Nabokov: "For me a work of fiction exists only insofar as it affords me what I shall bluntly call aesthetic bliss, that is, a sense of being somehow, somewhere, connected with other states of being where art (curiosity, tenderness, kindness, ecstasy) is the norm."[36] In this sense, Nabokov's fiction is a faithful representation of his world; true to life and true to the author's aesthetic and emotional standards, if not true to reality and hard, dry, historical fact.

The unfolding of Kinbote in the novel, his "desdoblamiento," is not dissimilar to that of Don Quixote. Both take the deceptions of books for historical reality and are better for it. They exchange the deceptions of reason for autonomous deceptions, and in the process their erstwhile drab existences as scholars and librarians fall away in an enchanting fable. In Kinbote, however, more clearly and obviously than in Don Quixote, this "desdoblamiento" in the mirrors of fiction takes on a strong narcissistic tinge. Nabokov's hero is addicted to the company of beautiful young boys. His love for women is dependent on their possession of slim, masculine good looks. Thus, the king rejects Fleur, the pretty, boyish friend of his youth— "the sight of her four bare limbs and three mousepits (Zemblan anatomy) irritated him" (p. 80)—for his boy pages, seeking out the "faunlets" whose "bold virilia" contrast with their "girlish grace" (p. 89). His relationship with his queen is equally unsatisfactory. "He forced himself with aphrodisiacs," says Kinbote, "but the anterior characters of her unfortunate sex kept fatally putting him off." Unregenerate, the king returns to his pursuit of faunlets and to his enjoyment of "our manly Zemblan customs" (p. 148). While Nabokov himself firmly rejected Freud and his insights, the discussion of the exiled king's homosexual preferences can profit from recourse to Freud's observations. In his writings on homosexuality, Freud mentions "the high value set upon the male organ and the inability to tolerate its absence in a love-object" that leads to the "depreciation of women, and aversion from them." Furthermore, Freud points to three factors that rule the "psychical aetiology of homosexuality"—"attachment to the mother, narcissism, fear of castration"[37]—which are applicable in broad outline to Kinbote's psychosis. While a more extended discussion of this perceived "aetiology of homosexuality" would be profitable, it is beyond the scope of this study. Here, I merely wish to note that of the three factors described by Freud, narcissism provides the most fruitful, immediate point of entry into Nabokov's novel and reveals an underlying thread in the narrative. Kinbote's obsession with mirrors and crystals, his attraction to subjectively perceived reflections and transparencies of all kinds, is a crucial aspect of this narcissistic compulsion. As with the faunlets, so too with Shade's poem: Kinbote's love is reserved for reflections/projections of some aspect of himself.

The game of *Pale Fire* is played almost entirely on the flat surface of the mirror, and like the warped mirrors of the funhouse, it is often difficult to establish the degree of distortion. Kinbote observes that "the name Zembla is a corruption . . . of Semberland, a land of reflections, of 'resemblers,'" (p. 187), and the mad king clearly identifies himself as a double of Gradus in his explanation that "kinbote" means "a king's destroyer" (p. 189): the role Gradus seeks to play. Kinbote is himself a double character, as he wishes us to remember. He is both king and college professor, a scholar who sank "his identity in the mirror of exile" (p. 189). At one further remove, he is also the dark shadow who brings the poet's work to light by co-opting it as his own. As Shade, appropriately enough for him, notes to another colleague, "Resemblances are the shadows of differences" (p. 187). Shade and Kinbote are the light brother and his dark shadow, in a charming reversal of the implications of their names. Kinbote's magic and his madness are inextricably interrelated. For him, as for Don Quixote, Foucault's words hold true: "Magic, which permitted the decipherment of the world by revealing the secret resemblances beneath its signs, is no longer of any use except as an explanation, in terms of madness, of why analogies are always proved false."[38] This is undoubtedly the case in Kinbote's mad ravings about the analogies between Shade's poem and his real? fantastic? Zemblan experiences.

The duplications of Kinbote into Gradus and Shade are humorous, but they also have an ominous aspect. Shade is the happily heterosexual double; Gradus is coldly asexual—he once attempted self-castration. Kinbote is constrained by these narrative projections, and unreason gives free rein to violence. The resemblance he sees in the mirror of his madness is an illusion; the reflection is not the same but the Other, the dark double, the feared and hated twin described by René Girard in *Violence and the Sacred*, a twin who generates violence and death. In *Pale Fire*, Gradus (Kinbote's double) kills Shade (the complacent heterosexual twin). Kinbote, as a critic, murders Shade after his death through his unskilled exegesis of the poem, since the poem is also a true double in this play of reflections. "Writing," says Foucault, ". . . automatically dictates that we place ourselves in the virtual space of self-representation and reduplication. . . . a work of language only advances more deeply into the intangible density of the mirror, . . . discovers in this way a possible and impossible infinity, . . . maintains it beyond the death which condemns it." [39] Only one member of such an intolerable pair of twins can survive; thus the book that the protagonist strives to imitate is ultimately responsible for the deaths of his twins and for his own death-in-life in the motor lodge.

This death-in-life also becomes a life-in-art as the release from his shadows allows Kinbote to more fully identify with his original narcissistic double: the book. Kinbote has early indicated his interest in the mirror-world of literature and, as King Charles, frequently describes his adventures by reference to already existing stories. Thus, during his escape from Zembla, he encounters a "gnarled farmer and his plump wife who, like personages in an old tedious tale offer the drenched fugitive a welcome shelter" and allow him "to dry himself in a warm kitchen where he was given a fairy-tale meal of bread and cheese" (p. 101). The mad commentator constantly searches for evidence of such correspondences and is never remiss in recounting instances in which life imitates art. The comfort derived from such imitation is clear: literary expression, in Kinbote's mind, reduces the plethora of experience to the rigid and arbitrary orders of art. Living beings are assimilated to immortal forms: "We are absurdly accustomed to the miracle of a few written signs being able to contain immortal imagery, involutions of thought, new worlds with live people, speaking, weeping, laughing" (p. 204). It is one of the strange paradoxes of the library that the brutal alphabetization of knowledge permits access to so many living beings, although it is perhaps only in the eyes of madmen like Kinbote and Don Quixote that such a transformation can fully take place. There is a further irony as well. The library, the repository of these living texts, is pre-eminently a product of the printing press by which books were mechanically and cheaply produced for sale to a large market. Alonso Quijano had access to the chivalric world by means of the printing press, and the life he perceives is the result of a process of bookmaking whereby for the first time in history the body was not directly involved in its production.

While both Kinbote and Don Quixote recognize that books are living, they are hampered by a too-strict application of literature to life. In his poem, Shade indicates that a balance of life and art is more fruitful:

> . . . not text, but texture; not the dream
> But topsy-turvical coincidence,
> Not flimsy nonsense, but a web of sense. (p. 44)

With these words, Shade expounds what is essentially a negative theology in which the gods and their chess games do not matter: "No sound / No furtive light came from their involute / Abode" (p. 44). This negative appreciation, "not text but texture," emphasizes what is not there—surely an appropriate stance for John Shade, the shadow or ghost of a kingly presence. "What is a ghost?" asks Stephen Dedalus referring to *Hamlet*. It is an impalpable Shade, a text/texture of sense.

But a Shade's formulation of the relationship between art and life is only of marginal interest in the context of the novel as a whole. It is the literature-ridden madmen in both *Pale Fire* and *Don Quixote* who have the largest claim to the reader's attention, and they are not the originators of the text, but merely the custodians, who in their literal applications of art to life violate the nature of that art. Kinbote concludes his foreword to Shade's poem with the remark,

"To this statement my dear poet would probably not have sub-scribed, but, for better or worse, it is the commentator who has the last word" (p. 19).

Though the commentator has the last word, the play is still sym-metrical, reason and madness alongside each other, at some point reflecting each other, but not identical. In *Speak Memory*, Nabokov writes of his artifice and the artifact that is his fiction as "the spiral unwinding of things."[40] Where Nabokov unwinds his symmetries and releases rigid orders into chaos, Flann O'Brien takes the op-posite approach, winding up chaos into a perdurable form: "If I paint you a still life . . . this canvas can be placed *beside* any similar 'natural' object, a flower, a shell, a leaf, in *competition*, not in imi-tation. . . . A shell, in its accidents, is the phenomenal expression of a design . . . which is rigid, logical, coordinated. . . . In the human scale, my paintings must inevitably exhibit the same characteris-tics."[41] Both O'Brien and Nabokov discuss their art in terms of the same image; a spiral (or a shell), rigid and coordinated or unwind-ing. While the process each follows is distinct, the initial impulse is approximately similar: the logic and rigid orders of the world are set beside a nonmimetic representation of reality. And in both, the "beside" indicates a disengagement which, while in some sense complete, is still convoluted and complicit with the forms of life.

In *Pale Fire*, the juxtaposition of the two fables (Shade's and Kin-bote's) unfolds into a world of mirrors, of doubles doubled at every turn. In O'Brien, the lesson of the shell gives rise to a pattern of con-tainment; spiraling inward rather than unwinding. O'Brien's treat-ment of character is an exemplary instance of this inward-winding spiral. The student-author indicates that his idea of character por-trayal would be based on a pool of common characters that authors would draw upon at will, saving the original characters for cases of extreme inventive emergency. It is a policy followed throughout *At Swim-Two-Birds*, a novel in which figures from folklore and fairy tale mingle with Irish cowboys, fictionalized authors, and private detectives. In the trial of Dermot Trellis for misuse of his characters, Mr. William James Tracy is called upon to testify:

> About four years ago he approached me and represented
> that he was engaged in a work which necessitated the services

of a female character of the slavey class. He explained that technical difficulties relating to ladies' dress had always been an insuperable obstacle to his creation of satisfactory female characters. . . . Eventually I agreed to lend him a girl whom I was using in connection with *Jake's Last Throw*, a girl who would not be required by myself for some months owing to my practice of dealing with the action of groups of characters alternately. (pp. 287–88)

When this character was returned to him, complained Mr. Tracy, she was found to be pregnant, a condition for which Mr. Trellis refuses to accept responsibility although he is clearly the author of this seduction/rape. The complications of similar inward-turning spirals are potentially infinite. Mr. Dermot Trellis's forcible bedroom activities result in the birth of a half-human son, Orlick, who like his father becomes an author. Orlick borrows *his* central character from O'Brien's novel, visiting revenge upon his salacious progenitor by writing him into the novel as an inert, unthinking, dreamless body: "Dermot Trellis neither slept nor woke but lay there in his bed, a twilight in his eyes" (p. 236–37). Meanwhile, freed from the tyrannical bonds of Dermot Trellis's character portrayals, Orlick and company proceed to rearrange the tale and live ordinary, independent lives. Orlick's text, a rigid, logical, coordinated evolution of the student-author's premises and the windings of the plot, provides positive proof of the dangers of unwarranted originality on the part of a writer. It is also an impossible object, not dissimilar in nature from the Escher drawing of a hand drawing a hand. The text empties inward, reason and unreason come into ever-closer proximity.

O'Brien does not discard the sublime, although he does discount the "aesthetic bliss" and ecstasy that make a work of fiction valuable to Nabokov. Like Nabokov and Cervantes, however, O'Brien is clearly interested in the importance of language—language that is both empty and full—in the fictional endeavor. But O'Brien is not interested in language as beautiful; rather, he concerns himself with the skillful manipulation of words by capable artisans. Anthony Lamont, one of O'Brien's borrowed characters, restates a formulation of O'Brien's work-a-day sublime: "Whether a tale is tall or small I like to hear it well told. I like to meet a man that can take in hand to tell a story and not make a balls of it while he's at it. I like to know where I am, do you know. Everything has a beginning and an end" (p. 89). The inward spiraling is not atemporal; on the contrary, the rigor of a temporal progression from beginning to end is one of the outstanding features of this superficially chaotic text. The relationship in time is no longer an essential one, however; it is merely convenient, and this convenient relationship to temporal succession is consistently seen ironically in the text. It is a useful tool, and remains a powerful one. Time (history) provides Orlick Trellis with the most effective weapon against his father:

> Labyrinthine are the injuries inflictable on the soul. The tense of the body is the present indicative; but the soul has a memory and a present and a future. I have conceived some extremely recondite plans for Mr. Trellis. I will pierce him with a pluperfect.
>
> Pluperfect is all right, of course, said Shanahan, anybody that takes exception to that was never very much at the bee-double-o-kay-ess. I wouldn't hear a word against it. (p. 242)

Orlick Trellis fixes his progenitor at a point in the past, forcing him to become part of the library, or a member of the anonymous, interchangeable corps of characters. Though his body remains in the present tense, Trellis's soul joins the collectivity of memory from which present and future authors will draw their inspiration.

Just as O'Brien's inward spiral is halted by the limiting force of a will that imposes beginnings and ends and establishes historical lines of descent, so too Nabokov's outward spiraling is restrained by the two texts of *Pale Fire* that enclose and limit the doubling and reduplication of the protagonist. For both O'Brien and Nabokov—and Cervantes as well—outside or beside the fictional text stands another text or texts that are systematically misread by the protagonist.

Don Quixote's life work and central chivalric duty is double; first, to protect his beloved books from contamination by the world outside his study walls, and second, to prove their veracity by sallying forth himself to establish their correspondence to the work-a-day world of seventeenth-century Spain. The forced ending to the novel, in which Cervantes gratuitously murders his character, is ultimately unsatisfying to the reader because it is not in accord with the magnitude of the questions intimated by the novel and sidesteps the implications of the philosophical issues raised.

Don Quixote belongs to a doubled reality. He is both the impoverished mad hidalgo who makes us laugh, and he is a *sign* whose function is not the usual one of relating words to a concrete reality but of finding the correspondences between two systems of verbal signs. This strange play of language systems reaches its culmination in the opening chapters of the second part of the novel where the protagonists are made privy to the inscription of their own adventures. Furthermore, Don Quixote and Sancho feel honor-bound to protect their "true" story from the incursions upon their reality of an apocryphal Don Quixote, though in this effort they are only partially successful since minor characters from the *Quixote* of Avellaneda do meet and discuss this confusing affair with the protagonists of Cervantes's novel. Nevertheless, the problem of identity is an increasingly troublesome one for the principal characters of the novel since Don Quixote must accept the first part of his adventures as real and genuine and Avellaneda's continuation as false and spurious. This problem extends to the reader of the novel (fiction, "true history," or apocrypha) as well, a feature of Cervantes's masterpiece that has often been a subject of critical inquiry. Jorge Luis Borges, among others, discusses the uneasiness this fictional doubling causes: "Why does it disquiet us to know that Don Quixote is a reader of the *Quixote* and Hamlet is a spectator of *Hamlet*? I believe I have found the answer: those inversions suggest that if the characters in a story can be readers or spectators, then we, their readers or spectators, can be fictitious."[42] The bibliophile is subsumed in the fiction and appears therein as a bibliophile obsessed with maintaining the purity of the written word. This first step in a potentially infinite regression as well as the emptying out of the universe outside the book are notions dear to Borges.

The multiplication of fiction can be portrayed, almost emblematically, in the figure of Sansón Carrasco, the student (bibliophile) cum knight errant (a fictionalized parody of Don Quixote's true imitation). In his unassisted effort to cure Don Quixote of his madness, Sansón Carrasco confronts him as the "Knight of the Mirrors," wearing a disguise designed to cancel his own physical presence and turn the mad knight's reflections back upon himself: "Over his armor he wore a surcoat or cassock of a cloth that seemed to be of the finest gold, all bedizened with many little moons of glittering mirrors, which gave him a most gallant and showy appearance" (p. 621). It is a disguise that is meant to be impenetrable; the showy surfaces of the mirrors are designed to reveal the spurious identity of the beholder, Don Quixote. Sansón Carrasco fails despite his carefully considered approach. Don Quixote defeats the Knight of the Mirrors and penetrates the mirrored armor, only to discover "the very face, the very figure, the very aspect, the very physiognomy, the very effigy, the very image of the bachelor Sansón Carrasco" (p. 624). Don Quixote does not doubt that this appearance of his old friend and neighbor before his eyes is the work of evil enchanters, so the scholar, though unveiled, remains disguised and, rather than revealing to Don Quixote the falsity of his fictional world, his actions have served to further reconfirm its reality.

Carrasco's second sally, as the "Knight of the White Moon," is more successful. Again, the scholar assumes a disguise suited to Don Quixote's peculiar madness and adopts, as it were, the outward forms of his lunacy. His defeat of the unfortunate knight is effected in accord with the strictest rules of chivalric behavior. Carrasco is magnanimous in victory, allowing the name of Dulcinea of El Toboso to remain unsullied, insisting only upon the exact terms of the agreement decided upon before the joust. Yet, Sansón's behavior, instigated by the motivation to see his neighbor returned to sanity, is nevertheless highly ambiguous. To cure the knight, he enters into the knight's world and adopts his madness, thus valorizing and confirming Don Quixote's fictional existence. Even his defeat of Don Quixote and the subsequent cure depend for efficacy on the strictures of Don Quixote's madness: "as he is so punctilious and so particular in observing the laws of knight-errantry, he is sure to perform his promise" (p. 995). Sansón Carrasco, the man who cures Don Quixote of his madness, is also Sansón the scholar, who in some sense enters into a subtle complicity with that madness and becomes (by his entry into the continuation of the novel) a dupe of the fiction he sought to destroy.

As for Don Quixote, the emptiness he feels on being deprived of one literary fantasy propels him to the brink of another, pastoral, madness. This enchantment is equally deplored by the housekeeper and the niece who try to stifle his "longing to wander off into fresh labyrinths" (p. 1043) by citing the hardships real shepherds must endure. But the enchantments of madness do not easily give way to the blandishments of reason. It is significant that the madness of knight errantry that prompts him to see enchanters foiling his greatest accomplishments is not exclusive to the knight and Sancho Panza. Apart from Sansón Carrasco, who enters the fiction willingly, Don Quixote and Sancho meet at least one other person who reconfirms their fictional reality—this time, an unwilling participant in the novel.

In a most confusing confrontation, Don Quixote and Sancho meet a character from the spurious *Quixote* by Avellaneda, and this Don Alvaro Tarfe is similarly beset by evil enchanters. In their brief aquaintance, Don Alvaro mentions twice that his appearance in Avellaneda's novel must have been due to enchantments. "For my part," he says, "I believe that the enchanters that persecute Don Quixote sent the bad one to persecute me" (p. 1036). A little later, after further conversations with the good and true Don Quixote, Don Alvaro again disavows his relationship with the bad Don Quixote in a more ambiguous fashion. Don Alvaro "even suspected that he must have been under a spell, since he touched with his hand two different Don Quixotes" (p. 1037). With this curious declaration, the reader is left to decide which of the two Don Quixotes was the cause of his enchantment—to suggest that he was enchanted in the former case is to imply that he might also be enchanted in the present tale, a suggestion that could be borne out in the second quote.

Thus, Don Alvaro's two references to his enchantment are substantially different in type. The first clearly attributes his former confusion to the work of evil enchanters; the second is more ambiguous, and more suggestive of Nabokov's blue magic of imitation or O'Brien's theory of interchangeable characters. By forcing the world to correspond to the chivalric novels he loves, Don Quixote becomes the true enchanter in the novel, *Don Quixote*. It is he who, upon reading the false adventures written by a spurious pseudoenchanter, breaks free of the world of the book to enter upon his own version. The reader, who follows this play of imitation and willful disenchantment, is twice put under a spell; once when Don Quixote reads, and once when he is read. Don Quixote implicitly forces the reader to enter into his doubly enchanted world under the force of a magic both blue and black.

The false learning gleaned from dusty books reveals its most potent and most captivating form. Cervantes, Nabokov, and O'Brien stand alongside the excesses they describe, a part of and apart from them, driven by the library itself into an interplay between the two irreconcilables of irony and analogy. Madness and magic, humor and heuristics meet in these texts, provoking a laughter that becomes ever more self-conscious and uncomfortable.

CHAPTER 3

The Self and the Catalogue: Borges, France

THE MADNESS OF the books is paralleled by a madness of the catalogue; the labyrinth of the library stacks has its analogue in the even more intricate labyrinth of the catalogue of these books, in which the simple relation of one entry/one text is perversely multiplied in an unending game of cross-references. The additive effect of these internal games does not always, as the technologically oriented librarian may hope, result in a greater clarity and ease in the use of the books themselves. Instead, the game becomes ever more problematic. The proliferating catalogue takes off toward infinity, overwhelming the library it was intended to organize, developing a will and a purpose of its own that only make reading more obscure than it was before the advent of such an organizing mania.

In his notes on Raymond Roussel's "How I Wrote Certain of My Books," Trevor Winkfield recalls an instance demonstrating just such inadvertent obfuscation: "Pierre Schneider relates that he discovered copies of *Impressions d'Afrique* nestled in the travel section of his local library; they even found their way into the tropical pages of the Catalogue de Libraire 'Africana Histoire, Cartographie, Voyages, Ethnographie . . .' (no. 33) where *Impressions d'Afrique* is grouped with tomes on exploration and tales of missionary zeal under the heading 'Darkest Africa.'"[1] The orders of the catalogue disarticulate the orders that allow us to distinguish between the poet, the scientist, and the fool, effacing distinctions and equalizing them all in an identical incomprehension. The catalogue is, then, both immoderate and inadequate. It is immoderate in that the endlessly proliferating game of reference and cross-reference leads the researcher ever deeper into the twisting labyrinths of an artificial system; but it is also inadequate because these journeys into the maze of the catalogue bring the student no closer to the promised increment in knowledge. One fact, one name, leads to another, and then to another, and still another. But each of these names is empty of content, so thin that it leaves barely a trace in the reader's mind as he tracks his way through the maze, searching for that final, sufficient card in which the knowledge is summarized and the arduous search justified. Says Foucault:

> Writing, in Western culture, automatically dictates that we place ourselves in the virtual space of self-representation and reduplication, since writing refers not to a thing but to speech, a work of language only advances more deeply into the intangible density of the mirror, calls forth the double of this already doubled writing, discovers in this way a possible and impossible infinity, ceaselessly strives after speech, maintains it beyond the death which condemns it, and frees a murmuring stream.[2]

In the library catalogue, the murmuring stream of language is frozen; it is fixed and classified and analyzed. In the catalogue, the text is reinforced—but it is also effaced. It is inserted into history—but arrested by the eternal present of the equalizing order. Its force is redoubled; its poetry is discharged. Following the sequence (any sequence) of cross-references gives rise to a curious phenomenon: the apparently frozen text cannot remain still; it pivots, it slips back into the void feared by literary metaphysicians; it returns—a forerunner of its own language.

Jorge Luis Borges would seem to be most thoroughly delighted by this state of affairs. He has frequently indicated his fascination with the absurdity and with the minuteness of the cataloguer's task, and in a number of essays speaks longingly of such agile combinatory puzzles as "the staggering fantasy" of a universal library as envisioned by the nineteenth-century popularizer of science Kurd Lasswitz. Lasswitz, according to Borges, has imagined a "universal library which would register all the variations of the twenty-odd orthographical symbols, in other words, all that is given to express in all languages."[3] While he qualifies his delight in these verbal combinatorics with the warning that such toying with metaphysics and the arts leads practitioners of the game to "forget that a book is more than a verbal structure or a series of verbal structures" (L, p. 213), Borges goes on to describe the dialogue between reader and writer as infinite, indicating that the former, mathematical, game is less enjoyable than the reader-writer interaction essentially because it is more limited in scope. The disclaimer, however, does not mitigate Borges's interest in the all-inclusive library. The Aleph—a point in space that contains the universe—is a similar construction; and the story, "The Library of Babel," is built directly from Lasswitz's dream.

It is not necessary to pause with Lasswitz (or Raymond Lully or John Stuart Mill—the other two figures mentioned along with Lasswitz as creators of such combinatory fantasies), and indeed, it is curious that Borges does so. The reference to Lasswitz appears at the opening of an essay on George Bernard Shaw (which, typically for Borges, has little to say about Shaw), and it is interesting that Borges did not recall another, earlier Irishman, who is also admired by the Argentinian writer, and who also discussed the possibility of a nearly infinite language combinatory machine. Jonathan Swift writes of Lemuel Gulliver's astonishing visit to the grand Academy of Lagado:

> He [the professor] then led me to the Frame, about the Sides whereof all his Pupils stood in Ranks. It was Twenty Foot square, placed in the Middle of the Room. The Superficies was composed of several Bits of Wood. . . . These Bits of Wood were covered on every Square with Paper pasted on them; and on these Papers were written all the Words of their Language . . . but without any Order. [On] giving them [the handles of the frame] a sudden Turn, the whole Disposition of the Words was entirely changed. He then commanded Six and Thirty of

the Lads to read the several Lines softly . . . and where they found three or four Words together that might make Part of a Sentence, they dictated to the four remaining Boys who were Scribes.[4]

Borges's only objections to this eminently practical Lagadoan reconstruction of the arts and sciences would be that the scribes did not record *all* the possible combinations rather than merely the ones that made the most sense to them, and that the machine suffers from the deficiency of employing only a recognizable human language rather than an arbitrary combination of alphabetical symbols.

Borges's interest in the universal library is coupled with an analogous interest in a universal catalogue. Like the library, the catalogue would be, by definition, infinite. But the very fact of its universality makes the catalogue theoretically eternal as well. The all-inclusiveness of the catalogue devalorizes linear time; since everything has already been included, no new elements can be created to augment the set. The passage of time in such a context theoretically reflects an eternally recurrent Viconian cycle or a Nietzschean eternal return, a theory that Borges often cites with favor. As in the Library of Babel, the nearly infinite number of archetypal elements recur again and again in a combinatory game as vast and as limited as the rotations of a kaleidoscope. History is invalidated or, rather, history operates in the contrast between the immense duration of the single cycle and the inevitability of its total recurrence. Typically, Borges cites with approval Nathaniel Hawthorne's dream of "Earth's Holocaust." In Borges's summary of the story, the aspect of an immense catalogue is emphasized:

Men come from all over the world. They make a gigantic bonfire kindled with all the genealogies, all the diplomas, all the medals, all the orders, all the judgements, all the coats of arms, all the crowns, all the sceptres, all the tiaras, all the purple robes of royalty, all the canopies, all the thrones, all the spiritous liquors, all the bags of coffee, all the boxes of tea, all the cigars, all the love letters, all the artillery, all the swords, all the flags, all the martial drums, all the instruments of torture, all the guillotines, all the gallows trees, all the precious metals, all the money, all the titles of property, all the constitutions and codes of law, all the books, all the miters, all the vestments, all the sacred writing that populate and fatigue the Earth.[5]

Borges, like Funes the Memorious, the protagonist of another of his stories, is enthralled by such a comprehensive list; the mere enumerative rhetoric is an immense source of pleasure. Even more, however, Borges is impressed by Hawthrone's recognition that the bonfire provides no definitive destruction, that the fire only destroys the individual exemplars of the things heaped upon it, that the archetypal (eternal) essence of the things consumed by fire remains untouched in the human heart, and thus, that the immense catalogue of the burning will give way on the morrow to a new, revised catalogue, identical to the last, of all the things that exist on this earth. Furthermore, in Borges's interpretation of the fatigue and overpopulation of the earth described by Hawthorne, analysis is overlaid and filigreed with the silent language of death, as that language flows into a murmuring rhetorical stream and is subsumed into the primary narcissism of man standing before the mirror of his own creations.

Even more than is the case with Cervantes and Nabokov, in Borges and, as we shall also see, in Anatole France, emphasis shifts from a library world to a world that is included in the category "library." In a reversal of the *abecedarium naturae*, the world is effectively catalogued and summarized in language. Myth degenerates to fiction (compare the title of Borges's most famous collection of short stories—*Ficciones*—and the nature of Sylvestre Bonnard's "crime" in Anatole France's novel) when rhetorical and linguistic classifications replace a lost sense of the absolute. We can perceive, thus, the irony in Borges's use of a biblical title for his story, "The Library of Babel," since the re-creation of Babel portrays the absolute entity in a fictional rather than a mythical setting. It is, however, an absolute described in the negative, by its undefinable qualities: "The universe (which others call the Library) is composed of an *in*definite and perhaps *in*finite number of hexagonal galleries. . . . From any of the hexagons one can see, *in*terminably, the upper and lower floors. The distribution of the galleries is *in*variable" (my emphases) (L, p. 51). The cumulative effect of this series of words beginning with the prefix "in", a series preserved in the English translation of Borges's story, is to cause the reader a slight uneasiness in the presence of a universe so alien and so mysterious. The universe is an *in*verse of our own eminently tactile physical world; an immense systematic order that exists outside of our time. The details used to describe the stairways, galleries, closets, and bookshelves do little to dispel this first impression. The stairways sink and soar beyond the narrator's comprehension; the galleries are quite possibly infinite in number; no distinction is made between the two small closets, one to be used to sleep standing up, the second to "satisfy one's fecal necessities" (L, p. 51). Even the bookshelves, described as to location, number, and distribution, are "scarcely" higher than the normal librarian—leaving the reader to ponder what a "normal" height would consist of for a narrator who had spent his entire life surrounded by hexagonal galleries and in scant contact with others of his kind. Thus it is that the library's feature of eternity affects all the substantive features contained within it, causing the narrator to double back and forth between precision of detail and deliberate indistinctness. As the librarian reflects upon the vast library that is his home and his prison, he allows the reader only a few more substantive details, but these details, like the former ones, alternate between the definite and concrete and the eternal and infinite, preventing either the librarian or the reader from conquering the space so described.

The historical being, existing in an ahistorical place, cannot help but ponder those two basic mysteries—"the origin of the Library and of time" (L, p. 55)—which are nevertheless incompatible. The first mystery refers to the work of an absolute that existed before time began, that perhaps continues to exist, like the library, in a time that does not elapse, a time that *is*, but does not *become*. This atemporal realm is indifferent to the time of the solitary librarian, who creates, as the narrator of the story does, a useless and inevitable historical system, a system of which the librarian becomes the sole prisoner. The library itself, because it is eternal *and* substantive, scoffs at the efforts of the substantive, but time-laden librarian, his metaphysical anxieties, and his narrative games. The library is a closed, inert, inaccessible world—but it is also, as the mirror in the entrance hall seems to suggest, a faithful and symmetric duplicate of the librarian; a solid, atemporal narcissistic projection. The unnamed librarian muses, "Men usually infer from this mirror that the Library is not infinite (if it really were, why this illusory duplication?); I prefer to dream that its polished surfaces represent and promise the infinite" (L, p. 51). The infinity discerned in the mirror's reduplication of appearances can only be a false infinity. Like the experience of the infinite, eternal Aleph, which is revealed in the final lines of the story to be a false Aleph, the timorous hopes and hesitant ecstasy that the librarian feels in the presence of this mirrored vestibule are mere literary simulacra of the hope and the ecstasy that could theoretically be felt in the presence of the true Aleph, the eye of God, or an infinity not given through the duplication of "appearances." It is an impossible ecstasy of which the solitary librarian dares not dream, surrounded as he is by mirrors, writing words that are merely simulacra of the unique Word, living at the heart of the false infinity of books.

These appearances—galleries, mirrors, books—weigh heavily upon the librarian, leading him (and us) to consider the impossibility of writing new thoughts under such circumstances. The librarian cannot forget the unbearable presence of these books, true and false, which surround him. The necessary and impossible process of forgetting what has been written in order to free the writer from this creative paralysis concerns Borges as much as his character. As Piétro Citati finds, "He who wishes to write a new book must possess a force of imagination immense enough to make him forget the existence of the Library; but Borges does not have this imagination."[6] History, and his inability to ignore the past, become Borges's enemies. Through his librarian, Borges discusses this intellectual obsession. The inability to forget is epitomized by the eternal library that contains past, present, and future. The librarian is not even allowed to merge into anonymity despite his namelessness; as he turns a corner, he will inevitably come into contact with his own face reflected in the mirror. The library is paradise—but it is also hell, a fact that the protagonist humbly recognizes. Says the librarian, "If honor and wisdom and happiness are not for me, let them be for others. Let heaven exist, though my place be hell" (L, p. 57).

The library is heaven for only one hypothetical librarian, the "Man of the Book," a librarian who discovered "a book which is the formula and perfect compendium of *all the rest*: some librarian has gone through it and he is analogous to a god" (L, p. 56). This Man of the Book would be the perfect librarian, in contrast to his imperfect counterparts, and a fitting complement to the eternal, all-inclusive library. However, the Man of the Book is a theoretical concept, bringing consolation to his imperfect fellows; the failure of generations of systematic searching does not prove or disprove his existence. It is, perhaps, the imperfection of the narrator's own existence that prevents him from finding this perfect librarian.

This is a suggestion that is borne out in the story that follows "The Library of Babel" in the *Labyrinths* volume. "Funes the Memorious" is an analogue of the perfect librarian, the Man of the Book; his infallible memory makes him godlike and remote. Unlike the Man of the Book, however, who possesses the key to the vast library in the form of a Platonic book of books, Funes was, "let us not forget, almost incapable of ideas of a general, Platonic sort" (L, p. 65). The Man of the Book is godlike because he is able to forget all extraneous material and focus on the single, essential book. Funes is godlike because he, like the library, is all-inclusive: Funes cannot forget. "Let us not forget," says the narrator—but of course we do, and thus we can do no more than glimpse the "stammering grandeur" (L, p. 65) of Funes's world. Funes, let us not forget, achieved this stammering grandeur following a fall from a horse, which left him paralyzed.

For the narrator of "Funes the Memorious," meeting the protagonist of the story alters his concept of memory completely and finally. No human memory can be anything but a pale reflection of Funes's prodigious memory; the narrator's stylized clarity of detail only serves to reflect upon Funes's intolerably precise observations. In a gesture of desperation, the narrator uses the phrase, "I remember," six times in the first five sentences of the story, and with varying frequency throughout the text, although he realizes, humbly, that when he says "I remember him," he has "no right to utter this sacred verb, only one man on earth had that right and he is dead" (L, p. 59). The narrator's memories are flawed and partial; they chart a process of forgetting, as Funes, now deceased, disappears into the twilight remoteness (L, p. 59) that characterizes the narrator's memories of him. The narrator's transcript of his most extensive dialogue with Funes is recorded with this humility very much to the fore: "I shall not try to reproduce the words, which are now irrecoverable. I prefer to summarize with veracity the many things Ireneo told me. The indirect style is remote and weak; I know I am sacrificing the efficacy of my narrative" (L, p. 63). Like the narrator of "Funes the Memorious," the narrator of "The Library of Babel" summarizes what he knows about the history and present existence of the library, hoping for efficacy in his summary, but suspecting the veracity of his tale. Funes's biographer is terrified at the realization that his words and his being are exactly reproduced in the mind of Ireneo Funes. The librarian of Babel is terrified and consoled by the recognition that he and his words are likewise reproduced in the books and mirrors of the universal library.

In both stories, this infinite, eternal experience (or simulacrum thereof) can only be expressed in negative terms. The library is indefinite, infinite, interminable; the Latin syllables pronounced by Funes were feared to be "indecipherable, interminable" (L, p. 62). The textual source of these Latin words is singularly appropriate— and not at all reassuring for the biographer. The subjects under discussion are history and memory, and the Latin text is also couched in the negative: "they formed the first paragraph of the twenty-fourth chapter of the seventh book of the *Naturalis historia*. The subject of that chapter is memory; the last words were *ut nihil non iisdem verbis redderetur auditum*" (L, p. 62). The biographer, like the librarian, might wish to forget this aggressive negativity, this resounding, absolute indecipherability, but although he recoils from such a terrible exhaustiveness, he cannot forget. And both the biographer and the librarian must forget in order to survive. Both Funes, with his inability to forget, and the library, with its closed infinity of mirrored galleries, repeat the *nihil non*, the "nothing not" in a rhetorical void. Mind and mirror capture the evanescent shades passing by them, but they possess no capacity for reflection upon these images.

Anatole France's Sylvestre Bonnard is also memorious, though not in the prodigious manner of Ireneo Funes. His defective memory is more closely allied to that of Funes's biographer, who imbues

the words "I remember" with the gentle nostalgia of all the multitudinous detail he has forgotten. Bonnard's memory, like that of the
biographer, recalls an imperfectly remembered past; it does not,
like that of Funes, make the past once again present. But with Bonnard, reminiscence always begins or ends in the library:

> I want, for example, before I die, to finish my "History of the
> Abbots of Saint-Germaine-des-Près." The time God allots to
> each one of us is like a precious tissue which we embroider as
> best we know how. I had begun my woof with all sorts of phi-
> lological illustrations . . . So my thoughts wandered on; and at
> last, as I bound my *foulard* about my head, the notion of Time
> led me back to the past; and for the second time within the
> same round of the dial I thought of you, Clementine.[7]

Thus, as Bonnard embroiders his cloth, or weaves the warp and
woof of the fabric of his life, the strong threads of memory are inter-
spersed with the interstices of its lapses. The historian's strong sense
of time is joined to a deep regret at its passing, and a profound sense
of nostalgia for the lost selves of youth and for the absent, beloved
Other, Clementine. The experience of Funes obviates history, but
the historian's and the biographer's labor of recollection restores
to us the consciousness of a time that is long past, and nearly
forgotten.

It is Bonnard's historical sense that prompts him upon the appearance of the fairy in the library. The old scholar's first instinct is
to pick up the most salient threads of her story and embroider a
historical tapestry before her eyes with the solemn gravity that
would befit such an auspicious visit. The exercise of this art of remembrance would be, to his mind, a sovereign compliment (p. 110).
The fairy, however, causes him to forgo this pleasure by throwing
nut shells at his nose: "I did what the dignity of science demanded
of me—I remained silent" (p. 111). This novel method of damping
the pretensions to science of the old scholar is more fully explicated
in the fairy's dissertation on the importance of the imagination.
Bonnard, a scholar and a historian, likes to think of himself as a
scientist; the fairy reminds him of the importance of the imagination to his scholarly weavings and recalls him to a recognition of

this faculty that is wonderfully developed in children but lamentably lost in the "old spectacled folks in your Institutes and your Academies." "To know is nothing at all," continues the fairy, "to imagine is everything" (p. 113). This is a judgment that is borne out again and again in France's novel and is repeated specifically in the last pages of the book. Gélis, Bonnard's brilliant young disciple and son-in-law, admonishes the older man that "history is not a science; it is an art, and one can succeed in that art only through the exercise of his faculty of imagination" (p. 297).

It is the use of the imagination to reconstruct the past that, paradoxically, makes history more real than any of Funes's exact reproductions. Funes himself, imprisoned by his bodily paralysis and his prodigious, infallible memory, is less real than the imperfect biographer who visits him. Funes *knows*, as Bonnard aspires to know; but France's librarian learns the lesson of the fairy on the necessity of the imagination. Like her, Bonnard exists more fully as he becomes closer to the imaginary. As with the librarian in Borges's Library of Babel, this imaginary existence is counterpointed by the solid walls of government buildings, and the no less solid walls of habit and custom: "Old clerks point me out to each other as I go by like a ghost wandering through the corridors. When one has become very old one finds it extremely difficult to disappear" (pp. 200–201). The wanderings of a ghostly Bonnard in the corridors of the Institute and the dream appearance of the fairy in another library recall once again the *Naturalis Historia* of Pliny the Elder, who, in the chapter referred to by Borges, describes a similarly wandering imagination: "let sleep creep at any time upon us, [memory] seemeth to be vanquished, so as our poor spirit wandereth up and down to seek where it is, and to recover it again."[8] But for Funes there is no escape in imagination. "My dreams," he says, "are like you people's waking hours" (L, p. 64).

The wanderings of spirits in dreams turn concrete once again in a later story by Borges, "The Book of Sand." The story, insists the author, "*is* true," and the book described therein "can't be, but it *is*."[9] In the emphasis on the verb of being, Borges intimidates us into the acceptance of the impossible as possible. And why not? As Herbert's poem "The Collar" (used by Borges as an epigraph to this story) implies, impossibility frequently displays an inner substantive nature:

> . . . leave thy cold dispute
> Of what is fit, and not forsake thy cage,
>   Thy rope of sands,
> Which petty thoughts have made, and made to thee
>   Good cables, to enforce and draw.[10]

If habit turns man into a ghost, if custom is for Herbert an insubstantial rope of sand, still, as France realizes, the ghost is the most perdurable of beings, and, as Herbert reminds us, the sterile exercise of knitting up ropes of sand can result in the manufacture of the most binding of cordages. It is thus with the Book of Sand; it is an impossible text that encloses all possible texts, a closed and fettered form of art that nullifies all further scholarly researches. Yet, in enclosing all, it also lets all slip away. It is a Book of Sand, as knowledge is a thing of sand, as man, in Foucault's words, is "a face drawn in sand at the edge of the sea"[11]—a rope of sands, a cable to enforce and draw, a chain of convenience and custom rather than of necessity.

Specifically, Borges's later story draws upon the last footnote at the end of "The Library of Babel," enforcing the lesson of those few lines, making the sturdy cable of a story line from the idle musings of an afterthought:

> Letizia Alvarez de Toledo has observed that the vast Library is useless: rigorously speaking, *a single volume* would be sufficient, a volume . . . containing an infinite number of infinitely thin leaves . . . the handling of this silky *vademecum* would not be convenient:[12] each apparent page would unfold into other analogous ones; the inconceivable middle page would have no reverse. (L, p. 58)

The silky pages of this infinite book remind us of the less mysterious, but nonetheless infinite, text of *Don Quixote* that begins with an aborted trip to a silk merchant. The threat posed by both these books is similar. The slippery, silky pages elude the grasp of the reader like a rope of sand or an imaginary tapestry, undermining logical thought, destroying years of careful organization, and, ultimately (as is the case with Pierre Menard), eroding the ego.

In "The Book of Sand," an aged bibliophile and retired librarian is visited, like Bonnard was visited in the opening pages of his novel, by a bookseller. While France's character sells obscure texts and cheap pornography, Borges's character is a Bible salesman who offers the old librarian the priceless infinite book. This book, as might be expected of such an uncanny treasure, bears with it an implicit curse, in this case one that makes the owner a virtual prisoner in his library. Like Don Quixote, he spends his days and nights reading it, and the book nearly drives him mad. Finally he recognizes the demonic nature of the book and the weird enchantments he has suffered through contact with it: "I realized that the book was monstrous. What good did it do me to think that I who looked upon the volume with my eyes, who held it in my hands, was any less monstrous?" (BS, p. 121). He has been contaminated by this monster; he must save others from a similar contamination. But how to destroy its power? He is fearful of the results of submitting the book to a quixotic bonfire. Would not such an infinite text, upon its conflagration, destroy the universe in its flames? The world itself is somehow implicated in the "obscene" silky pages, and their destruction might bring about the end of the world. Instead of burning the book, the old librarian devises a more elegant solution; he hides the book in the stacks of the National Library where the chance of finding it again among the 900,000 other books is not nil, but at least reassuringly slim.

But the solution also poses a problem. The book still exists, its problematic unfathomed (probably unfathomable). By hiding the infinite book, which corresponds to the universe, in the library (already figured in other stories and essays as the universe), the world loses its reality and is converted into the metaphor of a metaphor, into a twist of figurative language with a void at the center, into an inconceivable Möbius strip of a center, a middle page with no reverse. The crystallization of language into the infinite book represents not only a double of the universe, but also its annihilation. The world is converted into a book, as Mallarmé may have desired, but the book slips away through silky pages. It is the avatar of nothingness—we never learn a single scrap of information about the contents of the Book of Sand, despite the old bibliophile's exhaustive catalogues.

In "The Book of Sand" as in "The Library of Babel," Borges tends to annul grammar, syntax, and language itself by dissolving the syntactic chain that unrolls and develops in time. The infinite library, or the book of sand, is an analogue of the world. Like the world, this book and this library are dream children, fixed by the threads of memory, attenuated by a discredited theory and syntax of language and time: "We have dreamt it [the world] as firm, mysterious, visible, ubiquitous in space and durable in time; but in its architecture we have allowed tenuous and and eternal crevices of unreason which tell us it is false" (L, p. 208). By questioning the invisible ropes of sand of time and syntax, Borges puts everything else to the question as well and approaches those disturbing heterotopias described by Foucault as endemic to the Argentinian's writing: "heterotopias (such as those to be found so often in Borges) desiccate speech, stop words in their tracks, contest the very possibility of grammar at its source; they dissolve our myths and sterilize the lyricism of our sentences."[13] Borges himself describes his motivations with a nostalgic pensiveness:

I enter the Library. At once, in an almost physical way, I feel the gravitation of the books, the quiet atmosphere of ordered things, the past rescued and magically preserved. [Borges enters the office, discusses his works briefly (before the dream dissolves) with a precursor poet, now dead.] My vanity and my wistfulness have set up an impossible scene. This may be so (I tell myself), but tomorrow I too will be dead and our times will become one . . . and in some way it may be true to say that I once handed you this book and that you accepted it.[14]

Where France's more traditional concept of history rebels at the idea of an imaginative reconstruction, but terminates in the construction of a history that is also a work of art, Borges's histories are almost pure imagination, with no more substantiality than the fairy of Sylvestre Bonnard's dream. Yet these imaginative worlds are held back from the point of dissolution by the scientific orders, the desiccated and preserved time of the library.

The ordering method devised for the collection is just as revealing (if not more so) as the actual contents of the library. Foucault, on the first page of *The Order of Things*, speaks of the influence exercised on his imagination by Borges's recapitulation of the ordering system used in a certain apocryphal Chinese encyclopedia. In "The Analytic Language of John Wilkins," the article in which Foucault discovers this idiosyncratic catalogue, the dazzling taxonomy of the animal kingdom is followed by a second, equally quirky, though less striking, catalogue:

> The Bibliographical Institute of Brussels also resorts to chaos: it has parcelled out the universe into 1000 sub-divisions: Number 262 corresponds to the Pope; Number 282, to the Roman Catholic church; Number 263, to the Lord's Day; Number 268, to Sunday schools, Number 298, to Mormonism; and Number 294, to Brahmanism, Buddhism, Shintoism, and Taoism. It also tolerates heterogeneous subdivisions, for example, Number 179: "Cruelty to animals. Protection of animals. Moral implications of dueling and suicide. Various vices and defects. Various virtues and qualities." (OI, pp. 103–4)

Such arrangements, as Borges correctly observes, "exercise chaos" under the guise of order; they plunge the entire collection into absurdity.

The Chinese encyclopedia, the catalogue of the Bibliographic Institute, and the analytic disorders of John Wilkins are not to be rejected out of hand. Rather, Borges delights in them, revels in the blindness and the microscopy exercised in their formulation, enjoys the whimsical classifications for their own sakes as poetic constructions, and, as Foucault intimates, for the sake of the synchronic view of history that emerges. The actual function of such classificatory manias is not only to read history, but to rewrite it under the illusion of summarizing and repeating realities.

The catalogue is vaster, hence more inscrutable in the Hawthorne of Borges. Borges recalls that Hawthorne's diaries annotate "thousands of trivial impressions, small concrete details (the movement of a hen, the shadow of a branch on the wall); they fill six volumes and their inexplicable abundance is the consternation of all his biographers" (OI, p. 63), and one might add, of all his bibliographers. This Hawthornian profusion is, perhaps, the model for Ireneo Funes's even more excessive and absurd abundance, an abundance that is also the despair of biographers and bibliographers. Each of Funes's memories is precisely drawn, each is tinged, not by the imperfections of memory or perception, but by the singular point of view of the individual observer. Like Hawthorne, and unlike the bibliographic institutes and encyclopedias of the world, Funes has no urge (and indeed no ability) to fit these multitudinous details into an overall scheme or table of groups and subdivisions. Yet Funes, motivated perhaps by a similar classificatory instinct, "decided to reduce each of his past days to some seventy thousand memories, which would then be defined by means of ciphers." This mental equivalent of a catalogue, says the narrator, is senseless, but betrays "a certain stammering grandeur" that "permit[s] us to glimpse or infer the nature of Funes's vertiginous world" (L, p. 65). Funes has envisioned a system of references not unlike that of the Bibliographic Institute of Brussels in form, though far more extensive in actual scope. It is a system of references that imprisons the maker in a vain and misleading verbal net of signification, in which a cipher becomes the double of the memory. The arbitrary number supplants the original true and essential word, substituting an approximate, meaningless form for the pure recollection—a tautology, but an incomplete and particularly dangerous one, since it masks the individual's laborious compilations of existence under the artificial unity of a cipher. It is the enterprise of a confused and fallen Adam in a world that came into existence after the destruction of Babel, an Adam painfully conscious of linguistic variation. Where Adam named the things and animals of the earth, thus classifying them in the first of the catalogues of existing beings, Hawthorne and Funes reindividualize the species, recognizing only the singular item, filtering it through their perceiving consciousness. Funes takes this perception yet one step further, by subsuming all the products of his mind in a vast, meaningless system, which is, as Borges notes, the opposite of a Platonic one. No species are redefined; rather, the world is given over to the abstract indifference of numbers. The impossible catalogue is as vast as the experience it supposedly delimits, but with the personal element removed.

There is an analogous hopelessness attached to the catalogue of the Library of Babel. The librarian realizes that such an all-inclusive collection necessarily contains "the faithful catalogue of the Library, thousands and thousands of false catalogues, the demonstration of the fallacy of those catalogues, the demonstration of the fallacy of the true catalogue" (L, p. 54). Maurice-Jean Lefebve explains:

> Let us suppose that the volumes are ordered in the following manner: first all the works whose first letter is A, then all those whose first letter is B, etc. In the group A, those whose second letter is A, then those whose second letter is B. And so on. One sees immediately that a catalogue must mention, in order to describe and situate any particular work, *all* the letters of that work. In other words, the catalogue of Babel must reproduce, to designate each volume, the entire volume. The catalogue is, then, a second library identical to the first and contained in it. Which is hypothetically impossible, if all the works are different. The conclusion is that a finite and total world cannot contain its image.[15]

And yet, there are mirrors at the end of the entrance halls that "faithfully duplicate all appearances" (L, p. 51), so that images are already doubled at least once in an illusory mirror space. A similar power of duplication is inherent in Ireneo Funes's memoriousness. The result, as Mary Kinzie recognizes, is to transform Funes into the bearer of such a catalogue of catalogues; not a Man of the Book, but a god nonetheless: "Funes is not memorious; he is more than memorious. Incapable of ordering the trivia that come his way, he does more than order them—he perceives things so intensely that they become vast. . . . Funes' mind is, given the negligible transforming of scale, identical with God's."[16]

Funes, like God, imposes a form over the vast chaos of the universe, and despite the biographer's reference to his "fear" (L, p. 62) on hearing Funes's voice resounding in the darkness, the story of the memorious gaucho has no tinge of the uncanny. Such an "indecipherable, interminable" fear is dissipated in the minuteness of description, in Funes's partial register of the chaos in terms of objects impeccably observed and permanently engraved in his memory. "My memory, sir, is like a garbage heap," says Funes (L, p. 64), making the fearful banal. Nestor Ibarra agrees: "But even for Borges the writer, let's not speak of the *Unheimlichkeit*. Outside of a few rare exceptions Borges does not disturb or frighten us."[17] Despite the obfuscation following upon his use of abstract modifiers instead of adjectives that denote concrete qualities, Borges does not linger in the realm of the dark and unknown. With Funes's biographer, the reader shakes off his fear, crosses the dark patio, and awaits the slow coming of light. Borges's statement at the end of "A New Refutation of Time" is to the point: "Our destiny . . . is not frightful by being unreal; it is frightful because it is irreversible and ironclad" (L, pp. 233–34). The precise detail has more power to affect the reader than any uncanny, ghostly presence. When the reader is led to expect profundity, he is misled with a superficial clarity of detail, and vice versa.

Literature for Borges, as for Scheherazade, becomes a refuge. In the case of the Persian queen, fabulation forestalls death, buying enough time to produce a son to her cruel and desolate husband, and the long nights of story bear various fruits. For Borges, destiny is ironclad, but he, like the queen, is wily enough to engineer his escape through literature. The world is frightfully real, but in the refuge of the library, Borges can manipulate the geometries of art. He attributes to Herbert Quain his schematic summary of the rules of this game: "'I revindicate for this work,' I heard him say, 'the essential characteristics of all games: symmetry, arbitrary rules, tedium.'"[18]

The game is symmetrical. In the second paragraph of "The Library of Babel," the unnamed librarian repeats the "classic dictum: *The Library is a sphere whose exact center is any one of its hexagons and whose circumference is inaccessible*" (L, p. 52). Each player, each librarian, begins at the exact center of the library, each proceeds through long and exhaustive searches back to that center. While some philosophers derive justifications for hexagonal rooms in an inaccessible sphere, others dream of a circular chamber with a circular book as the perfect and unique center of the library. The protagonist has already rejected such idle speculation: "I am preparing to die just a few leagues from the hexagon in which I was born" (L, p. 52). The game is not only symmetrical, but as the mirrors in the entrance hall have already suggested, circular and closed. Progress leads to a regression, limitless space closes around the player.

The game is arbitrary: "This much is already known: for every sensible line of straightforward statement, there are leagues of senseless cacophonies, verbal jumbles and incoherence" (L, p. 53). While the combinatory basis of the library has been adduced, the librarians come no closer than before to understanding the norms by which they were ruled. The laws remain arbitrary and as inaccessible as the outer walls of the spherical library. The books remain perpetually cryptic and unreadable.

The game is tedious. The librarian recognizes that the combinatory rules of the library have resulted in a vast number of books. He also recognizes that this number is not, alas!, infinite. In order for the game to be completely closed and symmetrical, as befits an eternal, spherical library with an inaccessible circumference, the books cannot end with the using up of all the possible combinations of orthographic symbols. The librarian's futile searches are vindicated only if they are completely purposeless—otherwise tedium cannot be absolute, and neither can the library. Thus, he hopes that the library is both unlimited and cyclical, that "if an eternal traveler were to cross it in any direction, after centuries he would see [if he were as memorious as Ireneo Funes] that the same volumes were repeated in the same disorder (which, thus repeated, would be an order: the Order)" (L, p. 58). The algebraic and geometric symmetry of such a search would copy the symmetry and arbitrariness of the library, leading, as well, to a perfect tedium. Structure is vindicated, though its precise nature remains unknown.

While the library in which Sylvestre Bonnard passes his life in no way duplicates the ominous wasteland of Borges's Library of Babel, France's librarian is also cognizant of the rules of the literary game as Herbert Quain has enumerated them. Bonnard, like Borges's librarian, knows that the essential nature of life is cyclical; in his moments of discontent he realizes that scholastic endeavor is not:

I felt saddened to think that, whatever effort we scholars may make to preserve dead things from passing away, we are labouring painfully in vain. Whatever has lived becomes the necessary food of new existences. And the Arab who builds himself a hut out of the marble fragments of a Palmyra temple is really more of a philosopher than all the guardians of museums at London, Munich, or Paris. (p. 102)

It is not surprising, therefore, that Bonnard often longs to leave the dusty works of a dead past to their well-deserved oblivion and to devote his scholarly studies instead to some endeavor more closely allied to the cyclical progress of nature. The double pull is never resolved. Bonnard does dedicate his waning years to a treatise on insects and plants, but he also takes a disciple, young Gélis, to initiate into the historical researches that occupied the greater part of the elderly scholar's life.

Furthermore, Bonnard's study of life takes the form of another scholarly treatise. The last page of this work is reproduced in the last pages of the novel, a last page that is footnoted "by the French Editor" in a very Borgesian manner:

Monsieur Sylvestre Bonnard was not aware that several very illustrious naturalists were making researches at the same time as he in regard to the relations between insects and plants. He was not acquainted with the labours of Darwin, with those of Dr. Hermann Müller, nor with the observations of Sir John Lubbock. It is worthy of note that the conclusions of Monsieur Bonnard are very nearly similar to those reached by the three scientists above mentioned. Less important, but perhaps equally interesting, is the fact that Sir John Lubbock is, like Monsieur Bonnard, an archaeologist who began to devote himself only late in life to the natural sciences. (p. 307)

The excerpt to which this note is appended is the only excerpt we are given from any of Bonnard's works, and the footnote that refers to it is the only footnote in the 310 pages of the novel. Both are thrust into a position of prominence by their placement at the end of the book and the beginning of the last chapter. What are we to assume about this footnote? Was it appended to the study of insects and plants in the published version of that scholarly work as its position might seem to indicate? If so, it would seem out of place in a reproduction of the old historian's private journal. Or was it written specifically for inclusion in this publication of Bonnard's journals? It would then be an intrusion that calls attention to itself because it is so obviously out of place in the context. And what was Anatole France's purpose in associating his fictional character with three well-known scientists of the time? Perhaps its function is merely to add a note of verisimilitude at a point in this improbable story where improbability is about to dissolve into melodrama. The melodrama is distanced both by the quotation from Bonnard's text and the footnote reflecting on that quotation. Suddenly, Darwin, Müller, and Lubbock intrude upon the fairy tale, splintering and reinstating the illusion of truth. The final scene of the novel is envisioned from the vantage point of this distanciation. Bonnard says that he has chosen to write about insects rather than historical documents and monuments (it is curious that the "French editor" identifies both Lubbock and Bonnard as archaeologists whereas Bonnard is more strictly a historian) in order to feel close to the cycle of life, yet little Sylvestre's empty cradle alienates us from that unknown life; the child was born and died, the grief at his passing assuaged and distanced before Bonnard recounts it to the readers.

The page from Bonnard's history of insects and plants indicates a parallel distanciation. He speaks of his subject with affection, but not with passion, falling back into the role of a scientific observer (like Darwin, Müller, and Lubbock) with the ease of many years of practice in his historical studies. How different is this distanciation, including the discussion of young Sylvestre's death, from the earlier passion provoked in him by the presence of books! When he decides that his books must be sold to provide Jeanne's dowry, his grief and reluctance are far more immediate. He worries about the new owners: Will they care for the books properly? Will they recognize the special merit that can be derived from reading these books and respect them accordingly? The scholar's books and manuscripts are living beings to him, coparticipants in an almost erotic fancy:

I have taken great pains to collect and preserve all those rare and curious editions which people the City of Books; and for a long time I used to believe that they were as necessary to my life as air and light. I have loved them well, and even now I cannot prevent myself from smiling at them and caressing them. Those morocco bindings are so delightful to the eye! Those old vellums are so soft to the touch! (pp. 222–23)

The passion that rules his life becomes his life, as Bonnard is well aware: "Our passions are ourselves. My old books are me" (pp. 183–84). The passion for books stands in the place of other passions more directly channeled toward living beings. In his exposition on insects and plants, and in his love for Jeanne, Bonnard attempts to overlay his first passion (for books) with a second passion (for living beings). Yet, this second passion always returns to his first—his love of Jeanne is bound up in his delight in the sensual textures of his books, his affection for fragile insects and plants is expressed in a learned treatise. Bonnard, no less than Borges's librarian, is a permanent resident of his Library of Babel. He is detained among his bookshelves as surely as if they were the walls of a prison. Perhaps a world exists beyond the walls of the library, but Bonnard's excursions from his home give us no way of being certain. He travels, but he carries his library with him, surrounding him like an invisible aura. Like the librarian of Babel, who has traveled extensively only to discover countless identical hexagons, Bonnard's infrequent trips out of his library merely carry him into other libraries, parallel simulacra of the world. Michel Butor explains further:

> The library gives us the world, but it gives us a false world; from time to time fissures are produced, reality revolts against the books; through the intermediary of words or of certain books, an exterior beckons to us and gives us the feeling of being locked up; the library becomes a prison.[19]

"My old books are me" is less a liberating proposition than a limiting one. Bonnard's solitary existence, like that of Borges's librarian or of Funes the Memorious, emphasizes his characteristic isolation within a closed environment. In effect, Bonnard is saying, "I am my world," and like that unique and individual construction, he is incomparable. Anatole France's librarian would seem to anticipate the contemporary injunction that the uniqueness of a text resides in the reading of it rather than in its writing. In fact, however, the implication of Bonnard's statement is very different. He proposes no tyranny of the reader over the written word—quite the reverse. As with Borges, readable and unreadable texts tyrannize over the solitary librarian, but their overlordship is subtly expressed. Borges mentions once, at the opening of the story "The Library of Babel," a mirror in the entrance hall of the library. Bonnard tells us that he and his books are identical, establishing a metaphorical mirror in which he can caress his books, that is, himself.

As Bonnard is a prisoner of his books, so too is Ireneo Funes a prisoner of his peculiar mental library. His biographer recalls: "Twice I saw him behind the iron grating of the window, which harshly emphasized his condition as a perpetual prisoner: once, motionless, with his eyes closed; another time, again motionless, absorbed in the contemplation of a fragrant sprig of santonica" (L, p. 61). Sylvestre Bonnard, the nameless librarian, Ireneo Funes: the image is almost the same. The "literature" they espouse points to a cryptic knowledge that transcends the real (fallacious) world in a search for truth. Yet, in this search, art is produced at the cost of life, and reality must eventually revolt against such an outrage, as Butor intimates. The two librarians, France's and Borges's, are enclosed in and mirrored by books in their old age. Funes dies of a pulmonary congestion in his youth, but already he has lived a long life in the darkened room that could represent a uterus, or a tomb, or a labyrinth, and is a house, and a mirror, and a prison. In one of his essays, Borges felicitously quotes from Hawthorne's journals:

And now I begin to understand why I was imprisoned so many years in this lonely chamber, and why I could never break through the viewless bolts and bars; for if I had sooner made my escape into the world, I should have grown hard and rough, and been covered with earthly dust. . . . Indeed, we are but shadows. (OI, p. 63)

This shadow life spent as the prisoner of books and writings is more explicitly the fate of the scholar-librarian of "The Book of Sand." The infinite book occupies all his waking and sleeping hours: "I had only a few friends left; I now stopped seeing even them. A prisoner of the book, I almost never went out any more. . . . At night, in the meager intervals my insomnia granted, I dreamed of the book" (BS, p. 121). The structure of this impossible book is labyrinthine in the most complex manner conceivable. It is absolutely indecipherable. The scholar wastes considerable time studying the construction of the book; it is a manifestly futile endeavor. Speculation on the possible origin of the book can lead to no satisfactory conclusions. The Book of Sand is necessarily the work of some being(s) who existed outside history and time. Its mere existence in our time is horrible because it contaminates all of human history.

Yet, how is this book different in essence from those books that the scholar habitually consults? Clearly, its horror resides in a difference of degree, not of kind. Like Hawthorne, the narrator of "The Book of Sand" has long been a prisoner of his "viewless bolts and bars"; like Bonnard, his remembered excursions into the world represent little more than an illusion of escape, since the prison is carried with him in all his actions. Furthermore, the book itself only explicitly reveals the implicit nature of all literature. As Borges says in another context, "Literature is not exhaustible, for the sufficient and simple reason that a single book is not" (OI, p. 164). Eternity and infinity are the habitual modes of existence of the library. Of what library, of what book, is Borges himself the solitary prisoner?

Like his fictional librarians, Borges cannot be sure if the enchantments of books are of a beneficent or of a demonic order. However, like Nathaniel Hawthorne, like Sylvestre Bonnard, like Ireneo Funes, he has become used to the solitary chamber he inhabits and which he carries with him wherever he travels. He is accustomed to the labyrinthine passages of the Library of Babel and grew up in his maze like a second Minotaur. As Borges explains it in *Evaristo Carriego*, the library, the labyrinth, and the city come together once again: "I believed for many years that I had grown up in a suburb of Buenos Aires, a suburb of adventurous streets and showy sunsets. The truth is that I grew up in a garden, inside a wrought iron fence, and in a library of unlimited books."[20] Like the Minotaur in Borges's story, or Rappaccini's daughter in Hawthorne's, the characters' ignorance of the enchantments worked upon them allows them to be comfortable in the labyrinths that are their homes. It is a labyrinth from which Borges never escapes, since he moves from amateur librarian in his parents' home to professional librarian as the director of Argentina's National Library. Nor does he wish to escape: "I, that imagined Paradise / As a type of library."[21] His powers, like those of his fictional librarians, are derived from long dedication to books.

He is a humble scholar not always certain of his powers and ready to efface himself in favor of the library itself. In "The Library of Babel," the librarian states as the first principle that the library exists *ab aeterno* and continues, "This truth, whose immediate corollary is the future eternity of the world, cannot be placed in doubt by any reasonable mind. Man, the imperfect librarian, may be the product of chance or of malevolent demiurgi; the universe [i.e., the Library] . . . can only be the work of a god" (L, p. 52). There is, then, an originary difference between the perfection of the library and the imperfection of the caretakers, a difference that could also be called the original sin. The original imperfection accounts for all the rest: the inability to understand the books contained in the infinite hexagonal galleries, the incomprehensibility of the mirror in the hallway, the nagging concern about the mysteries of the origin of the library and of time. The librarian accepts his imperfections and imperfectibility humbly, hoping only that his searches are not totally worthless, that the library has an order though it is not given him to perceive it, and fearing that the incomprehensibility of the universe might extend to him as well. He voices this fear in an ambiguous, if typically Borgesian, aside: "You who read me, are you sure of understanding my language?" (L, p. 58). Borges's paradise is twinned with Borges's hell; the librarian cannot speak a word that does not already exist in the omnifarious texts of the library. He lives surrounded by the already written, and his recognition that he can add nothing new to the vast store of knowledge vitiates the desire for discourse through the realization of its inescapable redundancy.

Sylvestre Bonnard admits that he is a very bad storyteller and tells the readers of his novel: "if I were—by some impossible chance—to take it into my head to compose a novel, I know I should never succeed" (p. 152). Borges and his librarians could say the same. They are bad storytellers; they can only recount portions of those stories that have already been told elsewhere. These stories as retold are incomplete, full of memory gaps, buttressed by references to other authorities—a scholar's tales and not a novelist's. Borges's stories suggest their own superfluity; they remind us that what we are reading is merely a gloss on some other prior text. His art, therefore, consists in the skillful and organized replay of some portion of the library.

This redundancy of fiction further illuminates the librarian's nature as an unwilling mirror image of his books. Yet, while the librarian is doomed to repetition in his works and in his life, Borges can find no consolation in mirrors. On the contrary, in Borges's work, the reader is introduced to the darker side of the mirror. Even a clear reflection is shattering and horrible:

> Infinite, I see them, elemental
> Executors of an ancient pact
> To multiply the world like the
> Generative act, insomniac and fatal.[22]

Nabokov's duplication of Kinbote into Gradus and Shade is humorous; in Borges, the doublings resulting from the mirrors and words take on more ominous overtones. The copulation that reproduces life, the mirrors that reflect the image of life, the art that is a simulacrum of life are all equally abominable. Borges is obsessed with the darker implications of mirror reflections; thus, his own writing, so obviously mirrored from an absent source, is twisted slightly from faithful duplication. In "Funes," in "The Library of Babel," and in "The Book of Sand," it is the very impossibility of the exact duplication of reality that is the author's salvation. Thus, Funes, who by nature and circumstance would seem to be a perfect mirror of his environment, is actually a Narcissus in reverse: "His own face in the mirror, his own hands, surprised him every time he saw them" (L, p. 65). Funes does not recognize repetition; to him, each event is separate and unique. Likewise, he finds no narcissistic projection of himself in the clear waters of the river. On the contrary, it is in such waters that he seeks the dark oblivion of sleep: "To sleep is to turn one's mind from the world. . . . He would . . . imagine himself at the bottom of the river, rocked and annihilated by the current" (L, p. 66).

The incapability of telling stories directly is a hidden asset that prevents the librarian from approximating the mirrorlike duplications of life abhorred by Borges. Recognized redundancies redound to the author's credit. As Carter Wheelock observes:

> Borges' stories in the aggregate comprehend, almost omnisciently, the abstract form of literature and its creation and its manner of being. It is almost as if Borges had uttered the hundredth word, calling the summational Name of literature; but courteously, he speaks it obliquely, as if to spare literature the humiliation of fulmination.[23]

The stories, therefore, are purposely distorted, purposely incomplete. But is such a literature possible? Under what conditions can literature as an intellectual construct, without external referent, even enter the realm of the thinkable? The paradox of this impossible literature is detailed by Tzvetan Todorov in his book *The Fantastic*:

> For writing to be possible, it must be born out of the death of what it speaks about; but this death makes writing itself impossible, for there is no longer anything to write. Literature can become possible only insofar as it makes itself impossible. Either what we say is actually here, in which case there is no room for literature; or else there is room for literature, in which case there is no longer anything to say. As Blanchot writes in *La Part du Feu*: "If language, and particularly literary language, were not constantly advancing toward its death, it would not be possible, for it is this movement toward its impossibility which is its condition and basis." . . . And yet literature *exists*; that is its greatest paradox.[24]

The obliqueness of literary language is both a blessing and a curse, leading inevitably toward the play of possibility and impossibility described by Todorov. Borges is not alone in his recognition of the impossibility of literature, but in his character as a librarian he gives this interplay a peculiar twist and a special immediacy, as the death that is forestalled through literature becomes as well the death that advances its infinitely appealing oblivion. The life and the death (postponed, forestalled) are equally a part of the Borgesian simulacrum. Says Gérard Genette: "Literature according to Borges does not have a ready-made sense, a revelation to which we must submit: it is a reservoir of forms that await their sense, *it's the imminence of a revelation that does not take place.*" [25] Or, as Borges describes the situation in "The Library of Babel," the library is perfect and eternal, man is flawed and mortal. Therefore, when this imperfect librarian is unable to find the text he requires among the vast collections of the library (it is a condition of his caretakership that he cannot, by definition, find the book he seeks), he, like Borges, undertakes to write that text. But because he is flawed by an undefined original sin, the text he produces must also be flawed in some imperceptible manner. It is this flaw that defines his efforts—and condemns him to an infinite fall in death. "I suspect," says the aged librarian of the story, "that the human species—the unique species—is about to be extinguished, but the Library will endure: illuminated, solitary, infinite, perfectly motionless, equipped with precious volumes, useless, incorruptible, secret" (L, p. 58).

This silent grandeur of the abandoned Library of Babel is parallel to the "stammering grandeur" of Funes the Memorious, but where the library is incorruptible in time, for Funes, time is a crucial substance in his vision. The biographer notes that Funes remembers not only the individual object, but also each stage in its temporal metamorphosis. Thus, he could call to mind at any moment "not only every leaf of every tree of every wood, but also every one of the times he had perceived or imagined it" (L, p. 65). His waking life represents a perpetual state of total recall. Funes's memories, however, are empty; they crush the subject with their quantity and vividness, but they do not *connote*. The grandeur is necessarily reduced to stammering, and it is clear why Ireneo Funes's tale can be summarized in only a few paragraphs.

The intriguing aura of empty grandeur that clings to Borges's description of the Library of Babel and to his biography of Ireneo

Funes is an effect frequently sought after by this classifier of nonexistent texts. Borges is deeply concerned with the layering of events in a single moment of time, and notoriously stubborn about providing his reader with substantive detail. Thus, the librarian's discussion of life in the unimaginable library is, as the librarian himself recognizes, merely one of several alternative histories, all equally valid—that is to say, equally invalid. Likewise, Funes's prodigious memory for objects is only a subset of his incredible sense of time— we recall our introduction to the "chronometrical" Funes occurs with the "tripartite" phrase, "It's four minutes to eight, young Bernardo Juan Francisco" (L, p. 60). With this phrase and the ironic gesture that accompanies it, Ireneo Funes reveals not only his sense of time, but also the futility of that sense. There is no simple answer to Bernardo's question, "What time it is, Ireneo?" for a man of Funes's peculiar sensibilities. His sense of time is cognate with Borges's own:

> Reality is so complex, history so fragmentary and so simplified, that an omniscient observer could write an indefinite, and almost infinite, number of biographies of a man, each of which would emphasize different facts; we would have to read many of them before we realized that the protagonist was the same man. . . . A history of a man's dreams is not inconceivable; or of the organs of his body; or of the mistakes he has made; or of all the moments when he imagined the Pyramids; or of his traffic with night and with dawn. (OI, p. 137)

We recover in this enumeration of possible histories the typical Borgesian approximation of infinity, the suggestion of a *mise en abîme* that is also apparent in Funes's simple, ironic response to a question of the time of day and in the Babel librarian's vertiginous perspective of texts that refer to other texts that refer to other texts.

For Anatole France, time and space are not expanded toward infinity, but compressed into a single image. Says Sylvestre Bonnard, "My world is wholly formed of words. . . . Each one dreams the dream of life in his own way. I have dreamed it in my library; and when the hour shall come in which I must leave this world, may it please God to take me from my ladder—from before my shelves of books!" (p. 94). Despite their differences, both Borges and France identify the book and the world. For librarians, subject to the sovereignty of the written word, the world must necessarily disclose itself between the covers of a book. And for such portentous disclosures, an infinite library is a hindrance, an infinite book an abomination. Hence, the true counterpart to the story "The Library of Babel" is not "The Book of Sand," but another story, "Undr," in which a dying bard bequeaths to his disciple a single word which includes all the rest and which is unique to each individual (BS, p. 87). If the Babel librarian had halted his searches for the catalogue of catalogues, if he had overcome his obsession with words in the inner recognition of the one Word, the entire library would have ceased to exist.

In some sense, Sylvestre Bonnard does discover this one Word—or, in the approximate post-Babel fashion, a nearly perfect facsimile thereof—in his discovery of Jeanne. Because of his relationship with the young girl, Bonnard is finally able to leave the library. The books can be dispersed; they are no longer necessary to his existence or to his comfort. "Behind there we have a nice little room," he tells Jeanne, "you are going to take the place of the books which used to be in it" (p. 280). In France, the magnificent solitude of introspection gives way to a descent from the refuge of art into the other world, to the practice of interrelations between the self and some other person. However, it is an interaction that ultimately, inevitably, refers back to the unique and solitary word, to the self-possession that is the possession of self by self. The other is the double, reflected in the mirror, and the librarian who thought he had escaped from the refuge and prison of art finds himself back in the Library of Babel, staring at the entrance hall mirror: "A man proposes to himself the task of drawing the world. . . . Shortly before death he discovers that the patient labyrinth of lines traced the image of his face."[26] In Borgesian geography, that which is alien must refer back to the self. In France's psychology, the daughter of a lost love becomes more than a daughter to the aging scholar. In both cases, that which seems most strange and unknowable reveals not only a personal tie to the librarian, but an unsuspected degree of intimacy with him.

The yearning for infinity, the movement to abstraction that is a common motivation of both Borges's and France's librarians, is countered subtly by the reader's recognition that this expansion to the infinite is necessarily coupled with an extreme reduction within the self. It is not surprising, then, that this systole and diastole of expansion and reduction is captured in both authors through the use of the same metaphor—that of dream. In his "New Refutation of Time," Borges comments on the nature of the "unstable mental world," describing it as "a world of evanescent impressions; a world without matter or spirit, neither objective nor subjective; a world without the ideal architecture of space; a world made of time . . . ; an indefatigable labyrinth, a chaos, a dream" (OI, p. 175). By annulling personal identity at the same time he reaffirms it, Borges not only dissolves the Other, but eliminates the self in the annulment of all possibility of fruitful communication. This is the message of "Everything and Nothing" (L, p. 249), a message stated and repeated throughout the works of Borges: just as the Other dissolves in the Self, so too the Self must evaporate into Nothingness. The librarian-narrator of "The Library of Babel" accepts this extreme individualism and this anonymity; others of his kind are not so accepting: "I know of an uncouth region whose librarians repudiate the vain and superstitious custom of finding meaning in books and equate it with that of finding a meaning in dreams or in the chaotic lines of one's palm" (L, p. 53). These librarians, like the dreamer-priest in another of Borges's stories, wish to dream a son and impose him upon the world. The narrator of "The Library of Babel" condemns the *hubris* of those other librarians, not the validity or invalidity of their efforts. It is, he implies, futile to spurn one truth for another, taking a stand and making a judgment as to the respective value of two modes of perceiving reality. The lesson of the all-inclusive library is that books and dreams are equally real—and equally unreal. The labyrinthine corridors and the lines of the hand trace parallel "indefatigable labyrinths" of the oneiric.

For Sylvestre Bonnard as well, the dream of life, the dream of books, and the dream of Jeanne come together in one comprehensive dream. As he has variously indicated, Bonnard's passions are himself, his books are himself, and in the person of Jeanne his passions and his books take on a human form. This young girl, who so fortuitously conjoins Bonnard's passions and his dreams, is fore-shadowed in the text by the fairy, who visits Bonnard to discuss the relationship between reality and illusion. But this debate between the conflicting realms of the real and the imaginary has an earlier point of reference in the novel—Bonnard's Don Quixote cane. As Bonnard recognizes: "if the incomparable knight and his matchless squire are imaged only upon this cane of mine, they are realities to my inner conscience," and the debate he conducts between them in his mind is possessed of far more reality than his recounting of many of his actual conversations. He readily admits that Don Quixote's *dream* of life (like that of the fairy), which so closely approximates his own, is far more seductive than the more sober counsel of Sancho Panza: "Within every one of us there lives both a Don Quixote and a Sancho Panza to whom we hearken by turns: and though Sancho most persuades us, it is Don Quixote that we find ourselves obliged to admire" (pp. 136–37).

These self-founded, self-sufficient dreams-labyrinths-refuges in-evitably convert themselves into prisons. Thus, Bonnard's library must be dispersed, and Borges's great Library of Babel exists on the edge of fulmination. This threat of burning is carried out in a later story in which Borges rewrites Hawthorne's tale of "Earth's Holo-caust" in the form of a vast "Congress of the World," whose mem-bers, as their principal endeavor, assemble a library consisting of all the most essential books in the world. This library, once assembled, is put to the flames with an epigrammatic remark by one of the Congress's participants, a remark that comes as something of a rev-elation: "Every few centuries, the Library of Alexandria must be burned down" (BS, p. 47). The book burning was inevitable from the moment in which the collection process was initiated. The li-brarian of Babel, who does not burn his sanctuary, is condemned to a ceaseless mapping that is disjunctive to the realities of the world, and in this activity he loses himself both inside and outside the li-brary walls—and in the text of Borges's story.

Borges admires the contact between the real and the imaginary realms, and these points of contact are not, for him, evanescent, but sculpted in enduring stone. Life is a dream, but it is also, as for Foucault, a monument and a document. Borges himself points to the antiquity of this notion in referring the reader to Virgil, where Aeneas, shipwrecked in Carthage, is brought face to face with the monumentalization of himself (OI, p. 52):

> . . . Waiting the queen,
> He stood there watching, under the great temple,
> Letting his eyes survey the city's fortune,
> The artist's workmanship, the craftsman's labor,
> And there, with more than wonder, he sees the battles
> Fought around Troy . . .
> And he saw himself there, too, fighting in battle[27]

Aeneas confronts one monumentalized image; he does not directly confront the documentary counterpart to these marble carvings, that is, Virgil's own recounting of Aeneas's future adventures in Rome. Borges employs a similar technique in his description of the library/librarian and his reduplicated texts, and in the final observation on Ireneo Funes by his biographer: "he seemed to me as monumental as bronze, more ancient than Egypt, older than the prophecies and the pyramids" (L, p. 66). These spatial representations seem like dream constructions, so solid and yet so evanescent are they in the reader's mind, and time appears to be suspended in these interpenetrations of reality. And with good reason. As Mary Kinzie has discovered, in this monumentalization/documentalization of Funes, Borges is once again able to advance arguments for his refutation of time, and for his denial of the possibility of writing any new literature:

> Borges is also drawing an echo from the Roman poet who desired, in stating a hope, to create a reality, asserting simply that "he will not entirely die," that he had made something as indestructible as bronze out of mere words:
>
> > *Exegi monumentum perennius*
> > *regalique situ pyramidum altius. . .*
> > (Horace, *Odes*, III, 30)
>
> I have built a monument more enduring than bronze,
> Loftier than the royal pile of the Pyramids.[28]

Borges, always the librarian, adds still more layers to these layered documents: "According to Mallarmé, the world exists for a book; according to Bloy, we are the versicles or words or letters of a magic book, and that incessant book is the only thing in the world: or, rather, it is the world" (OI, p. 120).

CHAPTER 4

The Refuge Turns Noxious: Sartre, Beckett, Goytisolo

THE VAST, INHUMAN impersonality of the library cannot be encompassed by any one librarian, and, as we have seen, a number of strategies are employed to maintain sanity in the face of this potentially infinite system. One method of control is exercised through naming, thus attempting to define that which lies at the limit of knowledge. A second, and related strategy, is that employed by Borges in his unceasing (inverted) repetition of the already written, thus adding no new element to the library and sterilizing the influence of the past. Both of these solutions are in some sense mechanical ones; their divisions and subdivisions unwittingly enter back into the mechanized discourse of the library catalogue. Consolation for these librarians comes through the completion of the catalogue, which allows them an illusion of mastery over this monstrous whole, and which permits the feints and delaying tactics that keep the librarians from prolonged contact with an infinity that can only cause their madness.

Such extended self-delusions are not always possible. The precise mechanical orders are, as Borges and France admit, inadequate to encompass the reality facing them. Edward Said also recognizes that the library is not a comprehensible machine, but a locus of interactions that "holds together . . . a staggeringly vast array of discursive formulations, an array whose essence is that no source, origin, or provenance, no goal, teleology, or purpose can be thought through for it."[1] How then can the library be quantified, qualified, attributed? The abstract machine of the catalogue always threatens to convert itself into an insane destructive mechanism that conducts war against its developers.

This war is fought on several fronts, by various different means. In Borges, the abstraction of the book/library/machine outstrips man's power of comprehension and unrolls itself in the vacuum and the horror of the infinite book, of the eternal library. That which was living and organic becomes in Borges's hands dead and abstract. The threat is distanced, and thus, diminished.

A second strategy confronts the peril of the library on the opposite tack. Rather than reinforcing the abstract, this tactic reintroduces organic elements into the structure of the library. With his essay on plants and insects, Sylvestre Bonnard seems to be making some feeble attempts in this direction. This organic approach is also the choice made consciously by Goytisolo's Julian, unconsciously by Sartre's Roquentin, and unwillingly by Beckett's Krapp. The reintroduction of the organic, however, can also lead to a situation that ranges out of the librarian's control. The vegetation of learning becomes actual vegetation, the readmission of Dionysus into the sphere of Apollonian abstraction can lead to intoxication (Krapp's alcohol, Julian's hashish) or madness (Roquentin's hallucinations) and death or death-in-life:

> And where there was gunwale there now was vine-trunk,
> And tenthril where cordage had been,
>   grape-leaves on the row-locks,
> Heavy vine on the oarshafts,
> And, out of nothing, a breathing,
>   hot breath on my ankles,
> Beasts like shadows in glass,
>   a furred tail upon nothingness.[2]

The organicism of myth traverses the rational world like a shudder. That which was too complex and too extensive to be understood is not delimited by such an organic rebirth, but made even more elusive.

Roquentin's diary is also a tail/tale upon nothingness, an attempt to grasp the cool, clear abstractions of music when forced to face the hot breath and heavy vegetation that he discovers around him, within him, and which he is forced to face in the reflecting glass of his mirror. Roquentin cannot "catch time by the tail":[3] even with the ostensible ordering system of his diary, his personal past does not arrange itself neatly into a personal history. "You have to choose," says Roquentin, "live or tell" (p. 39). It is this discrepancy between life and the tale of life that Roquentin tries to conceal by writing both a diary and a history; the first to record the contingencies of a life as lived in the recognition of the indeterminacy of the future, the second to alleviate the anxiety accompanying this incompleteness of the temporal sequence by telling a story of a life already completed. By reminding us that lived time is irreducible to language, he already admits the futility of this double effort. Life disclosed and made clear through literature is not life as lived, but a betrayal of life through fictionalized anecdotes. Similarly, the history of M. de Rollebon does not reflect the truth of a story now completed, but the distortions of reality as seen through the vegetation of learning (in the impulse to make one man the center and pivot of an epoch) and through the distorting glass of a narrator's voice (that forces the subject of the history to become a double of the teller of the tale). Roquentin leaves the fiction of his life and the fiction of history unfinished; his diary is set aside in the aspiration to regain the past and fix the future by writing an impersonal novel, a fictional account that makes no pretense of factuality. Roquentin's novel is not written within Sartre's novel, however, and Roquentin's actual future remains unknown.

Roquentin's writing, then, is deeply implicated in the processes of time and memory as captured (or buried) in history and in the novel. By the very fact of writing, however, Roquentin entangles the reader in this web of time, and the re-creation of history must involve the reader's past as well as the narrator's. Given this intricate interpenetration of different pasts, the question arises: What makes Roquentin's anecdotes and stories a more privileged vehicle for the implicit salvation through art than those of his reader? There is nothing in Roquentin's narration that serves to assure us that the small library of his stories, and our perceptions and interpretations of his stories, do indeed occupy such a privileged position, other than the tacit acceptance of the premises of the book that we make when we are diverted from our story to Roquentin's within the framework of Sartre's novel.

The case is clearer in relation to the biography of M. de Rollebon. Roquentin uses M. de Rollebon as a lever to pry up a bit of the past in order to establish a rational, yet viable, relation to it. He is, perhaps, not aware of the importance to this endeavor of his own insecurity about the nature of temporal succession, but he is aware of the pleasure derived from his work—a pleasure that is related to the scholarly task of ordering the past, and to the discovery of necessary relationships between things and people that were once obscured by apparent contingency.

Roquentin finds that "man is always a teller of tales, he lives surrounded by his stories and the stories of others" (p. 39). Given this belief, it is not surprising that Roquentin's researches are totally devoted to the reconstruction of the life of a single figure to the point that "de Rollebon now represents the only justification for my existence" (p. 70). As a typical historian-librarian, Roquentin is obsessed with the control he exerts over documents and with his efforts to order scattered information. Because his interests are biographical, however, it is only to be expected that the peripeteia in his story would be accompanied by his decision to try his hand at novel writing. Sartre's novel closes at this point, but it is as false a closure as that of *Don Quixote*: the hero apparently exerts his free will to change the course of his life, but the change reverts back to the beginning of the story in an ironic circle. Alonso Quijano dies as the squire to become Don Quixote; in the end, the process is reversed—with the added twist that the shock kills the good country squire. Roquentin, in rejecting history for the novel, is repeating himself in another genre with only the superficial difference of recognizing as fiction what he formerly would have ascribed to learned intuition.

Roquentin does not study history because of his great love for the subject or because of his fascination with the object of his researches; instead, he looks to books and historical documents for stability and permanence in an uneasily contingent world. For this hero, books and the library provide a refuge, since in them everything is classically connected, dissonances are disallowed, time is flattened out and spatialized. When this last bastion of permanence begins to crumble, the nausea invades even the library and Roquentin becomes disenchanted with his objectivized substitute for reality:

> The books were still there, arranged in alphabetical order on the shelves with their brown and black backs and their labels *up lf* 7.996 (For Public Use—French Literature—) or *up sn* (For Public Use—Natural Science). But . . . how can I explain it? Usually, powerful and squat, along the stove, the green lamps, the wide windows, the ladders, they dam up the future. As long as you stay between these walls, whatever happens must happen on the right or the left of the stove. . . . Thus these objects serve at least to fix the limits of probability.
>   Today they fixed nothing at all. . . . I got up. I could no longer keep my place in the midst of these unnatural objects. (pp. 76–77)

In Roquentin's ordinary, pre-nausea world, the objects to which he devotes his life are similar in nature to the hero's personality. His fascination with documents is at least partly a result of the fact that they, like him, give nothing—the enigmatic de Rollebon remains intractable despite years of effort dedicated to researching his motivations.

On his departure from the library where he conducts his researches into the life of M. de Rollebon, Roquentin goes immediately to the Bouville museum (p. 82). In the museum, the portraits of town notables provide an alternative to the vision of "truth" found in the books of the library. Like the books, the paintings serve to fix the limits of probability; they are both dead and alive: "Nothing alive in this great rectangular room, except a cat who was frightened at my approach and fled. But I felt the looks of a hundred and fifty pairs of eyes on me" (p. 83). The painted faces on the walls cannot "really" exchange glances with Roquentin; their "looks" are abstract metaphors for a sensitivity on the part of the observer to the presence of the past in the present, which the historian also experiences in relation to the library. Yet, despite this rationalization of his response to the paintings, the impression remains that Roquentin has attracted the attention of those historical figures. He realizes that objectively, these notables from Bouville's past possess nothing of life, but, nevertheless, they manage to make Roquentin (as we, the readers of his diary, do likewise) the cynosure of all eyes, thus confirming his own contingency and his factitiousness, and restating the terms of his commitment to and his confinement in art.

In a more obstinately mechanized age, the library begins to give way to the instant retrieval systems of computer technology, but man's obsession with the accumulated weight of the past remains unchanged. At age sixty-nine, Krapp, the protagonist of Samuel Beckett's drama, *Krapp's Last Tape*, believes that everything has already been written (or recorded) on his ubiquitous tapes: "Everything there, everything on this old muckball, all the light and dark and famine and feasting of . . . (hesitates) . . . the ages!"[4] His tapes, however, are no more able than Roquentin's stories to capture the whole of the past—all Krapp succeeds in salvaging are the fragmentary bits of debris of a wasted life, the eroded memories of youthful dreams. Like Roquentin, Krapp has made his life into the type of prison Beckett discovers in Proust's time-ridden masterpiece:

> Proust's creatures, then, are victims of this predominating condition and circumstance—Time; victims as lower organisms, conscious only of two dimensions and suddenly confronted with the mystery of height, are victims: victims and prisoners. There is no escape from the hours and the days. Neither from to-morrow nor from yesterday. There is no escape from yesterday because yesterday has deformed us, or been deformed by us. . . . The future event cannot be focussed, its implications cannot be seized until it is definitely situated and a date assigned to it.[5]

Krapp's mind is an analogue of his tape, coiling and uncoiling backward and forward in time without growth; he reviews his life from a two-dimensional perspective with no gain in understanding, and he remains imprisoned by the life he has chosen, his language sterilized by the strict, endless repetition of the same memories. Even the older, disillusioned Krapp cannot completely abandon the dreams of his youth as tendered by the tapes: "Lie propped up in

the dark—and wander. Be again in the dingle on a Christmas Eve
. . . be again on Croghan on a Sunday morning . . . Be again, be
again. (Pause.) All that old misery. (Pause.) Once wasn't enough for
you. (Pause.) Lie down across her" (pp. 26–27). Krapp's identity,
lost within the past as lived before the deforming tapes were made
to interpret it, evades him as it holds him captive. He can neither
escape from nor redeem time past.

While the brief play, *Krapp's Last Tape*, records the wreckage of
an entire life, Juan Goytisolo's novel, *Count Julian*, records the de-
tritus of a single day in the life of a Spaniard exiled in Tangier—a
town infamous as Europe's garbage dump. Appropriately, an epigraph from Jean Genet's *The Thief's Journal* introduces the narration: "I dreamed of Tangier, whose proximity fascinated me, and
the prestige of this city that is more or less a favorite haunt of traitors."[6] The narrator of *Count Julian* (Julian? Alvaro?) is now relo-
cated in this land of traitors, from which city he obsessively looks
out across the straits to his homeland and plots his revenge. This
dream of revenge is made even more bitter by Julian's memories of
the manner of his expulsion. He suggests that he was expelled from
his mother country like bodily wastes, and the narrator, made to
feel like abandoned fecal matter or an unwanted fetus, decides to
take advantage of the role thus thrust upon him. He is seen as foul;
he will become a defiler. Throughout the novel, the reader is made
aware of the symbolic interconnection between treason and the defilement of language, between writing and defecation.

Julian is a historian and a librarian in reverse. He seeks, not the
preservation of the sacred texts, but the annihilation of a fossilized
literature. He seeks to free himself from the weight of history by
desecrating and consciously falsifying that history. He does not
need to plan a new military invasion of Spain in the tradition of the
fabled traitor whose name he takes; instead, Julian's enterprise entails the sacking and rape of the library. As an exile from his homeland, isolated in the city of traitors, Julian maintains no link with
his country other than the tenuous and powerful link of language. It
is this language that becomes, then, the object of his destructive
frenzy, this language of his childhood that bears not only personal
memories, but carries along with it the history and culture he wishes
to besmirch. The destructive urge is also a ritual exorcism, and an

act of suicide: "your irredeemable hatred of the past and the bastard child that represents it / calls for a sacrificial death, and a splendid magic ritual to accompany it" (p. 180). This history, then, is perceived not only in terms of an oppressive past, but as a living force oppressing the present, a weight that is felt in the blood and bones and sinews of the protagonist. His anticultural enterprise is antinatural as well as unpatriotic. The history and language that must be exorcised are felt as an immediate bodily presence; their befoulment is undertaken by a parallel perversion practiced on the body: sodomization followed by a murder-suicide.

This attempted annihilation of history is evident in the structuring of the novel; the author describes *Count Julian* as "a closed, circular, totalizing work which does not allow, or tries not to allow, any loose ends and which obliges the reader at each step to return to a series of elements which apparently had already completed their mission of information."[7] The very circularity of the novel (a day like all the other days, beginning and ending a daily ritual within the confines of the narrator's room in Tangier) reinforces the ahistorical (or antihistorical) impetus of the narrator. The novel opens with the narrator opening his eyes on a morning identical to every other morning; it closes with the closing of his eyes on this very ordinary day, assuring the reader of the fact that this ritual will be repeated once again the next day, and every succeeding day:

> as yesterday, as today, as every day: you will push the door of the building open, press the buzzer, immure yourself within your apartment: . . . it is time for the torrent of Pompeian lava, for the dipteral and hymenopteral hecatomb: once the ritual is completed, you will turn out the light, having first made certain, as a scrupulously careful huntsman, that escape is materially impossible, that your trap is absolutely perfect: . . . you close your eyes: as you know, all too well: tomorrow will be another day, the invasion will begin all over again (pp. 203–4)

This reversed history, this sodomized, defiled history, is the substance and motivation of the novel. In Julian's hashish-induced hallucinations, history is rid of its temporal associations and enters into the service of ritual, of myth.

The focus of Julian's anticultural, antihistorical frenzy is not the actual homeland he imagines to the north of him across the straits of Gibraltar, but its literary counterpart, the paper representative of Spain that becomes the object of his traitorous rage. Thus, every morning, the protagonist begins his daily ritual with a glance toward Spain (a perverse Mecca) and a visit to the local library accompanied by his "volunteers," namely, "all sorts of different winged species, done in by a powerful insecticide as the inhabitants of Herculaneum and Pompeii were annihilated by the lava pouring down from the roaring volcano: . . . dying in the midst of performing their digestive or reproductive functions: . . . all ready to be slipped into your jacket pocket and taken with you on your daily walk to the library" (pp. 10–11). Once he has collected these freshly killed insects in a pouch, he is ready for his daily walk.

Fearing that the poisons of syphilis have contaminated his blood, Julian pauses at a pharmacy for his daily penicillin injection, then continues on to the library, passing through the doors that say "ENTER WITHOUT KNOCKING," slipping by the "drowsy old custodian: imbedded in his chair, as though expiating a fatigue that is centuries old" (p. 21), and stopping at the shelves that contain the classics of Spanish literature. These books are the solid representatives of his enemy, the Spanish language and Spanish culture that he has sworn to destroy. He contemplates them, meditates on their "perpetual state of rapture," comments on the organization of the library that has placed such books before him: "capital carefully preserved here behind glass cases: catalogued, arranged in the proper order, lined up in neat rows: on shelves within reach of your hand" (p. 23). His dreams of destruction are counterpointed by his aspiration to join the ranks of these books: "if only some day you can get your name on the roster, to be put on the promotion list!" He imagines what brilliance the future could hold for him as a member of this select society, "strolling about in the company of an illustrious cadaver, clad in the mantle of the virtue of an untouchable!" (p. 24).

This passionate attraction to the library is matched by Julian's equally passionate hatred for it. The illustrious cadavers become "the refuse heap of history," their ecstatic rapture is discounted as "spiritual eructations, flatulent rumblings of the bowels." Despite his dreams of becoming one with them, Julian's primary goal is not

to join the admiring society of devotees of the books, but, perversely, to revile these proliferating excrescences, these word cancers. The
narrator is momentarily dazzled, but he is not deflected from his
mission. The long rows of Spanish classics recall Julian to his original extralinguistic purpose: "the intoxicating summons to action:
remember, Ulbán: violence is mute: to pillage, to destroy, to rape, to
betray, you will not need words" (p. 133).

Julian takes action. The murdered insects are buried within the
illustrious cadavers of Spain's literary past; the poisons ingested by
the insects are merged with the poisons of the Word, and symbolically become one with the traitorous, syphilitic, poisonous blood of
the protagonist. With his insects and his tainted blood, Julian hopes
to besmirch the virtue of the classic untouchables and leave upon
them the visible sign of his disdain:

> you search in the left-hand pocket of your jacket for the fateful,
> carefully concealed little pouch: your meager capital: rapidly
> calculating the modest but encouraging range of possibilities:
> houseflies, ants, bees, horseflies: perhaps a fat, hairy spider or
> two: . . . reaching for the first volume in the pile and deposit-
> ing an ant and six flies inside it: . . . suddenly closing the vol-
> ume and crushing these seven insects: . . . then opening the
> book and unhurriedly contemplating the result, with the finical
> appetite of the connoisseur: squashed flat, their guts spattered
> all over: indelible stains blotting the dramatic episode, con-
> taminating it with their sluggish, viscous flow (p. 26)

For Julian, exiled in the deserts of Africa, all that remains of his
homeland is this library, and the only focus for his destructive urges
is these books, these literary and historical texts, that bear the language and preserve the culture the narrator has rejected.

Appropriately, Julian's novel is a text created out of the love for,
and hatred of, these other sacred texts. He cites them endlessly—
but in an altered form. In his hands, the illustrious cadavers are defiled, marked with the guts of insects, stained by contact with his
impure hands, perverted by translation through the prism of his
mind. His own sought-after identity, that of the traitor Count
Julian, is derived from a squashed and desecrated myth. But this

myth is only one of many cultural stains that indelibly mark the narrator. Like other of his countrymen, Julian has himself been raped (sodomized) by Seneca, and by Lope de Vega, and Cervantes, and Isabel la Católica, and the countless other historical and literary figures that make up Spain's rich cultural heritage. As the flies and other insects ingest the sugar Julian sets out to lure them and are killed by the poison that imbues it, so too Julian gorges on the sweet content of literary texts, only to find that in his veins this delicious nectar mingles with a deadly poison. The wordless desecration by poisoned insect corpses is a partial expiation of the violation Julian has suffered in the past. Future voyeurs in the shelves of Spain's untouchables will be infallibly reminded by these insect stains of the fate that befell one of their fellow countrymen through exposure to these texts.

Goytisolo gives this warning one final twist at the end of Julian's novel. The author steps back into the text after the close of Julian's hallucinatory day and, in a final notice, he recognizes the contributions of a series of literary and historical figures to the creation of his text. In an informal bibliography, Goytisolo lists the contributions of figures as disparate as Ortega y Gasset and Ian Fleming, Virgil and Luis Buñuel, Umberto Eco and Alfonso X el Sabio (p. 205). After vilifying the library and making of it a poisonous trap for impressionable minds, the author reverses himself and (albeit tongue-in-cheek) recalls the reader to that refuge of the disinherited.

For Roquentin, beset with the contingencies of temporality and defenseless against the nameless things that impinge upon his consciousness, the library is not a poisonous trap but a refuge. Time and space are not contingent in the library; everything is controlled, organized, and ordered. It is the sense of power and rigor derived from the contact with books that Roquentin would like to carry to his relations with the organic and inorganic objects that touch the carapace of his solitude. Outside of his historical researches, his relation to the world is strained and hesitant. The second dated entry of his diary, Tuesday, January 30, is inspired by just such a hesitation in his relationship to an insignificant object. Roquentin reflects on the desirability of power and control as opposed to his felt inability to pick up a tempting bit of paper. In the course of these meditations he comes to his first realization of the nature of the affliction that gives title to his story by suffering "a sort of nausea in the hands" (p. 11).

The incident is trivial, nothing at all, "not even an event." Yet it deeply impresses the narrator; he feels that his freedom is being circumscribed, and he "tried unsuccessfully to get rid of this idea at the library" (p. 9). The library is well lighted, organized, subject to human control; that Roquentin gravitates to the library for refuge from the clinging nausea of the hands is instructive. In its four book-lined walls, the omnipotence of the human restates itself once again; here, if anywhere, the inorganic, inhuman objects will recede once more into insignificance.

The library does not fully triumph over things in accord with Roquentin's expectations. The nausea is not dispelled by the visit to the library; instead, the first insignificant episode of inanition is followed by a series of other moments of unease and inability to act increasing in severity until that slight nauseated discomfort becomes the full-fledged nausea of unfreedom that sends Roquentin careening through the town in the search of a cure. On the day of the fog, nausea seems to envelop the entire town of Bouville in its vague, penetrating grasp. Roquentin feels instinctively that the library would provide a bulwark against the creeping nebulosity: "the fog filtered in under the door, it was going to rise slowly and penetrate everything. I could have found light and warmth at the library" (p. 73). But on this occasion, Roquentin does not test his theory, perhaps fearful that the library would be no more useful in dispelling the fog than it was in ridding him of the slighter nausea of the hands. Consequently, a defense mechanism switches into operation—the library must not be tested against the fog since its failure to provide a refuge would be, at this stage in the novel, more devastating than the nausea itself.

For the Self-Taught Man also, the library serves as a refuge. Like Roquentin, in his selection of books from the shelves of the Bouville library, the Self-Taught Man devises timeless barriers to combat the fog and flux of existence with the vision of absolute truth and stable fact. He does not even fall subject to Roquentin's twinges of doubt and hesitation. For the Self-Taught Man, books can provide the true and complete definition of man. He feels that his own incomplete understanding is due to the limitations of his reading, and he is confident that upon finishing the last of the books of the Bouville library he will have gained the full knowledge of all human and inhuman foibles that will allow him to act and think appropriately in all circumstances. The refuge of the Bouville library will then give way to a more convenient refuge—that of a library in the head, equally complete, equally well ordered according to the principles set forth by the master librarians.

The books in the Bouville library, like the portraits in the museum, offer no actual, living content to either Roquentin or the Self-Taught Man. Both books and portraits are endowed with an illusion of life and truth, but Roquentin's diary clearly demonstrates that these ossifications of once-living truths are no longer either valid or helpful to the modern student. They provide merely temporary stays against the overwhelming confusion of living and provide no permanent barriers against the viscosity of the onward flux of history. As the novel opens, Roquentin hides in the documents that form the backbone of his biography, gradually discovering in his reflections on his work that it is not M. de Rollebon who attracts him but the book that is now in the process of being written: "It is the book which attracts me. I feel more and more the need to write—in the same proportion as I grow old, you might say" (p. 13). The sense of his own personal historical presence is perhaps at the root of this shift in attitude. The subject recedes into relative unimportance as Roquentin's need to write becomes the controlling factor. Still later, this need to write, which can be understood as a desire to arrest the flow of his personal existence in a permanent form, is also recognized as an ineffective measure. The words no longer seem to belong to him: "The letters I had just inscribed on it were not even dry yet and already they belonged to the past. . . . I had thought out this sentence, at first it had been a small part of myself. Now it was inscribed on the paper, it took sides against me. I didn't recognize it anymore" (p. 95). Though ostensibly attracted by the thought of completing a definitive record, Roquentin's underlying love (and fear) is for the flux of life. The book that once attracted Roquentin now repels him, the words that were once a part of him are alienated as soon as they are set down on the paper.

There is a hint of this eventual alienation even in the historian's earlier affection for his work. He recognizes that the police reports, letters, memoirs, and other documents he has gathered on de Rollebon's life are silent. He knows that such historical records show nothing in and of themselves and that the book he is engaged in writing is as much about his own thought processes as those of M. de Rollebon: "the facts adapt themselves to the rigor of the order I wish to give them; but it remains outside them. I have the feeling of doing a work of pure imagination" (p. 13). Just as the facts are implicated in Roquentin's account, but remain opaque and recalcitrant, so too his sense of identification with the product of his own imagination gradually distances him from the historical facts that make up his account. He comments, "I'd be better off writing a novel on the Marquis de Rollebon" (p. 58), and, finally, Roquentin abandons all pretense of factuality, opting for pure invention— "something that could never happen, an adventure" (p. 178), hoping to outwit the alienation of language by abstracting himself entirely from the text. An event that could have happened, or might happen, as recorded in a history book or a diary, is incessantly alienated by a false objectivity, an objectivity that hides an actual inability to place or order the perceived facts in any absolute manner. Thus Roquentin chooses the opposite extreme, that of a work of pure imagination, a necessarily alienated form valuable precisely because it can never turn into a physical reality.

It is the experience of the nausea, felt as an actual physical blow, which inspires this shift from an appearance of factuality to an acceptance of contingency. But this acceptance is only partial. Roquentin begins and ends the novel in the belief that the world can be fixed through language; that words, like the music of jazz, embody the clean, cold, clear dryness of a world without fog or nausea. "Through the lack of attaching myself to words," says Roquentin, "my thoughts remain nebulous most of the time" (p. 7). He implies by this statement that if he so desired he could use his linguistic abilities to fix his thoughts (and his world) for all time. This assumption, untested throughout the novel, is similar to Roquentin's feeling that the fog of his nausea cannot penetrate the warm, lighted reaches of the library, and it remains implicit in Roquentin's closing appeal to the rigor of the fictional medium. Significantly, he makes no decision to actually write a novel—he merely considers it, as he had considered employing the power of words to chase away the nebulosity clouding his mind and as he had recalled the refuge of the library as a barrier against the fog of nausea enveloping the town.

Krapp demonstrates an even deeper confidence in the significance and reality of words. Says Ronald Hayman, "His own past self is only real for him in the form of words on a tape, and the pleasure he enjoys most in the present is the pleasure of words."[8] Krapp's delight in the sound of the spoken word is even more extreme than Roquentin's love for the written text. These words, furthermore, are most fully enjoyed when they are abstracted from their context, as if the old man takes specific pains to rid language of its association with things and enjoy it, as Roquentin proposes to enjoy it, as an analogue to a musical theme. Thus, the only two times in the play that Krapp speaks of anything "with relish" is when he is savoring the taste of contextless words on his tongue. In the first episode, Krapp has been puzzled by the meaning of the word "viduity," a word used on an earlier tape and now forgotten. He looks up the word in his enormous dictionary, puzzles over the correct definition, and attaches himself instead to an inappropriate, but more aesthetically pleasing, sense of the word. "Also of an animal, especially a bird," he reads, "the vidua or weaver bird . . . Black plumage of male . . . (He looks up. With relish). The vidua bird!" (p. 18). In the second episode, the favored word is repeated twice; once to himself, once for the tape: "Box . . . thrree . . . spool . . . five. (He raises his head and stares front. With relish.) Spool! (Pause.) Spooool! (Happy smile. . . .)" (p. 12). In the taped repetition of this moment, Krapp further elaborates: "The sour cud and the iron stool. (Pause.) Revelled in the word spool. (With relish.) Spooool! Happiest moment of the past half million" (p. 25). By proximity and by a similarity of sound the meanings of the two words "stool" and "spool" become intertwined. Krapp's tape library is symbolically related to his retained excrement, the release of a spool/stool is a deeply gratifying sensual experience.

Like Roquentin, who is obsessed with soiled bits of paper, Krapp dreams of the "unattainable laxation" offered and refused him by the debris of his personal past as recorded on his tapes. In *Krapp's Last Tape*, the rotting documentary evidence of a personal history proves as inaccessible to objective analysis as the fragmentary bits of paper in Bouville's library and on Bouville's side streets. The alienation resulting from a life dedicated to such excremental archaeology is resolutely ignored. Like a child, like Roquentin, Krapp is content to play with a lifetime's stored feces.

Krapp's taped words and Roquentin's written text converge, eventually, at a zero point of dissolution; both are closed cycles that are finally reabsorbed into an originary silence. The same funeral cycle is repeated in the story of Julian, who is reborn only to reenact the destructive frenzy of the first Count Julian, burying his individual life in the historical mausoleum prepared by his own attention to the details of ritual and ceremony. Julian is murderer and surgeon and priest, performing the autopsy and conducting the last rites upon the freshly killed cadaver of his culture. This destructive/reconstructive action, like that of Roquentin and Krapp, gives precedence to the murder/suicide of language: "your lexicon must be rescued: the age-old linguistic fortress must be dismantled: the circulation of language must be paralyzed: its sap must be sucked dry: words must be removed one by one until the crepuscular edifice, bled dry, collapses like a house of cards" (pp. 165–66). It only remains to be noted that in this excess of linguistic destruction, Julian's stated motives are not to be accepted uncritically. As T. S. Eliot said of Baudelaire's attraction to satanism, such a devotion to evil is necessarily suspect;[9] blasphemy on some level is almost equivalent to prayer. Thus the narrator of *Count Julian*, in his excessive vilification of the Spanish language, reveals his own tormented love for this last link to the homeland with which he is still viscerally identified.

Because this is a novel, that is, a vehicle for words, about apostasy and treason and murder, language is not only the enemy to be destroyed, but also the weapon to be used for this destruction: "the marvelous language of the Poet, the linguistic vehicle most appropriate for treason, your beautiful native tongue: . . . a sharp pointed (insidious) weapon that drives off (exorcises) the African army and increases (whets) its irresistible appetite for destruction" (p. 56). Julian imagines himself at the head of a new invading hoard, armed with these linguistic swords, "the keen-bladed weapons of treason" (p. 115).

For Julian, as for Roquentin, the dream-world of adventure is the same, and in Julian's mind, as in that of Sartre's historian, music and knives are joined on the African soil to furnish the insidious pricks of contact with a reality that for once perfectly meshes its interior and exterior versions. Thus, fittingly, Roquentin's first attack of nausea is dispelled by the cutting edge of musical notes, and he recalls the previous memory of an attempted stabbing ("with an enormous knife" [p. 37]) in Morocco as one of the great moments of his life, a moment that can be relived through the time-annulling services of cafe music, "with its dry little points" (p. 21).

Similarly, Julian's first contact with reality upon awakening conjoins the appeals of music and the knife:

> once the window is opened, a melody pours into the room: a single sustained note sometimes, or perhaps a brief arpeggio: played on the shepherd's flute of one of Pan's disciples, a companion of Bacchus and a pursuer of nymphs: a spare, subtle, haunting melody: full of suggestions, temptations, promises: . . . all sorts of regrets and nostalgias condensed in a simple chord that the itinerant knife-grinder tirelessly repeats, day after day. (p. 8)

This primitive reed flute appears again and again in the novel, its sustained note becoming a leitmotiv in Julian's thoughts. The knife-sharpener merges with other devotees of Pan and Bacchus, reappearing in the guise of a snake charmer (p. 52), who also plays a panpipe to enchant the venomous (phallic) cobra, suffering a metamorphosis in the latter part of the novel and becoming Julian, the wolf (the serpent) seducer of a small, male Little Red Riding Hood who is lured to Julian's lair by the haunting power of his music (p. 184). Finally, at the end of the novel, as Julian returns to his room to sleep, the last sound he hears in the silent city is the "flute of the knife-grinder . . . heard in the distance, a melody so faint as to be unreal: full of sly hints, invitations, promises" (pp. 201–2).

For both Julian and Roquentin, music and the knife appeal to a cold, hard reality, as far removed as possible from the nauseating vegetative world of change. Julian identifies himself with the sharp cutting surface and professes a horror of the merely organic in words that recall Roquentin's similarly expressed hatred of his own human face perceived in a mirror: "you're alive! still alive!: not in the protean kingdom of the flaccid and formless, of obscene creeping flora, of filthy outpourings of the inorganic: but instead contemplating smooth polished surfaces, successfully contriving to avoid flabby, unnecessary excrescences of flesh" (p. 70). Roquentin, a historian by profession, and Julian, also a historian of sorts, share this hatred for the temporal manifestations of historical change, associating that change with decomposition and with the vast, warm, penetrating force of nature.

In Roquentin, this horror of the natural world is repeated in a horror of living things and in a hatred for the soft, fecund life of consciousness he feels within himself. The library and the museum, as the sanctuaries and mausoleums of the absolutely fixated object, are natural refuges against the pressures of the spontaneous burgeoning of nature he discovers around him.

The situation is somewhat more complex, however. While on the one hand, Roquentin loves books because they are dead objects that he can order and control, on the other, he realizes that the documents are not dead at all, and his efforts to order them are subverted by the books' own sly recalcitrance. The objects take on life, a life that is both monstrous and attractive. In his last trip to the library, he suddenly has "the delightful feeling that I was going into an underbrush full of golden leaves" (p. 161). Because his objects come alive, Roquentin cannot truly possess them. He is the librarian, but the books in the library slip out of his grasp. The pleasure he feels at their encounter is as satisfying but as fleeting as the near ecstasy he experiences on picking up stray filthy bits of paper from the street. The library eventually becomes intolerable to him because he realizes that it is full of living, unstable beings that violate the rigid orders imposed on them by the librarian. In this sense, the library and the city of Bouville are parallel constructions. "My God!" exclaims Roquentin when overlooking the city on his last night there, "How *natural* the city looks despite all its geometries" (p. 160). In Roquentin's pre-nausea world, the library and the city were both objects. After the nausea, they became imbued with subjectivity. The books were transformed into "unnatural objects" (living beings), and Bouville absorbed some of the teeming life within it to soften its harsh geometries and give it a more "natural," living aspect. In both cases, the "natural" has a monstrous, even obscene, side:

> What if something suddenly started throbbing? . . . the omens are present. For example, the father of a family might go out for a walk, and across the street, he'll see something like a red rag, blown towards him by the wind. And when the rag has gotten close to him he'll see that it is a side of rotten meat, grimy with dust, dragging itself along by crawling, skipping, a piece of writhing flesh rolling in the gutter, spasmodically shooting out spurts of blood. . . . Or they might feel things gently brushing against their bodies, like the caresses of reeds to a swimmer in a river. And they will realize that their clothing has become living things. And someone else might feel something scratching in his mouth. He goes to the mirror, opens his mouth: and his tongue is an enormous live centipede, rubbing its legs together and scraping his palate. (pp. 158–59)

If for Roquentin the city is monstrous because alive, for the Self-Taught Man it is simply monstrous; and more so because he fails to recognize its monstrosity. This insensitivity to the living force of things is revealed in his brutally mechanical method of study. For the Self-Taught Man with his alphabetical association to literature, the objects can never recover any real life. Since he is not blessed with the least glimmer of understanding and merely accepts the librarian's artificial orders as necessary and natural, for him there is no escape: "He walks, he must walk. If he stopped for one instant the high walls of the library would suddenly rise up around him and lock him in" (p. 171). The library, for him, is purely and simply a prison.

The walls of the library, which once gave refuge against the fog, now describe the restrictions of a life given over to the madness of order. For the Self-Taught Man, the refuge has revealed itself in the form of this self-imprisoning madness. Roquentin, in his recognition of the fatal attractiveness of the golden leaves, acknowledges the infiltration of magic and madness into the preserve of science and reason. It is a transformation earlier presaged in the living look given Roquentin by the painted figures of the museum and in the historian's attempt to use the word "library" as a talisman, as a magic word to counter the namelessness of the unclassifiable nausea. Roquentin feels that the changes going on in the material world could be controlled if only they could be properly restrained in language. It is typical of the nausea that it be accompanied by linguistic slippage—Roquentin simply cannot grasp the experience and define it according to a series of preset categories.

It is in the context of this helpless linguistic slippage in the face of the nausea that we can more easily understand Roquentin's fond memories of Anny. With her closed universe of "perfect moments" (p. 62) in which each gesture takes on a magic significance, Anny became for Roquentin an embodiment of a life lived fully in rigorous control of her surroundings. Her life progressed according to a series of tiny, independent events that were constantly and carefully mediated by the larger abstractions. This orchestration of her life assured her that nothing was extraneous, nothing was gratuitous, nothing was left outside the bounds of her subjective power of incorporation.

The Anny Roquentin recalls does not allow language to fail her; for Roquentin, on the other hand, the comforts of the magic word become increasingly unattainable in the throes of the nausea. The root of the chestnut tree observed in the park undergoes just such an evacuation of the name as the magic words that would stay the rising tide of nausea are lost in the larger myth of burgeoning nature:

> The roots of the chestnut tree were sunk in the ground just under my bench. I couldn't remember it was a root anymore. The words had vanished and with them the significance of things, their methods of use, and the feeble points of reference which men have traced on their surface. . . . The word absurdity is coming to life under my pen. . . . Absurdity was not an idea in my head, or the sound of a voice, only this long serpent dead at my feet, this wooden serpent. . . . In vain to repeat "this is a root"—it didn't work anymore. (pp. 126–27, 129)

Roquentin's gaze actively engages the root in a battle for domination. He attacks the problem of its existence with a historian's weapons, seeking the form that would consolidate the discontinuous, fragmented perceptions. In so doing, he is attempting to construct a "monumental" history of the root, a narration that automatically orders itself according to a predetermined scheme.

This scheme, apparently so simple, is subject to almost infinite ramifications, however, for as Hartwig says of Master Janus in *Axel*, "what he says, although always simple, seems like the reflection between two mirrors: one would lose oneself in the infinite images." And he adds a pertinent warning: "Look! The best thing is not to think too much about the doctor—if we mean to keep our wits about us till we die."[10] The simplicity of the root's structure and the simplicity of the historian's schema are parallel, impenetrable mirror surfaces. Natural truth faces man's impulse to order reality in a simple, but infinite, relationship whose implication is madness. That serpent, that absurdity, is both alive and dead under Roquentin's pen. The succession of metaphors he employs unsuccessfully in an attempt to circumscribe the object with language possesses no magic to penetrate the simple "being" of the root, and Roquentin's entire metaphoric structure crumbles against the inexpressible fact of the observed object. The intransigence of the root further reveals the bankruptcy of Roquentin's scientist concept of historical accuracy (a concept that he clutches desperately in the face of the nausea), which sees history as a mirror of past events rather than a mirror to an infinity of multiple truths.

The root is a monstrosity. Neither form nor formlessness, "this long serpent dead at my feet" is life that will not stay itself in death, but must be constantly changing and pushing itself into unnamable new configurations. Nausea invades the writer as he is once again dispossessed of his position of strong, masculine control over objects and events. Says Edith Kern in her translation of a line from Nietzsche's *Birth of Tragedy*: "man now detects everywhere nothing but the ghastly absurdity of existence . . .: nausea invades him." She points to the significance of the fact that "the terms 'absurdity' and 'nausea' are used both by Nietzsche and Sartre and that both thinkers see man's experiencing of them as resulting in inaction."[11] By the confrontation with the absurd, nauseating serpent of wood,

Roquentin is pushed one step further in his eventual rejection of history for the more straightforward fictions of literature.

The monstrous root, a natural fact, an absurdity, a fiction, is also a vaguely threatening sexual instrument. It is a powerful, inert mass with a radical function:

> There are radicals and endings, or if you will, roots and
>   stems.
> Grammar is a gardener.
> Thinking radically, an intervention where it's pushing up,
>   at the root.
> Flowers are for assholes: Their desire's ending
> But who can claim that he holds the root
>   that he is the radical
> Clearly, all this is bursting with sexual contents.[12]

The root of the chestnut tree calls to mind an earlier episode, that of Roquentin's feverish nightmare in which the soldier with the hole in his head indicates his prospect for the bouquet of violets he was given: "I'm going to stick them up your ass" (p. 59). The root whose essence escapes Roquentin can be associated with the violets (violation) of a dream of power.

In *Count Julian*, the myth is reversed as the serpent that escapes imaging by language becomes the weapon wielded by the protagonist against that very language. Julian sets out to destroy men like the historian Roquentin, contemptuously calling them "hollow, useless men: fencers without foils" (p. 121), men who, like the hero of Sartre's novel, stammer and wave their arms when faced with a lethal reality. In Goytisolo's novel, the old scholar Don Alvaro is the first victim of this serpent-inflicted linguistic paralysis. Confronted by the desecration of the library books perpetrated by the protagonist, words abandon Don Alvaro, his pulse fails, and he dies stammering in the arms of the master librarian:

> the custodian of the library takes his pulse and predicts the fatal end that awaits him . . .: Don Alvaro's . . . pale tongue protrudes tensely from between his teeth as he desperately attempts to pronounce a word: CU, he stammers: CU-CU-CU:

cuna, culebra, culpa, cupletista, cubil, curandero?: his voice fades with a dying fall . . .: the custodian of the library closes Don Alvaro's eyes and respectfully bares his head (Spanish text, p. 181).

Don Alvaro's dying "CU-CU-CU" in the library repeats, in Spanish as in English, the song of the cuckoo bird (cuclillo), a terrible and ironic bird to preside over the deathbed of a respected scholar. The cause of death is further revealed in the interpretations put by the author on Don Alvaro's dying stammer; cuna-cradle, culebra-serpent, culpa-guilt, cupletista-ballad singer, cubil-lair, curandero-medicine man. To this list it is simple and appropriate to add those other two obsessions of Julian that bear upon the cause of death and also begin with "cu": cuchillo-knife and culo-ass, which reflect the triple theme of sodomization by a serpent, poisoning with syphilis, and death by stabbing.[13]

Although his morning ritual includes a visit to the pharmacy for a penicillin injection, Julian's habitual attitude is to regard his syphilis (real or imagined) as the potent, deadly venom of his penis/serpent/knife. Thus, Julian's infected semen and urine gain a ritual value in the novel as Julian signals his ultimate disrespect for his defeated enemies: "the snake will energetically pump out its abundant, fluid, yellow disdain" (p. 189). This ritual urination on, or necrophiliac sodomization of, the bodies of his defeated enemies becomes a perverse baptism, initiating these cadavers into a deadly order that mimics the dead and deadening order of the illustrious cadavers of the books, desecrated by the corpses of poisoned insects.

Yet the protagonist, while identified with Julian, the keeper of the deadly serpents, and with the unnamed custodian of the dead, deadly books, is also metamorphosed into Alvarito, a small Don Alvaro, the sodomized child. The story of Alvarito-Little Red Riding Hood links the various themes of sexual perversion, murder, and thirst for vengeance against the homeland with the attack on and perversion of literature and language.

Like Roquentin, Julian is a storyteller; his story is the "new psychoanalytic version" of the fairy-tale story of Little Red Riding

Hood, "complete with mutilations, fetishism, blood." Julian, waking beneath the blade of the guillotine, pleads with the executioner for time to spin this modern fairy story: "invent, compare, lie, make up stories: repeat Scheherazade's marvelous exploit spanning a thousand and one brief, inexorable nights: once upon a time there was a darling little boy, the most delightful youngster imaginable: Little Red Riding Hood and the big bad wolf" (p. 5). The story resurfaces and is continued later in the novel: Alvarito visits his Granny, previously raped and murdered by the wolf (or serpent) in preparation for this moment. The traditional questions and answers follow the boy's discovery of the wolf in his grandmother's bed, with the addition of one novel exchange: "oh Granny, what a big snake you have! the better to penetrate you with, you stupid little idiot! and as you utter these words, you will bury the serpent in the child's body and slit his throat with your gleaming Toledo blade" (p. 177). This ritual death is only one of several alternatives offered in the novel, as the child is resurrected again and again to undergo various related ritual mutilations, all of which suggest sodomization, emasculation, and death. The child repeatedly falls victim to "the arduous copulation of carnivores" and is forced to submit to Julian, "haughtily pumping out the disdainful yellow fluid" (p. 81). In another version of this ritual death, syphilis attacks the child, filling him with the repulsive inner and outer sores of Julian's affliction. Made desperate by the foul disease, the child obligingly commits suicide, a self-destructive act carried out to the music of Chopin's *Les Sylphides* (or "Xopin's *Les Syphilides*" or "Xopen and his syphilis" [pp. 199, 200]).

In Julian's reenactment of the legend of the Moorish conquest of Spain, and in his rewriting of the tale of Little Red Riding Hood, the violated female element (the mother country, the daughter of the original Don Julian, the little girl of the folktale) becomes a sodomized male, reflecting not only the rape of the female language (la lengua) by the masculine books (el libro), but, more significantly, their subsequent desecration by Julian.

In *Nausea* as well, the violated female becomes the sodomized male in Roquentin's hallucinatory reenactment of the rape of little Lucienne, and that rape of a helpless girl child/adult male corresponds to Roquentin's earlier dream sodomization involving the author Maurice Barrès (p. 59),[14] and to the Self-Taught Man's later defilement of the library by his attempted homosexual advances toward a schoolboy. There is a further, related correspondence. Roquentin, the historian-librarian and dream rapist/sodomized child, has a deep, peculiar affection for paper "probably" soiled with excrement. Goytisolo's Don Alvaro is more direct: "Don Alvaro leans down, picks up a goat turd, raises it to his broad nostrils, and ecstatically inhales the odor emanating from it . . . [he says], the *capra hispanica* is the incarnation of our purest essences, didn't you know that?" (p. 67).

In *Krapp's Last Tape*, the very name of the protagonist suggests excrement. Krapp too breathes deeply of the aroma of the spool/stool that represents the essence of his wasted life. In choosing the "iron stool" of his vision, a vision given form in a book that sold only seventeen copies, over the light and fire of a life truly lived, Krapp trades the lucidities of women's eyes for the unassimilable darkness, and for the literary fire that is soon extinguished by lack of fuel. Like Julian, Roquentin, and the Self-Taught Man, Krapp is held prisoner by his choice of a life lived through books. He consciously throws away his hope of happiness for a romantic vision of enhanced creativity, a vision which, in his old age, demonstrably fills him with nothing but impatience. While the middle-aged Krapp indicates that he gladly sacrificed his hope of happiness to the service of the creative fire (p. 28), the older Krapp is not so sure. Throughout the play, Krapp recalls happy moments with women— not moments of creative inspiration—and in his final recording speaks of recent cool summer days when he sat in the park "drowned in dreams" and "scalded the eyes out of me reading *Effie*" and recalled his lost chance of happiness (p. 25). Krapp's experience of the tapes is limited to the evidence of his ears; his review of his magnum opus and other texts is restricted to the sense of sight. He participates in these recreations of his life in a limited manner, taking no action, identified with and at the same time detached from the drama unfolding before him. The aged Krapp is now quiescent, but he remembers a time when an opportunity for fuller participation in life was vouchsafed him. Never mind the fire of literary aspiration; what Krapp desires now is merely the "unattainable laxation" (p. 17) and the renewal of the recalled magic contact with the eyes of the girl in the punt.

In this detachment from life, Krapp, like Roquentin, lives "on the surface of solitude" (*Nausea*, p. 8). Other people exist for them as tree roots and pebbles exist—they touch the surface of consciousness, but make no lasting mark upon the inner man. For this reason, despite all his tape recordings, Krapp can say with Roquentin, "I have only my body: a man entirely alone, with his lonely body, cannot indulge in memories; they pass through him." This imperviousness to the past is a direct result of Roquentin's (and Krapp's) earlier abnegation of life in favor of art. Roquentin continues, "I shouldn't complain: all I wanted was to be free" (p. 65).

Roquentin is no more free than Krapp in this solitude. One prison is exchanged for another. Krapp is trapped by the meaningless repetition of recorded memories that call up before his indifferent eyes a portrait of his younger self; Roquentin is trapped by the empty surface of his reflected image in a mirror, "a white hole in the wall" (p. 16), that is, a window. As he gazes at his face in the mirror, he comes to the realization shared by Krapp that his desired freedom is a dead freedom, that his possibilities are closed. Glued to the window of his miserable flat, he makes a similar observation about a passing woman: "I *see* the future. . . . This is time, time laid bare . . ." (p. 31). The sickening vision of freedom impaired by time that brushes its surface is part of both of Roquentin's two visions—that of the mirror and that of the window. The old woman seen through the window, the self seen in the mirror; both reflect a reality that is metaphorically an eternity long. Says Fredric Jameson in his book on Sartre: "Violent figurative events swarm around the drama of the look without becoming any more material: our faces, our world are *stolen* by the eyes of other people; without the surface of the world changing, it suffers an internal *hemorrhage of being* and we go on existing in an unchanged but now alienated landscape."[15] Roquentin sees the woman and describes her, sees his own face, and describes it, but the description does not penetrate his surface solitude; like Krapp, he sees and hears without illumination. Jameson continues his analysis with an allusion to Sartre's book on Jean

Genet: "Genet's acts are ways of not acting, of contaminating the concrete acts of others until they become in their turn unreal, of operating precisely that internal hemorrhage of being which a look was enough to provoke."[16] It is not surprising that both Krapp and Roquentin turn to writing as a gesture to hold the fearful eternity at bay, to exhibit themselves before an audience of spectators and transfix time itself with a stylized, alienating stare. "Writing," says Jameson, "with its twin faces of concrete activity and dreaming, becomes the ultimate place of this process of 'irrealization,' but in its beginning it requires nothing but a look."[17]

In *Count Julian*, the "irrealization" is carried even further. After his encounter with Don Alvaro and the subsequent conversation about the fabulous qualities of goat dung, the protagonist of Goytisolo's novel continues his interior (surface) journey: "penetrating deeper and deeper: wandering farther and farther . . . by way of the twisting, turning paths of the urban labyrinth: as in the hall of trick mirrors at a fairground" (p. 73). The mirror-maze is both exterior and interior to the protagonist, reflecting both an urban reality and Julian's twisted mental structure. It is a peculiar property of the hall of mirrors that the labyrinth itself is simple, but the *look* makes it difficult to discern the underlying simplicity. Similarly, the protagonist's illusion of penetration into his mind and into the depths of the city signals a mistaken identification of the look that skims the surface of existence and results in the internal hemorrhage of being with a true physical and psychological dissection that would eternally alter the surface of perceived reality.

From the mirror-maze of the city, Julian allows himself to be led by a Moorish guide to the *mirador* (lookout point) of Bab-el-Assa to see dim outline of his homeland, and to the sacred grotto, where he sees and penetrates the female mysteries:

> you wanted to see how it [the snake] gets inside, isn't that
>   right?
> no, no
> do you know where the grotto is?
> no!
> right here!

> grabbing his head with one hand and raising her skirt with
>   the other:
> forcing (him?) to enter the Virgilian cavern
> . . . .
> it's the cunt all right
> the national emblem of the country of stupid cuntery
> (pp. 82, 145)

Julian, exiled from his country, expelled from the womb of his
motherland, looks upon his native country with mixed frustration
and longing. His penetration into other bodies at the site of fecal
expulsion, his staring into the mirror of himself reflected in these
sodomized bodies, indicates a reverse narcissism similar to that af-
flicting Krapp (through his tapes) and Roquentin, who looks at his
face in the mirror only to suffer a more definitive alienation from
the reflected image. As Roquentin, who in his dream sodomization
of Maurice Barrès unconsciously reveals the connection between
the eye and the anus, so too Goytisolo reveals a similar connection;
implicitly in *Count Julian*, explicitly in *Juan the Landless*:

> for just as the Eye of God radiates light and snow-white purity,
> so the bestial anus, the eye of the devil, emanates infection and
> fetor, filth and sin: their respective functions are absolutely ex-
> clusive and diametrically opposed: so the angelic Saint Thomas
> Aquinas tells us: what is corrupted in part is corruptible in
> toto, and such an eventuality would be regarded as odious, sac-
> rilegious, even by the most stubborn heretics: this is clear, and
> indeed self-evident: neither the Redeemer nor the Virgin ex-
> pelled fecal matter: . . . ah, if only one could see the gentle,
> smiling, pearly Eye that the Virgin conceals beneath her
> heaven-blue mantle[18]

Face and anus; each possess eyes. The first has the property of producing a celestial, penetrating gaze, to the second is left the fate of
being blindly penetrated. The first represents the light and fire of the
vision dreamed of by Krapp, Roquentin, and Julian; the second indicates the necessary poisoning of that vision by the infection of a

body that is not eternal. The light above, the darkness below; the clarity of the written texts preserved in the library, the nausea provoked by the decomposing wastes sniffed so delicately by Don Alvaro and his companion scholars. What is the solution, the resolution, of this conflict? Krapp stares off into space at the end of the play, Roquentin proposes to write a novel, Julian prepares to repeat his daily ritual of smashing insects in books and smoking hashish. We must look outside these texts for evidence of action that can be taken when the place of books becomes identified with the dark eye of the devil.

CHAPTER 5

Burning the Books: Williams, Canetti

WHEN THE LIBRARY somehow becomes disgusting or fear provoking, the desire to extirpate and purify the edifice gains force. The most efficient way of effecting this purification is by fire since, as Bachelard notes, fire is quintessentially the element of quick change.[1] It was by fire that the corruption of the biblical cities of Sodom and Gomorrah was quickly cleansed from the earth; it is also by fire that the predicted final destruction of the world is to come about. On another scale, such is the motivation that has moved book burners throughout the ages, from Egypt to China, from Don Quixote's library to Hitler's Germany. To burn the books is not only to excise the canker discerned (rightly or wrongly) at the heart of society, but to change history itself and set society forward once again in a desired new direction. But how did history become the enemy and the library its minion?

The conflict derives from the confluence of the two concepts of history briefly discussed earlier. As long as history could be viewed as a seamless sequence of linear representations, as a tightly knit continuous order, there was no threat. Succession becomes the movement from one near-identity to another, with moments duplicating each other in their likenesses and in their adherence to an overall plan. Even major apparent differences can be, to continue the metaphor, knitted up into the fabric in such a manner that the knots and discontinuities of the skein disappear into the smooth continuous product. Minor imperfections do not mar the finished work; it is only when the skein is tangled beyond repair that it is tossed into the fire. In the words of Hayden White:

> The historical process is seen to be not a process at all but a series of moments, each of which is related to what came before it and what will follow it by the intentions of the agents on the scene at that time. The idea is to destroy not only all teleology [and all theology] but all causality as well.[2]

The historical process, then, is a series of willful negations, what Bloom calls "lying against time"[3] in order to preserve man's power over history.

The newer historical sense has, as Foucault points out, several uses. These uses also become the phases in a movement toward destruction. The first movement is parodic, defined by Foucault as "directed against reality" and "oppos[ed to] the theme of history as reminiscence or recognition."[4] This is the moment of carnival, "an interval of timeless formlessness"[5] according to Norman O. Brown, an interregnum when rules are temporarily abandoned. It is a passing moment (and must be so) since it attains its timeless and formless characteristic only in contrast to the strict chronology and stable form of the surrounding periods. As Mikhail Bakhtin realizes, the carnival is always "linked to moments of crisis, of breaking points in the cycle of nature or in the life of society and man,"[6] and it is thus that the lawlessness reaffirms law, immorality reasserts morality, and timelessness becomes timeliness. Nevertheless, despite this ultimate reaffirmation of order, in the parodic interregnum the first serious tangle appears in the smooth skein of history.

The second major moment (or second use) of history represents a further break. Foucault calls this the dissociative use and says it is "directed against identity, and opposes history given as continuity or representative of a tradition."[7] The overarching cycle is lost and the powers of synthesis forgotten. The theme of the mask is essential to this phase. Under the mask differences are at one and the same time ignored and redefined. With a mask the weak individual identity is subsumed in the crowd; the particular one is merged in the many. Yet, at the same time, the identity so obtained is illusory, as both Foucault and Bakhtin discover. For Bakhtin the mask "is connected with the joy of change and reincarnation, with gay relativity and with the merry negation of uniformity and similarity,"[8] while for Foucault the unification of the mask inadequately covers its plurality, under the mask "history will not discover a forgotten identity, . . . but a complex system of distinct and multiple elements, unable to be mastered by the powers of synthesis."[9] If the first moment (or use) is that of carnival, the second, with its uncovering of relativity, is spacetime. In the first, difference is proclaimed but it mingles and dissolves in the cycle of the same, while in the second moment, similarity only further asserts distinction, and chronology is definitively broken.

The apparent harmony of the masker can only erupt into violence, a violence that is foreseen in Foucault's designation of the third use of history as sacrificial, which he describes as "directed against the truth and oppos[ed to] history as knowledge."[10] The formlessness of the first moment and the transformations of the second are channeled together and magnified in the Dionysian passion of the third. In the sacrifice the momentary fear of formlessness is thrust upon a single form, difference is reassured with the exorcism of difference, growing madness signals a return to normative sanity. The interregnum ends with the violent death of Dionysus, the uses of history are used up, the tangled skein is replaced by a smooth one: "for modern thought is one that moves no longer toward the never-completed formation of Difference, but toward the ever-to-be accomplished unveiling of the Same. Now, such an unveiling is not accomplished without the simultaneous appearance of the Double, and that hiatus, minuscule and yet invincible, which resides in the 'and' of the retreat *and* return, of thought *and* the unthought."[11]

In a footnote to his famous explication of the *fort-da* game of the small child, Freud mentions a potentially more revealing game which involves not a wooden reel, but the child's double as perceived in a full-length mirror. The Same is discovered, and the hiatus given a preeminent place in its recovery:

One day the child's mother had been away for several hours and on her return was met with the words "Baby o-o-o-o!"

which was at first incomprehensible. It soon turned out, however, that during this long period of solitude the child found a
method of making *himself* disappear. He had discovered his reflection in a full-length mirror which did not quite reach to the
ground, so that by crouching down he could make his mirror
image "gone."[12]

In the child's game the temporal metaphor of history is reexpressed
in spatial terms. The mirror reflection is different from the child; he
sees it as someone else whom he can manipulate and make disappear at will. Yet this realization that the mirror image is someone
different is paralleled by another realization that what he is seeing
in the mirror is also, somehow, the same as himself. He both is and
is not in the mirror, by a trick of optics he is both *fort* (gone) and *da*
(there) at the same time. The game of reflections is potentially much
more disturbing than Freud's principal example of the wooden reel.
The reel is alternately here and someplace else, but the image of the
self is in perpetual hiatus. It is always there, always gone, always (as
it becomes more stable) imposing itself on others, always maintaining its distance: the model for sameness and difference. The child's
innocent game of self-destruction and resurrection is profoundly
Dionysian in its ambiguous relationship to form, and it is not surprising that as a spatial model it stands opposed to the rigidity of
the windowless, airless, time-ridden library.

Yet this description of the import of the child's game must be
qualified further. The child negates himself by making himself
"gone," and thus separates self from self, absenting the object of his
contemplation from existence for an interval. The child creates not
only a temporal syntactic relationship—here, gone, subject, object—but also in the interstices of absence he makes his first commitment to the creation of a system of signs, to an image hypostatized in memory and recalled even in its absences. Bloom quotes
Kojève on Hegel:

For Hegel it is precisely in this annihilation of Being that consists the Negativity which is Man, that Action of Fighting and
Work by which Man preserves himself in spatial Being while
destroying it—that is, while transforming it by the creation of

hitherto unknown new things into a genuine Past—a nonexistent and consequently nonspatial Past.[13]

In the mirror, the child plays out a game of power, of knowledge, of signs created and of a history alternately wooed and rejected.

The window is the analogue of the mirror in many cases and also serves to entrap the solitary librarian in the *fort-da* game of history and space. Such is the case with Elias Canetti's librarian, Peter Kien, who has no patience with mirrors and, in a memorable, descriptive passage, orders the walling up of the windows of his flat to make more room for book shelves. A similar dislike is found in Sartre's Roquentin who expresses in no uncertain terms his nauseated abhorrence of those two falsifiers of resemblance.

The window, says Foucault, both opposes and reinforces the mirror,[14] and this trick of vision through glasses transparent and reflecting is clearly expressed in Beckett's *How It Is*: "I watched him after my fashion from afar through my spy-glass side-long in mirrors through windows at night."[15] The artificial lens becomes the mediator for the eye, and the act of seeing is refracted to its ultimate extent. "Reality" becomes a kind of optical illusion circumscribed by the perception of the character and the workings of creative imagination upon the reality described. Things, if they can be said to exist at all, cannot be perceived except through the mediation and distortion of the play of mirrors.

By immuring himself in the windowless space of the library, does the librarian then condemn himself to the splintered illusions of a Beckettian spyglass vision, or do his works of art allow him a clearer vision by virtue of such self-imposed limitations on sight? For Ortega y Gasset, the work of art is a metaphoric window onto a delightful garden:

> Looking at the garden we adjust our eyes in such a way that the ray of vision travels through the pane without delay and rests on the shrubs and flowers. . . . The purer the glass, the less we see it. But we can also deliberately disregard the garden and, withdrawing the ray of vision, detain it at the window. We then lose sight of the garden; what we still behold of it is a confused mass of color which appears pasted to the pane.[16]

This to-and-fro adjustment of vision from within a room (a library?) is comparable, says Ortega, to our shifting perceptions of a work of art. He does not stress, though the conclusion seems obvious, that this double possibility for focusing vision is to be deplored as well as celebrated. Ignoring the pane, the librarian functions under the illusion that the garden seen through the window is a whole and coherent entity, a complete and ordered cosmos rather than merely a small fraction of the world outside. Focusing on the window, the librarian recognizes the illusion as the whole content, but he is cut off from even the partial vision he once enjoyed. While the library serves as a shell and a cloaking device to protect the librarian's vulnerabilities, it also entraps him into a limited range of experience without hope of escape. The spyglass or the window of a work of art, no matter how apparently transparent and pure, is still a barrier interposing itself between the viewer and the garden outside. An act of willful forgetting is required to erase the pane from the perception of the garden, and this act is tantamount to the librarian's imposition of his reflected image upon that garden.

In walling up the actual windows of his flat (making them "gone"), Kien reaffirms his desire to open only such windows as he permits through the imposition of his books and himself upon a fictive or a historical reality. Kien accepts no reality that does not concur with the visions he has composed. He chooses the static rigidity of being and the illusion of timelessness over the lessons of history and change. His book becomes his mirror, his window, his very self.

The mirror is fundamentally different from the window, however. In its transparency, the window unites in some degree the observer and the observed on either side. The mirror falsifies an appearance of communication; it gives the illusion of an observer-observed relationship to the small boy in Freud's story through the agency of mere perceptual trickery. Although it separates, the essence of the window is its function as a connector; it allows one reality to merge with another through the flimsiest of barriers. The mirror (the book) can only give an illusion of such a communicative flow since it operates on the basis of stagnation and trickery. The reduplication of speech in writing is one of the most basic of these tricks.

Foucault calls it the "mirrored reflection upon death," which causes speech to seek its own image, and he finds that "the figure of a mirror to infinity erected against the black wall of death is fundamental for any language from the moment it determines to leave a trace of its passage."[17] But the growing chaos of writing and its attendant confusion only intensify the reality of death. Everything is endlessly repeated in the printed text—nothing is reproduced. The apparent symmetry of the library is false. Rather than denying death, the proliferation of the written word only stresses it more.

The window, as we saw earlier, is also an illusion, but at least partially a life-enhancing one. The act of mirroring from a distance, like that performed by Beckett's protagonist in *How It Is*, forces the image back into a continuous, unchanging integrity equivalent to the stasis of death. It is not surprising that primitive peoples are often afraid of reproductions of their image. Primitive man is caught up in movement and change; repetition (twins or photographs) is a perversion of the process of differentiation that insists on a reality that cannot be reproduced. He finds that a disembodied image is necessarily the result of evil magic. The twin banes of introjection and projection, already evident in the child's mirror game, are mercifully absent from the primitive mythic world, at least in their abstract manifestation; the true primitive accepts change and death easily and naturally. Gustav Gusdorf observes that "the mirror is absent from primitive cultures," and continues, "The North American historian Mumford claims that the vogue of autobiography as a literary genre dates from the moment when the technique of manufacturing good mirrors was learned."[18] History, and the history of the self, are dependent upon such *fort-da* games as that of the child with the mirror. Fear of reproduction gives way to a game based on duplication of the self. Furthermore, this game has a temporal (and therefore historical) dimension—the image is "there" and then it is "gone" in a succession that reflects that most common of temporal successions: the alternate "tick" and "tock" of a clock.

These considerations are borne out in the recognition by Jacques Lacan of the importance of the experience of seeing one's own image reflected in the mirror, and in the statement from Roland Barthes's autobiography crediting his work to such an experience: "And all this happens, as is obvious here, through the Mother, present next to the mirror."[19] The mirror reflects the dream of the perfect text and prevents that dream from being fulfilled. It shatters the illusion of oneness earlier experienced at the mother's breast and inaugurates the machinery of illusions of the hopeless search for a return to that early pleasure. A substitute and perverse pleasure is found in reading, and writing, and death, something López Velarde expressed in his verse:

> Voluptuous melancholy:
> it coils around your morbid waist
> Pleasure its calligraphy
> and Death its scrawl.[20]

The poet describes the union of Pleasure and Death under the signs of calligraphy and of the scrawl and forces us to recognize that the pleasure of writing remits us not to life and reality but to death, the library, and other writings. Thus Roquentin warns us to "beware of literature"[21] and clings desperately to the still living unwritten stories: "For a hundred dead stories there still remain one or two living ones. I evoke these with caution, occasionally, not too often, for fear of wearing them out."[22] What Roquentin really fears is that words will begin to infiltrate the mental structure of his dreams, congealing a living story into what is essentially another dead record. Literature becomes a death mask for the living story. Faust, another master librarian, shares this fear of the dead word despite his own lifelong devotion to books: "The word expires in passing to the pen / And wax and sheepskin lord it over men."[23]

The final destiny of all literature is the same: to become dead works written in living tongues stored in the labyrinthine space of the libraries. The library, and its keeper, represent life frozen, changed into mere words. The labyrinth, with its waiting monster at the heart, becomes a symbol of the passage from life into death; the mirror-maze of the library is the place where the dead are buried. Writing and living are irrevocably split; the person who chooses to devote himself to the librarian's task is choosing to divorce him-

self from the world and pass his life among the dead. Faust is aware
of this, as is Roquentin, and William Carlos Williams:

> Dead men's dreams, confined by these walls, risen,
> seek an outlet. The spirit languishes,
> unable, unable not from lack of ability—
> ....
> but from that which immures them pressed here
> ....
> The Library is desolation, it has a smell of its own
> of stagnation and death.[24]

These words described by Williams are dead words, doubly killed
by their enclosure in books and in libraries. They are given a semblance of life through the writer's machinations, but like the living
dead of legend, end by seeking the peace and escape of a true
mausoleum. Meanwhile, confined in the library, they remain "books
/ that is, men in hell" (p. 115).

The library does not synthesize or summarize the universe; it
merely presents it in its most terrifying details. The babble of the
library is nearly incomprehensible to all but the initiates, and its adherence to a strict inhuman logic is countered by what amounts to
aesthetic terrorism. The terrorist hopes to destroy the existing system in order to be able to return to a pristine beginning and remake
history in his own image (that is, a new mirror game). The library is
the enemy of this effort since it represents the walls of tradition
standing between a projected bright future and an unregenerate
present. It is not surprising, as Borges notes, that "burning books
and erecting fortifications is a common task of princes."[25] The first
activity symbolically destroys the past, the second represents the
beginning of a new library for the future.

In every social system, there remain those who do not adhere to it
implicitly, and they often seclude themselves in the more restrictive
systems of the libraries where the search for ancient, forbidden
knowledge becomes the object of their life's work. Such is the situation of the historian-librarians, such, in an even more intense degree, is the nature of the recondite studies of the magicians and al-

chemists. The life of the historian-librarian is characterized by the quest and its frustration, by fatigue and by a feeling of futility, which may give rise to strange fantasies. Historian-librarians shun the company of others and are generally ignored by the society that surrounds the isolated enclave of the library. The magicians are perceived as more iconoclastic since their public adherence to another system poses an implicit threat to the very founding principles of that system. The terror and revulsion experienced by the system-builders prompt the same hysterical reaction to the enchanters as to their libraries. The system-builders would deliver to the flames those who oppose the current system based on the theory that the familiar has divine sanction and that which is alien must be the work of the devil. In "Language to Infinity," Michel Foucault poses with his characteristic precision the double bind of the library's threat and the dilemma that results:

> The space of language today is not defined by Rhetoric, but by the Library: by the ranging to infinity of fragmentary languages. . . . But within itself, it finds the possibility of its own division, of its own repetition, the power to create a vertical system of mirrors, self-images, analogies. A language which repeats no other speech, no other Promise, but postpones death indefinitely by ceaselessly opening a space where it is always the analogue of itself.
>
> Libraries are the enchanted domain of two major difficulties. They have been resolved, we know, by the mathematicians [as in the librarian's calculations on the extent of the library of Babel or in Beckett's discussion of the permutations of the victim/oppressor relationship in *How It Is*] and tyrants [the indiscriminate library burners described by Borges and Canetti] (but perhaps not altogether). There is a dilemma: either all these books are already contained within the Word and they must be burned, or they are contradictory and again, they must be burned. Rhetoric is a means of momentarily postponing the burning of libraries.[26]

Rhetoric is, then, the heir to the rational aesthetic and to what Foucault calls the Classic approach to history. The assumption of discontinuity leads to a radically different approach proceeding from parodic through dissociative to the destructive/sacrificial phases. The Futurist artist Filippo Tommaso Marinetti argued for such a Dionysian solution. He argued that since science and technology have caused such profound changes in the human experience of reality, art should do likewise, and as a logical conclusion called for the destruction of such bastions of order and continuity as museums and libraries.[27] Marinetti's "thanatopraxis" is more overtly political and less subtle than Derrida's, but more immediately perceptible in its effects.

Lafcadio Wluiki, the post-Nietzschean protagonist of Gide's novel *Lafcadio's Adventures*, is a practitioner of this revolutionary thanatopraxis. He is a literary man who rejects literature in favor of, one would presume, bombing libraries. Even before the shockingly gratuitous murder at the culmination of his antisocial trajectory, Lafcadio pointedly and symbolically destroys and burns the few books and papers he possesses, thus defining his nature as a library burner and iconoclast. Violence and illogical behavior become the logical response to technology. The burning of the books is both a pivotal and a peripheral act: ambition, eroticism, and the death instinct acted out in the shadow of the flames.

Lafcadio's attempt to commit a murder that is free from what Walter Benjamin would call its characteristic aura of significance fails, of course, as it must. After the murder, Lafcadio is forced by circumstances into behaving very much like the murderer in a conventional novel despite his efforts to the contrary and in spite of readers' expectations. The case is similar with other purported revolutionaries. The historian who publishes his version of history attempts to make a tabula rasa of all anterior books; that is, to burn them—or rewrite them. Such too is the role of book burners throughout history. In condemning the past to flames, they are rewriting it and, more often than not, reaffirming it. Historiography merely becomes more devious.

In his review of Foucault's *Madness and Civilization*, Derrida makes a related point. He says: "Although the silence of madness is the absence of a work, this silence is not simply the work's epigraph, nor is it, as concerns language and meaning, outside the work. Like nonmeaning, silence is the work's limit and profound resource."[28]

In a sense, history could not exist without the burning of the books that clears the way for newer models of historiographic fiction. It is the necessary elimination of essential objects that is crucial to renewed comprehension. This recognition that understanding comes only with willed limitation is essential to Wallace Stevens's poem, "Of the Surface of Things":

I

In my room, the world is beyond my understanding;
But when I walk I see that it consists of three or four
          hills and a cloud.

II

From my balcony, I survey the yellow air,
Reading what I have written,
"The Spring is like a belle undressing."

III

The gold tree is blue.
The singer has pulled his cloak over his head.
The moon is in the folds of the cloak.[29]

The opening lines of this poem express the poet's desire to take possession of his world, so he collects and orders a few facts without concerning himself about their inward implications. This is a severe limitation, but a very prudent one since the world, he recognizes, will always remain an enigma and must be accepted in terms of such innocent apprehensions. The reflective lucidity of the poet is diluted, however, when he turns from walking to writing, where the ordering of things becomes, whether or not he so wills it, the travestying of the pure forms observed on the walk. The creation becomes an emanation, description of nature becomes the implicit creation of the poet's own existence and his re-creation of the world. "On the Surface of Things" reveals the threat of the dictionary and the encyclopedia as well as that of poetry. Writing transparently, recognizing and accepting the limitations of the self and the indecipherability of the world, is no panacea. It is, rather, the ultimate madness of the dream of sanity that further reveals the monstrous power of books. It is this power of books that Borges examines in his story of the fabulous encyclopedia of Tlön. The encyclopedia, man's imperfect catalogue of the world, recreates the world and becomes the only world in which mankind can now live.

It is this concern with the suprareality of invented worlds that gives Canetti's *Auto-da-Fé* some of the fantasmagoric intensity common to Borges's stories. Like Borges, Canetti demonstrates a tendency toward fanciful classifications of knowledge and eccentric combinations of real and imagined events. But in Canetti the intensely envisioned artificial world is layered with another level of artificiality. Like Beckett and Nabokov, Canetti has chosen to write his novel in a language that is not his mother tongue, determined, as Steiner observes, "to achieve in it a style of uncompromising purity superior even to that of the native speaker."[30] In Canetti, this eccentricity and purity are combined with still another element: conscious political involvement. Thus, in his novel, poetics combines with politics to create an eerie nightmare world in which things become autonomous, almost on the order of Roquentin's nauseated visions of inert matter come to life, while retaining a curious embeddedness in space and history. The processes of power and those of paranoia are inextricably combined. Fittingly, it was a political revolt that inspired Canetti's superficially apolitical book. The critical event occurred on July 15, 1927:

> From all parts of the city, the workers marched in closed processions to the Palace of Justice, which with its sheer name embodied injustice for them. . . . When they set fire to the Palace of Justice, Mayor Seitz, standing on a fire engine, tried to block their way with his right hand raised high. His gesture was futile: the Palace of Justice was *burning*. The police were ordered to shoot, ninety people were killed. . . . In a side street . . . a man, very sharply distinguished from the crowd, stood with high flung arms, wailing and moaning over and over again: "The files are burning! All the files!" "Better than people!" I told him, but that didn't interest him, all he could think of was the files. It occurred to me that he might have some connection to the files, an archivist, he was inconsolable.[31]

The mayor and the archivist, both with upflung arms; in politics, as in poetics, they are individuals standing apart from the united mass of the crowd, themselves united in their sense of disaster. The burning of justice (or injustice) merges with the burning of the files; the shooting of the people is of lesser importance than the loss of their records. Controlled blindness is the norm; defective vision is raised to a cosmic principle. In *The Great American Novel*, William Carlos Williams reaches a similar conclusion that points to the correspondence between the representative of justice and the archivists: "Card-index minds, the judges have. Socialism, immorality, and lunacy are about synonyms to the judge. Property is sacred and human liberty is bitter, bitter, bitter to their tongues."[32] The burning of justice by the masses indicates their desire to bring the old state of blindness to a conclusion. to destroy the old history and bring about a change and a renewal. The seeing eye of the author stands in opposition to the blind eyes of the archivist and the mayor among the spectators of the fire. It is, according to Foucault, the upturned eye that "discovers the bond that links language and death at the moment that it acts out this relationship of the limit and being."[33] Thus, for Canetti, political poetic language recovers some of the lost significance of languages before Babel. It is both logos and *physis*, carrying both meaning and the movement of discovery. He acknowledges both history and the veil thrown over history by politics and the library. As a political act, then, is the tyrant always and absolutely unjustified in burning the books?

By pronouncing a death sentence on the book/Book, the book burner takes fullest possession of that writing. In the Dionysian fire that penetrates to the core of things, the destruction is a prelude to a new germination. The burning of the Palace of Justice and its files is a reappropriation of justice for the people; a true revolution, though sadly abortive in this historical instance. Nevertheless, the burning is far more effective than mere denunciations that simply cast an Apollonian light on the surfaces of things. Thanatopraxis annuls this feeble light; flames and death speak from behind the mirror of imperfect resemblances. The destruction of justice can be conceived against a background of madness, of the limiting condition of silence, and of politics seen in vaguely religious terms. At the core of this burning flame, as Blake recognized, is lust and lust for power:

> Reader! *lover* of books! *lover* of heaven,
> And of that God from whom *all books are given*,
> Who in mysterious Sinai's awful cave
> To Man the wondrous art of writing gave:
> Again he speaks in thunder and in fire!
> Thunder of Thought & flames of fierce desire.[34]

Or this from Ralph Waldo Emerson:

> All writing is by the grace of God. People do not deserve to have good writing, they are so pleased with bad. In these sentences that you show me, I can find no beauty, for I see death in every clause and every word. There is a fossil or a mummy character which pervades this book. . . . Give me initiative, spermatic, prophesying, man-making words.[35]

For Canetti, for Blake, for Emerson, textuality becomes a body image comparable to other body images of power and presence; not just the feeble reflection seen in a mirror but the essence of man discerned in the living flames of language.

Elias Canetti, the Bulgarian-born son of Ladino-speaking Sephardic Jews, must have felt with deep poignancy the cultural and linguistic confusions of our post-Babel world. His family was exiled from Bulgaria to various countries of Europe. Canetti's own first schooling was in English because of his family's removal to Great Britain. He was later drawn to Vienna as his cultural and spiritual home. These confusions of language are mirrored in the title of the first American edition of his novel: *The Tower of Babel*. In effect, the displacements of the title of the novel in its various translations also encompass on a metaphoric level that original failure of communication. It was originally called *Die Blendung* (the blinding, the dazzling, the delusion), reflecting the hallucinatory displacements of madness; and retitled, in its first English translation (by C. V. Wedgwood "under the personal supervision of the author"), *Auto-*

da-Fé, reminding the reader of the immolation by fire of heretic threats to the power structure of the Church. The relation of the failure of language to paranoiac delusion, to the abuse of power, and to the remembered historical event of the burning of the Palace of Justice is crucial. The protagonist, Peter Kien ("pinewood") is a caricature of life lived solely by the will until that will to power drives him into a lonely and peculiar madness ending with his self-immolation. He is, perhaps, the avatar of Don Quixote in a verbo-centric, abstracting society.

Kien reserves his passion for books, allowing no other love to break the temper of his lifetime of austerity. Kien's intense connection to books is by far the most important aspect of his personality. For him, "the best definition of a home was a library,"[36] and when by choice or necessity he leaves his sanctuary for some short time, he always carries a number of those books with him on his excursions: "Kien tapped his own well-filled brief-case. He clasped it tightly to him, in a very particular manner which he had himself thought out, so that the greatest possible area of his body was always in contact with it" (p. 11). Kien demonstrates his power over books in his possession of them, a power he asserts tactilely and passionately in his daily walks.

The equation home=library is expanded to world=library as Kien in his orderly way expands his passion for books to include all disparate exterior phenomena in his interiorized scheme. Yet even the books themselves are only tools, unnecessary but useful, for Kien's scholarly endeavors. "It would be unscholarly to deny that the almost terrifying memory at his disposal had been remarkably useful in his learned researches. He did indeed carry in his head a library as well-provided and as reliable as his actual library" (p. 20). The real library in his apartment is merely a mnemonic system, useful primarily for the gratification it gives to Kien's tactile instincts.

His passion for books as material objects does not disappear with his expulsion from the library. The place of his real books is taken by the second, imaginary library that he materializes in his increasing madness. The library in the head has become the only library—an indestructible one, but sadly lacking in sensual pleasures. It is a lack that Kien immediately tried to fill. The library in the head becomes for him a real, material library that must be painstakingly unpacked at night and repacked each morning. Canetti details the growth of this obsession with the growth of the library.

> At first, when his liberty was yet young, he was not concerned with the kind of room he had taken; it was after all only a matter of sleeping and the sofa could hold his books. Later he used the wardrobe as well. Soon the library had outgrown both. The dirty carpet had to be used so he rang for the maid and asked for ten clean sheets of brown paper. He spread them out on the carpet and over the whole floor; if any were left over he covered the sofa with them and lined the wardrobe. . . . The books built themselves up higher and higher, but even if they fell they would not be soiled for everything was covered with paper. Sometimes at night when he awoke, filled with anxiety, it was because he had most certainly heard a noise as of falling books. (p. 170)

Dreams of orderliness do not dissolve with the increasing bulk of his imaginary library. Instead, books are carefully lifted in and out of his head in a predetermined order, according to lists of Kien's devising. As Kien's proliferating library in the head demonstrates, the library itself dooms the protagonist, not by the fact of its internalization, but by virtue of its incomprehensibility. More and more books are constantly added to the weight in his head, condemning the protagonist to a seemingly infinite additive process. Kien's failure to accommodate this increasing burden drives him deeper into madness. The orderly library borders on labyrinthine chaos. The dilemma encountered by Kien is similar to that foreseen by Foucault in the passage from "Language to Infinity" quoted earlier: "either all these books are already contained within the Word and they must be burned, or they are contradictory and, again, they must be burned." Furthermore, "Literature begins . . . when the book is no longer the space where speech adopts a form . . . but the site where books are all recaptured and consumed."[37] Kien evades the dilemma by his mad, metaphorical consumption of the library in the head and in his literal consumption of the actual library by fire.

William Carlos Williams, with his interest in the particular, with his "local pride" ("the great world never much interested me"),[38] with his search for the roots of a new poetic language in American speech, would seem to provide an absolute contrast to the universalist, cosmopolitan, polyglot Canetti. Williams repeatedly deplored the transplantation of American talent (Eliot, Pound, and others) to Europe and tried throughout his career to avoid the pernicious transcultural, transhistorical, and international influences that operated so strongly on his contemporaries. Yet Williams, with his insistently American focusing of the poetic impulse, is not immune to the pressures of the universalizing library. The dilemma of the word that must be burned is one that he too must face in *Paterson*, and while Williams and Canetti seem to approach the problem from opposing perspectives, the poet's man-city-giant is no more capable of resolving the dilemma than the novelist's sinologist.

The form of *Paterson* is itself that of an archive. It is a file of scattered and selected bits and pieces of information welded together according to some larger order. Helen Vendler observes that Williams, like the other librarian discussed above, uses data "in a socially self-conscious and deliberately archaeological fashion, as fragments shored against ruins."[39] Williams's fragments are not Eliot's fragments, nor are his ruins the same as those of his expatriate contemporary, yet fragments and ruins certainly exist, in America as in Europe, and in both places the poet's task is roughly similar: first to discover, then to excavate the site. Vendler's use of the word "archaeological," which is also a key word in Foucault's lexicon, is critical. Like Foucault, Williams interprets the past spatially, almost geologically. He takes in the physical implications of the documents he describes, and they are layered in the poem like the strata of an archaeological dig. This archaeology of knowledge is, furthermore, not unlike that described by Foucault in his definition of the temporally and spatially specific archive. In both, there is a "rolling up out of chaos" in the quest for the "rigor of beauty" (*Paterson*, p. 3). The implicit dilemma in this notion is similar to that stated by Foucault. The rolling motion suggests the poet's fascination with improvisational free form, but letters and clippings from various sources are carefully orchestrated in a manner that suggests a fixed form. There is a tension between the continuous movement of rolling up and the dread of formlessness implied in the appeal of rigor. Williams is aware that by artificially imposing limits on the free motion of rolling, he risks cooption into the rigid structures of the library which must be burned. Rigidity is the beginning of *rigor mortis*. Yet, on the other hand, Williams's ambiguous relation to form and pattern is evident from the first line of *Paterson* in his emphasis on the rigor that is the essence of true beauty. The problem, then, lies in the choice of system. Williams recognizes the need for structure—he only hopes that the system can be one he develops and freely chooses rather than a library structure imposed from outside. The construction of such a personal archive is a delicate endeavor. The poet must transform public material into his own private vision, and out of stark newspaper clarities create an original palimpsest.

Like Foucault, Williams finds the burning of the library essential to this task. He is a witchhunter and a terrorist. The destruction of the contradictory babble of past systems unburdens him for the quest of the one "Beautiful Thing," which hell's fire deflowers and the purifying flame causes to reflower again (p. 118). The burning of the library is a complex image for Williams since it symbolizes at once the rape of knowledge by the tyrant, the purification of the self that symbolically ensues in the body politic from the exorcism of spirits, and the reendowment of human passions to the maddening cold of dead books. In this complexity, the all-consuming passion of Williams differs from that "demoniac erotomania" described by Huysmans in his novel *Against the Grain*. Des Esseintes's passion heats but does not consume. Huysmans's hero does not look for the young and the fresh, but enjoys the over-ripe treats of the dead library-mausoleum. He especially prizes "those gamey flavours, those stains of disease and decay, that cankered surface, that taste of rotten ripeness"[40] that are anathema to Williams.

Williams is no Orpheus who loves and sings to bring the dead back alive, and in this, perhaps, he proposes an alternative to the librarian's plight. As Barthes reminds us, "All literature knows that like Orpheus, it cannot, on the pain of death, turn around to look at what is behind it: it is condemned to mediation—that is, in a sense, to lying."[41] Williams turns his back on the dead, and although it would seem that his poem is still contaminated with the litter of our civilization through his use of passages from newspapers, letters, histories, and so forth, his intention is clearly other. Williams advises that the only answer to the impingements of the library on poetry is to "write carelessly so that nothing that is not green will survive" (p. 129). His bits and snippets from the Paterson archive do not represent, at least in his mind, the debris of a decayed past, but the reflowered plants growing up in the ashes of the purgative fire. Whether or not his results match his intention is another matter, the further exploration of which would lead back to the greenery of Eden, on the one hand, and to the noxious grotto of Goytisolo or to the obscene garden library of Roquentin on the other. The green Williams longs for can be lost among the golden leaves that delight and repel Roquentin, and we are reminded of Mephistopheles's advice to the student: "All theory, my friend, is grey, / But green is life's glad golden tree."[42] This advice would seem to lend its support to the natural "green" life favored by Williams, but the actual effect of its deliberate confusion is to alienate the student from the true, tactile surface of the object described. It is, perhaps, to this famous observation that Stevens refers in his own statement of the confusions of poetic abstraction in "Of the Surface of Things": "The gold tree is blue."

This problem, while present throughout the whole of *Paterson*, is most clearly focused in Book III, "The Library." It is this book which details the attempts of the present to escape into a past that crushes it. The image of an order driven back through time, seeking to escape in history, is contrasted with the nonrationalistic presence of the African women on the official log where past and present exist without conflict in a fecund continuum of presence. The women exist within a historical syntax of a sort, but in their elementary relations to their natural origins and to each other they evidence a recovery of a primary system of exchanges lacking in the power-hungry disunities of the library. Their actual continuum exposes the fictitious continuum of the library. The women on the log flourish in the open air; the library is a closed space, stale and airless. The women unquestioningly embrace the elemental rhythms of flow and growth; the library contains only stagnant repetitions, lacking the elemental. The motionless stabbing force of the women contrasts with the library's inertia, its closed history. Their "thick lightnings" are the counterforce that rise up metaphorically in the form of flame to open up the mysteries of the dead men confined within the library's walls. The purgation of the books by fire is also, then, a lending of life and heat ("Fire is the ultra-living element," says Bachelard[43]) to a cold past.

The temptations offered by the library are real; if they were not, the burning of the library would have no significance. Paterson entered the library in good faith, hoping to find respite from the besetting riddle of the falls, but he soon brings into question the "virtue" of the library and finds its silence defective. The creative fires have long since died in the static, ordered books on the shelves, and only an effort of imagination can bring some feeble light back to their existence. Such enfeebled longing does not compare to the careless indifference with which the African women hurl their infinitely more powerful bolts. Paterson must be wakened from his reverie, so as not to sink more deeply into the drugged stupor of books.

Elias Canetti's protagonist, Peter Kien, is an example and a warning to those who heedlessly enclose themselves in the silence and stagnation of the library. Until his last action in the novel, the merest hint that flames might touch his precious collection (or any book) is enough to arouse his deepest and most unreasoning anger. Such a horrible thing cannot, must not, will not happen to him— and the very pathological force of his vehemence is enough to assure the reader's belief in the inevitability of this unthinkable event. Kien takes the implicit assumptions of *Paterson* seriously and literally. Through his books, he has leaped the abyss of time from the vulgar present to the more appealing distant past. The past has crushed out all hint of the present and is itself totally, physically present for him. It is, as we may expect, an isolated and sterile madness disallowing subjection to the immutable universal laws of time and place. It is not that Kien recognizes no difference between past and present; for him there is no present, so totally overwhelmed is he by the force of his chosen past. He totally evades the quotidian process of grappling with conventional reality; upon such trivialities and minor interruptions he imposes the severity of his own superlative order. With his library in the sky he feels master of history. He is both immersed in it and outside of it by virtue of his presumed superior control of the languages and the orders of books.

It is crucial that Kien's ordering process be strictly literary—the spoken word is contemptuously rejected: "The greatest danger which threatens a man of learning is to lose himself in talk. Kien preferred to express himself in the written rather than the spoken word" (p. 17). He allows no "green" (to use *Paterson*'s term) carelessly written word to escape his pen. His meticulousness with language matches his meticulousness with the library. Each word must be killed and fixed in its proper place so that no possibility of linguistic slippage might exist: "he took no decision, on a single letter, a word, or an entire sentence, until he was convinced that it was unassailable" (p. 18). One is reminded of a similar care on the part of James Joyce who set a historical precedent for Kien's concern with the minutiae of written expression. In Kien's case, however, the words of his logomania do not serve for communication, but for definition.

Yet, even in his logomanic madness, Kien longs for the wordless freedom of absolute silence, a longing that his conscious mind relentlessly suppresses. His longings return, nevertheless, in the form of the fear of fire, which haunts his waking moments and takes early shape in the conspiracy of silence his books wage against him. His formal declaration of war on his housekeeper is met by the obdurate silence of the works of Gautama Buddha; a silence upon which he had once modeled his own frequent silences. The fecund silence of the Buddha confronts the silence of madness and defeats it (pp. 95–96). This first silent threat to Kien's authority foreshadows the later hallucinatory rebellion of the books when, at the end of the novel, they rise up silently against the tyrant Kien to act out their declaration of independence from his repressive intransigence. In this mock-heroic Battle of the Books, Canetti once again dissolves pathology into politics, disclosing the dreams of power to which Kien aspires. The imaginary burning of the pawnshop shifts into the burning of the scholar's library, and both reflect on the historic burning of the Palace of Justice, which likewise substituted corrupt intransigence for the strictness of moral purity. Inertia and closure have here, as in Paterson's library, led from the cool of books to the stench of death.

For Paterson, since the source of logos lies in the original myth of history, the logical response would seem to be a return to this starting point, destroying what exists and reshaping everything anew. This longing, exemplified in the library fire, is impossible to fulfill. There is nothing clear cut, there is never any pure and simple solution to the dilemma outside the fictions of madness. The dead words in the books testify to their reality; if they are corpses, then they once had life, and alive or dead they maintain a solid presence in reality. Live, green, and dynamic, or dead, opaque, and static, the word is a fact in its own right. With its metaphorical death, the word collapses and lapses into the unknown—but it does not lose itself in the void. The living green of action and change becomes the dull, deadened, false, spatial order:

> The polis is polished
> civilization is polite
>   is policed.[44]

The dream of marriage is inseparable from the actuality of divorce. Man's historicity and his distance from the original desired union are part of the post-Babel paradox of men coming together to divide themselves from their original unity with nature. As Babel is the name of a place that does not exist, yet defines our being, the whole of man's history is determined by a fixed (negated) center, which like the deadened word of the books is nothing without being nothingness. The poet places himself temporally, but also spatially, in the heart of this problematic. In clarifying his moment in time, Paterson (and Williams) further intensifies the sense of place, making of the poem the very opposite of the green, living presence he declared for it. Richard A. Macksey finds that "there is no temporal depth to the experience or to the poem. Time past can only be represented spatially, as a collage of juxtaposed presents." Further, "this temporal as well as spatial contraction into an indestructible moment" provides the poet with a "stay against the volatility of experience,"[45] that is, a hardening rigor and order that can come to mimic (or mask) the rejected orders of the library. Time is flattened out, stratified, and stacked according to the laws Williams carries in his library in the head. This personalized historical sense enfolds traditional historical time in a mythic reinterpretation. Williams's gleanings from the documents of the past are at least partially parodic, in Foucault's sense of the parodic use of history, and tend toward the dissociative mode.

Fittingly, *Paterson* begins with a regathering of the scattered fragments of a myth of place, working from the "particulars," to the "thing itself," to the sleeping giants. He seeks in the close observation of particulars an approximation of timelessness and an elucidation of unity through multiplicity. Williams's effort approaches that of the theological poets described by Vico who, "by means of their logic . . . invented languages; by morals, created heroes; by economics, founded families, and by politics, cities; by their physics, established the beginnings of things as all divine; by the particular physics of man, in a certain sense created themselves."[46] Paterson, like the giants discussed by Vico, is a wanderer, learning about himself and his environment and summing up the particulars in his long walks. His wandering mirrors the wandering of those sons of Cain, those builders of Babel described by the Italian philosopher. Biblically (or mythologically) the wandering is sparked by an original crime of violence against a brother (see, for example, Rene Girard, *The Violence and the Sacred*). Psychologically, says Freud in *Totem and Taboo*, the fratricidal crime reflects back on an initial paternal murder, as the sons sacrifice the father in the first homicide, which is also the beginning of history. Significantly, Paterson's wandering stops outside the library, the temple of history set within the labyrinthine city constructed by men. He has become leaden, drifting with the stream of mass existence like the dead dog, longing for the "peace that comes of destruction: / to the teeth / to the very eyes / (cut lead)" (p. 132). The wandering poet's desire to build a city (and himself) from the "particulars" of experience is thwarted by the polite, polished exterior of already existing cities and selves. William Nelson's *History of the City of Paterson*, source of many of the particulars, becomes *The Book of Lead*, its pages so heavy with anticipated death that the poet cannot lift them (p. 134). Instead, the poet closes his eyes, willing blindness, willing death, willing the Dionysian destruction that will lift him from the leaden stupor of historical immersion to a new ecstasy of beginnings.

The leaden heaviness of the poet before his purification by fire significantly parallels the breakdown of uranium into lead; a parallel that Williams is at pains to point out:

> . knowledge, the contaminant
>
> Uranium, the complex atom, breaking
> down, a city in itself, that complex
> atom, always breaking down .
> to lead. (p. 178)

The man in the city, contaminated by the knowledge imparted in leaden books, is himself contaminated and finds his wanderings breaking down into a leaden descent. Thus according to Riddel, "the poet's measure, his names, function more like a Mendelief table of discrete and known difference, in which elements are arranged according to an arbitrary norm of relative atomic weight."[47] The search of the wanderer takes the form of nuclear chemistry, breaking down a complex unity to the elemental. But in *Paterson*, the breaking down is not simply a descent "leadward," but a sequence of change that at some point leads to a rupture and an ascension. The decay to lead represents a perversion of energy, a riddle of chemistry that parallels the riddle of leaden history and corrupt decaying cities: "Uranium : basic thought—leadward." The decay, however, is interrupted by violence: "Fractured : radium : credit" (p. 185). The poet's violent destruction of the self in a Dionysian frenzy of dismemberment leads to the other needed destructions: of physics, morals, cities, economies, languages invented by poets in other times. The dark flame and the messy stain at the bottom of the retort reveal their luminosity. Poetic fire, breaking down, closing itself into lead, rebuilds itself once again in creative potential. The heaviness of the lead contrasts with the weightless "nothing" of the stain.

But just as the closure of lead leads to the radiant opening, so too this opening signals another closure. Radium is the contaminant that signals a reemergent reality. It is itself a perverted, unnatural element, the product of a divorce. Its very discovery was due to a disharmony—"A dissonance / in the valence of Uranium / led to the discovery" (p. 176). The dissonance of radium realizes the extreme of linguistic dislocation and prefigures a similar temporal and spatial dissonance. The "nothing" of luminous radiance repeats the nothing of the books that in their leadward thrust complement and contradict the radiant stain. The sun/son of radium becomes the usurious Hamiltonian SUM; the healthy sexuality of Madame Curie—"with ponderous belly, full / of thought!" (p. 177)—is perverted into an infertile womb in the Solarium lecture on atomic fission:

> Smash the wide world .
> a fetid womb, a sump!
> No river! no river
> but bog, a . swale
> sinks into the mind or
> the mind into it, a ? (P. 171)

In a similar manner, the fire and the flood of the Paterson library do not create a fertile tabula rasa from which to begin creation anew, but rather a field of infertile muck, a "pustular scum" that "fouls the mind" (p. 140). The economics of usury returns to usurp the place of a healthy credit economy, and this economics too has its song—for "There is a poetry / of the movements of cost, known and unknown" (p. 109). Costs and poetry—both are "known and unknown," both are part of the luminous nothing that stains the bottom of the retort like the original violent crime.

The cycle of radium is an analogue of other similar cycles such as that of the rolling up of particulars into a sum that is intended to counteract the malevolent historical influence of the Hamiltonian SUM. The walk in the park ends, not in the construction of a new city (a new reality), but in a return to the past with Paterson's entry into the library. Even the run to the sea (a more desperate version of his earlier walk) does not produce "the final somersault" (p. 204), but curls back on itself in Book V, where "the (self) direction has been changed / the serpent / its tail in its mouth / 'the river has returned to its beginnings'" (p. 233). Within the library, the dreams of dead men, which should have been lost in the far-gone past, are instead confined by the walls, battering themselves against the illusion of freedom they see in the windows:

Flown in from before the cold or nightbound
(the light attracted them)
  they sought safety (in books)
but ended battering against glass
  at the high windows (p. 100)

Things—or parts of things—the spirits that inhabit the books, become eerily autonomous and flutter about unpredictably as Williams turns time (history) into space. The high windows do not provide a break in the stone walls; they are coterminous with and continuations of those walls.

The battered spirits of imprisoned dead men offer a fitting sequel to Paterson's visions of debased love in his walk through the park. Both are perverted by divorce. The high windows confine books in a stifling space when the spirits should be free to intermingle with the temporal sequences of nature. And love in the park "is no comforter," says Williams, "rather a nail in the skull / . reversed in the mirror of its/own squalor, debased by the divorce from learning" (p. 81). The window and the mirror once again come into play as near correlatives, both serving to pervert and corrupt the natural and harmonious interrelation of things and thoughts, of natural love and the spirits that reside in books.

In *Auto-da-Fé*, Canetti adds the fillip of madness to the pressures of confinement. In an autobiographical account of the writing of this novel, Canetti explains the importance for his book of a specific room he inhabited in Vienna in 1927: "I was thrilled with the view. . . . On the other side of the valley, on top of the facing slope, there was the walled town of the mentally ill, Steinhof. I made up my mind at first sight, I had to be in this room, I discussed the details with the landlady in front of the open window."[48] In Williams's poem, the books batter themselves against the high closed windows, in Canetti's novel, the spirit of the work is derived from an open window that restricts the author's view to a windowless space of confinement. Love is the nail in the skull for Williams; for Canetti the madhouse served a similar purpose: "the daily view of Steinhof, where six thousand lunatics lived, was the thorn in my flesh. I am quite sure that I would never have written *Auto-da-Fé* without that room."[49]

This walled space makes a symbolic appearance early in Canetti's novel with the walling up of Kien's apartment, allowing for the confinement of madness and the spirits of books within his rooms:

> The windows had been walled up several years before after a determined struggle with his landlord. In this way he had gained in every room a fourth wall-space: accommodation for more books. . . . The temptation to watch what went on in the street—an immoral and time-wasting habit—disappeared with the side windows. Daily . . . he blessed both the idea and its results, since he owed to them the fulfillment of his dearest wish: the possession of a well-stocked library, in perfect order and enclosed on all sides. (p. 23)

The windowless walls of Kien's library represent a perfect spatial correlative for his grotesquely walled-in self. The books serve as a shield for the scholar against the feared contact with the immorality of ordinary life. Within these familiar walls, Kien feels that he can control space (by equating the library with the universe) and time (the library is history within the grasp of a single man).

While Kien walls himself in with his books in a windowless (and also, it is worthy of note, a mirrorless) space, his housekeeper, Therese, suffers from a mirror fantasy. She is as little able as Kien to look out upon the world and employs her piece of mirror as Kien uses the books that cover his windows—as a substitute for a reality she refuses to see. In Therese, the dynamics of psychic projection are particularly strong. As she looks into the mirror, she sees both herself and her beloved from the furniture store, with the fantasy growing so strong that she exchanges places in her fantasy, and becomes "Mr. Puda" staring at the lovely young woman of the mirror:

> She balanced up and down before the mirror. It made her feel how beautiful she was. She took off her skirt and had a look at her magnificent hips. How right he is. . . . He's not only superior, he's everything. . . . She'll give him something, she says. Back to the door she goes, and fetches the bunch of keys hanging there. Before the mirror, she hands over the present with a jingle, and says he can come to her rooms whenever he

likes. . . . She calls. . . . He says nothing, he can't tear himself away from her hips. (pp. 271–72)

Kien's madness is all for words; he is a logomaniac and a biblio-phile. Therese's erotic fantasies about her mirror reflection evidence her affliction by a parallel obsession. Just as there are no windows in Kien's physical or mental libraries, there are no windows in Therese's love-mad mental or physical worlds. Both are totally turned inward, endlessly reflecting self-perceptions. Both are inflex-ible and uncompromising. The pressure of this madness, as the claustrophobic atmosphere is increasingly compacted in the novel, forewarns the reader of the final violent explosion. Raymond Wil-liams feels this rigorous compression of madness and wonders about its impact. "There is a point," he says, "where the diagnosis of delu-sion can become itself deluded, with a kind of relapse into a disin-tegrating vision of a controlling violence and madness."[50] Williams leaves open the question of whether this reaction is a challenge to the author's choice of expression, especially in the third part of the novel, or whether it is an act of self-protection against the tempta-tions of insanity and violence. As with Borges, who mirrors books but skews the reflection to save literature (and us) from fulmination, Canetti forces the final movement of withdrawal felt by Raymond Williams as a similar ploy, slanting the reader away from a world that too closely resembles our own. Williams's response is willed both by the scholar-author and his scholar-reader in order to divert the critic out of the too-familiar Kienian world back into the quoti-dian life where libraries do have windows, and they open out on to something other than madness.

The compulsion to escape is likewise built into the novel in the form of Kien's repeated dreams of primitive rituals of human sacri-fice. A typical dream opens with Kien's presence at an Aztec ritual in which the priests of ancient Mexico are disguised as jaguars. When the jaguar-priest drives an obsidian knife into the breast of the victim, along with the heart-blood, books come forth out of the wound, with the victim's heartblood, and the redness of the blood is transformed into the redness of fire; the books "fell to the ground, they were clutched at by viscous flames. The blood had set fire to the wood, the books were burning" (p. 39). The human sacrifice does not affect the scholar emotionally—it is the burning of the books that filled him with horror. Kien leaps into the flames only to find the books converted into screaming men. Having no patience with mere human suffering, he contemptuously leaps out of the fire. Suddenly, the men are changed into books again—he rushes back into the fire to rescue them, only to find himself once again surrounded by the same mass of human bodies. Again and again he escapes the flames, only to find that the books continue to be martyred on his exit.

Kien's own "logical" explanation of this extraordinary dream is woefully inadequate, associating the terrifying events with recollections of recent studies. Kien's mechanistic dissection of the dream, while superficially employing the techniques of Freudian dream analysis, is totally beside the point. His dissection of the dream ignores the irrational elements, the emotional supercharge in the scenes of violence and aggression, elements that he suppresses in his own conscious life as well. As Bachelard notes, the fire dreams of lonely men are "among the clearest, the most distinct, those for which the sexual interpretation is the most certain."[51] Likewise, Kien remains ignorant of the import of his dream on still other grounds. For Freud, not only is the anxiety dream a frequent precursor to a delusional outbreak in a prepsychotic person,[52] but the nature of the dream reveals the dominant factor of the delusion: "a dream is a (disguised) fulfillment of a (suppressed or repressed) wish."[53] Further, despite his interest in historical artifacts, Kien is only a half-hearted archaeologist; he ignores the purificatory nature of fire festivals, which point not only to destruction, but to a renewal of communication between men and of cooperation with nature and the gods. This is not the blindness of purer sight that Kien imagines that he employs in his logical analysis, but that of delusion.

The frenzy of motion in this dream is followed, after his marriage to Therese, by a period of immobility. Kien feels it incumbent upon himself to enter into a course of petrifaction in order to save himself and avoid the vile female encroaching upon his territory. He embarks upon this experiment with all the considerable power of his mind: "His efficiency in stiffening grew greater from day to day. As soon as he reached the consistency of stone, he tested the hardness of the material by lightly pressing his thighs against the seat of the chair. This test for hardness lasted only a few seconds, a longer pressure would have crushed the chair to powder. . . . From nine in the morning until seven in the evening Kien retained his imcomparable pose" (p. 161). In his immobility Kien did not neglect his studies—he was, after all, the proud possessor of a complete library in his head and did not require external aids to compose his texts. He had found a presumably safe haven in his reincarnation as an Egyptian statue of a priest, and his knowledge of history saved him from the vulgarities of the present. His only regret was that he did not have a mirror with which to inspect and admire his startling metamorphosis, a mirror which would have served not for self-knowledge but, as in Therese's case, for the inner reflection of an exterior fantasy.

When Kien, upon his expulsion from his library-home, finally does see his face in a mirror by accident, he sees the face of his petri-faction: "His forehead, ridged as a rock-face, from which his nose plunged at right angles towards the abyss, an edge dizzily narrow. At its base, almost hidden, cowered two minute black insects. No one would have guessed them to be nostrils. His mouth as the slot of a machine" (p. 173). Kien's self-description as a rock or a machine with two insects for nostrils is similar to, if not as extreme as, the heights of Roquentin's hallucinatory vision in which things and living beings exchange places. Kien, however, is machinelike in his physical appearance, indicating that his madness reflects that of society. In his face is legibly inscribed the meaning (or meaningless-ness) of the machine-oriented society in which we live. This machine face is the perfect image for the dissociative mask described by Foucault as the second use of history, in which the moment is disconnected and chronology is lost.

But with the sight of his inhuman face in the mirror, Kien becomes aware of something else—his loneliness. Desperately, he searches for human company to take the place of the company of books whose presence has been denied him. His blindness to his surroundings lifts, and he reads a tavern sign, "Zum Idealen Himmel" ("The Stars of Heaven" in the English translation), and associates this misnamed heaven with the forbidden heaven of his library in the sky. It is, in actuality, the sign of his descent into the Hades of a monstrous, subhuman thieves' underground. Kien's exit from this company is heralded by another glimpse of himself; this time in the mirror held up to him by a police inspector intent on wringing a criminal confession from the hapless scholar:

> Quick as lightning he pulled out his pocket mirror and held it out towards Kien, not so near but that he could see himself almost full length.
> "Do you know who that is?" he asked. . . .
> "It is . . . I, myself," stammered Kien. (p. 312)

One would expect that here Kien's original limitations would be mitigated to a certain extent, his delirium broken by the accusing mirror of the police officer. Such is not the case. The lonely, deluded machine-man is, with this glimpse of his face, definitively alienated from human kind. All that is left is the hallucinations of his delirium, the marvelous delusions of a total holocaust buried in the visions of his desire; the death and dismemberment of Therese, the destruction of his library.

Paterson's descent into Hades is also presaged by a sign; the SILENCE sign that represents the failure of language in the library. It too, like "Zum Idealen Himmel," is the sign of a criminal, antihuman place. The silence imposed by the library is malignant, keeping spirits entombed, preventing them from acting against the library. There is no virtue in it, neither evident nor hidden.

> But the pathetic library (that contained,
> perhaps, not one volume of distinction)
> must go down also—
>
> BECAUSE IT IS SILENT. IT
> IS SILENT BY DEFECT OF VIRTUE IN THAT IT
> CONTAINS NOTHING OF YOU (p. 122)

Like the sordid tavern into which Kien plunges in his misery, Paterson's library is a closed space. The name of the thieves' dive is a beautiful illusion, a fiction that does little to cover the harsh reality. Similarly, the reverent silence of the library in the presence of the

Word becomes itself an illusion that covers a lack of virtue, a deficiency of the beauty that is alone worthy of reverence. Paterson feels no compunction in shouting down that corrupted silence, a silence that serves no purpose in protecting beauty or the Word. "The language is missing them . . . / They may look at the torrent in / their minds / and it is foreign to them . . ." (pp. 11–12). Patch's fall into history at Passaic Falls parallels and predicts this fall into silence at the library: "his body wavered in the air—Speech had failed him. He was confused. The word had been drained of its meaning. . . . He struck the water on his side and disappeared. A great silence followed. . ." (p. 17). Sam Patch's historical place is defined by this failure of language. He is always caught in that silence, frozen for all time with the dead spirits of the library, displaced from earth and sky in a voiceless middle world. Books, says Paterson, "will give rest sometimes against / the uproar of water falling," (p. 97) but to what purpose is that preferred rest? Williams intimates that we drown just as surely in books as Sam Patch did in his silent fall at Passaic, and that this dangerous situation must be reversed by an inverse cataract, "the waterfall of the / flames, a cataract reversed, shooting / upward" (p. 120). Emerson, however, has issued a warning that is much to the point and counteracts this incendiary optimism. "You are a very elegant writer," he observes, "but you can't write up what gravitates down."[54]

Sam Patch remains unburied—worse—he is petrified in the winter ice; his perpetual presence frozen in his historical existence. For Williams the failure of language can only be rectified when this frozen presence is definitively made to disappear. "Therefore / present, forever present," Williams's helicopter "searches the Hellgate current for some corpse, / lest the gulls feed on it / and its identity and its sex . . . / . . . be no longer decipherable / and so lost . / therefore present, / forever present" (p. 161). The library is this Hellgate current, Williams's imagination the helicopter that pursues the spirits of the past in the grotesque cemetery, seeking to unite scattered bits of corpses into a decipherable order for burial and for the cessation of the intolerable presence that chokes words back and perpetuates the silence. The library, like the Hellgate current, destroys life: "white hot man become / a book, the emptiness of / a cavern resounding" (p. 123). They are the ghosts and dreamwalkers, empty and impotent, "locked and forgot in their desires—unroused" (p. 6).

In Williams's poem, fission, generally seen as an evil because it leads to divorce, can also be a constructive force, as in the splitting of the uranium atom-city to produce the radiant gist. Marriage, likewise, is not a universal good; beyond a certain point fusion is not even desirable. As Richard Shiff observes in his comments on metaphor, "Our concept of life . . . seems to demand that our works of art be incomplete, flawed, or imperfect; otherwise death will result."[55] It is this insight that Williams obeys in his call for a green, careless writing. Nevertheless, it is clear that Williams's own project is not green or careless, but carefully crafted according to the poet's concepts of the rigor appropriate to aesthetic form. Williams does not resolve the riddle of how analytic synthesis is to be reconciled with discontinuity, but the question bears further exploration.

Paterson opens in the space of ritual, of myth, but the poet's opening myth is not that of fusion in a paradisiacal garden, but rather of a primal division. History for Williams begins in divorce and ends in a sum. A virgin is whored, a woman is taken in love— fusion has many forms, one being the goal toward which the poet strives, but many of the forms of fusion are false sums that must be deplored and avoided by the living poet. The drowned man is not, as in Shakespeare's *The Tempest*, converted into a rich work of art. Instead, the poet finds himself sprouting unhealthy growths:

> His ears are toadstools, his fingers have
> begun to sprout leaves (his voice is drowned
> under the falls) .
>
> Poet, poet! sing your song, quickly! or
> not insects but pulpy weeds will blot out
> your kind. (p. 83)

Man and nature intermingle in death, creating a sum or a fusion that is counterpoetic. In this passage, the poet struggles against inhabitation by noxious forces. He is still writhing under the shock and violation of fusion.

Fission, the Dionysian dismemberment, is preferred to this violent interpenetration. Thus, Williams showers the reader with masses of fragments, turning to history for disconnected details to buttress the poet against the threat of fusion into an undesirable sum. Williams is an archaeologist in the Foucaultian sense. He does not return to the concrete object, the ruins of ancient monuments, but to the memories of them captured in documents, which are themselves rocks, to which he would give voice and song:

> Oh that the rocks of the Areopagus had
> kept their sounds, the voices of the law!
> Or that the great theatre of Dionysius
> could be aroused by some modern magic
>   to release
> what is bound in it, stones! (p. 201)

Like Foucault, Williams points to the shift from monuments to documents in traditional approaches to history and expresses his nostalgia for the silent ruins. In his poem he hopes to transform the documents of American history into monuments through song, and to perpetuate memory in the restitution of thingness to ideas through poetic discipline.

The suicide leap of Sam Patch is intimately related to this process. His leap into the falls is a self-perpetuating act, locking him for all time into the local histories of Paterson, transforming him into a document. Furthermore, as the idea of the leap is conserved in a document, so too is the objective thingness (the body of Patch) preserved in a monument—his petrifaction (conversion to stone) in a cake of ice. His agony has, in the poem, the same structure as pleasure. His leap, a passing form, is stabilized in a poetic creation, albeit a sterile one. This is an underlying fear haunting Williams's poem throughout, namely, that rigor and beauty cannot converge, that poetic creation is a sterile form suspended between life and death, between the document that has no spirit and the monument that cannot sing.

Williams is forced back to his original task, to reengage the problematic of rolling up the sum though the means are defective. The revelation of the radiant gist is one aspect of this sum, a starting point for the poem, a stain that gives evidence of the original fission, yet illuminates the whole. Williams rejects the analytic sum, the preimposed design that is repeated in the orders of the city or the catalogues of the library. These are the excremental sums, fetid and infertile, that give rise only to the most noxious plants. "Money: uranium (bound to be lead)" (p. 182) is the product of that inhuman design, the heir to the Hamiltonian Society for Useful Manufactures. Hamilton's SUM is the defective sum of technology, imposed without thought for the particulars of the area, thus creating in effect the city, the library, and, paradoxically, the numerous divorces.

The problem of the Paterson poet is to free history and space from this old SUM in a manner that does not negate the past but uses it freely to reestablish a new human measure. Williams undermines confidence in the old arithmetic that adds one and one and, most logically, reaches two. What is needed is a new mathematics expressing a new sum "by multiplication a reduction to one." Neither life stilled in the cycle of history nor art captured in the singing stones is an operable solution: both lead to death. In the first there is no change, in the second no growth of meaning. Williams's new mathematic of particulars shifts back and forth between them, hoping that the motion itself will indicate the new, desired sum. A static moment surrounded by the dynamism of life; a silence, imbued with the memory of rustling winds and singing coming forth from the rocks. In such a manner, Williams allows his form freedom and yet keeps it in check. He compels us forward to the edge of the falls, then moves back from the abyss.

For Canetti's Kien there is nothing but the abyss; his wandering in the inferno of the city leads him back to the inferno of his library. Living in such a hell, it is not strange that his most debilitating fear is that his private library may someday go up in flames. Not only is he subject to anxiety dreams in that vein, but in the daytime he broods about the burning of the library of Alexandria and carries within him constantly the memory of the Chinese counterpart of Alexandria, which was burned by the Chinese emperor in 213 B.C. Since Kien specialized in Chinese studies, this disastrous burning was particularly painful to him.

The ancient book-burning is strikingly relevant to Kien's own situation. Shi Huang Ti, the king of Tsin, unified the six kingdoms of

China under his rulership, arrogated to himself the title of First, and took the name of the legendary creator of writing, Huang Ti. He burned the books, that is, he abolished the past, because opposition to his rule persisted in invoking memories of ancient rulers in order to defame the present. He ordered "that all the libraries of poetry, history, and philosophy, except those under the custody of the Eruditi, be sent to the officials to be destroyed; that all people who recite poetry or discuss history be executed; that all those who raise their voices against the present government in the name of antiquity be beheaded together with their families."[56] The books were burned, leaving the only remaining complete set in the imperial archives, which was itself burned in 206 B.C. This burning was said to have lasted three months.

The memory of that colossal catastrophe remains alive for Canetti's scholar: "To this very day, I tell you, the smell of that burning stings my nostrils" (p. 91). The history that the emperor tried to destroy was the same history that memorialized his actions in the documents that tell of his fall and in the Great Wall that still stands today as a monument to his vainglory.

Clearly, as is the case with China and Alexandria, the fire that Kien sets at the end of the novel burns more than his 25,000 books. The historical fires afford glimpses of the dark abyss into whose depths the scholar must fall, and the desire to fall into that abyss is the hidden content of his life. The fire he foresees throughout the novel is the fire that consumes him at its close. George, the psychiatrist brother, who appears on the scene like the deus ex machina of our time to set aright the disorders of Kien's life, fails to recognize the logomanic abyss over which his brother hangs, and thus dooms the Chinese scholar and speeds the inevitable holocaust. Yet despite his blindness to the severity of his brother's condition, George unknowingly gives some insights into the aberrations that spark Kien's fiery end in his analogy of the love frenzy of the termites:

> I can imagine nothing more poignant than an orgy in a colony of termites. The creatures forget . . . what they really are, the blind cells of a fanatic whole. Each will be himself . . . the madness spreads, *their* madness, a mass madness. . . . the whole mound burns with unsatisfied love, they cannot find

their partners, they have no sex, the noise . . . attracts a storm of red ants; through the unguarded gates the deadly enemies press in, what soldier thinks of defending himself, they want only love; and the colony which might have lived for all eternity—that eternity for which we all long—dies, dies of love. (p. 432)

Peter Kien, like the sexless termites, burns with an unrecognized, unrequited love madness. The madness, and the impossibility of its fulfillment, presses upon the artificial eternity Kien has constructed within the library, allowing the invasion, presaging a death through an excess of love. Like the Chinese emperor Shi Huang Ti, Kien perverts his lonely superiority and his longing for immortality into a frenzy of destruction, inserting himself into history through burning the past, assuring future immortality with the loss of the last burning documents.

For the ancient emperor to declare such a wholesale destruction of the books entailed a full recognition of the power of the written word. Kien shares this recognition, although his reaction is initially quite different. The thing most important to him is the safeguarding of the written word. Between and beyond words there is nothing. Kien seizes upon language as though it were a fist that held the entire world within its grasp. His obsession with calling each word, each concept by its scrupulously correct name reveals at once Kien's recognition of the power of words and his assumption of superiority over them: "You have but to know an object by its proper name for it to lose its dangerous magic. Primitive man called each and all by the wrong name. One single and terrible web of magic surrounded him. . . . Knowledge has freed us from superstitions and beliefs. Knowledge makes use always of the same names, preferably Graeco-Latin, and indicates by these names actual things" (p. 385). Kien prides himself upon his ability for abstraction, an ability that he finds lacking in more primitive man. For primitives, the world consists of a bewildering array of sensual phenomena that cannot be subsumed into a unity since such people do not possess the ability to generalize experience or abstract common qualities from it. In the absence of such stable fixed points of reference, the primitive tends to be overwhelmed by, or caught in the web of, the multiple separate sensations that wash over him. For Kien, the root of the problem lies in an incorrect naming, and with Ernst Cassirer, he points to the power of reason to overcome this error. Cassirer describes an intellectualized representation of the world in which "the direct grasp gives way to new and different types of acquisition, of theoretical and practical domination: man has entered the path from physical to conceptual 'grasping' (from *Greifen* to *Begreifen*)."[57] Cassirer's belief in the powers of reason does not, of course, extend to such extremes as Kien's. The novelistic scholar substitutes a myth of reason for the primitive myths he despises, reaching by this inversion of myth, a curiously similar final result. Like the primitive man described by Cassirer, Kien somehow conceives of the word as identical to the thing it stands for. As primitive man expects to attract animals through the magic of a hieroglyph depicting them, so too for Kien, a word is not a mere rhetorical device, but the concrete and exact representation that will call up the thing it names. He has power over objects and concepts because he can name them. Kien can literally grasp concepts as he grasps the books that contain them in their printed pages.

A deep belief in the power of words—not just words in the vernacular but those inscribed in the taxonomic orders of a dead language—permits Kien several interesting options for exercising his power over language (and therefore over the world). He can block out unwelcome intrusions, such as that of his housekeeper, through his facility for selective blindness, and he can actually make the abhorred presence disappear by killing her in his mind, through words, and blotting her out of his conscious life. Moreover, as he extends the linguistic distinctions from his library to the outside world, he is able to mingle the two realms without any check on his invention. Books come to life, and reality imitates art. Thus he neither sees nor hears the pigeons on his daily walks, effectively walling himself off from contact with extraneous elements he had not yet put into words. On his first walk after an enforced six week rest following a beating administered by his wife, he is in an unusually receptive mood. He notices the pigeons and hears their cooing for the first time: "For twenty years he had not heard these sounds; every day on his morning walk he passed this spot. Yet cooing was well known to him out of books. 'Quite so!' he said softly, and nodded as he always did when he found reality bearing out the printed original" (p. 123). The vast compendium of knowledge that Kien had extracted from books has brought no wisdom. The word does not describe reality but precedes it. There is, in fact, no reality beyond the mediation of language, and mental concepts can be made to exclude experience. The grim dedication and rigid perseverance with which Kien maintains this illusion demonstrate his self-assertive blindness, his will to power.

The episode of the pigeons is followed by other similar examples. Life copies art once again when, in another excursion into the outside world, he suddenly "becomes fully conscious of the word 'Roses'" (p. 246). This word, like the cooing of the pigeons remembered from his books, brings about an instant recollection of their context in the printed texts he studies: "he took one of the roses . . . remembered their sweet smell which he knew from Persian love poetry, and raised them to his eyes; it was true, they did smell" (p. 246). It is important that Kien confirms the smell of the roses by lifting them, not to his nose, but to his *eyes*. It is a reaction similar to his recognition of the cooing sound made by pigeons. Kien gives no credence to the idea that his ears might be involved in the earlier sensual perception. For him, the essential (and only) sense is that of sight, since it is the only sense he requires for his studies.

It is, then, not surprising that Kien's money and energy are devoted to the preservation of the written word. In the absence of his private library in the flat, the mad scholar dedicates himself to a new endeavor—that of rescuing books from the unhappy confines of the pawnshop (or Theresianum). These books, unlike his own, are imprisoned under a broiling roof with no one to care for their needs. His life once again has purpose: "His first task was to ransom the unhappy books, his second to reform a bestial mankind" (p. 219). The order of these two goals is important; for Kien, the rescue of the books is a necessary prior condition without which the second task can never be attempted. The inviolability of books ensures the salvation of mankind. He is aided and abetted in his first task (but not his second) by the sly maneuvers of the hunchbacked dwarf, Fischerle. By his serene and simpleminded idealism, Kien stands as a virtual Don Quixote to the earthy, debauched dwarf. In a scene that closely parallels similar scenes of knightly courage in

Don Quixote, Kien takes up a militant stand in the entrance to the pawnshop, determined to rescue the defenseless books from that hell, as Fischerle and his accomplices pander to his obsession by re-selling him the same packet of books over and over again.

Yet this part-time pimp, full-time confidence man has, like San-cho Panza, his own idealistic streak. Fischerle dreams of chess as Kien dreams of books, and in what is perhaps the scholar's only as-tute observation on another human being, Kien recognizes this. "Chess is his library," he realizes (p. 185), and it is, though not ex-actly in the manner Kien envisions. Fischerle's dream of becoming the greatest chess master in the world is linked, as Kien's dream of books is not, to concrete visions of worldly success. In this, Fischer-le's dreams are not unlike Therese's dreams of success and love, and Fischerle and Therese are further associated by their affection for the telltale color blue, which, in this novel, stands for greed. With the money he steals from Kien, Fischerle buys a coat, choosing "a colour which reconciled the yellow of his shoes to the black of his hat, a bright blue" (p. 353). His fantasies of becoming a chess grand master, like Therese's dreams of love, are connected to visions of becoming a millionaire, at which time "he'd buy eleven more shirts, all blue" (p. 355).

Williams, like Kien, embarks upon a course of action intended to encompass the salvation of mankind through the salvation of books. He is, of course, less naive, less simplistic, less idealistic in his ap-proach. His preservation of fragments and his burning of the books indicate an obsession less extreme than Kien's but similar in form. Through poetic inspiration, Williams breathes spirit once again into the dead words. The resistance of the books to the wind of his fertilizing breath is analogous to the resistance of the virgin to the whoring by her husband ("Haven't you forgot your virgin purpose, / the language?" he asks, to which the female voice responds, "What language? 'The past is for those who / lived in the past,' is all she told me." [p. 187]), and the resistance of the poet's world to the will's forward thrust in its drive to mastery. Riddel finds that, for Williams, "art is not the incarnation of the new Word, but a repeti-tion of old words violently broken free from their 'text,' the old dream of presence."[58] In this manner the poet can justify his use of fragments, the violent wrenching of excerpts from their context.

The poet visits the library attempting to derive "spirit" and inspiration from the books of the past, only to find that they are corpses. His song, like that of the African women of the Ibibio tribe, is meant to extract fertility from a corpse (pp. 143–44), or to re-inspire the corpses of books with the breath of life and song. Williams's fragmentation of the books is necessary in order to give his own language a name and a voice against the background of the silence of the library and the meaningless noise of the falls: "The words have to be rebricked up, the / —what? What am I coming to ./ pouring down?" (p. 143).

In contrast to Kien's bestowal of primacy to the eyes, Williams gives primacy to the ear. His poem operates not on the basis of a sight-blindness spectrum but one of noise-silence. Somewhere in the conjunction of these opposites Williams's own will to power impels him to mend the divorce in song:

> What language could allay our thirsts,
> what words lift us, what floods bear us
> > > past defeats
> but song but deathless song ?
> . . . .
> Who am I?
>
> > > > —the voice! (p. 107)

The power of the poet to breathe life into dead words is recognized and praised by Emerson, for whom poetic perception (sight) gives words and symbols new power, "putting eyes and a tongue into every dumb and inanimate object."[59] The poet is empowered to accomplish this because he, more than a mere librarian or archivist, is the original creator as well as the caretaker of language: "The poets made all the words, and therefore language is the archives of history, and, if we must say it, a sort of tomb of the muses."[60] Emerson's observation is too strikingly similar to Williams's practice to be ignored. For Williams as well, the poet is the master of language, the word-smith who creates new life through his ear and breath, cross-fertilizing the dead words and symbols, impregnating the muses whom he has, by virtue of his power, brought forth from the

Hades of the library shelves. Says Joyce, "In the buginning is the woid, in the muddle is the sounddance,"[61] and Williams answers in true Dionysian spirit, expressing his will to power in the interplay of death and life, yet cloaking it with the Apollonian measure:

> We know nothing and can know nothing .
> > but
> to dance, to dance to a measure
> contrapuntally,
> > Satyrically, the tragic foot. (p. 239)

For Kien, who does not hear pigeons or smell flowers except as they are given to him in books, the measure is all, and he cannot imagine a counterpoint rhythm. Williams is more vividly aware of the interaction of the mythical with the ordinary stuff of reality. In the measure and the counterpoint, Williams indicates that myth is not extraneous to reality but that we live coterminously with myth and symbol all the time. Furthermore, just as the counterpoint sets up a contrast to the basic measure, so too destruction accompanies the work of creation.

In Williams's poetics, reality does not conform to the words set down in books. Reality is the green plant that persistently subverts (and is subverted by) the language of poetry. The green of healthy growth and the green of putrefaction come together in the living, livid green of the bud. It is a mode of existence that the poet imitates in his contrapuntal, "satyrical" dance. Living writing approaches death while acting as a counterpoint to the already written. Writing, says Riddel, "becomes a kind of drunkenness or madness"[62]—a Dionysian frenzy of creation and destruction. Language comes out at random, obedient only to the imagination's free play, destroying and remaking the written words of the past.

One of the more important symbols of this free play of the imagination upon created forms and its consequences is the bottle found in the library fire. The bottle, shaped by man and imprinted with his thought, has become a solidifed reflection of that thought—a geometrical object obedient to human rationalization. In the bottle, nature is controlled and harnessed to man's purpose, essential elements are shaped by fire into useful, symmetrical shapes that resist

further transformations. Yet the poet is able to take this rationalized shape, and by submitting it once more to the fires of his invention, annul its power to resist. Bachelard, in his book, *The Psychoanalysis of Fire*, quotes D'Annunzio on a similar creative frenzy
experienced while contemplating "the shining vases, still slaves of
fire, still under its power." He continues, "Later, the beautiful frail
creatures would abandon their father, . . . they would grow cold
. . . would lead their new life in the world, enter the service of plea-
sure-seeking men, . . . follow the variations in light, receive the cut
flower or the intoxicating drink."[63] The bottle, removed from the
creative fires, grows hard and dies, becoming a mere receptacle for
the living (dying) flowers of that liquid fire, the firewater that precedes the Dionysian festival. A similar connection is made by Williams. The flame of invention touches the written word, the poet
consumes alcohol, the bottle itself is intoxicated by the flames:

> The night was made day by the flames, flames
> on which he fed—grubbing the page
> (the burning page)
> like a worm—for enlightenment
>
> Of which we drink and are drunk and in the end
> are destroyed (as we feed)
> . . . .
> A bottle, mauled
> by the flames, belly-bent with laughter;
> yellow, green. So be it—of drunkenness
> survived, in guffaws of flame. All fire afire! (p. 117)

The drunken bottle, unbottled in the fires of its own Dionysian self-
immolation, is reshaped by the yellow and green living flames and
reimprinted with the rainbow colors of the new flame as it is "reflowered" by another creative imagination. Only in the fire does the
bottle gain life; once it has cooled it dies and becomes merely another empty cavern, another book.

It is a testimonial to man's Apollonian aspirations that he cannot
tolerate the beauty of the unbottled bottle. The poet, like the others,
seeks to separate the living sexuality of the bottle from that of the

fire. It is an identity "from which / we shrink squirting little hoses of / objection—and / I along with the rest, squirting / at the fire / Poet" (p. 120). The poet applies his own poor sexuality to the joyous sexuality of leaping flames, his poetic prowess to the poetry of fire.

The heat of the fire that created the rainbow light in the bottle also served as the instrument to separate the radiant gist from the uranium atom. The light of radium, like that of the bottle, is inseparable in the poet's mind from the fire that brought it into being. Both are unstable, living elemental forces, most beautiful when in an advanced state of decomposition. Living once again is identified implicitly with lividness.

Throughout the poem, Williams returns again and again to the image of radium. Like the radii of a circle that extend out from the center like the spokes of a wheel, as if defining that center and holding it in place, Williams's predilection for the radium image serves as a similar radius of pure energy, defining and locating the objects that compose his poetic ground. But while the radium/radius is the center for his ruminations, it is a highly unstable center. The beautiful thing, the bottle unbottled, the radiant gist, exist only in transition and are endlessly elusive. As the poet works to strip away the impurities from these rare and precious elements he finds that what was obscured was not any single object he can grasp but rather a pure potentiality, an energy node revealed as light. The poet as well, by his absent presence in the poem, approaches the state of radium as a centered function. Says Derrida, "I believe that the center is a function, not a being—a reality, but a function. And this function is absolutely indispensable. The subject is absolutely indispensable."[64] Similarly, for Williams, every place reveals, if trouble be taken to penetrate surface impurities, the radiant gist that illuminates it. The radium becomes an ordering principle and the supreme aspect of the poet's will to power. Each thing is mirrored in and illuminated by the subjectivity of the poet, an insight shared by Wallace Stevens:

> The moon rose in the mind and each thing there
> Picked up its radial aspect in the night,
> Prostrate below the singleness of its will.

That which was public green turned private grey.
At another time, the radial aspect came
From a different source. But there was always one[65]

For Williams, as for Stevens, the radiant aspect is determined by the imposition of will. Therefore, it is not timeless or eternal, like an archetype, but varied in relation to the field from which it is recovered and to the poet who accomplishes the recovery. The radiant gist functions much on the order of a metaphysical filing system by which the particulars are integrated into a new dynamic system that preserves life by constantly revising itself toward death.

Whereas Williams aspires to the condition of light, Kien moves in the opposite direction. His goal is to turn himself into something opaque and unassimilable like a statue. In his obduracy, he turns his craft against himself to take up his stand at a distance from other human beings and make himself impenetrable.

Kien's true opposite and double in the novel is not Therese, or Fischerle, or George, but a character that is glimpsed only briefly, a patient of the psychiatrist's known only as the "gorilla." While Kien withdraws from people and their environment in an excess of egoism, the gorilla's ego is dispersed throughout his environment. He is as fluid and metamorphic as Kien is rigid and unchanging. Where Kien's powers lie in emotionless abstraction, the gorilla merges subject and object, investing his surroundings with his own emotions. The gorilla shares with Kien the overwhelming concern with language, but he "hates the French language. . . . He's been working for years on one of his own" (p. 403), in contrast with Kien for whom the precise use of language and concepts is crucial to his work and his life. For Kien, language is literature; for the gorilla, it is speech. Kien lives in the dry, statue world of books and fixed identities; the gorilla lives in a green, metamorphic world of universal intermingling. To Kien's obsession with the proper name, he counters with a nameless flux of emotion: "The two rooms and their contents were dissolved in a magnetic field of passions. Objects . . . had no special names. They were called according to the mood in which they floated. Their faces altered for the gorilla, who lived a wild, tense, stormy life. His life communicated itself to them, they had an active part in it" (p. 403). In gratitude to the sublime wisdom of the gorilla, the psychiatrist wisely renounces a cure that would have taken the patient from his marvelous, magic, synthetic world and replaced him in the dry, analytic life common to such as Peter Kien. Nevertheless, the option presented by the gorilla is not truly open to the sane, since the gorilla, despite his "magic participation" in his surroundings, exists permanently on the brink of chaos and cannot be released into society at large.

Neither is the metamorphic existence of the gorilla truly an alternative for the work of art, as Williams well recognizes. The unity with his environment and meaningful human contact of the gorilla's life are similar to the attractions offered to the poet by the formless flames and the radiant gist. Yet Williams realizes, as the gorilla does not, that for art to exist the form must be circumscribed by the measure or it will constantly be breaking down from the fluidity of light to the dullness of lead.

In their separate madnesses, the madness of fluidity and the madness of ridigity, the gorilla and Kien approach each other. Each is deeply and primarily concerned with the problems of linguistic expression, obsessed with the difficulties of adopting an appropriate name for the objects that surround them. Kien chooses words of perfect clarity, whose solid immobility expresses his own striving for monumentality. The gorilla, on the other hand, chooses the language of emotion, where the purity of gesture indicates his preference for the transitoriness of speech. Both choices show a studied unambiguity that, at its worst, cannot be distinguished from the brutal mechanization of the same that afflicts the "sane" members of an industrialized society.

The psychiatrist himself, seeing the madness of mechanized sanity, is motivated by an admiration of and a longing for insanity. He escapes as much as possible from the solipsism of sanity into the solipsism of madness by interring himself in his own library (or asylum) of madmen. In what is very nearly an exact reversal of his brother's obsession with books, George ruminates on his own investment in people: "One half of their vast paternal inheritance was locked up in dead tomes, the other in a lunatic asylum. Which half had been better used?" (p. 451). George does not share his brother's love for books—he has had enough of literature in his days as a gynecologist: "Reading was fondling, was another form of love, was for ladies and ladies' doctors, to whose profession a delicate understanding of *lecture intime* properly belonged" (p. 398). Literature he regarded in much the same light as his brother did ordinary life; it possessed for George a deadly sameness with no power to attract him. But where Peter's self-centeredness gives him a feeling of power and superiority, George's hunger for the countless rapid transformations that madness allows strips him of will, leaving him with no self of his own outside the roles he has adopted for his patients. He lives for them as Kien lives for his books, seeking in them the same nourishment and finding in their variety the unacknowledged reinforcement of sameness.

While George combats the mechanization of society by willing himself back into the haven of his asylum-library, Peter Kien, its embodied essence, must discover another way of escape. Just as the masses in Vienna were impelled to burn Justice, so too is Kien impelled by the urge to become that most metamorphic of elements— fire. First, the hard, utilitarian face of the Theresianum disappears in flames, then his own machinelike face is sacrificed. Throughout the novel, the word "fire" and the dream of fire exist for Kien in a tension of attraction and repulsion, a tension that is finally resolved as the termites maddened by love merge with the rebellious books: "Termites eat wood and books. The love riot among the termites. FIRE IN THE LIBRARY" (p. 459). Kien, the most lonely of men, is made even more lonely after his restitution to the reassembled library. Everything seems as it was, but the books, like termites maddened by love, refuse to obey his commands. Instead, they rise in rebellion against him: "A letter detaches itself from the first line and hits him a blow on the head. Letters are lead. It hurts. . . . A footnote kicks him. . . . Lines and whole pages come clattering on to him. They shake and beat him" (p. 463). Kien counters the passion of the books with a fire of his own, destroying their sanctuary as the invading red ants destroy the termite colony. Kien, the lonely scholar who thought he was and always would remain the same, brings about the ultimate metamorphosis of himself and his world by reducing it to ashes. Says Bachelard, "Death in the flame is the least lonely of deaths. It is truly a cosmic death in which a whole universe is reduced to nothingness along with the thinker."[66] In order to escape from the love riot among his books, Kien meets their fire with one of his own, both meeting their ends in the transfiguring embrace of the flames.

In *The Great American Novel*, Williams describes the challenge of the American artist as the need to rush into the fire and continues: "What is literature anyway but suffering recorded in palpitating syllables?"[67] The key here is the fire, which, like Kien's, confronts the dynamic words with the incarnate, yet transcendent, metamorphic qualities of flame. As Williams says in *Paterson*, his dream is just such a fiery transformation in the embrace of flames: "The person submerged / in wonder; the fire become the person" (p. 122). To escape destruction the poet must embrace it, to endure the flames he must become one with them.

In the presence of fire, each thing merges with its opposite. Kien, the archenemy of change, becomes the instrument of metamorphosis. Williams, the proponent of marriage, institutionalizes divorce (woman from man, books from the poet, the radiant gist and the lead from the uranium). Opposites are sharply differentiated—and they are indistinguishable. Like the photon in modern physics that is sometimes seen as a particle and other times as a wave, two mutually exclusive forms can define a single phenomenon. The confusion of language around such inexplicable natural manifestations seems designed to give proper names to unnamable processes, to develop a symbolic language to say, as Beckett would, what cannot be said.

At one extreme, the merging described by Williams and undertaken by Kien leads to an impossible androgynous presence. Thus Kien, helpless under the battering of his books, becomes feminized in his weakness, calling out for his brother George, the gynecologist cum psychiatrist. Paterson, the double male, both father and son, is feminized in contrast to the powerful mannish Corydon and transformed into an impotent, old-womanish man. In Phyllis, the object of both their lusts, the virginal silence of the page upon which the poet sows the seminal seeds of his language is transformed into the whored silence of the library, scarred, broken by whips, but still exerting the undeniable attraction of her beauty. Williams seems to concede regretfully that such divorces and destructive transformations are necessary to the regeneration of creativity. There is for Williams no return to the mythical original innocence of the garden. Like the bottle in the flames, all the poet can hope for with his destructive-constructive fires is to break down an unnatural form allowing it to reflower into a beautiful transitory shape that is, itself, a perversion.

This pursuit of transitory beauty, however, commits the poet to the quest for the inseminating trace. Perhaps because of the very incompleteness of the poet's task of healing the divorce, he is powerfully drawn to the few integrated images he allows the reader to glimpse: the African wife and Madame Curie. Both women are sexually potent and learned in the ways of fire, cleansed from taint by means of their potency but with a curiously androgynous, hidden side to their natures, visible primarily in their assumption of power in their relationships to the less potent males.

A sequence of three quotes from three different authors may help to summarize and clarify the relationships between the phenomenon of light as it is perceived by man's optical nerve and limitations of sight and sexuality that are necessary to the production of a work of art. The first is from Friedrich Nietzsche: "For both art and life depend wholly on the laws of optics, on perspective and illusion; both, to be blunt, depend on the necessity of error."[68] Second, Sigmund Freud transforms this error into an anxiety that is linked to sexuality: "A study of dreams, phantasies and myths has taught us that a morbid anxiety with going blind is often enough a substitute for the dread of castration."[69] Third, Jacques Derrida makes of this probable cause a necessary condition: "I believe that the risk of sterility and of sterilization has always been the price of lucidity."[70] In the first quote, Nietzsche points to the selective blindness that is the province of artistic endeavor; in the second, Freud finds that the limitation of sight for whatever reason can represent the loss of manhood; and in the third, Derrida brings the two together: the price of lucidity is sterility. Art, blindness, symbolic castration— these are three themes that are linked implicitly to the threat of fire (and of women) by Williams, more explicitly by Canetti.

These themes parallel, furthermore, the earlier Foucaultian triad discussed in the opening pages of this chapter; that of parody, dissociation, and sacrifice. Art is fundamentally a parodic genre, implicitly directed against reality in its presumption of an overlapping artistic (fictive) reality. Blindness as practiced by Kien is an obviously dissociative mode. The mad scholar confirms his identity by hiding it under the mask of willed blindness and the no less rigid mask of his own machinelike face. This blindness is parallel to the blindness of books described by Williams in the library scene. Such metaphoric blindness is a fitting precursor to the sacrifice that must follow—a sacrificial moment that entails the loss of sexual potency with the loss of the books.

For Kien, despite the enforced blindness that prevents him from seeing outside, the eye is all. He depends upon his eyes for his work and guards them carefully against indiscriminate use. He sees nothing of the outside world in his daily walks except what he chooses to see, believing that his capacity for work, his lucidity, is improved by this voluntary blindness. Nevertheless, while he abhors the indiscriminate use of sight as a distraction, he finds the confrontation with actual, physical blindness horrible. In the first chapter of the novel, while on his morning walk, Kien happens to notice a blind man and his dog. He disassociates himself from the unpleasant sight, protecting his own eyes by assuming the man is a fraud. Kien is forced to relinquish his assumption when he hears the blind man warmly thank a small boy when a button the boy threw in the blind man's extended hat clinks against the coins it contains with a metallic sound. The shock galvanizes Kien, stimulating a reexamination of the virtues of the eye as an infallible organ when compared to the weaker, less discriminating ear. Kien decides that he will kill himself if he is ever threatened by blindness. For Kien the loss of any other sensory organ would be a minor disruption, perhaps even a blessing. But the loss of sight! Kien determines to follow the example of Eratosthenes, the great librarian of Alexandria, who starved himself to death when he could no longer read his books (p. 22)—a fitting end for a scholar, to starve the body when the mind goes hungry.

The situation changes somewhat when the hated housekeeper invades his sanctuary. In reaction to her presence, Kien sacrifices his most vital organ, castrating himself as it were, to protect his mind as he cannot protect his rooms from her presence. Kien practices longer and longer periods of blindness, shutting out in a deliberate amnesia all signs of Therese and her hated furniture. Rather than being diminished by this loss of sight, he feels charged with a new power: "Learning flourished. Theses sprouted from the writing desk like mushrooms." Soon, the blindness adopted out of necessity acquires a theory and a justification: "Blindness is a weapon against time and space; our being is one vast blindness save only for that little circle which our mean intelligence . . . can illumine." He concludes from this that "it is his right to apply that blindness, which protects him from the excesses of the senses, to every disturbing element in his life." Finally, his newfound lucidity allows him to dismiss the existence of Therese and her furniture with a flick of philosophical analysis: "to be is to be perceived. What I do not perceive, does not exist. . . . Whence, with cogent logic, it was proved that Kien was in no wise deceiving himself" (p. 71). The sterilizing lucidity described by Derrida and the optical errors of Nietzsche combine to define Kien's reaction to the invasion of his senses by the castrating woman he married in an earlier, metaphorical, moment of blindness. The rationalization of willed blindness takes the place of suicide, providing a clear example of the way perceptual errors produce a figurative blindness and a loss of power.

This voluntary blindness contrasts with that of the secondary character, the blind man (perhaps the same one suspected by Kien of being a fraud in the first chapter of the novel). Kien adopts a voluntary blindness to aid in focusing his sight on his work. The "blind" man of the Stars of Heaven, who like Kien is not really blind, suffers from the opposite dilemma. His work is dependent upon sightlessness, and not only is he forced to endure the humiliation of thanking people for buttons thrown into his hat instead of coins, he is a compulsive voyeur—an extremely inconvenient neurosis in a supposed blind man. The paths of Kien and the blind man cross repeatedly in the novel as the bookman and the button-man confront each other in the entrance hall of the pawnshop on a daily basis as part of Fischerle's scam. But while Kien goes back to the hotel to unpack his beloved books from his head, the blind man uses his ill-gotten gains to purchase the services of the fattest prostitute he can find, blessing his "luck" with women as a compensation for the degradations of his seeming blindness. The trajectories of the two characters are exactly opposite. The pretend blind man is a voyeur, irrational, oriented toward sensual and sexual gratification. Kien, the truly blind man, adopts the shield of voluntary blindness so that he need see nothing, uses his powerful mind for the errors of self-delusion, and substitutes the surfaces of books for any other sensual pleasure. The blindness of an excessively lucid mind does indeed lead to sterility, and no phoenix arises from the flames it lights.

CHAPTER **6**

Women in the Library

IT IS CLEAR that the burning of the library entails more than a love/hate relationship to the written word, however important that component might be. Kien's linking of the love orgy of the termites and the fire in the library and the *Paterson* poet's efforts to quench the library fire with streams of urine point to another, sexualized aspect. Bachelard reminds us that the psychology of the pyromaniac is deeply imbued with frustrated sexual tendencies.[1] Freud points out the perverse nature of man's desire to exercise control over fire:

It is as though primary man had the habit, when he came in contact with fire, of satisfying an infantile desire connected with it, by putting it out with a stream of his urine. The legends that we possess leave us no doubt about the originally phallic view taken of tongues of flame as they shoot upwards. Putting out fire by micturating . . . was therefore a kind of sexual act with a male, an enjoyment of sexual potency in a homosexual competition. . . . It is remarkable, too, how regularly analytic experience testifies to the connection between ambition, fire and urethral eroticism.[2]

The relationship between ambition, fire, and a perverse eroticism reflects a psychopathology that involves social, metaphysical, and moral components. In the library, each one of these aspects is submitted to the double operation of another, superimposed, reality: that of writing and that of the criticism of that writing. Each written work is an attempt to conquer that triple pathology, each critical act is a revelation of passion reflecting on an attraction that is both religious (sacrilegious) and erotic (perverse) to the work of art. The social obsession of ambition, the metaphysical attraction to fire, and the moral component of eroticism metaphorically reveal the burning, blinding madness that afflicts the librarian.

Bachelard makes an important point in this respect. He refers to the sexualization of alchemy in a reflection that applies equally well to libraries: "We must not lose sight of the fact that alchemy is uniquely a science engaged in by men, by bachelors, by men without women, by initiates cut off from normal human relationships in favor of a strictly masculine society. . . . Its doctrine of fire is strongly polarized by unsatisfied desires."[3] Immortality was sought in the perversion of minerals, and the pleasure derived from the alchemists' work was independent of cults of religion and utilitarianism.

The immortality sought by the caretakers of books is more abstract; it is found in the immortality (immorality) of literature and is called "literary studies." The pleasure derived from the librarians' work of criticism, thus, stems from the triple transgression described earlier, of social, metaphysical, and moral perversion. Ambition (desire) is deplored as vulgar and commonplace. Fire is tabooed. Sexuality is suppressed in a manner that is equivalent to self-mutilation.

Freud considers the suppression of man's rage to extinguish the flames to be a sign of his control over fire, and thus, "by damping down the fire of his own sexual excitation, he had tamed the natural force of fire."[4] That is, by renouncing control over fire and giving the care of the flames into the hands of women, he controls and channels his own sexual desires into more socially and morally accepted outlets.

There is a further twist, however, since the librarian rejects these socially acceptable channels, funneling his passion, his creative fire, back into books. The book, written by men and perceived as male, becomes the body that receives this passion; the library space is the womb in which this creativity comes to fruition. The "strictly mas-culine society" is perversely sexualized. The librarian perceives him-self as a father-authoritarian figure in the library; the books are al-ternately his dead fathers, his living sons, his homosexual partners. The burning of the library, that most feared of all possible occur-rences, becomes practically inevitable in such a context.

Since the librarian's own immortality is ensured only if the books he uses and the books he writes are preserved for his heirs, he must repress that part of him that is drawn to fire, emphasizing only the living, spermatic stream that cancels and controls the flames. One flame must die so that the other can survive. But the librarian must, like a woman, tend the flames carefully since his own survival de-pends on allowing *none* of the books to slip into death. Books are bodies, are flames, are lovers; they are also desexualized dead ob-jects. Among such confusions the librarians make their home. They structure the feelings they experience in their encounter with books and use them to reaffirm the body's naturalness and reality. In this way the books, which are dead objects, are made to come alive through the exertion of the librarians' will. Such a powerful effort of will cannot be constantly maintained—books slip back into the object-world and living beings are, willy-nilly, carried along with them. Furthermore, in this willed denial of the unreality of books there is something necessarily perverse, as Roland Barthes openly admits when he speaks of the "perverse bliss of words"[5] and calls the text an anagram of the erotic body.[6] The librarian is not a liber-tine but a necrophiliac.

This perversity is compounded when we remember that the bliss of words is an incestuous pleasure, its eroticism derived from the use/misuse of the mother tongue. It is, furthermore, frequently a sa-distic pleasure, as William Carlos Williams recognizes. He signals and admires "a dry beauty of the page— / beaten by whips."[7] Herein, perhaps, lies the key to the confusions and perversities of the love/hate relationship that leads to the burning of books. Asks Freud, "Is it not plausible to suppose that this sadism is in fact a death instinct which, under the influence of the narcissistic libido, has been forced away from the ego and has consequently only emerged in relation to the object? It now enters the service of the sexual function."[8] In the librarians, the sexual instinct itself has been suppressed, leaving the desire for immortality to enter into the service of Thanatos. Further, the horror of mirrors that is so common to the librarians studied here, is in fact related to their narcissism. They do not want to see their human face, which is, as Freud reminds us in reference to the child's mirror game, *fort* and *da*. Their narcissism is reflected in the books which they are and which they will become. The books are both subject and object; the librarians are books and books are the objects of their forbidden affection. But the eternal presence of the books—which contradicts their own bodily present—becomes intolerable. The love they feel for themselves (their books) and the hatred they feel toward their books (their bodies) erupt in a sadism toward the objects of their love and in literal or figurative suicide.

The writing and the reading are interrupted, however. A woman penetrates the reserve of masculinity; the keeper of the fire enters the place where fire is disallowed, creating in the librarian a metaphoric urinary compulsion, a desire to quench the fire she carries within her. The apparition of such blatant sexuality in the library comes as something of a shock to the librarian and familiar boundaries slip away. The homey room/womb of the library becomes associated with that other feminine, thus fiery, womb. The male is enthralled by the female; the reading cannot continue. The revelation of the sexuality behind the library becomes apparent, and the librarian falls out of books into . . . What? Foucault gives us a hint:

> Perhaps the emergence of sexuality in our culture is an "event" of multiple values: it is tied to the death of God and to the ontological void which his death has fixed at the limit of our thought; it is also tied to the still silent and groping apparition of a form of thought in which the interrogation of the limit replaces the search for totality and the act of transgression replaces the movement of contradictions. Finally, it involves the questioning of language by language. . . . On the day that sexuality began to speak and to be spoken, language no longer served as a veil for the infinite; and in the thickness it acquired on that day, we now experience finitude and being. In its dark domain, we now encounter the absence of God, our death, limits, and their transgression.[9]

Thus, while in one sense the librarians' desire can be located in the death wish as mediated through the Other, which is the same as the Self, in another sense the origin of desire resides in language.

For Jacques Lacan also, the origin of desire can be found in language. In his famous essay, "The Insistence of the Letter in the Unconscious," he finds that "the speaking subject, if he seems to be thus a slave of language, is all the more so of a discourse in the universal moment of which he finds himself at birth, even if only by the dint of his proper name."[10] This emphasis on the introduction to language at birth with the bestowal of a *proper* name is indicative of a tendency throughout Lacan's work to use great caution in employing names of any sort and to be impatient with those who attach a lesser importance to "wording." He cites the case of another analyst who "is amazed by the fact of having obtained an entirely different result in the interpretation of one and the same resistance by the use . . . of the term 'need for love' instead of and in place of 'demand for love.'"[11] Lacan suggests that the amazement and confusion of the author with the results of such a careless use of the English language reflect back on his own ego (his own proper name). In both the phrases above, "love" is the mediating factor, and by not recognizing the difference between the two statements of need and demand, Lacan indicates that "this writer can push his practice of analysis to the limits of a nonsensical stuttering." Lacan defines these terms much more strictly, insisting that " 'need' and 'demand' have a diametrically opposed sense for the subject, and to hold that their use can be confused even for an instant amounts to a radical failure to recognize the 'intimation' of the Word."[12] Lacan amplifies this distinction in later works, indicating that "need" attaches itself to an object and is satisfied by it, while "demand" is the sign of an unsatisfied quest. Desire, like the word "love" in the earlier example, mediates between need and demand, partaking of some aspects of each.[13] Thus a child, on his introduction to language, quickly learns to translate his felt needs into demands, and in the shift from felt bodily needs into the abstract medium of language desire has its origin. For Lacan, therefore, desire is, in a sense, a translation factor. This distinction is not unique to Lacan, however. It was made centuries earlier, in related terms, by Giambattista Vico:

A man is properly only mind, body and speech, and speech stands as it were midway between mind and body. Hence . . . the certain began in mute times with the body. Then when the so-called articulate languages were invented, it advanced to ideas. . . . And finally, when our human reason was fully developed, it reached its end in the true. . . . This truth is a formula . . . which like light, informs in all the minutest details of their surface the opaque bodies of the facts over which it is diffused.[14]

Vico is obviously much more optimistic than Lacan about the possibility for a perfect conjunction of body (need), speech (demand), and mind (desire). Yet even for Vico, the truth, which illuminates the surface, does not penetrate into the interior of the opaque objects so revealed. Although he does not say so directly, in this realization Vico expresses the genesis of the alienation of the signifier and the signified that occurs when words *illuminate*, but no longer stand in the place of things as in primitive thought. For primitives, desire is theoretically nonoperative. Since words and things are perceived as equivalent, the mechanism of translation does not interrupt the flow between need and demand. Man needs because he has a body, he demands because he has language, but only desires when he is split between the two.

The alienation between need and demand becomes more acute in more advanced societies, paradoxically causing the two concepts to draw together in their perceived abstraction, until trained observers like Ernst Kris, the analyst referred to by Lacan, can no longer distinguish the concrete differences between them and are reduced to a stammering text. The dictionary and the library become necessary in such a forgetful society since they force memory back to linguistic distinctions in what could be considered the revenge of the proper name. This case is made with clarity and great good humor by Gabriel García Márquez's account of the progress of the plague of forgetfulness in the town of Macondo. In the beginning of the plague, the people of the town carefully marked each thing with its proper name; table, chair, bed, and so forth. As the forgetfulness became more acute, the simple identification of word and thing was no longer sufficient, and the production of texts began: "This is the

cow, it is necessary to milk it every morning so that it might produce milk and the milk must be boiled in order to mix it with coffee
and make coffee with milk."[15] Even abstract concepts and senti-
ments were recorded on such placards, with somewhat less success.
Inevitably, José Arcadio comes up with the idea of collecting these
texts in a "memory machine"—a library—that would allow him to
"review each morning and from the beginning to the end the totality of all the knowledge acquired in life."[16] Where other distinctions
seem to be fading in the plague of forgetfulness, the mediating force
of desire continues operable and is strengthened in respect to the
weakening of the other two poles. Desire is in the middle, making a
link between that which is foreign and that which is of the self. It is
the link, but ironically, at the same time it precludes any hope of
ever satisfying the longing to become one with the other that is the
motivating force of the desire. History, or the library, becomes, as
Françoise Gaillard reminds us in reference to an episode in *Bouvard
and Pécuchet*, "a neutral space where bits and pieces of a past for-
ever-gone accumulate. Its memory is full of holes, as though it were
attacked by a selective amnesia. . . . The text it stammers out is like
a vocabulary devoid of syntax."[17]

The further danger in this loss of the ability to make correlations
between objects, events, and concepts, says Lacan, is that of the
subject's "capture in an objectification no less Imaginary than before—of his static state or of his 'statue,' in a renewed status of his
alienation."[18] This alienation is unrolled in society, in history, as are
all other works of man, and Lacan finds the cure for this alienation—and the plague of forgetfulness—in a recuperation of history
that conjoins the Viconian emphasis on the revelation of truth with
the Foucaultian recognition of the importance of monuments and
documents in the movement of history:

> The unconscious is that chapter of my history which is
> marked by a blank or occupied by a falsehood; it is the cen-
> sored chapter. But the Truth can be found again; it is most
> often written down elsewhere. That is to say:
> —in monuments: this is my body. . . .
> —in archival documents also: these are my childhood memo-

ries, just as impenetrable as are such documents when I do not know their source.[19]

This truth is found through the motivating force of desire that is an irreducible manifestation of history, operating in and against the historical grounding. Desire is in perpetual osmosis with the animal (bodily) needs—the monumentalization, or "capture in objectification"—and the historical world as preserved in language, in documents. It is also in perpetual contradiction, and for this reason the domains of need and demand cannot be reduced to a single category, nor can they be used to explain totally the workings of desire.

The objectification is essential, for desire must have a static object. It is a social act that requires the presence of a lover and a beloved, even though the beloved is sometimes symbolic, or passive, or even imaginary. In terms of the child's game with the mirror, the pleasure and delight of mastery depend on the perception of the objectified presence in the mirror. Without the reflected "other" child, there is no desire. But this objectified child is not a concrete person but a shadow figure—the image of the child's desire. It is a desire, furthermore, that is displaced from an original desire for the absent mother. Anthony Wilden summarizes and amplifies Lacan's statement of the central issue of the relation between desire and desire of the other:

> The Other is not a person, but a principle. . . . According to Lacan, the Other . . . is the only place from which it is permissible to say, "I am who I am." The paradox of identity and autonomy which this involves—identical to or identified with what?—puts us in the position of desiring what the Other desires: we desire what the Other desires we desire. We therefore desire to TAKE THE PLACE of the Other in desire. When all is said and done, then, we do not desire objects; we desire desire itself. Desire is represented by the phallus, which is not an object, but a "signifier."[20]

This Other, which is identified with desire and with language, is, and must be, such an imaginary creation. Without the mirror there is no Other and hence no desire and no game. Says Lacan, "The Other with a big 'O' is the scene of the Word insofar as the scene of the Word is always in third position between two subjects. This is only in order to introduce the dimension of Truth, which is made perceptible as it were, under the inverted sign of the lie."[21]

The sign of the child's desire resides in the splitting of his ego, in the objectification of himself into two for play, in the distancing of self from self that reduplicates an original alienation from the mother at birth. In creating the structure of the game, the child is destroying another form. He expresses his pleasure at this creation and this destruction in the stammer of desire that is satisfied and unfulfilled in the same breath: "Baby o-o-o-o-!" The pleasure of the child rests upon a lie and upon distancing.

The psychological problem of closeness to and distance from the written Word as expressed in books is clearly the province of the librarian, where "intimacy" with the written word is possible only in the suppression of sensualization and desire. The result is a kind of madness that has already been discussed to some extent in reference to the protagonists of these works. The relationship between the librarian-author and that which is already written copies the relationship between one individual and another as instigated by desire. Language, as Lacan reminds us, is not simple and unproblematic. In the case of the librarians, the use of language gives rise to a level of encounter intimated by Lacan in his reference to the stuttering text of Ernst Kris, which is so careless of wording as to unconsciously confuse "need" and "demand." As is the case with the small child before the mirror, though with less justification, there is in Kris's text an insufficient recognition of distance, which allows one realm to slip into another against nature and language.

Desire, which operates as a translating link between two subjects, becomes more appropriately a lie in which we desire not the other, but the self in the guise of the other. Lacan makes this very clear. The essential element is the reflected surface acting on us from a distance and not the interiorized reality of the desired object. All of the force of desire is in this mirrored reflection, in the imitation of desire that makes desire more profound. Nietzsche recognized this essential psychological factor: "When we love a woman, we easily conceive a hatred for nature on account of all the repulsive natural

functions to which every woman is subject." Therefore, says Nietzsche, the lover sets himself up at a distance from the desired one so
that his admiration is not translated into disgust in the mirror of
nature: "The magic and the most powerful effect of women is, in
philosophical language, action at a distance . . . but this requires
first and above all—*distance*."[22] Thus, desire is a game that translates truth into a lie, illuminating only the opaque surfaces of the
desired one. What distinguishes desire from sexuality is exactly this
factor of distance. In desire, the look dominates the other senses,
objectifying and mastering the reflected imitation of the self. By setting natural functions at a distance, and by maintaining that distance, the artist not only perpetuates his longing but converts it into
a work of art which is, as Nietzsche observes elsewhere, dependent
for its existence on illusion and optical error.[23] The look always occurs with the eyes half closed.

These considerations of distance and proximity, language and
body, lie and truth, surface and interior, come together in Derrida's
recapitulation of Nietzsche's attitude toward women, a recapitulation that provides an outline for the pages that follow: "(1) Woman
is condemned, humiliated, and scorned as a figure or power of
truth, as a philosophical and Christian being, whether she identifies
herself with truth, or at a distance, whether she still plays with it as
a fetish." The woman as Sophia, as wisdom, must likewise be kept
at a distance since in a world that demands illusion, the truth is under suspicion as a contaminant. Thus, "He was, and he dreaded,
such a castrated woman." "(2) Woman is condemned, humiliated,
and scorned as a figure or power of lying. The category of accusa-
tion is now set forth under the name of truth . . . of the credulous
man who advances truth and the phallus as his own attributes." Because her nature as lie contradicts his own self-established image of
truth, "He was, and he dreaded, such a castrating woman." The
third possibility, while it breaks the negating and negative roles of
the first two, is perhaps the most to be feared: "(3) Beyond this
double negation, woman is recognized, affirmed, as an affirmative,
dissimulating, artistic, and Dionysian power." However, "she is not
affirmed by man; rather she affirms herself and in man" and the
possibility of dismemberment by such an affirmative woman always
threatens the male. Derrida quotes *Ecce Homo*: "the perfect woman

tears to pieces when she loves."[24] Because this powerful woman is both affirmative and castrating, one might modify Derrida's third summary statement to a slightly different parallel of the former two and say that he loved, and he dreaded, such a Dionysian woman. To write is to pay the price of this dismemberment, to stammer out partial truths or total untruths in a stuttering, hesitant text that approaches the negative and negating fringes of lunacy.

"He was, and he dreaded, such a castrated woman."

In Cervantes and Anatole France, the woman is perceived at an extreme distance. Her presence is almost ineffable or unreal, and though she exercises a strong effect on the protagonist-librarian, she is more of a ghost or a shadow than a real woman. These women are infinitely desirable, but because they are so distanced they are impossible to possess. Furthermore, it seems that the librarians are most comfortable with this kind of idealized Platonic relationship. The woman can be worshiped from afar, idolized at a safe distance. Around her figure the librarian is able to mold a statue, converting the living woman into a work of art, which, like his books, is loved but does not return affection. Because she is desired from a distance, her presence offers no threat to the library. She can, in fact, be readily incorporated into the library space as an embodiment of the muse—cold, essentially indifferent, infinitely to be wooed, never to be won.

For Don Quixote, this factor of distance is comically crucial. Dulcinea of El Toboso is his muse and his inspiration, the primary energy source from which he derives all his bravery and his noble chivalric impulses. Don Quixote is well aware, however, that her power is in direct relation to the distance that separates them. He adores her, longs for her, idolizes her—but he is prohibited from drawing near. We see this very clearly when the love-stricken knight, through his faithful squire, receives a missive from his beloved begging and commanding him to come to her side. What knight would not fly to his lady upon receipt of such a tender recall? Yet, Don Quixote postpones the meeting, inventing a series of excuses to maintain the required distance from the object of his desires. He expresses these doubts and equivocations in conversation with Sancho:

> . . . what do you think I ought to do about my lady's order to go and see her? For although I perceive that I am bound to fulfill her behests, I find myself prevented by the boon I have granted to the princess who accompanies us, and the law of chivalry forces me to satisfy my pledge rather than my pleasure. On the one hand, my longing to see my lady disturbs and perplexes me; on the other, my plighted word and the glory I stand to reap in this enterprise incites and spurs me on.[25]

What is clear from these meditations is that Don Quixote does not want, nor does he intend, to go to El Toboso. The knight is himself uneasy with his explanation of the course of action incumbent upon a knight faced with the heroic dilemma of love versus duty.

Don Quixote's imaginative powers wane sharply as distance is closed between him and El Toboso. At his convenience, in order to make the real world accord with the literary one he prefers, he is capable of turning an inn into a magical helmet. Nevertheless, at the gates of El Toboso, he is completely incapable of transmuting peasant girls into his beloved and her attendants, despite the fact that he frequently makes similar transformations both before and after this incident. His dearest desire is also his most feared encounter; the distance cannot be closed between Dulcinea and himself. This is a condition of his love that cannot be translated or traduced.

Dulcinea is not only distanced; her reality is much more tenuous than that of the other damsels with whom Don Quixote comes in contact. There is a doubt whether either Don Quixote or Sancho has ever seen the real life prototype of the lady, and if they have, it is certain that neither has ever spoken to her (pp. 61, 583), so that any knowledge they might have of the peasant girl, Aldonza Lorenzo, comes from hearsay and perhaps two or three casual glimpses at a distance. On this tenuous basis, Don Quixote builds his firmest and most lasting attachment, flying in the face of enchantments and even his own doubts of her existence. In answer to a question put by the Duchess about the reality of his beloved, Don Quixote answers, "God knows whether Dulcinea exists on earth or not, or whether she is fantastical or not. These are not matters where verification can be carried out to the full" (p. 760). Clearly, the most essential aspects of Don Quixote's faithful love for Dulcinea are his distance and her spiritualization.

One might recall, by way of contrast, the role of women in the chivalric romances that serve as models for Don Quixote's own behavior. In his primary model, the *Amadis of Gaul*, love is sentimentalized, but it is never relegated to a purely Platonic spiritualization of passion. The essential theme of the *Amadis* is fidelity in love, the unbreakable loyalty of the knight to his lady in the face of the most difficult tests possible. To this degree, Don Quixote provides a faithful imitation. He strays in two important aspects, however. The model knight obeys his lady in all her requests, putting her whim before considerations of honor and duty. But Don Quixote, by ignoring Dulcinea's letter, fails to fulfill this knightly code. Second, the theme of the romance of chivalry is not a spiritualized but an erotic attachment. Fidelity is not an empty emotion. It is based on an actual sexual relationship; the knight carnally possesses the damsel to whom he is to dedicate his life and works. It is a secret love, but it is deeply imbued with sexuality, and the goal of the knight is an eventual open union with the lady of his heart. *Amadis* is a case in point. Oriana is the knight's first and only mistress; she later becomes his wife but not before bearing a son, Esplandian, who has nearly reached adulthood by the time his parents are finally married. Such relationships are the rule rather than the exception: Amadis's own mother did not marry his father until long after her child was born. This is such a typical situation that one of the great intrigues of the romance is the mystery of the child's origins and the discovery of his parents. This circumstance does not indicate desire at a distance, but a full consummation of love.

Marthe Robert signals another pertinent aberration in Don Quixote's spiritualized love for his distant lady: "Don Quixote is at fifty a confirmed bachelor, a secret misogynist in spite of, or precisely because of, his jealous devotion to the eternal principle of femininity."[26] On the one hand, his lady's distance and ineffability permit him the joys and sufferings of love without the problems of consummation, while on the other, his fidelity to her image excuses him from participation in the enjoyment of the fleshly temptations that he encounters in his travels. Thus, at the inn, Don Quixote resolves to remain faithful to his lady, using Dulcinea as a talisman to protect him from the dangers of forbidden love: "he began to feel anxious as he reflected on the perils his honor would suffer, but he resolved in his heart not to be guilty of the least infidelity to his lady, Dulcinea of El Toboso, even though Queen Guinevere herself . . . should appear before him" (p. 157). Don Quixote's vows to his imaginary lady serve as a barrier to keep other women at a distance as well. The landlady's daughter, apparently a reasonably attractive young woman, arouses the knight's passions to just such a curious declaration of love that functions on the basis of attraction and subsequent distancing: "I shall forever keep engraved in my memory the service you have done me, and I shall be grateful to you as long as I live. Would to high heaven that love had not enthralled me and subjected me to its laws . . . else would the eyes of this beauteous damsel here bereave me of my freedom" (p. 155). This declaration reveals the knight's ambivalence in his relationships with women. The compliments and the declarations of love are real, but they are prefaced by a distancing condition, "If I were not in love, I would love," allowing Don Quixote the harmless pastime of indulging his amorous instincts while remaining at a safe distance from the object of his attention.

A similar ambivalence rules his subsequent contact with the noxious serving wench, Maritornes. As she brushes by his bed on her way to a midnight assignation, Don Quixote sits up despite the pain from his recent fall, stretches out his arms, seizes the lady, and pulls her toward him. Don Quixote himself, in this case, closes the distance between himself and the woman, only to back away and reestablish that necessary space:

> . . . clasping her fast, he began to court her in a low, tender voice, saying: "I wish, fair and noble lady, I were in a state to repay so great a boon as thou hast given to me . . . but Fortune has seen fit to lay me in this bed, where I lie so bruised and battered that, even though I were ready to satisfy my wish it would be impossible for me to do so, for there is still a more invincible obstacle, namely the faith I have plighted to the peerless Dulcinea of El Toboso. . . . Had this obstacle not intervened, I

should not . . . let slip the happy opportunity thy great bounty
has bestowed upon me. (p. 158)

The reader is left to puzzle over this ambiguous statement. Don
Quixote clasps the woman in his arms, makes a declaration of love,
and assumes she is offering her body for his exclusive pleasure. The
grounds for his refusal of this assumed offer are curious: he cites
Dulcinea, the habitual censor for forbidden contact with other females, but also his recent injuries. Both merge together in the same
breath. Which carries the most weight in his polite refusal (while
tightly embracing her) of her services? If he were uninjured, would
the memory of his love for Dulcinea be strong enough to prevent
infidelity? Later, he speaks to Sancho of this episode, citing his
strength in overcoming temptation, bragging of "those other hidden
things I shall let pass untouched and unspoken, to keep the faith I
owe to my lady, Dulcinea of El Toboso" (p. 161). But what hidden
things were uncovered in his midnight explorations of Maritornes's
body, and what unspoken thoughts were kept silent in his fervent
declarations of love to both her and the innkeeper's daughter? With
Dulcinea as a screen behind which he can retire, Don Quixote is
free to indulge in the game of forbidden love through verbal declarations and surreptitious embraces.

Don Quixote's preference for sterile embraces and empty declarations of love reveals another facet of his impotence, an impotence
that was earlier made evident in his inability to create original literature outside the structure of his chosen models. This sense of impotence, on all levels, is intensified after the enchantment of Dulcinea.
Don Quixote is helpless in the face of Sancho's invention, a helplessness that is reflected in his vision, upon his descent into the Cave
of Montesinos, of a Dulcinea still under enchantment. This vision of
the ugly peasant version of his beloved is a tacit recognition by the
knight of his own inability to reorder his world: his will is no longer
able to sustain the enchantments; he is incapable of integrating visual representations with their ideal images. This feeling of impotence when faced with the enchanted Dulcinea leads, indubitably,
to the final disillusionment that kills the knight at the end of the
novel.

In "The Daughter of Clementine," the second part of Anatole France's novel *The Crime of Sylvestre Bonnard*, a similar situation obtains. While cataloging a friend's library for sale, Bonnard is visited by just such an ineffable presence: a fairy riding a sixteenth-century folio volume like a horse. She is charming, beautiful, lovable, and—by her own admission—completely imaginary. As with Dulcinea, being imaginary does not make her less real—rather, more so. In Cervantean and Borgesian fashion she declares the advantage of such ideal images over the mundane facts: "To know is nothing at all; to imagine is everything. Nothing exists except what is imagined. I am imaginary. That is what it is to exist, I should think! I am dreamed of, and I appear. Everything is only a dream; and as nobody ever dreams about you, Sylvestre Bonnard, it is *you* who do not exist."[27] This fairy who so delightfully visits Bonnard in the world between sleep and waking appears again in the novel in another guise. Her quicksilver dream existence is transformed into concrete reality at the hands of young Jeanne. The fairy is rendered in the mundane world in the form of a statue, that is, a wax figurine. And the girl, Jeanne, so significantly introduced through the mediation of the fairy, is herself transformed by Bonnard's desire into the shape of his dream-love. Her figure becomes for him the metaphoric wax in which a remembered imaginary love is re-formed. There is scarcely a transition between the dream figure, the wax figure, and her human embodiment in the form of the young girl.

In Bonnard's dream, Jeanne becomes her mother, Clementine, the woman he loved at a distance and who was denied him by political disputes. His renunciation of his love had, in the past, taken the form of a sublimation in books; now he envisages a reverse operation, telling Jeanne that "you are going to take the place of the books [that used to be in the little room]; you will succeed them as day succeeds night" (p. 280). Bonnard, however, remains distanced from his new object of desire, adopting a paternal tone and exercising parental authority over the girl. He insists that only he, as the adopted father, should provide the dowry for Clementine's daughter (p. 125), a dowry which he pays in the self-same books.

As Bonnard reveals the story of his relationship to his beloved Clementine, the reader realizes that this love, like that of Don Quixote, is an idealized love sprung from the society of books, nourished by distance and by Sylvestre's inability to declare his passions. Clementine and Sylvestre were drawn together in the library, united by the fact that both assisted Clementine's father in his work as a cartographer of antiquity. The girl herself, Bonnard readily acknowledges, demonstrated nothing but indifference to him (p. 154), a fact that inflamed rather than abated his ardor. His love was lost to him through the agencies of his Uncle Victor, the prototype of the man's man, a Napoleonic hero of the old school. She was lost—and yet she remained more deeply his. The love that the young Sylvestre felt for Clementine was given no chance to deteriorate with the vicissitudes of time; rather distance and time purified and enhanced it.

This same Uncle Victor, blamed by Bonnard for the loss of the great love of his life, is also responsible for a prior, equally cutting deprivation, the story of which is detailed in the first part of the novel. This earlier episode of Sylvestre as a child reflects back on the later experience of Sylvestre as a young man, and both bear upon his relationship to Jeanne in his old age:

> I can see once more, with astonishing vividness, a certain doll which, when I was eight years old, used to be displayed in the window of an ugly little shop of the Rue de Seine. . . . I was consumed with longing for a doll. . . . I was quite conscious in my own way that this doll lacked grace and style—that she was gross, that she was coarse. But I loved her in spite of that; I loved her just for that; I loved her only; I wanted her. (pp. 22–23)

The longing for this doll represents the first great passion of Sylvestre's life, a longing that he tries to disguise and struggles to overcome in attention to "manly amusements" like toy soldiers. Yet he is haunted by this doll; she fills his dreams, coming alive to stretch out her arms to him—he is forced to reject her. Finally, he timidly asks his uncle to purchase the doll for him, and the uncle's heartless response leaves him crushed and trembling. In the aftermath of this shame he renounces the doll. With the loss of the doll, he also renounces the possibility of fulfilled love, replacing it with an unfulfillable desire. He loved the doll and was forced to abandon her.

Bonnard's love for Clementine takes a different but parallel course. He longs for her, desires only her, but he does not confess his devotion until his uncle has made the fulfillment of it impossible. After the doll incident, Sylvestre established a barrier against femininity not unlike Don Quixote's barrier, which censors out close, sexualized contact in favor of distance, longing, and unfulfillable desire. Just as the wax figurine of the imaginary fairy comes to life in the form of its sculptor, so too the interdicted doll merges with the forbidden love.

Bonnard is, in effect, thrice rejected: by the doll, by Clementine, and by her daughter, an interdiction that in the third case is that of incest. Bonnard's fatherly affection for Jeanne is constantly undermined in the reader's mind by the nature and the intensity of his jealousy where she is concerned. When his visits are no longer permitted at the boarding school Jeanne attends, Bonnard perceives it as the revenge of a frustrated schoolmistress. While this is in fact the case, her accusations of Bonnard have a ring of truth: "Your assiduities in this house are being interpreted, by the most respectable and least suspicious persons, in such a manner that I find myself obliged . . . to see that they end at once" (p. 241). While Bonnard emphatically rejects such an interpretation of his behavior, the reader is more likely to see in the old scholar's exorbitant affection for the daughter of his lost love the stirrings of incestuous feelings.

The cat that Jeanne brings home to Bonnard's apartment becomes a focal point for this sexual undercurrent. Bonnard identifies the cat with his own Hamilcar, considering it a fit successor to the feline that he kept as his alter ego in the City of Books. If Bonnard sees the cat as another version of himself, Jeanne sees in it quite another person—the young scholar, Gélis. In his absence, Jeanne loads the cat with all the caresses she would like to give the young man, her own undeclared lover.

Bonnard's rival, Gélis, is also his double, a younger version of himself with the same scholarly interests. Gélis is a disciple of the older man, becoming in some sense, the son he had always longed for, the son who would carry on his work and his love for Clementine when he was no longer able to do so.[28] Further, while Jeanne associates the young man with her cat (the link felis-gelis was surely not unrecognized by France), Bonnard can be satisfied that the statuesque nature of desire and the required factor of distance will be preserved in these two adopted children. Jeanne is a sculptor, living partially through her creations, while Gélis, through the other association of his name with *geler*, possesses a cold, statuesque quality in his own nature. This coldness reflects the imposed coldness of a life lived among books. These two young people are, like the fairy, to some extent creations of the dreaming mind of Sylvestre Bonnard.

Significantly, the marriage of Gélis and Jeanne is followed by the birth of a new Sylvestre, a child who is doomed to die in old Bonnard's place as a sacrifice to his jealousy. As Geoffrey H. Hartman notes, "Scenes of nomination that affect men in Scripture tend in fact, as with Abraham, to be a call for child sacrifice."[29] This is no less the case with Bonnard. The baby Sylvestre is condemned before birth from his association with the doll-Jeanne and the ice-Gélis. A pretty, pale, sleepless child, his appearance in Bonnard's dream was premature, and it is not surprising that his birth, the scene of his nomination, coincides with the beginning of a new life (a new book) for his namesake. The end of the book on bees and flowers, as well as the conclusion of France's novel, fittingly coincides with the death of this small Sylvestre-image. The situation is not unlike that at the end of *Don Quixote* when the knight gives up his fictional name and assumes his real-life one—and dies. By putting himself in unmediated relation to the reality outside (the insects and flowers, or the name Alonso Quijano the Good and all it implies), the librarian expresses a desire to fix that reality for once and for all through the power of the name, a power that brings death in its wake.

Life for these librarians can only be maintained at a distance. In the first part of the novel, the "homunculus" Coccez dies with the birth of his son. Bonnard's own mother's death coincides with Clementine's birth (suggesting, perhaps, that Clementine is to take the place of the mother and therefore that Bonnard's affection for Jeanne is, in some twisted manner, Oedipal). Jeanne herself says that she has worked so long on a particular statuette because, "I had an idea that I was going to die as soon as my little Saint George would be finished" (p. 265). When the distance is closed, death can be the result. Hartman, commenting on the death of Tennyson's lady of Shalott, could be discussing the relation between the feminine, distancing, and death as it has been adduced here:

> She did not know that by her avertedness, by staying within representation, she had postponed death. The most art can do, as a mirror of language, is to burn through, in its cold way, the desire for self-definition, fullness of grace, presence; simply to expose the desire to own one's own name, to inhabit it numinously in the form of "proper" noun, words, or the signatory act each poem aspires to be.[30]

Desire becomes desire for the proper name, an unmediated, perfected correspondence of existence and essential being that in its closure would imitate the monumental immortality of language and art.

In *The Crime of Sylvestre Bonnard*, the feminine principle takes one other form, no less distanced, but in this case, extremely powerful. In his association with Mme. Coccez, the goodness implicit in Bonnard's name meets its first test through contact with a woman who carries with her a strong aura of the illicit and the improper. Like Clementine and Jeanne, Mme. Coccez is distanced from the librarian, but she is not the plaything of his dream-life. In her, strong mythic resonances combine the archetypes of the Madonna and the Whore, attributes of the potent, ambiguous Great Mother. Each time Bonnard comes in contact with her, it is as though he sees her from afar. She is enveloped in a cloak of mystery of her own making and can appear as awesome as a statue come to life or a saint stepping out of her icon.

The husband of this radiant and potent woman is, as may be expected, a total nonentity, the "homunculus Coccez." A bookseller by trade, he is in actuality a miserable salesman of quasipornographic books. Ironically (or prophetically), the majority of his books deal with illicit love affairs, with love that ends in death, or with castration (Abelard and Héloïse). This husband dies with the birth of Mme. Coccez's child, as the need for this symbolic castrate is obviated with the arrival of a healthy boy child to take his place.

Mme. Coccez's new husband, the Prince Trepof, is hardly more prepossessing than his predecessor. Like Bonnard, the prince is a collector; not, as Bonnard finds time to regret, of antique marbles or painted vases, but of matchboxes. Bonnard finds this circumstance somewhat comical, though he realizes that he "could not possibly make fun of them without making fun of myself" (p. 59). In their earlier acquaintance, Bonnard had supplied Mme. Coccez with a large Yule log since her husband was unable to provide the comforts of a Christmas fire. Her second husband is a somewhat better provider, but his collection of matches, the tiny sticks contrasting with the huge log, suggests that men in association with this potent woman are inevitably diminished by proximity to her.

While these men lose themselves by their relationship to the powerful female force, Bonnard loses himself in the longing for an old manuscript, searching for it like a desirable, desired, lost love. In finding the manuscript, he again comes in contact with a log (in which the manuscript is hidden), and Mme. Coccez (the potent woman), and her child. The association does not escape Bonnard: "In the oddest way the Coccez family has become associated in my mind with the Clerk Alexander" (p. 30). It is the Coccez child who, through the agency of his mother, now the Princess Trepof, delivers the manuscript to the scholar, thus completing the association of child-book (by the Clerk Alexander), which is repeated in the second part of the novel in the link between the girl-child, Jeanne (significantly, surnamed Alexandre) and the old man's library.

It is in this manner, therefore, that both Don Quixote and Sylvestre Bonnard approach their beloveds, obliquely, catching sight of them, as it were, in the dream-mirrors of their own desire. Significantly, both men ignore the proper names of the women they love; Don Quixote calls his peasant girl "Dulcinea," and Bonnard recalls in his adopted daughter the form of the fairy-doll-Clementine that is for him the embodiment of his library. These women are idolized, but they are castrated figures, monumentalized as emblems of truth and beauty, but helpless to effect any change in their own states.

In Mme. Coccez (or the Princess Trepof), the reader catches sight of a different type of woman, one who is feared for her castrating powers. Neither is her proper name revealed in the text, and for this reason her essence cannot be captured. Throughout the text, her potency is felt from a distance, her existence veiled under the only names by which she is known, both of them names of less potent consorts. This potency felt as a negative, castrating force becomes the major feature of the second group of women who intrude upon the librarian's solitude.

"He was, and he dreaded, such a castrating woman."

The women admired by Don Quixote and Sylvestre Bonnard were desired from a distance, extravagantly praised, and idealized-idolized. While there may be, as Robert suggests, more than a hint of misogyny in such a fervent love for an impossible object, Don Quixote and Sylvestre Bonnard differ greatly from the more openly misogynistic attitudes of this second group of librarians. More adamantly solitary than either of the two protagonists just discussed, the heroes of this group are active, self-professed seekers of solitude for whom trespass upon their self-imposed distance from other humanity is an unpardonable offense. The women who come into contact with these librarians are also perceived in a different light. Rather than serving as sources of inspiration for the scholar-heroes, for Canetti, Sartre, and Beckett the women their protagonists encounter are vulgar, fleshy, antiartistic creatures—the very opposite of the beautiful, evanescent figures fantasized by Don Quixote and Sylvestre Bonnard. Furthermore, these earthy, vulgar creatures are not welcomed within the heroes' sanctuaries, but are emphatically pushed out of the libraries and the minds of the protagonists, where their submerged, suppressed presence operates as a malevolent influence.

This is clearly the case with Sartre's Roquentin. Women play a peripheral role in his novel and in his life; where present (for example, the patronne, Françoise) they service disgusting bodily functions and are subsequently shunted aside without a thought. Even his dream mistress, his Dulcinea, has shown the effects of the passage of time. No longer is Anny slim and attractive: like the landlady, she has grown fat and disillusioned. Nevertheless, while women play but a small role in the novel's conscious level, Roquentin is subliminally obsessed with problems relating to femininity and masculinity. Canetti's hero, Peter Kien, is an even more intense version of Roquentin whose mad, hallucinatory hatred of women spills out upon the figure of the hated housekeeper turned wife. Other secondary female figures in the novel are no less disgusting. All are perverted into grotesques, from Fischerle's ignorant, greedy slob of a wife who supports the family by prostitution, to the pathetic, ugly hunchbacked newspaper woman.

In *Krapp's Last Tape*, the suppression of women takes another form. Krapp insists on the unimportance of women and the romantic episodes in his life, preferring his present state of lonely inspiration. Yet, despite his impatience with his taped records of his past, the reader is ironically aware that although he reiterates his rejection of female companionship, his tapes (his library, his books) talk of nothing else. The return of the suppressed, repressed figure of the woman is not precisely uncanny, since in her vulgar, fleshy appearance there is little of the ghostly aura associated with such apparitions, but her intrusion into the male preserve of the library has a similar unsettling effect.

Krapp is an aging solitary, nursing the dregs of what must have once been a considerable intellectual talent. Like other Beckett heroes, he prefers solitude to the company of other men, and lonely fastidiousness to sex. His real (and symbolic) retention of excrement is an indication of this extreme fastidiousness; a once-erotic man perceives physical relations as a profanation and as an unworthy dispersal of his energies—he reserves his waning strength for pleasures of the mind. But his digestive problems reflect back on his intellectual sterility, and despite his rejection of love he is obsessively forced back by his tapes to an endless review of past sexual experiences, good, bad, and indifferent. In the present, all he has to look forward to are the regular visits of Fanny, but she's a "bony old ghost of a whore"[31] who drains the last romance out of sexuality. He barely sees her when she comes and goes, indicating in an offhand manner that he doesn't care much either. Krapp is reaching the end of a long unproductive (and unreproductive) life. "Couldn't do much," he says, typically, "but I suppose better than a kick in the crutch" (p. 25). His irritation with his earlier self and his earlier sexuality takes a similar form—he can't do much, but it's better than total impotency.

Krapp, his tape recorder, and his bananas inhabit a circle of bright light surrounded by darkness. Krapp himself creates this artificial situation, intending perhaps to force some meaning from the contrast of light and dark. The women in Krapp's life, as they emerge from the taped memories, represent to him a similar combination of light and darkness, of fluid life and rigid form, of challenge and death. John Fletcher and John Spurling find that "'Death and the Maiden' is the burden of Krapp's tape,"[32] and his relation to the two terms is one of ambivalent opposition and affinity. When the affinity for the presence of women becomes too strong, Krapp represses the memories with strong signs of disapproval and with the partial consolation of his withered lusts upon the body of the old whore. When the attraction of the dark (his death) becomes too strong, he freezes into immobility in his circle of light. Always in one realm or the other, he can choose neither a total darkness nor a diffuse light, refusing in this manner to confront reality by taking refuge in words. Krapp's life and his relationships to women are shaped in a large part by this basic ambivalence.

On the one hand, there is his retention of excrement, which is parallel to his youthful eschewal of sex in the expectation that seminal retention will serve the forces of illumination. On the other hand, his autoerotic toying with the banana and the wanton dispersal of seminal fluid in the nonprocreative body of the whore signal his attraction to the darker forces of death and dissolution through the fusion of the face with the sexual parts.

The first woman he speaks of at any length in the play, an ex-mistress with whom he apparently lived for several years, combines these aspects of light and dark. Eugene Webb notices that her name, Bianca, means "white" in Italian, and that her home was in Kedar Street, a word that means "dark" in Hebrew.[33] Krapp's subsequent recollections of his mother are also tinged with this contrast. He recalls on tape his experience of sitting and watching the window of the house where she lay dying, remembering her long mourning, her envelopment in darkness. He sits, drenched in sunlight, staring up at the dark window, recalling the dark, deadly, dying woman within. His meditations on his mother's window are interrupted by a comment relating to another young woman who, like Bianca, combines in her person the attributes of light and darkness, of new-springing life and funereal maternity: "One dark young beauty I recollect particularly, all white and starch, incomparable bosom, with a big black hooded perambulator, most funereal thing" (p. 19). His love/hatred of his mother, transferred to the maternal/funereal nurse, indicates his own ambivalent sexuality. The fulfillment of sexual desire is linked indissolubly to death, but seminal (excremental) retention indicates a regression to an earlier, also deadly, state. The triumph of death is assured whether the observer grasps that "incomparable bosom" to his own, or whether he regresses, with the suffocating maternity of the nurse or of his own mother to the funereal, undifferentiated sexuality of infancy. In the case of his relation to his mother as well as in his appreciation of the nurse, the opposites of light and dark mingle. Egoism joins with fear and is expressed in a depreciation of the other, the opposite, the female.

Nowhere is this situation made more clear than in Krapp's aborted relationship to the young woman of the punt. The aged Krapp is evidently fascinated by this scene of youthful lovemaking since he returns to it three times in the space of the short play. On this tape he recalls, when it is "past midnight," the lazy afternoon on the stream with the "sun blazing down." This episode represents a crucial turning point in his life, his final rejection of the dark, irrational feminity for the illumination of reason in his work. In his own words, Krapp chooses "unshatterable association until my dissolution of storm and night with the light of understanding and fire" over the darkness of woman in the dazzling noon-time light; "my face in her breasts and my hand on her" (p. 21). He prefers the dark fire of his vision to the fire of life that the young woman offers along with her dreaming eyes and still body.

Common to all these fantasies of women is Krapp's obsession with their eyes. He remembers little about Bianca "apart from a tribute to her eyes. . . . Incomparable!" (p. 16). The nursemaid is particularly recalled because of her eyes, "like . . . (hesitates) . . . chrysolite!" (p. 19). In the dark woman with the staring golden eyes that never seemed to leave his, the contrasts of light and darkness are again reaffirmed. Likewise, the girl of the punt is memorable particularly for her eyes that remained closed against the glare of the sun, then gradually opened as Krapp shaded her with his body. Now, in the present of the play, Krapp is "very near-sighted (but unspectacled)" (p. 9). Despite the problem with his sight, he "scalded the eyes out of [himself] reading *Effie* again, a page a day" (p. 25).

The light and fire that Krapp feels within him after his renunciation of women have been dissipated, leaving the shell of the author to contemplate a novel, not even his own novel—Krapp's masterpiece is nowhere mentioned in the play except to note that it sold only seventeen copies—about still another woman. Women's eyes, the feature that so obsesses Krapp, do not serve as windows to the soul, but as reflecting mirrors that shift back onto Krapp the responsibility for his own nearsightedness, for his own dark inability to penetrate within the woman's darkness to the light she is capable of bringing forth.

Krapp substitutes the concrete reality of things for a world of signs, turning his back on the bright eye of the sun for the artificial light of his desk lamp, giving up fruitful relationships with women for sterile encounters with the ghosts on his tapes, the ghost who visits him regularly to tend his waning sexual lusts, and the ghosts of words that scald his eyes in *Effie*. The passionate and chaotic times of his youthful sexual exuberance have been converted into a static, asocial, historical time of memories of failure and symbolic blindness. Krapp, who dreads women and recalls their eyes, sits at the end of the play "staring before him" into darkness and the eyes of the theater audience.

Peter Kien, who does not see pigeons or flowers except as they are given to him in books, brings this same intermediary to bear in interpersonal relationships. All of Kien's difficulties begin with the loan of a book, a battered schoolboy copy of *The Trousers of Herr von Bredow*, to his housekeeper after she maneuvers him into the loan. Such manipulation fills him with rage—he cannot bear to have even the least of his books touch uncouth hands. But much to his surprise, the housekeeper seduces him by the extreme care she takes in handling the wretched text. She wraps it in thick, clean paper, lays it on a specially embroidered velvet cushion, and handles it only with spotless white kid gloves. Kien is ashamed of his earlier rage and divines from this care that Therese's heart, like his own, belongs to the books. What recompense can he offer for this misjudgment, what better way to insure the well-being of his library than to marry her?[34] And marry her he does.

This misreading of his housekeeper's temperament is the first of his mistakes; the second is even more serious. Unlike his brother

George who recognized that "reading was fondling" (p. 398) and so ensured his success with women patients, Kien believes that fondling is nothing but reading—a deadly assumption to make in view of the highly sexed woman he has chosen for his bride. His first, fumbling approach to his wife on their wedding night is mediated by books. Books are love. Feverishly he covers the divan bed with a layer of books: "Inferior works he rejected, so as not to hurt the woman's feelings" (p. 58). Therese, of course, knows nothing of such delicacy or such refined substitutes for the sexual act:

> Therese caught his eye, she bent down and, with one all-embracing stroke of her left arm, swept the books to the floor. . . . Horror choked him. . . . Therese took off her petticoat, folded it up carefully and laid it on the floor on top of the books. Then she made herself comfortable on the divan, crooked her little finger, grinned and said "There!"
>
> Kien plunged out of the room in long strides, bolted himself into the lavatory, the only room in the whole house where there was no books, automatically let his trousers down, took his place on the seat and cried like a child. (p. 59)

Sexual excitement is not in Kien's nature. His passions are cold and sterile, reserved only for books and the written word. In his misreading of Therese's character and motivations, he ascribes a similar cerebrality of love to her, and expresses this phantom, sterile desire in his lavish wedding gift of a bed loaded with books. Therese responds to the rarefied purity of his desire with her own damp, vulgar sexuality, shattering the perfect moment Kien had prepared, forcing him into a realization of his own impotence in the face of such an overwhelming lust. While Krapp saw in the dark beauty of the nurse an attraction both maternal and fatal, Kien finds in Therese only the deadly mother who destroys his mastery and reduces him once again to childhood.

The shame and trauma Kien suffers at his first experience of a relationship unmediated by books poisons any further contact he has with his wife. His fear and hatred of her grow ever more intense with the physical restrictions set on his space as the woman begins to infiltrate his rooms. His impotence extends to all levels and spheres of his life. The sexual and emotional traumas are followed by equally devastating intellectual defeats as exemplified in Therese's vanquishing of his petrifaction. As his rage builds, the petrified Kien changes his position from a defensive to an offensive one. He decides that his existence as a statue is costing him weeks of work and that the unspeakably vulgar woman is guilty of causing the scholar to waste his precious time on his new art. This he can tolerate, but when Therese begins to tear up his papers his rage knows no bounds: "he would get up, a cold stone, he would crush her to fragments against himself." He feels the power of his righteous anger strengthening him, "he grasped himself, the Tables of the Law, and stoned his people with them." Kien becomes in his mind an avenging God who rises up and destroys his people, smiling grimly at the revelation that Therese's last words indicate her venal desire for money. Then the dream shatters: "They were not her last words. She grabbed his head and battered it on the writing table. . . . He felt it all. It hurt him. He was not a stone. Since she did not break into pieces, his art did. All was false, there was no faith in anything. There was no God" (p. 165). Kien, the fallen God, is expelled from the heaven/haven of his library into the hell of the streets by the vengeful female.

Physically powerless against attacks by the hated female, Kien takes another tack. His hatred of Therese grows into extreme misogyny. First, he destroys the female element lurking in words by relieving them of the absurd feminine gender that so inappropriately attaches itself to many of them (p. 159), then, analyzing the interference of the woman in his work, he concludes that "learning demanded her death." Learning also demanded his "free pardon and rehabilitation. Scholars of his standing could be counted on the fingers of one hand. Women, unhappily, may be reckoned in the millions" (p. 265). Since his own attempted destruction of Therese was thwarted, Kien kills her from a distance, through words. Acting from afar, the scholar masks his impotence, relishing his imaginary victory over his wife as Therese in his mind dies the death he has prepared for her with his words:

> She devoured herself. Piece by piece her body fell a prey to her greed. Day by day she grew thinner. She was too weak to

stand, but lay there in her own filth. . . . The blue skirt, which she always wore, covered her skeleton. It was starched, and thanks to this peculiarity held the repulsive remains of her body together. . . . No one was with her in her last hour. . . . Corruption set in before she was dead. All this happened in my library, in the presence of my books. I shall have the place cleaned. She shortened this process by no suicide. . . . You must seek out the remains on a rubbish dump outside the town. (pp. 316, 318)

When Therese appears before him after he has killed her off with his language, Kien, typically, refuses to accept the evidence of his senses. His words were always powerful—they will remain so. He repeats his version of her disgusting end over and over with only slight variations, even, to Therese's utter confusion, in the presence of that lady herself.

The pathological intensity with which Kien details the particulars of Therese's supposed death is equaled only at the end of the novel when his hatred of women comes to an emotional climax. In a remarkable sixteen-page passage of sustained rage, he relates to his brother George all the hateful aspects of the female sex with which his vast studies have made him familiar, listing feminine transgressions ranging from biblical (Eve, Delilah) to mythological (Helen of Troy, Circe, Clytaemnaestra, Kriemhild) to historical (Cleopatra, Messalina) to the natural world (spiders, gnats, bees) (pp. 433–49). Kien believes that God's benevolence was exhausted with the creation of Adam; his meticulous review of all subsequent relations between the sexes indicates nothing but the woman's hindrance of a man's work and her insane impediments to progress.

It is possible that the source and the inspiration for this amazing catalogue of the deadly effects of the female may have been Canetti's own mother who, by his own admission, filled Canetti alternately with fear and admiration. She exerted a powerful intellectual influence on her son's life, and her educational style included the symbiosis of reading in unison with the lacerating tensions of protracted debate. Her very presence could be annihilating. She despised women and their weaknesses; her loves and hates were implacable. Steiner quotes an episode from Canetti's autobiography that reveals the tensions she created and the cruelties of which she was capable. On their return to Vienna after the death of Canetti's father, his mother took upon herself the task of teaching the boy German:

> She sat around the corner to my left and held the textbook in such a way that I couldn't look in. She always kept it far from me. "You don't need it," she said. "You can't understand it yet anyway." But despite this explanation, I felt she was withholding the book like a secret. She read a German sentence to me and had me repeat it. Disliking my accent, she made me repeat the sentence several times, until it struck her as tolerable. But this didn't occur often, for she derided me for my accent, and since I couldn't stand her derision for anything in the world, I made an effort and soon pronounced the sentence correctly. Only then did she tell me what the sentence meant in English. But this she never repeated. I had to note it instantly and for all time.[35]

The mother, loved above all else, becomes the cruel taskmaster, whipping the boy with the very force of his love.

Kien's encyclopedic study of the malevolent role of women in all aspects of human and natural history is schematically summarized and placed back into the context of his sexual impotence in the final pages of the novel where the perpetual fever of hot blood becomes a burning in the trousers, referring Kien back to the book he loaned Therese at the opening of the novel, *The Trousers of Herr von Bredow*, and to the recollection that with the book she was trying to seduce him. The fires in the blood, recalled from his earlier anxiety dream, become the fires that burn in the trousers (both man and book) in a conflagration that is both literal and sexual. The destruction/seduction of Therese is inexorably linked to the trousers. Her dark blood stains him, stains his library, burns them both.

The sexual fire that Kien fears throughout the novel and that in his hallucination devours his rapacious wife is perhaps more accurate than he knows, though in a completely different sense. Therese meets her match in the sadistic expoliceman, who responds to her overtures with salivating eagerness as he "let her fall to the ground, broke open the starched skirt and had her" (p. 281). Even Kien recognizes the intensity of the sexual fire in the caretaker, associating the color of his hair with the burning red he imagines around him: "He had red pomade in a thousand different tubes. Under the bed in his closet was a collection of salve jars, red of every colour, red here, red there, red overhead. His head, yes, his head was FIERY RED" (p. 457).[36] Kien envisions this fiery red conquering the blue of the housekeeper and rejoices in it. He does not realize that this same fiery red that consumes his wife also consumes his books. He imagines that Therese devours herself but, with the complicity of the caretaker, she hauls away Kien's books to the pawnshop (the Theresianum) where they are devoured by the pawnbroker, leaving her with the beautiful money to satisfy her own lusts (p. 281).

Therese is as obsessed with respectability (which she defines in terms of cold cash) as Kien is with books. Money indicates decency; it also serves as an index of beauty, youth, and lovability. Canetti's devastating, brief description of her belies the image she has of herself: "She would have disintegrated into her chief components—skirt, ears and sweat—had not her hatred for [Kien] . . . become the core of her being" (p. 143). Out of this natural grotesquerie, Therese creates the illusion of a beautiful, vibrant femininity. Her experience of reading contributes to this illusion, but since her studies are limited to the personal and help wanted columns of the newspaper, in her mind the sentimentalized romances and the offers of good wages were joined: "'Love' in all its parts of speech was a heavy-type word in Therese's vocabulary. . . . 'love' still remained for her a foreign sound of wondrous import." Like Roquentin, for whom the use of the living stories is an infrequent indulgence, Therese rarely treats herself to the use of the word ("She rarely took the blessed consolation between her lips"), but when she reads it she cannot resist the impulse to linger over and meditate upon the word.

> At times the most tempting "situations vacant" were overshadowed by offers of marriage and love. She read "good wages" and held out her hand; joyfully her fingers curled up under the weight of the expected money. Then her eye fell on "love" a few columns further on; here it paused to rest, here it clung for broad moments. She did not of course forget her

other plans, she did not open her hand to return the money. She merely covered it over for a brief, tremulous space with love. (pp. 73–74)

Despite her grotesque looks, her vulgarity, and her immorality, her dream of love mitigates the caricature and lends Therese a pathetic, humanizing aspect. Her twin dreams of money and love, conjoined in the persons of Kien and the furniture store salesman, are ritually enacted in her fantasy in front of the mirror. Besides revealing Therese's own obsessiveness, the mirror scene exposes the motivations of a lonely, aging spinster. She imagines herself rich and therefore loved, the hand that grasps the imaginary money also deals out imaginary caresses. She fantasizes that these hands belong to someone else, caressing an actual woman (herself) behind the mirror-window. As always, in her obsession she neglects such insignificant details as her actual appearance, her actual solitude, bringing together in her mind the beautiful young man and the beautiful money in the imagined love that she perceives as her right.

The hand that caresses, that grasps the money, is also the hand that cleans and polishes the library to Kien's satisfaction, keeping it free from any speck of dust. This cleansing mania too can be related to her libidinous desires. Bachelard explains that the joy felt with rhythmic motion "is the indication of a specific affective power," and he continues, "In this way is explained the joy of rubbing, cleaning, furbishing and polishing that could not be adequately explained by the meticulous care taken by certain housewives. . . . Psychologically speaking, cleanliness is really a form of uncleanliness."[37] This tireless diligence of the housekeeper/housewife is revealed in other actions as well. Perceiving her husband's books as soluble assets, she begins to make an inventory of the library, thus marking each book as her own by her possession of a strip of paper listing its name. Even in her catalogues, her meticulousness and mania for neatness are evidenced. So as not to disrupt the beautiful symmetry of her writing, she made up the rule "one book, one line," and since she was unable to accommodate long scientific titles on her narrow strips, she ruthlessly abridged them, breaking off "in the middle of a name if she reached the end of the paper, sending the rest, which she did not want, to the devil." The most comic aspect of this strange inventory, however, resides in Therese's love for the letter O, whose style she perfected during three years in the same class at school. Therese feels a particular affection for the letter O in the titles of the books she appropriates to herself: "If a long title had a great number of Os she would count first, *how* many, then write them all down quickly at the end of the line and use what room there was left at the beginning of it for the title itself, duly deprived of its Os" (p. 116).

Therese's obsession with money and her love for the symmetrical letter O come together in her mania about Kien's will. Bitterly disappointed when she discovers that his fortune is far less than she imagined, Therese sees this reduced quantity as an insult to her beauty and decency, easily convincing herself that the number "12,650" is in error. Finally, after donning the kid gloves she purchased for her seduction of Kien through *The Trousers of Herr von Bredow*, she examines the will carefully and increases her fortune by adding two beautiful Os to the figure she finds there, regretting immediately that she had not written small enough to accommodate a third O. As in the mirror scene, her greedy hand again detaches itself from her body: "she struggled desperately with the pen which wanted to write," (p. 132) and finally her sense of moderation overcomes her greed. She drops the pen and hurries off to church, leaving behind the revised will that more truly reflects her valuation of her many attractive qualities. Therese's O can be identified with the Lacanian "big 'O'" of Other. Significantly, it is introduced into the novel at the scene of the Word (the library) and takes the form of a lie, a typical characteristic of castrating women, which is in its inverted form a sign of the truth.

Sartre's Roquentin is afraid of mirrors for the same reason that Therese is attracted to them. In the mirror, the individual is split into two persons, and the reflection can, frighteningly, take on its own reality in the mirrored space of reflections. The other, the self, becomes another person, different, even as to sex, separate and yet one with the protagonist. Therese, the masculinized woman, sees her double and opposite as the young man from the furniture store, Mr. Brute, and reads in the mirror the fulfillment she dreamed of when meditating on the word "love" as discovered in her readings.

This love born of pulp magazines turns back on the reader, becoming a self-love that is dramatically played out in front of the mirror.

For Roquentin, the danger of narcissism is much more clear and present since he, like Peter Kien, is deeply immersed in the metaphoric lovemaking of the scholar's work. While Therese masculinizes herself in her love for Mr. Brute, Roquentin is feminized in his relation to books, and specifically, in his relation to the historical figure of M. de Rollebon. Roquentin feels M. de Rollebon as a symbolic pregnancy, even to the point of suffering morning sickness (a wave of nausea) at the thought: "An immense sickness flooded over me suddenly and the pen fell from my hand spluttering ink. What happened? Did I have the Nausea? No, it wasn't that, the room had its paternal, everyday look. The table hardly seemed heavier and more solid to me, nor my pen more compact." Roquentin combats the creeping softness of femininity with the hardness and compactness of his masculine, "paternal" room. Yet, as the passage continues, Roquentin admits the pregnancy that weighs down his metaphoric womb: "He was still there inside me a little while ago, quiet and warm, and I could feel him stir from time to time. He was quite alive, more alive to me than the Self-Taught Man or the woman at the 'Railwaymen's Rendezvous.'"[38] It is not surprising that Roquentin avoids the mirror as a trap, fearful of finding in it the evidence of his own burgeoning female shape.

Like Canetti's protagonist Peter Kien, Roquentin hides this horror of feminine softness under the illusion of a hard, solid masculinity, a hardness and self-sufficiency that he reconfirms in his solitary life-style: "I live alone, entirely alone. I never speak to anyone, never; I receive nothing, I give nothing." This solitary firmness is analogous to Kien's adopted pose of petrifaction, but his hardness is no more real than that of Canetti's scholar. "I never speak to anyone, never," says Roquentin, but he follows this absolute statement with a qualifier: "The Self-Taught Man doesn't count." (Why not?) And then he describes a second exception—Françoise, the patronne, whom he occasionally invites for casual sex after dinner (p. 6). Roquentin's assertion of extreme individualism is followed by these immediate (disclaimed) qualifiers. The patronne can be dismissed as the vehicle for the mindless satisfaction of a mere physical desire, but it is more difficult to account for Roquentin's recognition of and subsequent dismissal of the Self-Taught Man.

The Self-Taught Man is another Roquentin, an image of what he hopes he is not and fears to become. Like Roquentin, he spends his time in the Bouville library, but unlike the self-image Roquentin has carefully built up for himself, the Self-Taught Man is flabby, ignorant, and pathetically grateful for other human companionship. Despite this apparent dissymmetry, when Roquentin is trapped by his own face in the mirror, what he sees is not the hard, rock face of his imaginary self-image, but a soft fleshy mass: "I see a slight tremor, I see the insipid flesh blossoming and palpitating with abandon. . . . that is not what I was looking for: nothing strong, nothing new; soft, flaccid, stale!" (p. 17). Like Freud's small child who feels lost and powerless in the absence of the mother and turns to the mirror for a substitute for the maternal presence and for a means of exercising power over another, Roquentin unconsciously seeks out the Self-Taught Man to reconfirm his own masculinity when the pressures of the mirror become too strong: "I had a ray of hope when I saw him; it might be easier to get through this day together." But the Self-Taught Man, perceived as an opposite that can relieve the solitary fears of the historian, is actually a double who only further intensifies the desire and the alienation. "But," says Roquentin, "with the Self-Taught Man, you only appear to be two." And how does he comport himself, this sought out double and mirror image? He is prone to most unmasculine behavior: he blushes easily and frequently, and in speaking to the hero, "his lips swayed gracefully" (p. 75). A proffered invitation to dinner is expressed almost as a seduction.

In choosing the company of the Self-Taught Man, who horrifies him almost as much as his own face does and whose presence aggravates the attacks of nausea to which he is prone, Roquentin is choosing himself in the guise of another, inclining, as Freud intimates in his discussion of homosexuality, "towards a narcissistic object-choice, which lies in every way nearer and is easier to put into effect than the move towards the other sex."[39] Furthermore, this attraction to the Self-Taught Man and the implied recognition that he is one with the protagonist indicate Roquentin's unexpressed ambivalence in matters of desire. Unconsciously, he "looks about for love-objects in whom he can re-discover himself."[40] Roquentin represses the feminine other he sees in the mirror, but searches for it again in the person of a maternal/homosexual denizen of the library.

Roquentin's narcissism and repressed femininity become an all-pervasive ontological problem in the novel. He would like to escape—or let himself go—but he cannot: "existence penetrates me everywhere" (p. 126). Since existence has become a penetrating force, Roquentin, in his nausea, becomes the receptacle. He is feminized in "soft, monstrous masses, . . . naked in a frightful obscene nakedness. . . . my very flesh throbbed, and opened, abandoned itself to the universal burgeoning" (pp. 127, 133). The Apollonian veneer with which the scholar disguises his own Dionysian longings is destroyed in such moments of nauseous clarity: "And suddenly, suddenly, the veil is torn away, I have understood, I have *seen*" (p. 126). The abstract categories that serve the scholars as protection against the sight of unmediated reality are dissolved, leaving the hero open to that which penetrates the strong narcissistic self-image, revealing its amorphous substructure.

This penetration by existence and the resulting clarity of perception are prepared for by an earlier recollection. Roquentin recalls the days of his youth, when he sat at the feet of the Parisian humanists, remembering the penetrating eye of Virgan, a philosopher who understood the sexualized nature of sight and the incisiveness of the direct stare: "He would take off his spectacles, as if to show himself naked in his man's flesh, and stare at me with eloquent eyes, with a weary, insistent look which seemed to undress me, and drag out my human essence" (p. 113). Virgan seduced the young Roquentin with that stare, branding him for all time as a son and as a lover, awakening in the young man an excessive regard that remained unparalleled in later experience. The old humanist's gaze blinded the young man, erased his nascent masculinity, and signaled him as a receptacle rather than a penetrating force. Appropriately, Roquentin himself takes on the role of the authoritarian, castrating, father figure for the Self-Taught Man, satisfying his desire to be the sought-after object of love rather than the desiring subject. The Self-Taught Man is a provincial humanist, and unlike the powerful father figure recalled from the past, his eyes possess no penetrating power. Roquentin comments disdainfully, "His soul is in his eyes, unquestionably, but soul is not enough" (p. 112).

Roquentin's moments of clear-sightedness toward his own nature do not bring calmness or acceptance. Instead, the nausea drives him to repeated attempts to disprove his own repressed nature through consciously acting out dramas imagined for the desired self. On the day that Roquentin contemplates his face in the mirror and feels the onset of nausea from the revelation of its soft femininity, he leaves his room for the tavern, planning to exorcise the vision of his flaccid softness through sex with Françoise. His face has become, in the mirrored reflection, a kind of nauseating female organ; he will dispel this unpleasant thought by proving his hypothesized hardness by penetration of a woman's soft body. His disappointment at being informed of Françoise's unavailability takes a curious form: "I felt a sharp disappointment in the sexual parts, a long, disagreeable tickling. At the same time I felt my shirt rubbing against my breasts and I was surrounded, seized by a slow, coloured mist. . . . I floated, dazed by luminous fogs dragging me in all directions at once" (p. 78). First, the unavailability of a woman to prove his masculinity causes him to slip further into the nauseated fog-world to which he closes his eyes, subliminally aware of the female burgeoning that would accompany such clarity of vision. This willed blindness is maintained at a counterproductive cost; the unpleasant tickling masculinity is followed by the second sensation: the tickling of his breasts. Serge Doubrovsky points out that "the word *breast* (and the Robert dictionary, I venture to add confirms it), especially in the plural and in the expression: 'the tips of my breasts,' refer [sic] to a fundamental signifier of femininity, one of its essential appendages and endowments. A man usually speaks of his chest."[41] Roquentin's failure to prove his ability to penetrate drives him deeper into the horrors of his rejected mirror image.

The reencounter with his aging mistress, Anny, nearly sparks a similar reaction. Like Roquentin, Anny is well aware of the power of the eyes to provoke disgust. "It isn't good for me to stare at things too long," she tells him. "I look at them to find out what they are, then I have to turn my eyes away quickly" (p. 145). She also realizes that a prolonged stare can uncover the nakedness of things and Anny, like Antoine Roquentin, has no desire to find herself penetrated by the force of existence. As an actress, she recognizes that their compatibility derived from just such a blindness to existence, that they played at role reversal because they did not want to open their eyes to the essential reality of the roles they had chosen. Thus as Anny tells her exlover, "I said; I'm a man of action" (p. 151). She plays at sensuous femininity as Antoine plays at impenetrable masculinity, while recognizing (with a sideways glance) that her essence is that of a man of action, while Roquentin is really an "old woman" (p. 146). The interview with Anny is deeply depressing for Roquentin. His shaky masculinity is further undermined by her newfound honesty, rather than being reaffirmed by her former play of sensuality. The onset of nausea is predictable: "I wanted to stop thinking about Anny, because imagining her body and her face so much, I had fallen into a state of extreme nervousness" (p. 155). He shakes off the imminent attack by engaging in a pastime that reaffirms his masculinity and his power over women: he looks through obscene books in secondhand book stalls, focusing on one entitled *The Doctor with the Whip*. His equilibrium is restored.

Roquentin was attracted to Anny precisely because of the core of masculinity hidden under her ultrafeminine pose. It made her exciting and dangerous, allowing the expression of his passion for masculine hardness and power, without crossing the bounds of a heterosexual relationship. His feelings for Françoise, despite his sharp disappointment when she is not present to satisfy his lusts, more habitually range from depreciation to aversion. He admits that the patronne "disgusts me a little, she is too white, and she smells like a newborn child." Mainly out of politeness, Roquentin feels compelled to play with her genitals, but when he does, "my arm went to sleep" (p. 59). It is the soft childlike odor that most displeases Roquentin, limiting the pleasure of proving his masculinity by subliminally reminding him of babies and reproduction and by what is, perhaps, a too-vivid evocation of his own metaphorical pregnancy.

Further evidence points to the fact that Roquentin wishes to vitiate this pervasive femininity repressed in himself and perceived in others. He clings to the memory of an adventure at Meknes where "a Moroccan jumped on me and wanted to stab me with an enormous knife" (p. 37). Roquentin saves himself from the knife attack by forceful action, but, with his would-be assailant, is chased to Souk Attarin by a band of dirty beggars. In his moments of power, Roquentin feels like the Moroccan knife-man, but he is unable (or unwilling) to act in so decisive a manner. During his dinner with the Self-Taught Man, he considers stabbing a cheese knife into his host's eye, but is detained (so he informs us) by an unwillingness to bring that superfluous event into existence (p. 123). This unwillingness, which may be a disguised inability, to penetrate the fog of existence tempers his most obvious gratuitous act—that of turning the knife upon himself in a rage to escape the soft, sticky neutrality of nausea:

> My knife is on the table. I open it. Why not? It would be a change in any case. I put my left hand on the pad and stab the knife into the palm. The movement was too nervous; the blade slipped, the wound is superficial. It bleeds. Then what? What has changed? Still, I watch with satisfaction. . . . Four lines on a white paper, a spot of blood, that makes a beautiful memory. (p. 100)

What has changed?—very little, if anything. Roquentin makes an attempt to possess himself, to become, in this sexualized sadomasochistic act, the self-penetrating lover. It is an index of his narcissism that he attempts such an act; an index of his ineffectuality as a lover that the knife slips, inflicting only a minor wound that soon coagulates. The illusion that Roquentin has devised in his mind to prove, once again, his masculinity and his potency, is dissipated in the execution of the act, revealing that the historian's power of invention, like that of Peter Kien, is insufficient to carry the imaginative man through his contact with reality. The Moroccan is remembered and admired because he was capable of carrying out the act that Roquentin merely contemplates. He does not stab the Self-Taught Man in the eye because he is incapable of it.

The tiny knife prick that so gratifies Roquentin's aesthetic sense for a brief moment is engulfed in a much more potent penetration, one that Roquentin can only imagine in his hallucinatory dreams. Little Lucienne has been raped and murdered; a double violation by existence. Roquentin, in one of his most sustained fancies, imagines himself alternately as the rapist and the violated girl, deriving an equal measure of autoerotic pleasure from each role in the drama. His wounded hand becomes her wounded body, his penknife becomes her attacker:

> I think that I . . . because . . . ugh! I flee. The criminal has fled, the violated body. She felt this other flesh pushing into her own. I . . . there, I . . . Raped. A soft, criminal desire to rape catches me from behind. Am I going to . . . enter into the existence of another . . . between the wet sugary lips weeping like eyes? . . . he runs, he runs like a ferret, "from behind" from behind *from behind*, little Lucienne assaulted from behind, violated by existence from behind, he begs for mercy, . . . pity, help, help therefore I exist. (pp. 100–2)

Doubrovsky indicates that the ambiguity of Roquentin's desire to rape and to be raped "is none other than the ambivalence of active/passive desire, is momentarily resolved for the benefit of a transsexualization which is phantasmagorically assumed by way of the *place* where desire takes hold of the subject: *from behind*."[42] Roquentin stabs his hand because of the sugary taste of his saliva; and in the following scene his sugary-tasting lips are associated with the sugary lips of the genitals of the raped girl, lips, which, furthermore, are also *eyes*. The girl is violated, and she no longer exists; Roquentin, on the other hand, is violated into existence from behind. Roquentin's mouth is a wound, like that on his hand; the girl's vagina is a mouth and a wound; the rapist's penis is a pen, is a knife cutting into existence, releasing the sugary-sweet blood of femininity.

This episode of the violated girl is crucial to an understanding of Roquentin's secret fears of castration and his secret desires for feminization. Doubrovsky finds evidence that throughout Sartre's text, the word "violet," on all its levels of signification, "is the emblem for a sexuality which is feminine and lethal."[43] Anny, that loved and feared masculinized woman, writes to Roquentin in violet ink (p. 60), recalling to his mind her old practices, and he had, in their past as lovers, promised not to see *Violettes Impériales*—a promise which he promptly breaks when she is too sick to prevent him from attending. A cashier with whom Roquentin is well acquainted is also associated with violets, and with Roquentin himself: "she's red haired, as I am. . . . She is rotting quietly under her skirts with a melancholy smile, like the odour of violets given off by a decomposing body" (p. 55). Earlier in the text, all these variants come together in a sequence that at once associates the various symbolic elements of mouth, genitals, violets, and a sadistic sexual attack from behind. Roquentin recounts his dream:

> I gave Maurice Barrès a spanking. We were three soldiers and one of us had a hole in the middle of his face. Maurice Barrès came up to us and said, "That's fine!" and he gave each of us a small bouquet of violets. "I don't know where to put them," said the soldier with the hole in his head. Then Maurice Barrès said, "Put them in the hole you have in your head." The soldier answered, "I'm going to stick them up your ass." And we turned over Maurice Barrès and took his pants off. He had a cardinal's red robe on under his trousers. We lifted up the robe and Maurice Barrès began to shout: "Look out! I've got on trousers with foot-straps." But we spanked him until he bled and then we took the petals of violets and drew the face of Déroulède on his backside. (p. 59)

Significantly, this dream-sequence follows a nightmarish sexual encounter with the patronne in which the woman's body transforms itself into a hallucinatory garden under his hands. His disgust at the "horrible animals" he imagines peeking out from the woman's genitals parallels the disgust he feels at the smell of the cashier's decomposing body. This nausea is counteracted by a dream of power in which Maurice Barrès is beaten and sodomized (penetration *from behind*) by a bouquet of violets.

Freud's discussion of the fantasy of a child being beaten is pertinent to Roquentin's dream. As Freud discovers, "this phantasy . . . was invariably charged with a high degree of pleasure and had its issue in an act of pleasurable, autoerotic gratification."[44] Furthermore, Freud points out that the person who does the beating is the father, although this fact remains known only to the unconscious because of the intensity of the repression, and instead of fantasizing the father in the role of disciplinarian, "the child who produces the phantasy appears at most as a spectator, while the father persists in the shape of a teacher or some other person in authority."[45] Thus, Roquentin imagines the family as an army, and the beaten child is not himself, but Maurice Barrès. Perhaps the most interesting observation of all, from the point of view of Roquentin's secret femininity, is that the masochistic tendency masks a repressed desire for sodomization. "The boy evades his homosexuality by repressing and remodeling his unconscious phantasy"[46] of being beaten by his father, but Freud notes that when this repression takes the form of a masochistic perversion, the sufferers "invariably transfer themselves into the part of a woman: that is to say, their masochistic attitude coincides with a *feminine* one."[47] Roquentin's disgust and hatred of the soft, decomposing feminine body is transformed, in his dream, into the desire to possess the attributes of the female sex; the hole in the head, the penetration from behind in which pleasure is permitted because the act is a violent one, a violation like that perpetrated on little Lucienne. In his waking life, this desire to become a female is repressed under the fear of castration. We recall once again that on his exit from the unsatisfying visit with Anny, the castrating female, Roquentin is forced to regain his equilibrium by vicariously participating in another beating fantasy in obscene books that so graphically display men of power beating women on their "monstrous naked rumps" with whips (p. 155).

The origin of all Roquentin's unhappiness derives from the separation described in his dream of face and backside. The face has no genital organs, so Roquentin devises one, the hole in the head which can be sexually violated. The violets, then, have two alternatives: "Put them in the hole you have in your head" or "I'm going to stick them up your ass," which represent a single dream reality. In the dream, Roquentin uncovers and beats the face of the backside that is usually blind and hidden from the sun. In his conscious life, he dreams of a parallel sadistic penetration of the eye (the "hole in the middle of his face") of the Self-Taught Man with the cheese knife. The uncovering of the face on Maurice Barrès's backside, and the reference to the hole in the soldier's head are equivalent to an identification of face and ass; it is the same as saying that the soldier has no face—his face is sex. This equation symbolically established between face and sex also reveals the connection between reading and anal eroticism. As the protagonist studies the life of M. de Rolle-bon, the marquis penetrates him (through the eye), symbolically im-pregnating the scholar and reinforcing his feminine nature. Ro-quentin can only avoid this optical violation by blinding himself—visual castration. Yet, even the willed blindness of self-penetration is inadequate to the problem, since there still remains the threat (and the pleasure) of an unseeing violation from behind.

This desired, feared anal eroticism corresponds to the various facets of Roquentin's excremental vision; his need for the sexual gratification provided by the patronne despite—or because of—the putridness he envisions around her genitals, and his other familiar fantasies about soiled bits of paper. Freud realizes that "excremen-tal things are all too intimately and inseparably bound up with sex-ual things."[48] Roquentin's unconscious identification of face and sex comes together once again with the masochistic enjoyment of excremental texts: "I very much like to pick up chestnuts, old rags, and especially papers. . . . with a little encouragement I would carry them to my mouth the way children do. Anny went into a white rage when I picked up the corners of heavy, sumptuous pa-pers, probably soiled by excrement" (p. 10). Roquentin is lost in his love affair with putrefaction. He condemns a reality that is excre-mental and nauseating, but at the same time is consumed by a de-sire for excremental things: the rotting cashier, the sodomized sol-dier, the obscene park of the patronne's genitals that smell of vomit.

Roquentin's perverse attraction to the more unpleasant products of animal life (feces, vomit) is a fitting correlative to his obsession with the engulfing nausea. Derrida recognizes that the two sensa-tions, physical and intellectual, have much in common, as Kant noted:

The first three senses are those of perception (of the surface), while the other two are senses of pleasure. . . . Therefore it happens that nausea, (*Eckel*) a stimulus to rid oneself [*entle-digen*] [by vomiting: *sich zu erbrechen*] of food . . . is given to man as such a strong vital sensation. . . .

However, there is also a pleasure of the intellect [*Geistesge-nuss*] consisting in the communication of thought. But when it is forced upon us [*uns aufgedrungen*], the mind finds it repug-

nant. . . . Thus the natural instinct to be free of it is by analogy
called nausea, although it belongs to the inner sense.[49]

In his discussion of this passage, Derrida highlights the negative
pleasure that derives from both the physical and the intellectual
forms of nausea. He finds that "Vomit is related to enjoyment [*jouis-sance*]. . . . It even *represents* the very thing that forces us to enjoy—in spite of ourselves."[50] It is this obscene interplay of en-
joyment and the violation of enjoyment that is so irresistible to
Roquentin. When all individuality begins to slip away, the immediate presence of the nausea provides the historian not only with a
perverse pleasure, but also with a means of self-identification—
even though it be purely through the reaction of disgust.

Derrida points to one further service provided by the physical
and intellectual nausea: "The word *vomit* arrests the vicariousness
of disgust; it puts the thing in the mouth; it substitutes, but only for
example, oral for anal."[51] It is this fluid orality, free from the stammering of a merely partial historical reconstruction, that Roquentin
aspires to achieve in his account of the life of the Marquis de Rollebon. Yet, in his historical researches, Roquentin is constantly confronted with the unregenerate silence of the documentary evidence
on de Rollebon's life. This silence contrasts not only with the sound
of his favorite jazz music, but also with the implicit *spoken* negativity of his nausea, which replaces the silent anal violation of his
existence with "a still internal negativity which does not reduce itself to silence; it lets itself be spoken."[52]

In contrast with his unconscious desires to merge with a warm,
palpitating dampness, in his conscious desires Roquentin yearns for
the reassurance of masculinity that drives away the nausea. Thus,
his attraction to putrefaction is checked by a love for the "inflexible
order" of jazz that counteracts the viscous happiness of nausea with
a more masculine joy: "There is another happiness: outside there is
this band of steel, the narrow duration of music which traverses our
time through and through . . . tearing at it with its dry little points"
(p. 21). This masculine happiness is typically hard, dry, and cold,
dispelling the viscous, damp warmth of the feminine nausea. Likewise, while the nausea is pullulating with noxious life forms, in the
music, Roquentin feels his body "at rest like a precision machine"

(p. 23). In the dry, cold reaches of art, blood does not flow with its sugary-sweet stickiness; it is frozen, it is ice, it is the purity of "a wave of icy air. . . . To be nothing but coldness" (p. 26).

This desirable coldness contrasts in Roquentin's mind with the flabby warmth of the Self-Taught Man, a contrast that is established on the first introduction of that character in the novel. Roquentin considers his hands, juxtaposing two incidents in his mind. On entering his room, he is stopped short "because I felt in my hand a cold object [the doorknob] which held my attention through a sort of personality." Immediately following this impression is another observation, relating to his meeting with the Self-Taught Man in the library: "I saw an unknown face, barely a face. Then there was his hand like a fat white worm in my own hand. I dropped it almost immediately and the arm fell back flabbily" (p. 4). The doorknob holds his attention; the Self-Taught Man is a virtual nonentity. The doorknob is cold and hard, has personality, signals the threshold of the paternal room; the Self-Taught Man is warm and soft, he has no face. This worm-hand reminds the reader of the ants and centipedes that run out from Françoise's genitals, and this verminous femininity is confirmed by other attributes of the retired clerk; his tendency to blush frequently, his long curved eyelashes, "like a woman's" (p. 30), his near attack of hysterics on being evicted from the library (p. 169). The worm-hand also recalls the male sexual organ, a connection that Roquentin ratifies later in the novel in the climactic scene of the Self-Taught Man's compulsive homosexual seduction attempt:

> I could see something out of the corner of my eye: it was a hand, the small white hand which slid along the table a little while ago. Now it was resting on its back, relaxed, soft and sensual, it had the indolent nudity of a woman sunning herself after bathing. A brown hairy object approached it, hesitant. It was a thick finger, yellowed by tobacco; inside this hand it had all the grossness of a male sex organ. It stopped for an instant, rigid, pointing at the fragile palm, then suddenly, it timidly began to stroke it. (p. 165)

Roquentin is not surprised by the act; his description of the scene indicates that the Self-Taught Man is only enacting a seduction that

Roquentin himself desires to undertake, but he is angry at his companion's lack of restraint. The desire is permissible, indicates Roquentin, but the demands of a hard, icy masculinity require that it not be satisfied. It is not surprising that when the Corsican asks, "Are you a fairy too?" (p. 168), Roquentin has no answer to give. His predisclosed disposition toward an optical/anal eroticism testifies to his own latent homosexuality.

It is quite likely that the homosexual act of the Self-Taught Man is merely a substitute for the kind of erotic gratification Roquentin receives from books. On an earlier occasion, Roquentin had noticed that the Self-Taught Man "observes me with respectful lust," (p. 30) and the scholar-historian has also compared his writing to a homosexual act: "the great Rollebon affair was over, like a great passion" (p. 97). Similarly, the expulsion of the Self-Taught Man from the library does not clear that space of homoerotic doubles. The Corsican remains, and, as Roquentin reminds us, he "likes students because he can exercise a parental supervision over them" (p. 163), a supervision that includes verbal chastisement. The attack upon the Self-Taught Man is as much a result of the Corsican's displaced homosexual impulses as it is of righteous anger. It is easy to imagine the Corsican in the clerk's place, caressing (or beating) the young boys in a homosexual frenzy of which the child's optical/anal seduction is a repressed form.

Finally, there is Anny, whose potency as a masculinized female has already been noted. She too is a double of Antoine Roquentin; she also is associated with the attractive, lethal color violet; she also exercises her erotic attraction with the eyes. Roquentin recalls her "superb look of Medusa, which I loved so much, all swollen with hate, twisted, venomous" (p. 144). The Medusa turns men to stone with her eyes, a consummation to be dreaded because it is linked with the fear of castration, but which Roquentin, perversely, loves and desires because it confirms the hardness and coldness toward which he strives in his conscious life. And further, Anny as Medusa confirms the perverse pleasure of Roquentin's nausea. Says Werner Hamacher: "Break, throw up [*Brechen*]—with me. . . . Indigestible, like stones, one of which has petrified the others—medusaized Medusas that wear one another down."[53] The Medusa's eyes, unlike his own which are penetrated by another, are penetrating weapons that reverse the feminization of face/backside and replace it with a masculine analogue: the head and the genitals become rock-hard, potent, stabbing forces. Roquentin can hardly complain of the woman's look that is capable of transfixing and freezing the object of its perception—he has frequently indicated his own desire to possess a similar power of petrifaction.

In the rigor of the jazz music, Roquentin imagines a pure, cold, sterile style that reflects his own ideal self-image. The look he envies belongs to the Medusa-mask of a frigid, infertile woman, and, like Perseus, Roquentin approaches her backwards, as it were, exposing himself to violation from behind but keeping his eye free from the envied transfixing gaze. Perseus slew the Gorgon Medusa and appropriated her potency in just such a manner; through the aid of a magic cap he is rendered invisible, and he destroys her with the aid of her reflection in a mirrored shield. The invisible Perseus, staring in a mirror, sees not his own reflected features, but those of the Medusa, which become his own as any mirror image, however distorted, belongs to the person looking into the mirror. Her petrifying glare passes through his invisible transparent body and is reflected back in the surface of the shield. Does Perseus really kill the Gorgon, or does she kill herself with that freezing gaze? At any rate, the head reflected in the polished surface is engraved into the mirror in the form of the Medusa's actual head which, when decapitated, is permanently attached to Athena's shield.

The Medusa's head is for Roquentin both a desired and a feared object, and Freud explains the reason for this ambivalence of affect: "the sight of the Medusa's head makes the spectator stiff with terror, turns him to stone." In this aspect, it becomes the incarnation of the evil eye that haunts nightmare visions. But, at the same time, "becoming stiff means an erection. Thus in the original situation it offers consolation to the spectator: he is still in possession of a penis, and the stiffening reassures him of that fact."[54] The Medusa's look deprives the spectator of life and will, but at the same time perpetuates the most sought-after sign of a potent masculinity. Roquentin's perception of jazz as a rigorous, cold, petrifying art form is associated with this desire for a Medusan seduction and is related to the deceptions of the Apollonian impulse described by Nietzsche: "What kept Greece safe was the proud, imposing image of Apollo, who in holding up the head of the Gorgon to those brutal and grotesque Dionysian forces subdued them."[55] This action reveals a monumental aspiration, a desire to turn the viscous, fluid mass of life into clean, cold, dead stone. Norman O. Brown describes the role of the spectator at such an Apollonian (Medusan) festival:

> The spectator is voyeur. The desire to see is the desire to see the genital; and the desire to see is the desire to be one. . . . To idealize is to idolize; to make an idol; to translate into a fixed image for contemplation; to turn into monumental form; to turn into stone. To concentrate on seeing is to turn into stone; Medusa's head; castration.[56]

The Apollonian man is happiest when he is able to create such idols for idle contemplation, to escape with the castrated image and enjoy it in comfort. He is overwhelmed by the coldness that reflects on his own coldness; he is entranced by the monument that proves his masculinity while also declaring his impotence: "the final goal of all monumental aspiration; the Stylites complex. Both castration and erection achieved, in a genitalization of death."[57]

Anny is an actress; Roquentin is a writer of historical fictions; both of them are closely associated with the aesthetic and political realms of representation. As Brown intimates, wherever there is representation, there is a lack of immediacy and therefore the spectator enters into the mediated vision of fiction. Anny's reactions are mediated by masks, which are not unlike the masks worn by actors of antiquity: "she changes faces; as the actors of antiquity changed masks: suddenly. And each one of the masks is destined to create atmospheres, to give tone to what follows. It appears and stays without modification as she speaks. Then it falls, detached from her" (p. 144). By virtue of her use of masks, Anny is distanced from the emotions she represents; her feelings and her voice are transformed into vehicles for the eye. The fat, aging woman is passive to this Apollonian force, and because she is passive to it, as Antoine is likewise passive, the Medusa-mask represents a castrating state of being. Says Brown: "the actor, the hypnotist, the representative person, turns us to stone by showing us Medusa's head: a genital that is both male and female and castrated."[58] The coldness and the rigor are essentially identical to death.

But while this petrified history *is*, and is dead, the death is not completely feared. Roquentin returns to his feared and beloved Anny to be reassured of his physical hardness and to be reconfirmed in his slipping mental ability to petrify time. As Sartre reveals in his autobiography, *The Words*, the *memento mori* is inherently pleasing: "The metamorphosis of that old woman [his grandmother Sartre] into a tombstone did not displease me. There was a transubstantiation, an accession into being."[59] Nietzsche explains that this attraction to the monuments of death is a universal trait of human nature and a necessary component of the historical impulse. The message of the *memento vivere* "is spoken rather timidly, without the full power of the lungs; and there is something almost dishonest about it. For mankind still keeps to its *memento mori*, and shows it by the universal need for history."[60] Roquentin carries his preference for the *memento mori* to a startling length. He does not accept being-in-history; instead, Roquentin wishes to *be* history, wishes to change the temporal flux of existence for the spatialized concreteness of a tombstone. Part of the attraction of the classical mask is that it resembles and prefigures the death mask.

There is another side to this Medusa figure, however, one which is equally terrifying, equally affirmative, but alive, disordered, antihistorical. The Medusa is not merely the castrated male organ, she is also a female, a mother (of the warrior Chrysaor and of the winged horse Pegasus, beloved of the Muses), and a grotesque. As such, she is a living force, and a Dionysian one. Freud reminds us that it is not Apollo who carries the Medusa head on his shield, but his warrior sister, Athena, and appropriately so, "for thus she becomes a woman who is unapproachable and repels all sexual desires—since she displays the terrifying genitals of the Mother."[61] Freud's insight holds true in the fiction. The female, as we have seen from *Nausea*, is quintessentially a being in constant flux, her genitals are filled with the sticky-sweetness of burgeoning life. She calls upon the male to face the Dionysian dissolution she represents, to "gaze into the horror of individual existence," says Nietzsche, "yet without being turned to stone by the vision."[62] This ambiguous, ambivalent Medusa figure, who appears only briefly in Sartre's novel, moves from a peripheral to a central role in Stendhal's *The Red and the Black* and William Carlos Williams's *Paterson*.

He loved, and he dreaded, such a Dionysian woman.

For Julien Sorel, the protagonist of Stendhal's *The Red and the Black*, physical and literary passions constantly cross paths, but the full strength of his devotion is given up to the ecstasy of books rather than to that associated with women. Of his scant personal library, Rousseau's *Confessions* and Napoleon's bulletins of the Grand Army and his *Mémorial de Sainte-Hélène* exercise the strongest spell on his imagination and the most profound claim to his devotion. Stendhal says Julien "would have died for those three works,"[63] compelled by a force of love that no mere mortal woman could ever hope to match. His first visit to a bookstore, in the company of his future mistress, Mme. de Rênal, displays just such a semiotics of passion in the presence of books. Julien stared "in amazement at the quantity of books he saw in the shop." Completely forgetting the woman at his side, he is lost in the ecstasy of books: "Far from trying to guess what might be going on in Mme. de Rênal's heart, he was . . . trying to find a means whereby . . . he might procure a few of those books for himself" (p. 49). This reaction in the presence of books is repeated in Book II of the novel with an even greater intensity. Julien's seduction by the delights of provincial society takes place in a local bookstore; his "First Taste of High Society" (the title of Chapter II, Book II) fittingly occurs in a similar literary setting: the impressive library of the Count de La Mole. Again, the ecstasy that Julien feels is a solitary one:

A few minutes later Julien found himself alone in a magnificent library; it was a delightful moment. So as not to be observed in his excited state, he went and hid himself in a gloomy little corner; from there he gazed rapturously at the shining backs of the books. . . . Julien ventured over to the books; he almost went mad with joy on finding an edition of Voltaire. He ran and opened the library door so as not to be caught in the act. Next he gave himself the pleasure of opening each of the eighty volumes. (p. 248)

Twice in this brief passage, Julien evinces his fear of being discovered; twice the attraction of the books makes him give way to his rapture. In his relationship to books, Julien takes the role of a secret lover. His passions are aroused by the fact of prohibition; it is the forbidden text that most excites him and most fills him with guilty pleasure.

One would expect this same delight in the forbidden fruit to transfer to his relations with women. It does, but only to a certain extent. It is true that both of Julien's mistresses are appealing to him because they are technically beyond his reach: Mme. de Rênal by the fact of her marriage; Mlle. de La Mole by virtue of her superior social standing. But they inspire a passion of an entirely different order from that derived from books. While Julien approaches a forbidden book as a desired lover to be wooed and won, his seduction of women is conducted under the screen of a military engagement. Where his passion (for books) crosses with his plan for seduction, he expresses the latter in the language of the former. Napoleon, through his books, is Julien's true beloved; he approaches his women through the language of Napoleon, a military vocabulary. Thus he considers it his "duty" to ensure that Mme. de Rênal's hand is not removed from his. Pleasure is not involved in the fulfillment of this action, but rather an exorcism of the persistent feeling of inferiority that afflicts the hero. When he achieves this goal, he feels that "he had done his *duty, a heroic duty*" (p. 63). The emphasis on duty is underscored by Stendhal, indicating that Julien's action is not to be misunderstood as a pleasurable impulse, but a tactical maneuver. As in the bookstore, he gives no thought to the woman he has thus conquered. She is the vanquished enemy, and once the battle has been won he can turn to pleasurable activities: "he locked the door to his room, and with an entirely new pleasure, gave himself over to reading about the exploits of his hero" (pp. 63–64). Mme. de Rênal is forgotten. His desire for her is evanescent, the product of his imagination and his twisted sense of what is his due and his duty. Based on his reading, "he planned a detailed offensive" for the seduction of his employer's wife. These readings on love and strategy are then transformed into a military operation, which he again expresses in the language of love through writing: "Since without admitting it to himself, he was very nervous, he wrote out his plan" (p. 90). Julien's sense of the pleasure of reading leads to the extravagantly literal application of literature to life. Like Canetti's Peter

Kien who is pleased to note that life copies literary originals, Julien Sorel writes out a plan for life based on the reading of Fouqué and the Bible. Books are his life and his life becomes a book in which the pleasures of reading are transferred (albeit imperfectly) to the physical pleasures enjoyed with his mistress.

The actual seduction of Mme. de Rênal is conducted according to the written plan, and Julien, after the act of writing, is left practically without volition—he must follow the dictates of the written text. He is subordinate to his plans, as a foot soldier is subordinate to his commanding officer. On leaving the room of Mme. de Rênal after the success of his seduction, he reviews his conduct "like the soldier who comes back from a parade" (p. 96). The palm of victory is awarded to the general, not to the subordinates who merely follow orders, and the success of Julien's seduction is due more to Napoleon and Julien's other literary advisers than to any ability of his own.

The military tactics that served him so well in his first encounter with women are employed once again in his campaign against Mlle. de La Mole. Julien thinks of this relationship as "an armed truce," and asks himself each morning, "Will we be friends or enemies today?" (p. 307). Clearly, Julien is much more comfortable thinking of Mathilde as an enemy to be conquered than as a woman to be loved. Her birth becomes for him a metaphoric "high hill, forming a tactical position between her and me" (p. 331). But in Mathilde's case, unlike that of Mme. de Rênal, the woman counters the attack with her own written weapons. Julien's own obsessive writing is mirrored in that of Mlle. de La Mole. Fittingly, Julien takes these words of passion, so like his own earlier writings, to be a plan for an offensive: "Then, around nine o'clock, Mlle. de La Mole appeared on the threshold of the library, threw a letter at him and fled. 'It seems that this is to be an epistolary novel!' he said, picking up the letter. 'The enemy has made a false move'" (p. 331).

Mathilde, more than Mme. de Rênal, is emblematic of the love affair Julien has with books. She is *read* more than physically possessed. Ignoring the fact that in this seduction by print Mathilde's nature closely approximates his own, Julien is exasperated at receiving three letters from his admirer in one day: "'What a mania for writing!' he said to himself, laughing, 'when it is so easy for us to talk!'" (p. 333). The mania for writing is precisely the point, however, since through her written texts Mathilde becomes the coauthor of this "epistolary novel" with Julien, the object of her desire converted into literature.

It is fully appropriate that this very literary affair take place in the city of fantasies, Paris, and that the love is consummated on a street in which the twin labyrinths of city and library are conjoined: the rue J. J. Rousseau (p. 239). Julien, already tacitly a creature of the book, here becomes more explicitly so; he is possessed by the library-universe and possesses a humanized book. Julien's affair with Mathilde takes on a totally literary cast. Like Julien, Mlle. de La Mole is a creation of the books she has read; the madness in which they engage is that of passion. It is clearly significant that the library provides the first important place of confrontation for this very literary couple: "Early the next morning, Julien was copying letters in the library when Mlle. Mathilde came in through a small private door, cleverly concealed by the backs of books" (p. 253). To Julien, then, it must appear that Mathilde has stepped right out of the books he so admires into his own fantasy library world. The excitement he feels in the presence of books is, fittingly, transformed into an erotic excitement. Like Julien, Mathilde gets her ideas on the nature of life and love from books rather than from her heart. She abets her predilection for the dangerous and forbidden literature through a mirror show of the illusory art: she "had found a way to steal books from her father's library without its showing" (p. 253).

Both Mathilde and Julien find the most delight in forbidden texts, and both hide these books from the eyes of possible censors. Mathilde and Julien are both, in Stendhal's words, "the unhappy consequences of too much civilization" (p. 89), where the word "civilization" could easily and appropriately be replaced by the word "reading." The library-labyrinth, which gives them an illusion of freedom, is actually the deepest and darkest dungeon.

Mme. de Rênal is exempt from this library-dungeon by her innocence of novels, but Mathilde proves the truth of the author's early statement that "in Paris, love is the child of fiction" (p. 46). She realizes she is in love by comparing her feelings to those she has read about in *Manon Lescaut*, the *Nouvelle Héloïse*, and so forth; in the singleminded strength of her imagination, Mathilde is able to imagine a grand passion from a trifling emotion. "This could be another Danton!" she exclaims (p. 315), covering her hesitation and boredom with a heroic veneer. If Julien maintains his passion on a literary level by feeding it substantial doses of Napoleonic lore, Mathilde is no less actively at work on her own fictions, converting the dross of her father's secretary into the literary gold of another Danton, or another Boniface de La Mole as befits her own literary orientation.

The consummation of such a literary affair can only take place in the domain of literature. Mathilde and Julien are so distanced from their passions by the mediation of literature that they become more spectators than participants in the sexual act, detached observers of the actions taken by the other:

> He resorted to his memory . . . and recited several of the most beautiful passages in the *Nouvelle Héloïse*. . . . Mathilde seemed delighted to find a topic of conversation. . . . "I must speak to him," she told herself at length. "It's only proper; one speaks to one's lover."
>
> She had made up her mind that if he dared come to her room, with the help of the gardener's ladder, as stipulated, she would be his. . . .
>
> To tell the truth, their raptures were a bit forced. For them, passionate love was still a model to be imitated rather than a reality.
>
> Mlle. de La Mole believed that she was performing a duty to herself and to her lover. . . . Despite the terrible violence she was doing her feelings, she was absolute mistress of her words. (pp. 342–44)

The love affair, though conducted in the privacy of Mathilde's bedroom, might just as well have occurred in a library, since the presence of books around them is more deeply felt than any physical desire for each other. Julien, typically, plagiarizes Rousseau; Mathilde follows the dictates of the literary precedents she has chosen for herself. Like Julien, she controls the linguistics of passion perfectly; like Julien she allows the physical side of passion to be erased in a mimesis of the literary text.

At the end of the novel, Julien makes his sole instinctive attempt to escape this textualized reality by shooting Mme. de Rênal, but engrained habit is much too strong. Almost immediately Julien transforms his actual prison into a literary one, recalling the sufferings of his mentor, Napoleon, and sitting down to convert the prison cell into a library: "And he set to making a note of the books he wished to have sent down from Paris" (p. 458). This fall back into the complacencies of fiction proves fatal to the young man.

Mathilde makes no similar effort to escape from the novelization that is her fate—and her blessing. With the death of her lover, a death that secretly perfects the love she feels for him, Mathilde is more deeply imbued with her fictive essence until she becomes a fiction at the end. Throughout her bored young life, Mathilde has dreamed of the momentous events of 1574 when Marguerite de Navarre recovered the head of her deceased lover, Boniface de La Mole, and buried it with her own hands (p. 304). Sorel's decapitation allows her to fulfill her most cherished dream, and at the same time reveals to the reader Mathilde's own essential nature as Medusa:

> The memory of Boniface de La Mole and Marguerite de Navarre gave her, no doubt, a superhuman courage. . . . By the time Fouqué had the strength to look at her, she had set Julien's head on a little marble table and was kissing it on the brow.
>
> Mathilde followed her lover to the tomb he had chosen for himself. . . . unbeknownst to everyone, alone in her carriage draped with black, she bore on her lap the head of the man she had loved so dearly. (p. 508)

This last image of Mathilde with her lover's head on her lap not only mimics the image she has chosen for her life from her reading in sixteenth-century history, but also monumentalizes that history, preserving its freshness in the living icon of the young woman. Once again, Mathilde is compelled to act by the fiction chosen to give form to her life; her whole being is thrown into the mimesis until her life becomes her art. As in her love affair with Julien, she is again more observer than participant of her actions, but while the episode in her bedroom is more comic than otherwise, this final scene partakes of a tragic mythic shimmer.

"To decapitate = to castrate," says Freud in his brief study of the Medusa's head,[64] and it is appropriate that Julien's decapitated head is carried apart from his body, between Mathilde's knees, where it is close to her genitals. This is a doubly fitting position in view of Mathilde's Medusa-nature, and also in view of the fact that it was Julien's tongue (his words) rather than his penis that was the real instrument of Mathilde's seduction, a seduction that is directly responsible, through a chain of circumstances, for his eventual execution.

The death of Julien through the perversion of his love for Mme. de Rênal and hers for him can be linked to an earlier episode in the novel in which forbidden love is associated with death. Mme. de Rênal's young son, Stanislas-Xavier, falls ill, and the mother is convinced that his illness is God's punishment for her adulterous love. She must either kill her love, or see her child die (pp. 120–21). The link between love and death becomes even more complex in Julien's relationship with Mathilde. In the case of Mlle. de La Mole, the discovery that she is with child is concurrent with the discovery of her love for Julien (pp. 430–31). This love is intensified at the thought that his head will soon fall, because his decapitation proves the pride of blood that has come down to Mathilde from her ancestors. In the clearsightedness that precedes his death, however, Julien recognizes that passion is merely accidental and that the death of his son would be a blessing to the same family pride that is the essence of his mistress's being. Thus, Mme. de Rênal, who was able to sacrifice her love for the life of her child, would make a more fitting mother to the child of Julien than Mathilde, for whom pregnancy has become a hindrance in the perpetuation of her proud myth. The baby might die in his mother's careless embrace, as the hero must and will, or, at the very least, he will be ignored: "In fifteen years Mme. de Rênal will worship my son, and you will have forgotten him" (p. 474). He requests that Mme. de Rênal take charge of his son, hoping to ensure in this manner the conjunction of a mother's love with the rebirth of passion in his reincarnated self, so that the younger version of himself might bask in a love without reprisals.

The link has an incestuous tinge, however, with Mme. de Rênal becoming the mother/mistress of her reborn lover. It is his own fate to be sealed to his Medusa-wife Mathilde in death, as she puts him in the place of her ancestor (her fore-*father*), enjoying an incestuous relationship with history and triumphantly carrying off the trophy head-penis-child[65] in her arms at the end of the novel. In death, Julien merges more completely with the spiritualized father-lover that Mathilde has chosen for herself, and by embracing the symbol of his potency within her body and outside it (in her lap) she is able to fulfill her fantasy in the reincarnation of the historical tableau that formed the basis of her prime obsession.

For William Carlos Williams as well, the seduction by words results in a symbolic marriage and childbirth. "The words must become real, they must take the place of wife and sweetheart. They must be church—Wife. It must be your wife. It must be a thing of adamant with the texture of the wind. Wife. Am I a word?"[66] Psychic and physical realities fold inward upon each other; the abstractness of words achieves an immovable density—"adamant"—while retaining the transient shape of a gesture felt invisibly: "the texture of wind." The word becomes real, solid; a wife pregnant with poetry. The self dissolves in the abstract space of words. Imagination crystallizes in a new form perfected and gifted to nature, and nature is inhabited by poetic consciousness. The father, who is also the mother, and the midwife, gives birth to his child (himself), a word-child, engendered and born out of the "sea of all knowledge"[67] rather than the feminine sea of blood.

This magical, mythical, metaphysical marriage of self (a word) to words (a wife) points to an endlessly solipsistic closure of a life totally given over to the narcissistic sexuality of writing. Such is the case with Krapp, with Kien, and, to a large extent, with Roquentin. In Williams, however, the word that signifies wife is the word most difficult to define, and since the word escapes him, the closure cannot be completed. A great deal of the content of *Paterson* consists of a manifest effort to give a name to the word-wife so as to more completely possess her and bring the various problems of discord, separation, and difference into a unity that gives a proper form to the patterns of desire. Without passion channeled into the form of marriage, the harmonious interrelationship of word and wife is torn apart by divorce and by perversions of passion that satisfy purely occasional lusts. In his desire to achieve unity and harmony, the virgin word is whored in the service of the poet, giving birth to a bastard child; the son/sun of the book that is doomed to languish inappropriately in the darkness of the library, a brothel (or a prison) of staggering proportions.

The situation is analogous to that of Julien Sorel, himself a series of plagiarized words searching for a name, an image, which would fixate him at a desired level in society. This name he hopes to achieve through his marriage with Mlle. de La Mole, not realizing that she is also nameless, that the name by which society calls her is an empty social function. Ironically, it is with the loss of his head that Julien achieves his true mythic name of Boniface de La Mole, while Mathilde ("for she has a head! a head!" [p. 304]) is herself imaged in the form of Maguerite de Navarre, "the most intelligent queen of his time" (p. 305). Mathilde exerts her fascination while nameless, but with the emergence of her true name, she is monumentalized and surrounded by a startling aura. In death, Julien becomes a Perseus who images the Medusa ("Queen")[68] in the shield of her fiction, thus naming and fixating her while harnessing her power, a power he can no longer employ, for himself. Mathilde keeps her head, but loses her identity in the silent petrifaction of her last iconographic portrait in the novel. Her obsessional, uncontrollable nature is circumscribed by the mastery of the word-husband.

In contrast with the monumentalization of naming that is incarnated in the library, Williams is unable to discover the identity of the object of his desire. The bottle unbottled in the fire is beyond his comprehension: "Things made of glass have no 'aura,'" says Walter Benjamin;[69] even the sex of the word-child, word-wife is uncertain. Says Williams, "they maled / and femaled you jealously / Beautiful Thing" (p. 127), indicating not only the whoring of the virgin word, but an ambivalence as to the nature of the violent rape. Does it represent the sodomization of a boy-child by a superior force, or the violation of a girl-child-wife by a stranger-lover-husband? Both of these alternatives and more are involved, as the dry beauty of the page (a female presence) is sadistically beaten by the whips (pen/penis) of the male writer, and this beaten female presence is somehow transformed into the implicitly male form of the spirits of books, battered against the library windows. And the windows—translucent, auraless glass, the same substance that gives rise to the mysteries of the bottle unbottled—resist the battering now by men, now by female forces:

> —and still he brings it back, battering
> with the rest against the vents and high windows
> (they do not yield but shriek
>   as furies,
> shriek and execrate the imagination, the impotent,
> a woman against a woman, seeking to destroy
> it but cannot, the life will not out of it) . (pp. 101–2)

He/she, the poet, battering and battered, is crushed against the nameless high windows, falling back into nameless impotence. "They maled and femaled you"—who? The shrieking, beaten forces of woman against woman? "She writes," says Derrida. "It is to her that style resorts. Even more: if style were man (as for Freud, the penis would be 'the normal prototype of the fetish'), writing would be woman."[70] Style and writing, man and woman, form and formless desire, are locked together in nameless patterns of attack and retreat, inclining toward marriage, flirting with divorce.

Beauty, says Williams, is "a defiance of authority" (p. 119), tapping against the library walls, undermining the library's foundation, mischievously introducing burning matches between the covers of books. But Williams also says, "To me beauty is purity,"[71] and the degraded women of the park have no beauty, "Unless it is beauty / to be, anywhere, / so flagrant in desire" (p. 71), because they lack the original dry purity of the page beaten and whored into submission. The passion of defiance and the cold purity of resistance meet in the activity of the verse. But the purity of beauty—is this not the same as the frozen, desireless wastes of the library? And the passion of beauty—can this not be identified with the degraded loves of the women in the park? Passion's fire must join with the purifying flame: "To me beauty is purity. . . . And for this you are willing to smash—Yes, everything."[72] The virgin is whored, not by any physical presence, but by the harsh purity of light (the radium) and the devouring flames that caress the bottle (Madame Curie's crucible, the witch's cauldron).

Like Julien Sorel, the Paterson poet is threatened by the loss of his head in the library prison, a decapitation that is equivalent to the loss of manhood. The cost of beauty involves the threat of castration and that of envelopment in the Apollonian veil of a beauty that is purely formal: pure, silent, and free from desire:

> Beautiful Thing!
>
> —the cost of dreams.
>   in which we search, after a surgery
> of the wits and must translate quickly
> step by step or be destroyed—under a spell
> to remain a castrate (a slowly descending veil
> closing about the mind
>   cutting the mind away . (p. 101)

The castrating woman meets the castrated man; lucidity, sterility, and death come together in the decapitated woman, the Medusa, whose head is carried on the shield of the infertile goddess of wisdom, who herself sprang forth full grown from the cloven mind of her father, Zeus, the god of lightning. For Williams, sexual encounters, even woman against woman or man against man, must contain as a minimum condition for decency and beauty the possibility of reproduction. Intellectual as well as physical intercourse must include this potential for procreation. All other relationships are perverse, horrible, death-dealing.

The Beautiful Thing, however, unlike the Medusa, devours what she destroys, merging the separate lucidities into "a nameless fire, that is unknown even / to yourself" (p. 121), a fire that the castrate poet with his "little hoses of objection" (p. 120) is ludicrously unable to control. In another sense, the flowing river of life is only the first metamorphosis of the Beautiful Thing, a metamorphosis that reaches its final form in the monumentalization of rock, which once, as volcanic lava, flowed in a river of fire, but is now captured in the solid shapes (the *named* words) of stone. The poet, voiceless in the face of the fire, lacking the words and names to free himself from the library prison, is equally voiceless in the face of the rock. He can only dream of the imprisoned voices buried in the stones of the great theater of Dionysus (p. 201). Medusa, the creator of stone, and Athena, the daughter of lightning, become "the whore and the virgin, an identity: / —through its disguises" (p. 210).

Woman against woman, maled and femaled, the Beautiful Thing "deflowers" herself as the female fire touches the female bottle in a violent rape that is also a consummation of love. Out of this violation, the bottle is reflowered, capturing the "concentric rainbows / of cold fire" (p. 118) in its new, permanent shape. Clearly, the woman as flower, which equals flame (lightning) is not fragile or helpless. The man counters with his whips in an effort to break down her resistance: "We can hope that the woman will be merciful, a kind of repose (and our rejection in part) for that for which she attacks. And yet there is no woman either to be kind or to live with a kind man, and rightly. The man who would come to her comes with his own weapons, and if he is not a fool, he uses them."[73]

Madame Curie and the queenly African first wife on the log are the poet's principal examples of such potent creative/destructive women. Significantly, the wombs of both of these women are fertile, indicating their function as life-givers, and both are also associated with the metaphoric powers of flame. Fire, the element that burned the library and transformed the bottle, embodies the paradoxical qualities of destruction and creation. While on the one hand it is representative of masculine potency, on the other it has important sexual connotations residing in the female: "the libido that flames up in sexuality, the inner fire that leads to orgasm, and which has its higher correspondence in the orgasm of ecstasy, is in this sense a fire resting 'in' the Feminine, which needs only be set in motion by the Masculine."[74] The ravages of the fire are a necessary prologue to the process of rebirth, but, as Williams realizes, the female fire, once released, can easily range out of control.

In the Madame Curie episode, the flame is needed "to dissect away / the block and leave / a separate metal" (p. 176). Analogously, the Paterson poet employs a flamelike erotic intuition that will bring about the interpenetration of mind and things necessary in order to burn away the sludge of surrounding language and separate out the luminous poetic metal. To the vegetative aspect of the female defined in the early parts of the poem (that is, woman: flower, as in "Innumerable women, each like a flower" [p. 7] and woman: log, as in the nine wives of the African chief astraddle the official log [p. 13]), is added the aspect of woman: flame. The potent first wife of the African chief sits tranquilly dealing "thick lightnings that stab at / the mystery of a man" (p. 21), and the potent female scientist creates a radium child in the female vessel through the mediation of a "luminosity of elements, the / current leaping!" (p. 176).

The aging body of the first wife of the African chief is a symbol of original beauty precisely because of this power gained through her age and experience. She has fulfilled her essential function as a woman by conceiving life within her womb. Nevertheless, this primitive beauty does not suffice as a model for the modern world or for the contemporary poet, since her beauty lacks the component of knowledge (head) typical of Athena, the conqueror and double of the Medusa-queen.

The frequent references to Sappho are to be understood in a similar sense. Where the African queen is all body, Sappho is all mind, representing an opposite and complementary tendency. Like the African woman, Sappho is too distanced—temporally, spatially, and culturally—for her creative/procreative drive to serve as a model. In Sappho, the mathematics of verse construction replaces the murderous poetry of stabbing lightnings, but in one of his prose interpolations, Williams describes her as having a "clear gentle tinkling voice. She avoided all roughness" (p. 217). The clear, gentle voice of the original Sappho contrasts strongly with the tough masculinity of her modern-day counterpart, Corydon, whose poem is introduced with a vulgar bit of prose: "'With that she split her girdle.' Gimme another shot. I always fell on my face when I wanted to step out" (p. 161). Yet, the classical poet can provide no model for a contemporary world—we "do not read her poetry particularly well" (p. 217) even with years of training—and the modern Corydon, despite her great vitality, is a perverse and corrupted product of the capitalistic environment. Corydon's unregenerate (and unregenerative) lasciviousness results in the damming up of her creative potential. She is "flagrant in desire," an empty shell without beauty or interest for the poet except as a warning. The clear inspiration of the Greek poet, the determination and drive of Corydon, and the fierce procreative urge of the African queen are combined in Marie Curie to produce a woman capable of functioning in and producing valuable discoveries for her society.

Madame Curie becomes a symbol of the muse who serves as a source of inspiration for the struggling poet: "(What I miss, said your mother, is the poetry, the pure poem / of the first parts .)" (p. 271). With these words, the muse reminds the poet that in order to reach the radiant gist he must clear away the debris accumulated around the poem and return to the "first parts" (the green, constitutive poetic elements untainted by the stain of the past as corrupted by the library), just as he had earlier celebrated a return to the "first wife" and the "first beauty" as essential life-giving concepts. Marie Curie's experience follows a parallel course to that of the poet as she eats "away a rind / of impermanences, through books / remorseless" (p. 172) in her successful quest for the luminous child she must bear to the world.

But Marie Curie is not only the mother, she is also the child, "a small Polish baby-nurse / unable" (p. 179). From her undeveloped potentiality (we must bear in mind that Phyllis is also a young nurse, though a perverted one), Madame Curie was able to make an astonishing discovery that will be linked to her name and will recall her efforts each time the radiant gist is released from the uranium atom. Historically, the identification is so complete that it makes the discoverer and the discovery almost interchangeable; Madame Curie is, in some respect, invented by her discovery.

In another sense, Madame Curie, the historical figure, is transformed in Williams's work of art and becomes a poetic as well as a scientific child through the poet's rediscovery of her importance as an inspirational force. Madame Curie thus functions as the scientific mother of a transient yet immortal luminous son, and as the child of this luminous son, since through him she is continually reborn and given new life. Similarly, as the mysterious poetic muse, she serves as the source of inspiration for the poet while being continually renewed in his poetry. In Book Five, the paradox is propounded along traditional lines: "—the virgin and the whore, which / most endures? the world of the imagination most endures" (p. 213). It is the transformed, poeticized Marie Curie that is the focus of interest rather than the actual woman. For this reason, while her concrete historical nature is simple to discern, the implications of her existence are complex and mysterious for the poet and the reader. As Kierkegaard observed, "he who is willing to work gives birth to his own father," to which maxim Harold Bloom would add that the child so begotten is conceived upon the body of his mother, the muse.[75] The nouns need only be changed in gender to make the spirit of this aphorism appropriate for Madame Curie. The poet's poem-child is, then, also a radiant son and can be compared to the radiant child of Madame Curie.

This valid immaculate conception implicitly contrasts with the earlier frustrated and perverted relationship between Paterson and Phyllis, in which the girl represents a modern virgin/whore rather than a maternal, life-producing force. As an impotent Paterson brutally strips Phyllis of her clothes, a sardonic narrative voice parodies the song of thanksgiving upon the discovery of the luminous son: "Glory be to God . / —then stripped her / and all his Saints!" (p. 155).

The parodic implications of this episode are further stressed by the introduction of the fishing theme and its concomitant mythic and religious associations with the Fisher King and the Fisher of Men. Corydon wishes to convert Phyllis to her way of life, and the means of seduction becomes the suggested fishing trip. Phyllis accepts the offer of the trip and its implicit sexual overtones with a spectacular indifference, an indifference that is maintained with her male lover as well as with her female one. She is incapable of reproduction, incapable of sensing the deeper undercurrents involved in human relationships. Thus, Phyllis goes blithely from Corydon, a perverse Fisher Queen, to Paterson, the impotent Fisher King, always skimming an indifferent, insignificant surface:

> Let us read, said the King
> lightly. Let us
>
> redivagate, said the Queen
> even more lightly   (p. 164)

Yet Phyllis, who cannot express herself sexually, serves as an introduction to Marie Curie, who is reproductive in both the physical and the intellectual senses. And Marie Curie recalls that other Mary, the mother of Jesus Christ, who combines in one person the physical flame and the intellectual light of creativity, and who remains the unique example of the virgin whored without ceasing to be a virgin. Through Williams's own poetic juxtapositions, therefore, a line of association can be drawn from the perverse and unfruitful whore queen, Phyllis, through the productive "movie queen" (p. 172), Marie Curie, to the beneficent and protective queen of the heavens.

This line of association from impotence to potency, from a negative infertile woman to the release of fertility in flame indicates that the poet's love for the inspiring muse is linked to a dread of her death-dealing properties. The poet must tread with caution in his approach to this ambivalent female force, or the wisdom he desires will become a sterilizing lucidity, and the hope for illumination will be dissipated in the monumentalizing gaze that leads to the impotent perpetuity of the library.

Phyllis and Corydon pervert the natural order; they are the epitome of "predatory minds un- / affected / UNINCONVENIENCED / unsexed" (p. 165), and the closure that defines their joyless existence is intimately related to the figure of the old woman wearing a "china doorknob / in her vagina to hold her womb up" (p. 238). They are empty, closed within a vicious circle of self and selfishness. These predatory, unnatural women are worse than prostitutes because they forestall the dissemination of the word by closing off their feminine space to contact with the masculine seed. Their bellies represent the reign of the soured seed, tightly packed in an infertile library-universe.

The intrusion of Williams's critique of the capitalist ethic is consistent with the poet's development of the theme of sexual perversion in the Corydon/Phyllis/Paterson relationship. In this relationship of the psychopathology of economic desire with the attraction to and repulsion from a Medusa/Athena figure, William Carlos Williams's insight into the sexualized psychic corruption of dirty money is similar to Stendhal's earlier linking of sex and ambition, and reflects back on the economics of human relationships and their implication in the processes of production/reproduction. Erich Fromm's theory of the connection between the development of capitalism and anal eroticism is apposite. The place of reproduction is intricately related to the conception of man's role in production, and although the relation has been partially effaced in the rationalist's work ethic, the physical and the symbolic cannot totally conceal their common origins. Octavio Paz discusses the paradox that necessarily arises from carrying Fromm's discovery to its logical conclusion: "Excrement is the *other* phallus, the *other* sun. Likewise, it is the decayed sun, as the sun is frozen light. . . . To store up gold is to hoard life (sun) and to retain excrement."[76] Money has a similar value in Williams's world. It is equated with "basic thought—leadward / Fractured" (p. 185), and Madame Curie, the genius, the creative female, is also a woman "of no importance" whose discovery serves the purposes of the degenerate state and helps solidify its corrupt order. Radium has phallic properties in its potency to "cure the cancer" (p. 179), and this life-giving value relates it to the earthly sun (gold) and to the heavenly sun. Nevertheless, the equation Uranium=Money, Radium=Credit is excremental and death dealing, and it is this aspect that the poet stresses in Book Four with his analysis of the attraction and dangers of perversion. The discovery of radium itself results in a kind of perversion, for Madame Curie's scientific curiosity is described as "an unhatched sun corroding / her mind" (p. 172). The undeveloped idea becomes a symbolic form of what Paz would call retained excrement. And the idea once developed, once hatched, seems to become equally useless, as Williams reveals in his early "Notes from a Talk on Poetry": "What is the discovery of radium to Mme. Curie today? . . . what is her discovery to her but a stale, useless thing, a thing she would forget in a minute if she could equal it with another as great? It is to her exactly nothing save the end of a circle, exactly where the beginning was—a serenity, a stasis."[77] The Muse once again melds with the Medusa, the attraction of original beauty is overlaid with the fear of the petrifying, dismembering grotesque.

It is thus that in Williams the desire for a "rigor of beauty" is joined with a fear of rigor insofar as rigor→asphyxiation in the technical sphere of form→the castrating Medusan gaze→death. But death, by another curve, brings the poet back into an ambivalent association with beauty: death→the death-dealing womb of the terrible Medusa mother→the fear of/desire for enwombment→desire to take part in the raw, quivering flux of nature. Rigor and beauty are married only in their relation to the poet's death (or castration). In life, rigor is annulled in the multiplicity of phenomena that con-

ιpinge upon consciousness. In life, beauty is divorced from
its association with a system of luminous, effervescent sym-
ιt are sensually apparent, but irreducible to mind:

> (then, my anger rising) TAKE OFF YOUR
> CLOTHES! I didn't ask you
> to take off your skin . I said your
> clothes, your clothes. You smell
> like a whore. I ask you to bathe in my
> opinions, the astonishing virtue of your
> lost body (I said) . (p. 105)

The beauty is attainable only at the cost of reducing it to prostitution—this is the economic factor—and by transforming its nature
through the traducing bath of knowledge that is foreign to it.

It is said that Perseus, when he went to slay the Medusa, was
given by Athene a resplendent mirror to escape the monster's
direct glance, which would have turned him into stone. Perseus, accordingly, looked in the mirror, cut off the Gorgon's
head, and from her blood there sprang the winged horse Pegasus which with one stamp of its foot produced Mount Helicon's sweet fountain, dear to the Muses. But the new Perseus is
a different kind of hero. He disdains or has lost Athene's mirror, and goes against the monster with naked eye. Some say
that, in consequence, he is petrified; others, that he succeeds
but that the fountain of Pegasus is a sweet-bitter brew.[78]

CHAPTER 7

Women of the Book: Brontë, Eliot, Lessing, Murdoch, Ozick, Wittig

ONLY THE STRONGEST of men, Perseus or his avatars, can approach the Medusa at all, can endure her penetrating gaze either shielded or unshielded, can possess her, can appropriate her power for himself. For most men, for most librarians, the confrontation with the Medusa is a dream vision that can never be enacted in the waking world. For most men, as Nietzsche realizes, all women are in some sense Medusas—or completely harmless. Most men belong to "a race of eunuchs; and to the eunuch one woman is the same as another, merely a woman, 'woman in herself,' the Ever-unapproachable." Perseus confronts the Medusa; the eunuchs confuse every woman with Medusa since all women are equally unapproachable. Because of this confusion, "it is indifferent what they study, if history itself always remains beautifully 'objective' to them, as men, in fact, who could never make history themselves." And so, in a final movement, these eunuchs draw history down to their own level, give it their own name, and make of it a mere neuter as well.[1] By styling woman (history) as the Ever-unapproachable (a single nameless name for all womankind), the librarian abrogates his rights and duties as a name-giver and devalues without demystifying the feminine presence in both its spiritual and corporeal aspects. Thus, Jean-Paul Sartre, who in his autobiography describes his future role as that of imposing names, is unable "to carve that glorious body in words,"[2] and thus: "I suffered the horrors of impotence. No sooner was I seated than my head filled with fog. I chewed at my nails and frowned: I had lost my innocence. I got up and prowled about the apartment with the soul of an incendiary. Unfortunately, I never set fire to it."[3]

The question at stake here is no less than an inquiry into the nature of art itself. Is art a nameless Ever-unapproachable, or is it a talisman to protect the wearer from impotence and incendiary passions, a magic mental charm to allow him to approach the Medusa obliquely and appropriate her power as his own? Or is art the abyss itself, so strikingly described by Artaud as a woman in labor:

> This flux, this nausea, these lashes, it is in *this* that the Fire begins. The fire of languages. Fire woven into twisted coils of languages in the shimmering of the earth that opens like a laboring womb, with bowels of honey and sugar. This slack womb's obscene wound yawns open, but the fire gapes above in twisted and burning tongues. . . . The earth is mother beneath the icy fire.[4]

This vast earth mother who gives birth, at one and the same time, to language, to the icy fire, to the flux of history, and to the nausea in one great, obscene gesture, is none other than the Ever-unapproachable described by Nietzsche, an unnamed, and hence, impersonal, mythic figure. Yet, while Artaud intuits the existence of the dim, driving force that gives life and destruction together in one vast uterine contraction, Nietzsche discovers the figure of desire hypostatized in a negativity without sexuality, in an oppressive feminine presence that resists naming and corporalization. Two versions of the same myth: the woman captured in the continual flow of an obscene gesture and the woman imprisoned in the ice of man's fear of impotence and desire for transcendence.

This woman, the Ever-unapproachable-Medusa-earth-mother, seen from the point of view of male custodians of books as described by male authors within the framework of the exclusively male system of the library, is represented as devastatingly powerful, yet ultimately helpless. In their texts, she achieves simultaneously the heights and depths of mythic and symbolic overdetermination.

But while male art can be described through the metaphor of the Medusa, the problem that remains to be explored is the relation of female authors to the library, and, even more specifically, the relation of female custodians of books to the texts and to the institutions that make up their world. How do literate women approach the institution, the eternal, infinite construction within whose physical/metaphysical walls reposes, theoretically, all of human knowledge? Along with this question, at some point, there is a still more disquieting problem that must be posed and confronted implicitly or explicitly in relation to these texts. Can a discussion of the female librarian even be undertaken, or is it a study whose organization is based on the shakiest of premises? Beyond the most banal associations, is not the grammatical construction "female librarian" itself an oxymoron?

While Charlotte Brontë and George Eliot may seem to differ greatly about the role of the woman in society,[5] their depictions of the relation of women to the library are strikingly similar. In both *Jane Eyre* and *Middlemarch* the refuge of the library is denied the intelligent woman, who must satisfy her cravings for knowledge (cravings often expressed in terms of physical hunger) with a vicarious relationship to books, with an inferior position as subordinate to and helpmate of the man, the master, the teacher. Yet, while apparently maintaining their position of subordination to a male will, Jane Eyre and Dorothea Brooke subvert that masculine impulse from beneath. Like Anny, who in *Nausea* strenuously maintains the validity of her mythic constructions in the face of the historian's mania for comprehensive, comprehensible biographies, so too, by the very fact of her almost passive refusal to participate, Jane Eyre frustrates the intent of her cousin-teacher-suitor to transform Christian myth into vulgar practice, and Dorothea Brooke resists the attempt by her first husband to force her to continue his fruitless work of killing primitive myth by cataloguing it according to exhaustive logical categories.

St. John Rivers and Causabon, in their obsession with rationalized structures and in their refusal of human passion, have distorted the world into a library world. Jane and Dorothea must resist the ultimate manifestations of these library worlds created for the convenience of the pious eunuch and the bookish fanatic, but at the same time they acknowledge the attractive power of orderly intellectual accomplishments. In rejecting the dry, bookish desires of St. John Rivers or the posthumous wishes of Edward Causabon, the women by no means reject the library. They have learned their lessons far too well; they return to a library, another library, to a slightly less perverse master, to further their education.

For Jane Eyre, these lessons learned and partially rejected affect the most basic structural determinations of her story. She writes her history, her autobiography, but is careful to remind the reader, in the first paragraph of Chapter 10, that "this is not to be a regular autobiography."[6] It is this irregularity, presumably, that provokes in her an ambiguity of intent. Her true history, like that of Cervantes's narrator, becomes fiction. Thus, Jane opens Chapter 11 with the words: "A new chapter in a novel is something like a new scene in a play" (p. 103). Jane's story alternates between autobiography and fiction, between history and myth; it is a personal drama figured as a play. Jane tells us the truth about significant moments in her past life as she remembers them, and she invents an adventure, a novel or a play, a work of pure imagination. She is doing both simultaneously, in an unconscious act of rebellion against the forms of her life and the forms imposed by books.

Jane's experience of libraries gives likely cause for this ambivalence in mode of expression. As a child, Jane finds the library a refuge from the helpless hatred she feels for the Reed family and a place to flee to when the restraints they force upon her become too burdensome. There she spends happy hours of oblivion when she is excluded from the family circle by her aunt and sent elsewhere to sit quietly and mull her evil ways. But the library is not purely a haven even then. When Jane obeys her aunt's injunction to leave the society of her cousins and retires to a corner to read Bewick's *History of British Birds* (airy Jane dreams of sharing not the birds' plumage or their history, but at least their power of flight), she is interrupted by her cousin John who forbids her the book and exiles her from the bookroom as well. Despite this prohibition, Jane returns to the refuge from which she was driven to "find nourishment for some less fiendish feeling than that of sombre indignation. I took a book— some Arabian tales; I sat down and endeavored to read" (p. 38). Thus, Jane, refused tenderness by her wicked aunt, forbidden access to the library by the order of her male cousin, turns back to the forbidden books for an exorcism of her forbidden passions. She is refused the history, the taxonomy, the catalogue of Bewick, so she turns instead to the fantasy, the mythic excess, the rich disorder of Scheherazade's tales. Significantly, in neither case is she able to achieve her goal; in the first episode she is interrupted by the authoritarian voice of the future master of the house; in the second, her own too-intense feelings prevent her from appreciating the book she has chosen.

The compulsion to return to the library, a compulsion made more significant by denial, by the fact of the multiple interrupted readings (a pattern which, as we shall see, occurs consistently in relation to Jane's approach to books) is given a perverse tinge when Jane is sent to Lowood, the authoritarian school for girls where Jane is to pass what remains of her childhood and adolescence. There, Jane's incipient interest in Helen Burns, a girl who attracts Jane because she is quiet and bookish, is marked by the episode describing Helen's whipping on the first day Jane is admitted to the classroom:

> When I returned to my seat, that lady [Miss Scatcherd] was just delivering an order, of which I did not catch the import; but Burns immediately left the class, and, going into the small inner room where the books were kept, returned in half a minute, carrying in her hand a bundle of twigs tied together at one end. . . . the teacher instantly and sharply inflicted on her neck a dozen strokes with the bunch of twigs. (pp. 56–57)

Jane's quivering anger, an anger that she is accustomed to exorcise in the bookroom, is contrasted to the restrained impassivity of Helen Burns. It soon becomes clear, however, that Helen also employs the book-closet as a place to privately release emotion; she returns to the classroom surreptitiously wiping a tear from her eye, a tear for which the contents of that same book-closet are responsible. The closet, then, is half feared because of the scourge that lies within; for a girl to be sent to the book-closet indicates that she is about to be severely punished for a real or imaginary minor transgression of the law. At the same time, by this very fact, the presence of the book-closet and its significance are branded indelibly on each girl's mind. Jane's longing for the knowledge contained in that room, her literal and figurative famishment, is linked to a fear of the painful plentitude that access to the room often brings. Jane's early attraction to the bookroom, although it was forbidden, because it was forbidden, is now conjoined to a fearful fascination with the Lowood book-closet where the knowledge bound into the pages of books is countered by the fear of the lessons taught by a bundle of bound twigs. It is only to be expected that in such a setting, Jane would grow to adopt the impassive exterior of her friend Helen who was unwilling to release her emotions until she retired to the privacy of the bookroom. Consequently, and not surprisingly, Jane would, at the same time, find nourishment at Lowood, and she would find the nourishment she derives from Lowood's books insufficient to satisfy her driving hunger.

Jane's hunger, similarly manifested in her discontent with Thornfield before the arrival of Rochester, is given a new source of nourishment with the arrival of the master of the house, her future teacher in the forbidden arts of sexual passion. "Thornfield Hall was a changed place . . . ," Jane reflects, ". . . it had a master: for my part I liked it better" (p. 131). The eventual outcome of these early forbidden lessons is indicated, though Jane is blind to the implications, in terms of yet another act of exclusion: "Adele and I have now to vacate the library: it would be in daily requisition as a reception room for callers." The schoolmistress and her pupil are tacitly excluded from the company of polite social callers; they are remanded to an apartment upstairs. Jane's accustomed location for building and releasing emotions is once again denied her; once again she is excluded from the library, and her feelings must find an outlet elsewhere. And where does the mistress turn but to the master? In an almost reflexive movement, Jane turns to the man now ensconced in the library, a man at once feared and fascinating. Before the arrival of Mr. Rochester, the library was a simple classroom; after Mr. Rochester appears to take control of his house, the library is separated from the schoolroom. With the master's appropriation of that room, the library regains for Jane the tension derived from an ambivalent fascination (the Reed boy, the Lowood scourge, the Thornfield master in the bookroom), which is for the schoolmistress a source of pain and perverse joy.

Her self-chosen exile from Mr. Rochester's house upon discovering his prior marriage to the madwoman, Bertha, leads Jane to her other cousins, the Riverses, whose home Jane approaches, typically, in a state of near starvation. Her first sight of Mary and Diane offers a scene of intellectual plenty:

> As they each bent over a book, they looked thoughtful almost to severity. A stand between them supported a second candle and two great volumes, to which they frequently referred; comparing them seemingly with the smaller books they held in their hands, like people consulting a dictionary to aid them in the task of translation. (p. 376)

Mr. Rochester's admission of his preexisting marriage makes Jane physically ill, and the violent indigestion she feels in their last interview—which occurs in the library—is purged in her wanderings and her near starvation. Thus, the surfeit she feels in his presence is dissipated, and once again she can approach a library scene with her former hunger. The library again provides nourishment for a starved mind: "I devoured the books they lent me," and with these learned females Jane recovers the sense of intellectual and spiritual equality that she felt with Mr. Rochester before their ill-fated engagement: "Thought fitted thought; opinion met opinion: we coincided, in short, perfectly" (p. 387).

In contrast with the sense of ease Jane feels in the company of the two women cousins she is deeply sensible of a distance separating her from St. John, a distance that is intellectual, spiritual, and physical. Eventually this distance is transformed into the student-teacher difference, and the aesthetically beautiful Mr. Rivers takes the place of the ruggedly unhandsome Mr. Rochester as Jane's instructor and as her suitor. This change in their relationship is initiated by his request that she give up the object of her studies to concentrate on his: "I want you to give up German, and learn Hindostanee" (p. 452). St. John appeals to Jane as to the good student; but Jane, despite her Lowood lessons in impassivity, knows herself to be naturally rebellious. And like the book-closet at Lowood, St. John's study contains a metaphorical whip along with the nourishing books. Jane is once again requested to join with an instructor in an impossible marriage, to become the helpmate of a man she cannot love, to maintain indefinitely the cold schoolmistress exterior she learned at Lowood at the side of an intransigent male, to continue her state of near starvation and her sense of inadequacy in the presence of forceful males and "books written by men" (p. 293).

The same love for learning that Jane Eyre experiences as a physical hunger animates George Eliot's Dorothea as well, but where Jane rebels against the spiritual paths of Lowood School and St. John Rivers, Dorothea dreams of starving the body to feed the soul: she "had strange whims of fasting like a Papist, and of sitting up at night to read old theological books."[7] Dorothea's hasty acceptance of the Reverend Edward Casaubon, whom she hopes will provide her with just the spiritual glut of learning she so desires, leads her into an orgy of hasty reading: "She was not only thinking of her plans, but getting down learned books from the library and reading many things hastily (that she might be a little less ignorant in talking to Mr. Casaubon)" (p. 43). But Edward Casaubon, whom Dorothea in her innocence had imagined a great historian and a monument of pious learning, belongs in fact, to that race of scrabbling eunuchs described by Nietzsche, who, unable to aspire to any true elevation (spiritual or physical), draw others down to their own pitiful level. Dorothea's twin hungers—the love of learning and her sexual passion disguised as religious ardor—go unfed. "Books were of no use" (p. 443) to feed her, and her own thoughts provided no sustenance: "It was another or rather a fuller sort of companionship that poor Dorothea was hungering for, and the hunger had grown from the perpetual effort demanded by her married life" (p. 442). The infrequent careless caresses of her husband chill rather than warm her; the small taste of married life she has experienced only makes her more ravenous for having to share the bed of a man who is, at the very least, a mental eunuch.

It is a sorry outcome for Dorothea's lofty aspirations. For Dorothea dreamed of being the submissive wife, the adoring assistant, the daughter-student to a brilliant husband-father-teacher:

> She felt sure that she would have accepted the judicious Hooker
> . . . ; or John Milton when his blindness had come on; or any
> of the other great men whose odd habits it would have been
> glorious piety to endure. . . . The really delightful marriage must

be that where your husband was a sort of father, and could teach you even Hebrew if you wished it. (p. 22)

It is curious that Dorothea's attraction to a marriage of painful piety and immortality by association should meld in her mind with the "delightful" idea of marriage to a father who is also her teacher. "I suppose," says Rochester in the last pages of *Jane Eyre*, "I should now entertain none but fatherly feelings for you" (p. 497). The blinded, fatherly Rochester is to become Jane's husband and tutor; Dorothea dreams of a grander fate as Milton's sexual and spiritual partner— and his daughter. In the closed society of Middlemarch, the Reverend Edward Casaubon, a holy and learned man, seems the closest approximation to a Milton that her age and circumstances can offer her in her search for glorious self-sacrifice. Furthermore, "the really delightful" aspect of Mr. Casaubon is that he is already half blind and in need of a daughter's assistance. "I have been using up my eyesight on old characters lately," he tells Mr. Brooke, "the fact is, I want a reader for my evenings." It is immediately obvious that Mr. Casaubon will have no affection to spare for other human beings, and his proud ego provides an opportunity for the sort of self-immolation Dorothea had in mind: "I feed too much on the inward sources; I live too much with the dead. My mind is something like the ghost of an ancient" (pp. 28–29). Half-blind, ugly, inward-turning, and learned in ancient books, Casaubon appears before Dorothea in the guise of a Milton. He is, moreover, "a good seven-and-twenty years older than" his fiancée (p. 49), and serves as a father figure to replace the father she lost when she was only twelve years old.

It would seem almost superfluous to recall that Dorothea is also half blind: "I am rather short-sighted," she admits to Sir James. She has, furthermore, been stifled by her feeling of uselessness in her uncle's house. Mr. Brooke's haphazard document collection needs arranging, by his own admission, but he is reluctant to leave such a thankless task in the eager hands of his niece. "I cannot let young ladies meddle with my documents," he tells her. "Young ladies are too flighty" (p. 31). When Mr. Casaubon indicates that he needs a reader and seems willing to allow her to share his treasured documents, Dorothea is excessively grateful. Her restless energy has found a focus.

The reader is early aware that Dorothea's hungers are hardly as simple as they seem to that young lady. While she (myopically) sees herself as a self-sacrificing amanuensis, her half-conscious intentions are quite different. Dorothea is seduced by the thought of learning itself, of achieving a pinnacle of masculine certainty that is traditionally denied to women. Thus when Dorothea humbly requests her husband's assistance in learning the classic tongues for the purpose of making herself more useful to him, she asks, "could I not learn to read Latin and Greek aloud to you, as Milton's daughters did to their father, without understanding what they read?" Clever Dorothea is more devious than she knows; for in begging for the little crumb of usefulness to a brilliant man, she keeps hidden the true motivation of her request, a motivation that would be grounds for a flat refusal by most men: "but it was not entirely out of devotion to her future husband that she wished to know Latin and Greek. Those provinces of masculine knowledge seemed to her a standing ground from which all truth could be seen more truly" (p. 70).

Dorothea is ambitious. Even Latin and Greek do not satisfy her: "Perhaps even Hebrew might be necessary—at least the alphabet and a few roots—in order to arrive at the core of things" (p. 70). It is at Dorothea's request, then, that her courtship follows the course already signaled in *Jane Eyre*; the young woman takes her subordinate place as a student to a learned man and is taught languages along with what passes for love in the scholar: "Mr. Casaubon consented to listen and teach for an hour together, like a schoolmaster of little boys, or rather like a lover, to whom a mistress's elementary ignorance and difficulties have a touching fitness (pp. 70–71). The equivocation, schoolmaster-lover/little boys-mistress, is a significant and revealing juxtaposition, inviting others: the schoolmaster and the mistress (schoolmistress?), the lover and the little boys. . . . The lessons are both socially incorrect and, through the perverse implications, startlingly appropriate. Both of the principals, however, her intellectual blindness changed to a pure inward sight through a reading knowledge of Latin, Greek, and Hebrew. Casaubon, one supposes, delights in the manipulation of the woman, in the sexless seduction of her virgin impulses.

Thus, Casaubon's courtship of his future wife runs a marvelously similar course to that outlined by Canetti for his hero Peter Kien, who is likewise a eunuch, likewise incapable of satisfying the urges of his chosen wife, and who attempts to cover this inadequacy with the subterfuge of a pile of books. It is, once again, the same strategy used by St. John Rivers in his attempted seduction of Jane. St. John Rivers has given his heart elsewhere; there are no warm sensual urges left for his proposed spouse. Instead, he offers her the perverse closeness of the student-teacher relationship and provides Hindostanee constructions instead of lovelike affection.

If the blank of her formerly useless life in her uncle's home (where she is not allowed to meddle with documents) is the force that drives her into marriage with the old scholar, Dorothea comes to feel a similar blank soon after her marriage, a blank that is intensified as her sense of aimless purpose is paired to the realization that her energies are being dissipated in deadly confusion. Before her marriage, at the height of her infatuation with her dream of a life as an adjunct to a great man, Dorothea "looked deep into the ungauged reservoir of Mr. Casaubon's mind, seeing reflected there in vague labyrinthine extension every quality she herself brought . . . , and had understood from him the scope of his great work, also of attractively labyrinthine extent" (p. 321). Dorothea confuses Mr. Casaubon's library in the head with a real library; further, she invents an attractively infinite labyrinth from the self-reflections of her own desire. Mr. Casaubon is again compared to Dorothea's great model: "for he had been as instructive as Milton's 'affable archangel'" to Dorothea and demonstrated to her the extent of his life work (*not* an original effort to be sure), which aimed at systematizing, not mere scattered documents, but all of myth, into a great reductionist model. These unmastered, unmasterable documents and fragments of devitalized myths are gathered together in a series of notebooks: "His notes already made a formidable range of volumes, but the crowning task [a task similar to the one her uncle would not allow her to undertake, but a task that she ultimately rejects as useless labor in her husband's case] would be to condense these voluminous still-accumulating results and bring them . . . to fit a little shelf" (pp. 34–35). Although warned by her own infatuated realization that Mr. Casaubon's mind is vague and labyrinthine, Dorothea yet sees in him the contradictory aspect of wide vistas; to these wide vistas she proposes to give her life, and to these tortuous labyrinths she offers herself in sacrifice.

The honeymoon in Rome raises in Dorothea's mind the first doubts about the validity of her dream, as the "young ardent creature" again is confronted with an immovable blank, the "blank absence of interest or sympathy" from her newly wedded husband. This affective blank is, unfortunately, paralleled by an intellectual one. Dorothea gradually "cease[s] to expect . . . that she should see any wide opening where she followed him." Mr. Casaubon is wholly, unproductively, unfeelingly labyrinthine: "Poor Mr. Casaubon himself was lost among small closets and winding stairs." Like Peter Kien, he immures himself in windowless rooms: "With his taper stuck before him he forgot the absence of windows, and in bitter manuscript remarks on other men's notions about solar deities, he had become indifferent to the sunlight" (p. 193). In Rome, the labyrinthine predominates: "Dorothea . . . felt with a stifling depression that the large vistas and wide fresh air which she had dreamed of finding in her husband's mind were replaced by anterooms and winding passages which seemed to lead nowhere" (p. 191). They are dark passages, moreover, in which Dorothea knows herself to be an unwanted, alien presence, blank empty corridors, vague dark tombs filled with unassimilated scraps of foreign material. Dorothea's vital qualities, her energy, her passion, recede or are repressed in the presence of her husband, and it is with a sense of lowered expectations that the young woman returns to England with her husband to take up her married life in his house at Lowick.

Her first married encounter with the house, and with the library where Mr. Casaubon passes his time, comes upon her almost with a shock of recognition. For this is a house that fits the vague labyrinthine nature of its owner, and any illusions about wide vistas to be gained at his side are further depressed. "How class your man?" asks the first gentleman in one of Eliot's chapter epigraphs, and the second replies:

> Nay, tell me how you class your wealth of books,
> The drifted relics of all time. As well
> Sort them by size and livery:
> Vellum, tall copies, and the common calf
> Will hardly cover more diversity
> Than all your labels cunningly devised
> To class your unread authors. (p. 125)

Dorothea is depressed by the gradual realization that the voluminous results of her husband's researches are "labels cunningly devised," are mere superficial scratchings that neither provide an insight into myth for modern man, nor preserve the myths in a useful
system. Recognizing her husband's limitations accelerates the advance of shrinking expectations for herself. Now returned to Lowick Manor after her disastrous honeymoon, "the volumes of polite
literature in [her] bookcase looked more like immovable imitations
of books" than storehouses of knowledge and delight, and "the
duties of her married life, contemplated as so great beforehand,
seemed to be shrinking with the furniture and the white vapour-
welled landscape" (p. 261).

The library, the center of the house for Mr. Casaubon, is fittingly
dark and shuttered, a narrow, "melancholy looking" and "small-
windowed" place. Tantripp calls it a "caticom," and her association of
the Lowick library with a tomb is in perfect accord with Dorothea's
sense of the shrinking landscape. Mr. Casaubon, "a little buried in
books, you know" (p. 47), makes of his bookroom a tomb; it is a
tomb, moreover, with a splendid monument to his name to be constructed by the patient efforts of his widowed wife: "he willingly
imagined her toiling under the fetters of a promise to erect a tomb
with his name upon it. (Not that Mr. Casaubon called the future
volumes a tomb; he called them the Key to all Mythologies)"
(p. 459). Dorothea follows her husband into the labyrinthine depths
of his private catacombs as far as her wifely duty forces her, but
hesitates a crucial moment before following him into the tomb to be
immured alive alongside him.

Jane Eyre also longs for wide vistas, and also fights the threat of
enclosure with an assertion of self. But where Dorothea learns to
hate the imprisonment with her husband in the dark, windowless
enclosure of the library-tomb, Jane, a well-trained (whipped) schoolmistress, is fascinated with the book-closet. Significantly, her early
experience of bookrooms combines enclosure in a small space with
wide vistas: "I mounted into the window-seat . . . and, having
drawn the red moreen curtain nearly close, I was shrined in double
retirement. Folds of scarlet drapery shut in my view to the right
hand; to the left were the clear panes of glass, protecting, but not
separating me from the drear November day" (p. 2). Jane is forcibly

removed from this partial seclusion in a small, windowed closet by her cousin John, who flies at her with all the force of his fourteen-year-old male authority: "Now I'll teach you to rummage in my book-shelves: for they *are* mine. . . . Go and stand by the door, out of the way of the mirror and the windows" (p. 5). For Jane's presumption in removing a book, for her effort to lose herself in the seclusion of a closed curtain and an outward gaze through a wide window, for her passionate rebellion against the master of the house ("I don't very well know what I did with my hands, but he called me 'Rat! rat!' and bellowed aloud" [p. 6]), Jane is removed from her self-isolation behind red curtains to imprisonment in the dreaded windowless red room, the room where her uncle had died and his coffin had been laid.

The room, made memorable (and horrible) as her uncle's final resting place within the house, encloses Jane in another version of a coffin, a coffin that is meant to kill the free spirit that is her proudest attribute. In the room at Gateshead, as in her exile at Lowood, Jane is to be taught the lessons of submission proper to a young woman. She is to abjure her pride and her dreams of power in her acceptance of the constraints society has placed on a woman alone and penniless.

Jane fully recognizes the limitations of her position, and in her engagement to the powerful Rochester dreams of an inheritance, an "independence" that would loosen the constraints her suitor is placing on her. For Mr. Rochester, though her spiritual equal, as Jane thinks, prefers to see Jane in an inferior role: as an elf, a fairy, a sprite—a diminished goddess. Jane's smallness and powerlessness make, for her proposed husband, a pleasing contrast with the figure of his first wife, who is both tall and physically powerful.

Nevertheless, as Gilbert and Gubar have discovered, the large, powerful madwoman is the double of the slight governess;[8] she exists in a repressed form within Jane's body. It is a parallel that Mr. Rochester has expended considerable energy in not recognizing. When Jane describes her wedding eve encounter with Bertha, Rochester patronizingly dismisses the vision as "the creature of an over-stimulated brain" and with all the arrogance of manly superiority tells her: "I must be careful of you, my treasure: nerves like yours were not made for rough handling" (p. 321). Yet what Jane has seen, though Mr. Rochester orders her to blindness, is a reflection of herself. During the visitation, the madwoman puts on a wedding veil intended for Jane and turns to gaze at herself in the mirror. "At that moment," says Jane, "I saw the reflection of the visage and features quite distinctly in the dark oblong glass." At the sight of the savage, discolored face, so like "the foul German spectre—the Vampyre" (p. 320), Jane loses consciousness.

It is little wonder that Jane's cousin John tells her to stand out of the way of mirrors and windows; for in the midnight reflection in a glass Jane will devise (if not recognize) the Medusa face that is and is not hers. The true transformation of the slight, powerless governess does not take place until the cycle of the coffin-room is completed, with the death of Bertha, burning in the flames of Thornfield, but more important still, with the death of the unknown uncle of Madeira who leaves her a fortune, the "independence" she desired so desperately during her engagement to the master of Thornfield. The news of her inheritance affects her as a glance from the Gorgon: "I thought Medusa had looked at you," says St. John Rivers, "and that you were turning to stone" (p. 435). Immediately, the submissive Jane dissolves; she becomes demanding. "I am a hard woman— impossible to put off" (p. 437), she responds to St. John's evasions. A hard woman, and a rich one, Bertha and Jane meld into one figure, a composite Medusa who must seek the man she has blinded, the monument of her own creation. The blind mate, a newly humbled Mr. Rochester, provides a perfect foil for the confident young woman, who maintains her attitude of submissive service while possessing the power she had desired and had been deprived of when her cousin John took away her book and when her cousin St. John forced her to give up her studies of German to learn Hindostanee. "Never did I weary of reading to him," says Jane (p. 515). Under the guise of a willing servant to his desires, Jane now directs the footsteps of her husband.

If Jane learned the lessons of apparent submission in the coffin-room of Gateshead and the book-closet of Lowood, Dorothea Brooke learns similar lessons in the catacombs-museums of Rome and the library at Lowick. For both women, the schoolmistress of Lowood, the mistress of Lowick, the effort of repressing their most vital instincts to the requisite passivity requires strenuous exertion.

The energy they possess, not expected and considered unseemly in a woman, is allowed partial expression when the women reach independence; Jane, by way of her inheritance, Dorothea by way of the widowhood that frees her from the importunities of both her uncle and her husband.

Like Jane, who carries with her the memories of two coffins, one that imprisons her, one that sets her free, Dorothea Brooke marries into a tomb and is freed by death. Dorothea, like Jane, longs for wide vistas, and in her short-sightedness thinks to find them in Mr. Casaubon, a man whose life among tombs and catacombs, documents and burial monuments, is aptly reproduced by his researches in his catacomblike home and tomblike library. He is a minor, underground scholar who thinks to excavate the immortal gods and thereby become immortal himself. For a man who has spent his life entombed, it is fitting that his work be described in terms that recall burial stones. Thus, his "Parerga" were considered even by him as "minor monumental productions" (p. 268), and Dorothea looks upon her husband's notebooks as "the weary waste planted with huge stones, the mute memorial of a forgotten faith," that is, as pyramids, or catacombs.

Casaubon is weighed down by all these monumental tasks: "he was prepared only for those amenities of life which were suited to the well-adjusted stiff cravat of the period, and to a mind weighted with unpublished matter" (pp. 193–94). His courtship of Dorothea and the social necessity of marriage and procreation also weighed upon him: "the hindrance which courtship occasioned to the progress of his great work . . . naturally made him look forward the more eagerly to the happy termination of courtship" (p. 69). Stiff and weighted by his desperate search for immortality, Casaubon feels himself petrified on the brink of great discoveries (or recoveries), hesitant to commit himself to the actual writing of his masterpiece lest in the realization of the project his dream be traduced: "the difficulty of making his Key to All Mythologies unimpeachable weighed like lead upon his mind" (p. 267).

Casaubon's unrecognized inadequacies prey heavily upon him; he is not equal to the great cataloguing task he has set himself. He is a man of microscopic capacities; his minor monuments, soon forgotten, are the only copies of himself he will ever leave behind. His blood is "all semicolons and parentheses," says Mrs. Cadwallader. "He dreams of footnotes, and they run away with all his brains" (p. 76). Dorothea herself, by way of contrast, has "the impressiveness of a fine quotation from the Bible,—or from one of our elder poets,—in a paragraph of to-day's newspaper" (p. 19). Mr. Casaubon, that laborer in tortuous, narrow pathways, is rightly compared to the dream of a footnote. There is not a speck of originality in this provincial would-be scholar; in place of creativity the myth-master possesses only the pedantry and the arrogance of Nietzsche's scholiast or eunuch historian. He is a semicolon aping a footnote; his wife, chosen because he needed a reader, is made of finer stuff. She is, as Will notes effusively, a living poem, a fine quote from a real Milton.

Mr. Casaubon's affinity for tombs and monuments, for death and for the desiccated corpses of myth, is reflected in his physical appearance as well. "He is no better than a mummy!" exclaims Sir James Chettam, the disappointed rival suitor (p. 65), and Dorothea, despairingly, is forced to come to a similar conclusion about the life's work that he wishes her to finish after his death as a monument to his vast, useless labor:

> . . . she looked with unbiased comparison and healthy sense at probabilities on which he had risked all his egoism. And now she pictured to herself the days, and months, and years which she must spend in sorting what might be called shattered mummies, and fragments of a tradition which was itself a mosaic wrought from crushed ruins. (p. 445)

Dorothea escapes this literary tomb by delaying in giving her unconditional promise to her husband, and she refuses to be buried alive in the catacomb-labyrinths of Lowick like a modern martyr. She escapes—or does she? In Casaubon the short-sighted Dorothea thought she devised the lineaments of a blinded Milton, needing the assistance of a daughter-secretary in order to compose his great works. In her second husband, Will, Dorothea chooses another version of the same figure, another diminished Milton, a dabbler at poetry and politics. Dorothea's uncle, Mr. Brooke, makes the comparison explicit. "He would make a good secretary, now," he tells Mrs. Cadwallader, "like Hobbes, Milton, Swift—that sort of man"

(p. 311). Mr. Brooke is most acute where most obtuse. Comparing Will Ladislaw, his secretary and the publisher of the local newspaper he sponsors, to Milton, the Secretary for Foreign Tongues to the Council of State, is equivalent to Dorothea's mistaken identification of her first husband with the same immortal statesman, scholar, and poet. If not precisely like Milton, however, Will is a good secretary, quietly and unhappily arranging Mr. Brooke's scattered documents, agitating (in a minor way) in the service of a justified cause.

In her second husband Dorothea does not choose blindly. Although Will's abilities are very limited, by the very fact of his scattering of interests, he presents a refreshing contrast to Casaubon, who was likewise limited in ability, but unlike Will, chose a single, empty line of inquiry for his superficial scratchings. Like Jane Eyre, who chooses the humble life of a reader to a disabled man rather than glorious martyrdom at the side of an ascetic, Dorothea abandons her girlish dream of assisting in the work of another Milton for the milder martyrdom of living as the solicitous wife to a lesser man. "I might have done something better, if I had been better," Dorothea tells her sister (p. 754). As Will is no Milton, neither is she a St. Theresa nor an Antigone whose unconventional daring earned glorious immortality. Dorothea, perhaps wisely, has decided that it is better to direct the footsteps of a weaker man than to languish in total submission to a stronger one. There is a more peaceful life in the "unhistoric acts" and a surer rest in the "unvisited tombs" (p. 768) than in the monuments of the great and the catacombs of the martyrs.

The meagerness of Dorothea's access to the literary world and the repeated ejections of Jane Eyre from the library partially, but only partially, reflect the historical constraints set upon the female creators of these two studious females. The library, which for Jane is associated with coffins, with bundles of twigs used in the name of pious obedience, with a passionate love forbidden because of prior commitment, is for Dorothea associated with labyrinthine tombs, with the pious endurance of the vagaries of a presumed brilliant man, and with the mental conflict between remaining faithful to an unloved memory or marrying the man for whom she feels a child's passionate desire. Although trapped by social expectations, each woman manages to flout society's demands to some small degree, but their transgressions (which loom so large in their narratives) are relatively minor; while the two heroines strain the boundaries of polite society, they do not break totally free of its strictures. Similarly, the two women remain tangential to the structure of the library, though they shift the focus of the lives of the librarians whose lives they touch in that small point of contact. Jane brings to St. John Rivers a renewed commitment to the missionary fervor that is his only true passion and to Rochester she brings the lessons of a youthful marginality that trained her will to mask her devouring hungers as a humble submission to the desires of her mate. The reader clearly notes, however, that it is Jane's clear superiority over her "master" that releases her own desires and provides her a measure of freedom. Dorothea forces Casaubon to recognize the futility of his life work and accepts a second marriage out of a passionate hunger that resembles Jane's in her determination not to be dwarfed or entombed again in life.

The library itself, so central to men, is necessarily marginal in the lives of these women; to some extent, it is for them the Ever-unapproachable, the "library in itself," utterly alien to their hungers. This marginality, this tangentiality has not been collapsed in more recent texts. Instead, Doris Lessing, Iris Murdoch, Cynthia Ozick, and Monique Wittig demonstrate how the woman's tangential relationship to the enclosed space of the library is increasingly attenuated, though the library still exerts an undeniable attraction on her.

In *The Memoirs of a Survivor*, Doris Lessing confronts directly the problem of a woman's relation in/to history. The unnamed female narrator of *Memoirs* is a survivor, whose writings are meant to offer a retrospective view to a period of time that has reached some unspecified end and to provide an alternative to the official (untruthful) histories of that time, histories that are supposedly also familiar to the reader: "But the *truth* was every one of us became aware at some point it was not from official sources that we were getting the *facts* which were building up into a very different picture from the publicized one" (emphases mine).[9] Yet these memoirs, which supposedly offer us "truth" and "facts" in contrast to the official lies, are also subject to the vagaries of memory and the tendency of the mind to elaborate on what fragments it recalls. "We all remember that time," (M, p. 3) says the narrator in the opening words of the book, drawing the reader into complicity with an unfamiliar future-as-past in memoirs that we are asked to see as more truthful, more faithful to fact than a spurious history that has not, cannot, reach our hands. In addition, we are warned that this survivor's memoir is necessarily flawed: "the past, looked back on in this frame of mind, seems steeped in a substance that had seemed foreign to it, was extraneous to the experiencing of it. Is it possible that this is the stuff of real memory?" (M, p. 4). But is "real memory" true? As Anna reminds us in *The Golden Notebook*, "what I 'remembered' was probably untrue."[10] The value and significance of the *Memoirs* as a historical document are seriously affected by the problematics of truth. For if the value of the woman's memoir rests on its claim to be more truthful than the official histories, how is the reader to judge the admitted contamination by a mind that invents as well as remembers? Furthermore, the woman's text *also* aspires to be read as a history: "This is a history, after all, and I hope a truthful one" (M, p. 110). The woman hopes without absolutes; her history may or may not be true, may or may not agree with the facts, but it is valuable in that its questioning of form is in itself more veracious than the monumental versions of official history.

Lessing's history of a future end is made yet more problematic by its chronicle of a simultaneous coexistence in another completed cycle: that of an Edwardian bourgeois family whose country house occupies a parallel universe, which the narrator reaches by dissolving a blank wall in her apartment. As the narrator shifts spatially from the apartment to the country house, from the world of the window to the world beyond the wall, the spatial dislocations (apartment, house) overlap in a temporal continuum (future and past as cycles which have ended). The formalization of her memories in a history, a memoir true or untrue, is paralleled by her consciousness of another space and time seen and experienced most intensely in endless child-time (M, p. 43), in a sequence which does not follow the day-to-day thread of a traditional historical narrative but travels back into a marvelous realm both intricate and infinite, memorable and immemorial. The motionless child-time is subject to even more extreme pressures than those felt in historical time, however, through its detailing of the repressive formalizations of family structure in Edwardian England.

The narrator's awareness of this split (future, past; adult, child; window, wall) in her consciousness of the proximity of the end invites ambiguities in her relation to truth and lie, to invented memoirs and official histories. Her intuition of a missing stage, a missing link (the present?), is most clearly concentrated in her uncertainty as to the nature of "it," the subject and motivating force behind her account of these times and places. "It" is variously, "the secret theme of all literature and history"; "a force, a power . . . distorting all thought by fear"; " 'it' . . . is the word for helpless ignorance, or of helpless awareness"; " 'it' . . . was, above all, a consciousness of something ending" (M, pp. 153–54). Beside the twin formalisms of a future-as-past coexisting with a past-as-future resides the unknowable, unnamable "it" that exerts its baleful influence over all the formalisms, destabilizing them without providing any outlet or relief. Lessing's narrator suffers from the infection of "it," from a surfeit of history, from an invasion by the future into the past, from a monumentalizing impulse and from the recognition of the futility of all efforts to construct a "true" history.

Iris Murdoch's novel, *A Severed Head*, also purports to be a memoir, but Murdoch distances herself more obviously from her first-person narrator. While Lessing recognizes her novel as an "attempt at autobiography," a visionary enterprise, Murdoch has made a self-consciously formalist choice by reviving the Restoration comedy of manners in a modern setting. The narrator, Martin Lynch-Gibbon, "got the best History first of [his] year"[11] at Oxford and continues to think of himself as a historian who only incidentally earns his living as a wine merchant. He dreams idly of writing a monograph on the comparative competence of Wallenstein and Gustavus Adolphus as military commanders in the Thirty Years' War, an imaginary study that is to be part of a larger project on efficiency in military leaders (p. 41). It soon becomes clear, however, that Martin's only completed historical enterprise is the writing of this memoir recounting his various relationships in a tone that is, for the most part, smug and self-satisfied, leaving the reader to discover "it," the secret theme written between the lines of this self-indulgent text.

In Martin's memoir, "it," the mystery that cannot be adduced, is embodied in the shape of Honor Klein, the Oxford anthropologist. If Martin, in his own mind, represents the enlightened historian, Honor, as a devotee of the dark gods, is figured as his absolute antagonist. Yet Honor, the Oxford don, the "remote and self absorbed deity" (p. 93) with eyes "like a cold sun" (p. 177), is not only Martin's antagonist, but is also the embodiment of his dreams, the self he has always wished to become. The anthropologist recognizes, as the historian does not, that "you cannot cheat the dark gods," that in matters of human relationships "you cannot have both truth and what you call civilization" (p. 64). In Honor's presence it is impossible to lie, but the uncivilized, primitive truth that she elicits runs contrary to the historian's truth and counters the lessons of history with irrational urges of dark gods. Martin, deluded by his own dreams of mastery, imagines himself Honor's master, "imagined that she must be virgin: that I would be the first person to discover her, that I would be her conqueror and her awakener" (p. 129). Instead, Martin is himself conquered (if not awakened) by Honor when he stumbles upon her and her brother in her rooms at Oxford, her position and his incontrovertible evidence of their longstanding incestuous relationship. No shrinking virgin awaits the coming of her half-feared lover; as Martin opens the door, Honor Klein is "sitting up in this bed and staring straight at me. . . . I took in her pointed breasts, her black shaggy head of hair, her face stiff and expressionless as carved wood" (p. 128). It is the brother who scrambles to cover himself, and Martin who turns away from the scene and leaves the room. The woman remains motionless, an index of her power, of her control.

While Honor Klein is a swordswoman, a student of the physical/spiritual art of handling a hideously sharp samurai sword, Cynthia Ozick's heroine is at the other end of the spectrum—a mere Puttermesser. Her Uncle Zindel advises her to change her name: "I say make it a name not a joke. Your father gave you a bad present with it. For a young girl, Butterknife."[12] Honor is the potent woman, the mysterious controlling force; Puttermesser is relegated to the "ignominy of belonging to that mean swarm of City employees rooted bleakly in cells inside the honeycomb of the Municipal Building" (p. 28). Like Honor Klein, Puttermesser is a Jewess in an uncongenial world, but unlike Honor, she is powerless; her knife has no cutting edge: "By us we got only *messer*, you follow? By them they got sword, they got lance, they got halberd. . . . Not to mention what nowadays they got—bayonet stuck on the gun, who knows what else the poor soldier got to carry in his pocket" (p. 34). Poor blunt Puttermesser is absorbed into the workings of power, but is powerless herself. At thirty-four, a brilliant lawyer demoted to a meaningless post, "something of a feminist, not crazy" (p. 21), Puttermesser has become a compulsive cataloguer, "organiz[ing] tort cases on index cards" (p. 22). She dreams of meaningful cases, dreams of making a contribution to the cause of Soviet Jewry, dreams of love, and daughters, and a house in the suburbs. But as these commonplace dreams slip further from her grasp, Puttermesser substitutes other dreams of a glorious literary afterlife:

> There, at any rate, Puttermesser would sit, in Eden, under a middle-sized tree, in the solid blaze of an infinite heart-of-summer July, green, green, green, everywhere, green above and green below, her self gleaming and made glorious by sweat, every itch annihilated, fecundity dismissed. . . . Ready to her left hand, the box of fudge . . .; ready to her right hand, a borrowed steeple of library books. . . .
> Here Puttermesser sits. Day after celestial day, perfection of desire upon perfection of contemplation, into the exaltations of an uninterrupted forever, she eats fudge in human shapes . . . , or fudge in square shapes . . . and she reads. Puttermesser reads and reads. . . . In Eden insatiable Puttermesser will be nourished, if not glutted. (pp. 32–33)

Thin, unironic, neurotic Puttermesser eats and eats and reads and reads in an ecstasy of guiltless indulgence. Fudge is for her what a ginger biscuit is for Beckett's Murphy: the most tempting, the most sensual of all foods. Puttermesser's weakness for fudge (and for the aroma of the binding glue used in the books of the Crotona Park branch library) represents for Ozick's heroine, as for Beckett's, the occasion for "a critique of pure love."[13] Murphy arranges his biscuits before him on the grass and meditates on the configurations of edibility theoretically open to him, on Shelley and Wordsworth, on the demeanor of sheep, and on the indiscretions of dachshunds in heat. Puttermesser gobbles fudge and Kant and Nietzsche, contemplates "Roman law, the more arcane varieties of higher mathematics, the nuclear composition of the stars, what happened to the Monophysites, Chinese history, Russian, and Icelandic" (p. 33).

Puttermesser's love for the sonorous names on her proposed reading lists is refracted in her weakness for the toothsome delights of fudge, and the two sensuous joys become one in a generalized love of language as an sensual object: "Puttermesser loved the law and its language. She caressed its meticulousness" (p. 82). She loves the legal jargon despite the fact that she recognizes its constructions are meaningless, that her very title, "Assistant Corporation Counsel" is an empty sound, "part of the subspeech on which bureaucracy relies" (p. 28). Yet Puttermesser allows herself to dream as she reads and eats her fudge; her title may be meaningless, without signification, but it is still poetry, "the poetry of the bureaucracy" (p. 84).

This bureaucratic language, this legal jargon, though so delightful in itself, is still a blank, an empty series of sounds, meaningless poetry. While Puttermesser loves the manipulations of these empty words, she is most profoundly affected by the potent, meaningful constructions of Hebrew grammar:

> The permutations of the triple-lettered root elated her: how was it possible that a whole language, hence a whole literature, a civilization even, should rest on the pure presence of three letters of the alphabet? . . . Every conceivable utterance blossomed from this trinity. It seemed to her not so much a language for expression as a code for the world's design, indissoluble, predetermined, translucent. The idea of the grammar of Hebrew turned Puttermesser's brain into a palace, a sort of Vatican; inside its corridors she walked from one resplendent triptych to another. (pp. 24–25)

From legal language Puttermesser derives the evanescent pleasure of surface manipulations, a pleasure as intense and as fleeting as the overpowering sweetness of a fudge cube melting in the mouth, an exercise as meaningless as the crossword puzzles that Puttermesser staples together and works indiscriminately. Through Hebrew, however, Puttermesser gains access to another world of profound significance: not meaningless poetry, but sacred monuments; potent, divine hieroglyphs whose power she can sense, though at some level (a Jewess in the Vatican) she cannot totally appreciate the religious reality that they hide and uncover. The labyrinthine mysteries of Hebrew are in some sense as lost to Puttermesser as Greek and Roman myth is lost to Edward Casaubon, who also wanders mutely in incomprehensible labyrinthine palaces.

Where Puttermesser, even in her dreams, is an essentially passive character, a blunt domestic instrument, the warrior-women of Monique Wittig's *Les Guérillères* are active forces, independent of man and the meaningless institutions he created. Like Murdoch's Honor Klein, they are sublimely indifferent to conventional morality; in fact, the case could be made that the potent female glimpsed in *A Severed Head* and distanced by the agency of Martin's memoirs, is seen directly in Wittig's book. Honor carries with her an aura of the primitive; there is no softness or sentimentality in her. She has a character that, as Martin surmises, has been developed through long contact with the subjects of her anthropological investigations. In Wittig we see practical anthropology (or archaeology—the time frame is never clear) face to face.

Les Guérillères is intentionally vague as to time and place. If Murdoch and Ozick refer to a stylized present, and Lessing to a survivor's memories of a future-as-past, in her novel, Wittig maintains a temporal indistinctness; her characters consistently speak in the present tense, but the overall effect is of timelessness. Linear temporality is refused as another trap of the rejected male social and political system. This effect of timelessness is intensified by Wittig's adoption of an antihistorical mythic method. The collective female voice recalls old myths, traditional stories suddenly washed new by memories consciously politicized: "You say there are no words to describe this time, you say it does not exist. But remember. Make an effort to remember. Or failing that, invent."[14] Memory is at best partial. The women, though they consciously berate and undermine the recognized male strictures of an unwanted societal organization, in their retelling (reinvention) of myths of the strong woman they consciously or unconsciously ignore the male sources of the myths they use as models. In their inventing and in their remembering, an inconceivable mythic past becomes a possibility, even a future reality. The break with a male-oriented, male-dominated society is effected through a recuperation of myth, through a reinstatement of the marginal as central. Nevertheless, the reinstatement of myth, though subverted, closes a temporal, political cycle. Instead of a male storyteller, we hear a female voice, frequently, but not always, an anonymous one. The women free themselves from the conventions designed to subjugate them, yet remain trapped by myth: "They are prisoners of the mirror" (p. 31), still working through the entanglements of a history that has been invented for them.

These women say that "they ignore the brain" (p. 70), and when man appeals to them in terms of intellectual constructs and formal categories they remain unmoved:

> He says to them throwing his head back with pride, poor wretches of women, if you eat him who will go to work in the fields, who will produce food consumer goods, who will make the aeroplanes, who will pilot them, who will provide the spermatozoa, who will write the books, who in fact will govern? Then the women laugh, baring their teeth to the fullest extent. (p. 97)

Yet while the women laugh at man's bestowal of importance on consumer goods, spermatozoa, and books, their rage and their love are also expressed in literary form, in the creation of Wittig's book and other books, the feminaries that contain a nonintellectualized womanly wisdom. The rejected social contract returns to haunt these women's books; the ghost of the academy is present in what is unsaid, imprisoning the women firmly in the mirror with invisible, uncanny ties. The new set of symbols to which the feminaries give pride of place is used, not to counter and destroy the library, but to "decipher" old legends (p. 45), thus reaffirming the library's centrality even while they subvert its contents.

Along with the reinterpretation of old words and old myths, new bibles are being produced: "The women are seen to have in their hands small books which they say are feminaries" (p. 14). These books, part journal, part cooperative effort, recall the breviaries carried by priests and indeed serve much the same function. Empty pages for unexpressed desires open the way for a return to a quasi-religious economy, and a hermeneutic code for reading and re-evaluating the library functions as an implicit philosophical system.

Then progress (or a retrogression) of sorts seems to occur; the feminaries, with their close ties to myth and religious sentiment, are judged no longer necessary. In their place, the women now have an assembly; the assembly is compiling a dictionary (p. 76).

Concurrently with the writing of the dictionary comes open warfare against the men, as if the crystallization of an ideological system implicit in the efforts of the dictionary-compilers (the assembly, or the academy) results in other rational formalizations as well; the amorphous community of female voices becomes an organized army with a well-defined program of aggression against a specific enemy. Likewise, the peaceful coexistence of revitalized myth with the unassimilated institution of the library is disrupted:

> The women say that it may be that the feminaries have fulfilled their function. . . . They say that thoroughly indoctrinated as they are with ancient texts no longer to hand these seem to them outdated. All they can do to avoid being encumbered with useless knowledge is to heap them up in the squares and set fire to them. (p. 49)

No longer are the women content to reinterpret and modify old myths. Now "all the books must be burned," and "every word must be screened" before it can be readmitted into the vocabulary (p. 134). At the highest pitch of their anger, the women "say, hell, let the earth become a vast hell destroying killing and setting fire to the buildings of men, to theatres national assemblies to museums libraries prisons psychiatric hospitals factories old and new" (p. 130).

Nevertheless, even while the women are attempting to burn out memories of the past and destroy the weighty encumbrances of useless knowledge, at the same time, what is scorched out of memory is not so much the old order, but their ability to recognize traces of it. The traces remain, however, as Wittig reminds the reader in her own subtle reversal/dispersal of a poem by Mallarmé on the second to the last page of her text. Early in her text, Wittig reminds the reader not of the danger, but of the fact, of women's imprisonment in the mirror. In the concluding passage of Wittig's book, the fire that burns the feminaries, the fire that burns the libraries (a fire, moreover, derived from the slanting circular mirror of the women's genitals [pp. 19, 28]) becomes the ice of Mallarmé's sonnet on the trapped swan; ice and fiery mirror converge in a single image.[15]

Appropriately enough, the myth that the women decipher by the aid of their feminaries is a cautionary tale that should warn them of the difficulty of their undertaking: the transvaluation of values followed by the active forgetting of the original, negated principle. The feminaries emphasize "the symbols of the circle, the circumference, the ring, the O, the zero, the sphere. They say that this series of symbols has provided them with a guideline to decipher a collection of legends they have found in the library and which they have called the cycle of the Grail" (p. 45). The Grail cycle of legends describes an epic "geste," a significant choice if we recall that the last words of the final poem in Wittig's original text are "GESTE RE-VERSEMENT." In the poem, the gesture is an overthrow of action in general, and also specifically an overthrow of the heroic enterprise, an overthrow as well of the truncated beginning of a gestation. The women in the novel, however, merely overturn the symbolic meaning of the Grail itself, seeing in it "singular attempts to describe the zero the circle the ring the spherical cup containing the blood" (p. 45), a gross oversimplification that is equivalent to actual blindness. The essence of the Grail quest is not found in the interpretation of the object that is sought, but in the reevaluation of the nature of the quest itself. For the Grail quest is not only a heroic "geste," it is also a perilous voyage of self-discovery in which the object of the quest becomes ever more immaterial. The essence is in asking the right questions. The women, with their feminaries, their dictionaries, their wars, their mirrors, operate on the basis of a simple reversal that does not, as Wittig intimates in her reference to Mallarmé, either uncover the mystery of the Grail or yet ask the necessary questions:

AGAINST TEXTS
AGAINST MEANING
WHICH IS TO WRITE VIOLENCE
OUTSIDE THE TEXT
IN ANOTHER WRITING

THREATENING MENACING
MARGINS SPACES INTERVALS
WITHOUT PAUSE

Society, consciousness, and the novel remain fragmented. Wittig's passion is intense, but the quest is just beginning, the proper questions have not yet been asked or answered; passion alone cannot create the new order.

In *The Memoirs of a Survivor*, the Grail, the unknown object of the quest, is figured simply as "it." "It" is the end that will collapse the narrator's dual quest into the worlds of the wall and the window; "it" will ask the necessary questions in invisible ink between the lines of the traditional legends. "It" is the "feelings of unreality, like nausea" that grip the narrator in those "moments when *the game we were all agreeing to play* simply could not stand up to events" (M, p. 19). "It," like the word, "Grail," embodies the blank helplessness the narrator feels as words lose their meanings with the dissolution of their societal context, what Lessing in *The Golden Notebook* calls "the thinning of language against the density of our experience" (GN, p. 302). Significantly, the dry tone used by Lessing to describe this "painful disintegration" is the very opposite of the passionate lyricism used by Wittig. *The Memoirs of a Survivor* bears witness to "the end" in a language that is flat and restrained; the narrator looks back on the lost world from (perhaps) the other side of the quest and is painstakingly, carefully honest in her uncertainty: "This was comic, of course. Unless it was sad. Unless—as I've suggested—it was admirable" (M, p. 20).

It is a quest that is not undertaken willingly, but one which is forced upon her by circumstances as the flaws in the system become fissures and the narrator, unable to depend on the society outside the window, is thrown back on the resources she discovers through the wall. The order that once existed "in pockets, of space, of time" (M, p. 18), is gradually dissipated, but the narrator turns away from the window to her housekeeping, her private order. The disorder of a disintegrating society is paralleled in the world through the wall as well, however, and again the narrator turns to an impossible task of keeping house as a means of keeping order:

Throughout this period, whenever I was drawn in through the flowers and leaves submerged under half-transparent white paint, I found rooms disordered or damaged. I never saw who or what did it, or even caught a glimpse of the agent. It was seeming to me more and more that in inheriting this extension of my ordinary life, I had been handed, again, a task. Which I was not able to carry through. (M, p. 64)

Yet, as the narrator notes, the discouragement she feels at this hopeless housekeeping task in no measure compares to the discouragement she feels in the "real" world; it is with a sense of liberation that she undertakes the cleaning of these Augean stables, for here, at least, she is filled with a sense of possibilities, of alternatives to be explored. Nevertheless, one housekeeping mania reflects the other; the wall world is a mirror reversal of the window world. It is an Alice-through-the-looking-glass-world of intense personal commitment, a means of salvation, a resurrected myth. It is also, as in Wittig, a trap; the woman remains a willing prisoner of the mirror. Thus, the narrator contemplates the life on the pavement, envies its freedom from rules, and dreams of joining one of the amorphous tribes: "What a relief it would be to throw off, in one movement like a shrug of the shoulders, all the old ways, the old problems. . . . Housekeeping now could be just as accurately described as cavekeeping, and was such a piddling, fiddly business" (M, p. 166). But the narrator, drawn back from the pavement by Emily, by the life beyond the wall, finds one excuse after another to delay the dreamed-of relief. Her rationalizations for this delay are less than honest; in fact, she does not wish to give up the housekeeping (especially the liberating housekeeping beyond the wall) for cavekeeping. She is, in addition, wise enough to recognize that this attractive chaos is only the primary swirling before the adoption of another form, one more suitable to the demands of survival than the outmoded laws of a dying society: "They would have to make for themselves some sort of order again. . . . Responsibilities and duties there would have to be, and would harden and stultify, probably very soon" (M, p. 167). The housekeeper dreams of the carefree chaos of a child's life, but responds intuitively to structure, or to the chaos of a messy house that is accessible to order.

With her dual residences, the flat with the window, the set of rooms beyond the walls, the narrator hopes to avoid unpleasant realities; in her memoirs, her retrospective reordering of that time, she tentatively draws the two into proximity, tidying up, wherever possible, upturned chairs and dirt in the corners. Yet her reordering of that time is no facile housekeeping job; the window world and the wall world remain separate entities, resisting the superimposition of a false unity. The text is disjointed, hesitant, refuses the mutilation that would inevitably result from such a forced union.

At the same time, however, the house and the flat serve as focusing forces; they become for the narrator the binding principle that spatially localizes and integrates her memories into a nonhistorical autobiography, into a truthful fiction. Thus, in each world, the narrator experiences a real transvaluation of values. From the near normality of a cycle of daily chores, interrupted and punctuated by food-buying excursions and gossip with the neighbors, the narrator's world slowly disintegrates into a jerry-built mechanism: "Everything worked. Worked somehow. Worked on the edge" (M, p. 183). At the same time, "while ordinary life simply dissolved away . . . the structure of government continued, though heavy and cumbersome and becoming all the time more ramified" (M, p. 182). Fear of the lawless mobs imperceptibly shades into its opposite; without conscious volition familiar words could slip out of key. The slippage in the vocabulary is one symptom of the generalized slippage in society's orders. Awareness finally dawns on the housekeeper: "how quickly things could change, we could change. . . . *Had* changed" (M, p. 181). Where formerly the neighbors were quick to inform the authorities of activities on the pavement, now, "Above all, what we feared more than anything was the attention of Authority—that 'they' should be alerted" (M, p. 181). Words slip out of key; "we" exchanges places with "they."

In her other world, the world beyond the wall, a parallel transformation occurs, and like the transformation on the pavement it is effected through the interchange of "we" and "they," the people who inhabit the narrator's flat and the people who live in her "personal" world. Like the change in the world of the pavement, the transvaluation (or transcendence, in this case) occurs as a change of key; the Emily who walks out of the collapsed world is "Emily, yes, but quite beyond herself, transmuted, and in another key" (M, p. 217). And thus we are warned that the *Memoirs* themselves, despite the meticulousness that the author gives to definition and word selection, are both familiar and estranged because written in another key. The two worlds, held in necessary tension throughout the book, display their ridiculously oversimplified nature in the presence of "that One who went ahead" (M, p. 217), One which we cannot follow. The One, nameless and beyond language, represents a mystic experience. She heals the housekeeper's dissociative breach nonverbally. Her simple, wordless gesture totalizes and collapses the two worlds, the inside and the outside, the self and the other, and forestalls (or precipitates) the end. And the survivor? Do her words reach us from the brink of collapse or from beyond it?

In *The Memoirs of a Survivor*, then, it is the second world, the presumably illusory world, invented, we hypothesize, as a reaction to the powerlessness of the housekeeper's life, that triumphs in the end over the "real" world of power relationships described in the breakdown and reintegration of hierarchies of authority. In Cynthia Ozick's stories, powerless Puttermesser also dreams/invents nodes of power interchange through which she can influence the most intimate structures of human relationships in the city of New York. The basis of Puttermesser's dream is not housekeeping, but Hebrew. Hebrew is all Ozick's heroine has to counteract the "blank" of America, so "twice a week, at night (it seemed), she went to Uncle Zindel for a lesson" (p. 33). Uncle Zindel, her mother's uncle, "kept his pants up with a rope belt, . . . lived without a wife, ate frugally, died [four years before Puttermesser's birth] with thorny English a wilderness between his gums" (p. 36). From her imagined Uncle Zindel, all she has of her Jewish ancestry, Puttermesser learns of the beauty and magic of the Hebrew tongue, learns of the mystic powers residing in "the bellies of the holy letters" (p. 35), learns to love the sounds of the Hebrew words as they fall upon her ears in the voice of her long-dead uncle. It is Hebrew in another key, Hebrew as she wishes she had learned it.

Her imaginary lessons serve her well. For among Puttermesser's extralegal accomplishments is the art of golem-making, an endeavor that involves a knowledge of the power of the Hebrew alphabet as well as a delicate attention to the detail of ritual. Puttermesser's brain is crowded with bits and pieces of knowledge from her voracious and eclectic reading, but she has a special interest in golem history, an interest that she would describe as purely scientific: "she was unattracted either to number or to method." What interested Puttermesser was something else: "it was the plain fact that the golem-makers were neither visionaries nor magicians nor sorcerers. They were neither fantasists nor fabulists nor poets. They were, by and large, scientific realists" (p. 103). So Puttermesser, seeing the disorder of New York, scientifically creates and gives birth to a golem, a word and clay daughter to take the place of the flesh and blood daughter she will never bear, an intellectual scion brought to life for the express purpose of fulfilling Puttermesser's "Plan for the Resuscitation, Reformation, Reinvigoration & Redemption of the City of New York." And, as she gives life to the golem, so too a sense of high purpose animates the golem-maker, filling her to the exclusion of all index-card torts and orgies of fudge and library books.

The golem, like Puttermesser, is a scientific realist. She makes Puttermesser mayor of New York. The golem does not accomplish this feat through some sorcerer's trick—this is the twentieth century—but by dint of charm and perserverance. Xanthippe organizes a petition, solicits signatures, and engineers her mistress/mother's election as an Independent candidate. From her post, the epitome of her dreams of worldly power, Puttermesser dispenses order, efficiency, honesty, peace, and all-night libraries. She recruits nothing but incorruptible visionaries for public posts; her awareness of the meaningless poetry of bureaucratic jargon inspires her, perhaps, to dream of poets in all key positions:

> . . . she yearns after Wallace Stevens. . . . How she would like to put Walt Whitman himself in charge of the Bureau of Summary Sessions, and have Shelley take over Water Resource Development. . . . William Blake in the Fire Department. George Eliot doing Social Services. Emily Brontë over at Police, Jane Austen in Bridges and Tunnels, Virginia Woolf and Edgar Allan Poe sharing Health. Herman Melville overseeing the Office of Single Room Occupancy Housing. (p. 130)

Puttermesser's dream, then, is to overlay the contents of New York's Crotona Park branch library directly onto the Municipal Building, blending the metaphorical relation of books into the twisted relationships of the impure game of power politics. This imposition of the library onto the political structure of city government through the insertion of poets into prosaic posts, also represents the appropriation of myth into science, an overlapping that Puttermesser dreams of in her lush green Eden and later puts into practice in her "scientific" creation of a golem. This coming together of poets and politics, of literary and scientific knowledge, is effected through the agency of the golem, Xanthippe, the concrete representative of all Puttermesser's inchoate dreams and longings, of all her desires: literary (her readings in golem lore), scientific (her imaging of a perfected political apparatus), and physical (her maternal yearnings for a daughter).

Yet Xanthippe, the embodiment of so many frustrated longings, is a highly ambiguous figure. She is born, a dead child, out of the morass of social upheaval figured in Rappoport's copy of the *New York Times* that Puttermesser carries to bed with her:

> It was as heavy as if she carried a dead child. . . . Affluence while the poor lurked and mugged, hid in elevators, shot drugs into their veins, stuck guns into old grandmothers' tremulous and brittle spines. . . .
>
> A naked girl lay in Puttermesser's bed. She looked dead. . . . Filth. A filthy junkie or prostitute; both. . . . When Puttermesser's back was turned, the filthy thing had slid into her bed. Such a civilized bed, the home of Plato and other high-minded readings. (pp. 93–94)

Xanthippe, who refuses the name her creator had chosen for the name of the most famous shrew in history, has an inauspicious birth amid meditations on sordid crimes, and from the first moment of her mother's conscious awareness of her, is mistaken for a living-dead exemplar of that truth that crawled into Puttermesser's bed from the pages of the newspaper. A blank slate, blank like the blank of America described by Uncle Zindel, yet not blank, Xanthippe is Puttermesser's intellectual as well as earthly daughter, born of mud emptied from flowerpots and from the mental slime of Rappoport's *New York Times*. In her, Puttermesser's high-minded principles war with Puttermesser's mistaken identification of her with a filthy prostitute. Still, Xanthippe is her creator's image; she engineers Puttermesser's success and guarantees her fall: "A golem cannot procreate! But it has the will to; the despairing will; the violent will. Offspring! Progeny! The rampaging energies of Xanthippe's eruptions, the furious bolts and convulsions of her visitations— Xanthippe, like Puttermesser herself, longs for daughters! Daughters that can never be!" (p. 145). The golem reflects her mother's own despair, her own helpless desire for impossible progeny. "Ruth, I came to make love to you!" says Rappoport. She answers, "All I wanted was to finish the *Theaetetus* first" (p. 79). Puttermesser's knowledge of books interferes with and substitutes for other, more carnal knowledge. Like the golem, blank and not blank, desirous of offspring but unable to create them, Puttermesser knows and does not know. She conceives and brings forth a golem daughter, the intellectual child of a physical imperative, but her grasping at poetic politicians, pure restructurings of impure impulses, scientific formulations of mythic constructs, is a conception without knowledge. Puttermesser does not *know*, and therefore cannot create and formalize children-literature-politics from within herself. Her grasping is all at straws. She does not know and cannot conceive. Thus, she must destroy the monstrous simulacrum of life she brought forth, kill her Medusa self in destroying her mirror image, her daughter, her mate, the Xanthippe to her Socrates.

Like Puttermesser, Murdoch's Martin Lynch-Gibbon stands for civilized values, for a scientific transcendence, for "sincerity," "honesty," and similar abstractions that are at the basis of his misconceptions about human nature and human relationships. If Puttermesser cannot bear daughters, neither can he father sons; the child he has Georgie "get rid of" is the nearest he comes to paternity. Martin found the "hideous business" of the abortion "quite uncannily painless" and suffers twinges of guilt because he has not suffered enough (p. 13). The faceless child his mistress never bore, sacrificed to a civilized necessity, looms large by the very fact of its absence. The aborted child becomes the figure for these memoirs, becomes the memoirs, becomes the civilized self of Martin Lynch-Gibbon, stripped from him by those Medusa-mother-wives, Honor Klein and Antonia.

Martin's wife, Antonia, is the epitome of all a civilized society man could desire in a spouse. Her connections are impeccable: "Her father was a distinguished soldier, and her mother, who came out of the Bloomsbury world, was something of a minor poet and a remote relation of Virginia Woolf" (p. 15). Antonia's vestigial religious beliefs, also derived from the "statelier" version of Antonia's mother, "may be described as a metaphysic of the drawing-room" (p. 17). She is a perfect wife in every way; connected to Bloomsbury (at one remove), but no threat to an aspiring historian's own intellectual efforts since her connections are to a *minor* poet, a *remote* relative of Virginia Woolf, another's *drawing-room* metaphysic. In addition, Antonia's beauty is of a time-ravaged sort; she "has more than once been taken for my mother" (p. 15). In his wife, Martin thus finds a comfortable society hostess as well as a mother to replace his own artistic mother (who died when Martin was sixteen), and a woman with vaguely literary connections but no pretensions to compete with his own amateur historical studies. In his memoirs, Martin is perfectly honest, perfectly sincere (in his civilized way) about his relations with his wife, but civilization has little to do with truth and still less to do with the mythic potency of incestuous titillation Martin finds so attractive in his attractive wife. More strongly than he knows, in his relations with his mother-wife, in his attraction to the girl with the man's name young enough to be his daughter, and in his interest in the unfathomable, incestuous Honor Klein, Martin is drawn to the illicit covered with a veil of civilized license.

Martin shies away from such knowledge of himself. In his brother Alexander's studio at Rembers, Martin recalls that in playing his mother's role, Alexander "was the real head of the family" (p. 39). Alexander, the head, is a sculptor, as his mother was a painter, a sculptor particularly interested in working on disembodied heads. Martin does not remember, however, the identities of the women captured in the two heads shown him for his edification by his brother-mother-head of the family. The first head is an unfinished clay bust that Martin views with distaste. The sculpture is arrested in that particular moment that "always seemed to me uncanny, when the faceless image acquires a quasi-human personality, and one is put in mind of the making of monsters." The second head is of an "Antonia that was not quite familiar to me," and in seeing this second bust, Martin "felt a shock of surprise even before I recognized it" (p. 43). It is an uncanny Antonia, one that also makes Martin uncomfortable. By the end of the chapter, Martin remembers at last the uncanny original of Alexander's other, unfinished head: "as I looked now at the damp grey featureless face I remembered what it was. When my mother had died Alexander had wanted to take a death mask, but my father had not let him" (p. 46). The unfinished head, Alexander's death mask of his mother, of himself, draws together the two unknown sculptures of the mother-wife, the painter and the poet's daughter, and reflects back as well on the faceless unborn (dead) child that Martin had carelessly given Georgie. Mother, wife, child, the faceless face breeds uncanny quasimonsters indeed, disembodied heads, monuments of civilized incest (recall that the Gorgon Medusa was born of an incestuous union between Ceto and her brother Phorcys).

As Honor Klein becomes more central to the telling of the memoirs, these images cluster around her. Herself a severed head, involved in an incestuous affair with her brother, she is clearly a Medusan-mother figure. In her book on Sartre, Iris Murdoch indicates her interest in the myth of the Medusa and hints at her dissatisfaction with systems that try to categorize or define her power:

> The striking symbol of the petrifying Medusa is interpreted by Freud as a castration fear (*Collected Papers*, Vol. V). Sartre of course regards as its basic sense our fear of being observed (*L'Etre et le Néant*, p. 502). It is interesting to speculate on how one would set about deciding which interpretation was "correct."[16]

Honor Klein combines both the sexual potency and the omniscience derived from her association with "the dark gods." There is no "correct" interpretation of her significance, however, for correctness, as Murdoch's ironic quotation marks signal, indicates that the question is merely one of social or librarianesque pseudoscientific interest, a category that Honor escapes altogether. She is the castrating female, the sword-wielding woman, and she is also the stone-faced impassive observer who seems to affect the course of events by her very presence. Her presence is sufficient to freeze the most dynamic situation into a sculptural tableau; she paralyzes the other charcters, allowing Martin to compose his memoir, and is paralyzed herself, an uncanny presence frozen on the threshold.

When Martin takes Georgie to see the house he has shared with his wife, the sound of a key turning in the front door "paralyzes" the couple. "It could only be Antonia," thinks Martin. He is filled with panic, shaken by feelings of nausea; "There was something here horrible, almost obscene." Martin goes into the hall to confront this obscenity and finds "Honor Klein was standing just outside the door. The appearance, so unexpectedly, of this absolutely immobile figure had something of the uncanny" (pp. 72–73). It is the uncanniness, the monstrosity of Honor that Martin is later determined to annex to himself so as to shore up his failing confidence in his masculinity with her Medusan hardness. "It was in truth a monstrous love such as I had never experienced before, a love out of such depths of self as monsters live in. A love devoid of tenderness and humour, a love practically devoid of personality" (p. 135); a monster love, devoid of personality, a love accompanied by revulsion, by fear and hatred, a love that inspires the same feelings that Martin experienced with a chill of recognition on seeing the death mask (that was not a death mask) of his mother. Honor Klein is a stone mask of a severed head, but as she is also a Medusa, her features must remain unfathomed. She is an observer and a faceless face.

It is Alexander who formalizes Martin's unvoiced objections to the bodiless head. "An illicit and incomplete relationship," he says. "Yes. Perhaps an obsession. Freud on Medusa. The head can represent the female genitals, feared not desired" (p. 44). From his first meeting with Honor, Martin fears her; soon he is obsessed with her as well. Yet she, like the unfinished head, is both uncanny and deadly: "I saw that without moving her head she was following me with her eyes. It was like the animation of a corpse" (p. 94). Honor herself would not disagree with this assessment:

> Because of what I am and because of what you saw I am a terrible object of fascination for you. I am a severed head such as primitive tribes and old alchemists used to use. . . . And who knows but that a long acquaintance with a severed head might not lead to strange knowledge. . . . But that is remote from love and remote from ordinary life. (p. 182)

"*She* certainly has power in her," says Georgie on the first mention of Honor in the text (p. 7), and Martin, fighting his obsessive love and his overpowering fear, wishes he could maintain a distance and knows that his helpless attraction to her will not let him stay away: "When it came to it I was scared stiff." Even the prospect of meeting Honor is petrifying: "when I pictured being in the same room with her my whole body became cold and rigid" (p. 156). Martin, like Roquentin, turns to the rationality of books to exorcise this irrational urge. He visits the public library, studies mythology, notes with satisfaction that brother-sister incest is common among the gods, notes as well that monstrous progeny result from such unions. At the conclusion of his researches, he is left still more in awe: "What lurid illumination I thus engendered served merely to display with a vividness which prostrated me the figure of Honor, aloof, frightening, sacred, and in a way which I now more clearly understood, taboo" (p. 153). Instead of dispelling the force of Honor's attraction for him, the researches intensify it further, giving him a "rational" (or a "correct") interpretation for his irrational impulses. Finally, in a convoluted sentence that displays the confusion of his own emotions, Martin at last voices to himself the nature of Honor Klein's hold over him: "I could, in the darkness and uncertainty into which we had been plunged by the mute withdrawal of the other two, just about do with, live with, the image of Honor: an image which might however become for me at any moment altogether a Medusa" (p. 156). By this understanding, Honor Klein would seem to be more than ever in danger of slipping into a mythic inaccessibility. Paradoxically, Martin's recognition of Honor's mythic potency acts on him as a stimulus; with this categorization of her nature, the nature of the mystery that surrounds her is revealed. Honor is elevated to myth, but demystified at the same time.

Martin's fearful recognition of Honor's Medusa nature complements his first impression of her as a "headless sack" (p. 57). If, on the one hand, she seems to him a severed head with a potent, piercing gaze, on the other, she is a sagging sack, a slumping, useless Medusa body, already slain by the intrepid Perseus. For Martin, the amateur historian, student of "what constituted efficiency in a military leader" (p. 41), undoubtedly sees himself in the role of Perseus, Medusa's master. Like her mythic counterpart, however, Honor

Klein is by no means defenseless against attack. "I know you have the temperament of an assassin," Martin says (p. 204), and while he apparently is the victor of their dreamlike drunken fight in the cellar, in a later dream scene it is Honor/Rosemary who holds the sword and threatens Martin's genitals directly: "As we danced I attempted to embrace her; but I was impeded by the sword which hung down stiffly between us, its hilt biting into me and causing a sharp pain" (p. 135).

As his perverse attraction to Honor grows, Martin becomes indifferent to both Georgie and Antonia; their "civilized" claims on him fade beside this new primitive, mythic force. When Georgie announces her intention to marry Alexander, Martin's only emotion is a passive nostalgia: "I reflected that we [Antonia and Martin] were like two aged parents wishing the young people well" (p. 162). Martin accepts the marriage of his mistress and the "head" of his family with passive equanimity under the benign influence of Antonia's metaphysic of the drawing room. Under the influence of Honor's personality, the parental affection of two well-bred members of society dissolves in a callous indifference to Georgie's fate. She becomes, indeed, the child he had aborted with such painless ease. He finds Georgie soon after she attempts suicide and realizes, "If she died, I had killed her" (p. 173). The thought pleases rather than shocks him, especially after Honor arrives with her closed, cold face and her precise, detached analysis of the scene: "I thought, she is pitiless. Then I thought, so am I" (p. 174). Martin, at this moment, feels as cold and as dispassionate as Honor herself, savoring the power to wound another human being, the power of life and death over his exmistress, his daughter.

In this same scene, the place of Antonia, his Bloomsbury connected, civilized mother-wife is definitively taken over, whether she will it or no, by Honor Klein, who also becomes a mother figure, though a monstrous one, to Georgie: "the two women composed for me for an instant into an eerie *pietà*, Honor with bowed head, suddenly gentle with concern, and Georgie slain, alienated, sleeping." Here, perhaps for the first time, Martin feels full control over a scene in which Honor, the observer, the catalyst, appears. It is he who assumes the painter's or the sculptor's role and composes the two women into a tableau. Honor, composing a pitiless *pietà* with

Martin's daughter, now hers as well, completes the last stage in the closing of the cycle that began with the aborted infant and Martin's displaced mother-love for Antonia. This pitiless uncivilized love, theoretically, is the sword that cuts him free from civilized entanglements and allows him to write this memoir: "Honor was still touching Georgie's shoulder. . . . I now felt able to touch her too. . . . But what I felt more, as in an electrical circuit, was the shiver of connexion between Honor's hand and mine; and I remember our two hands almost touching on the blade of the Samurai sword" (p. 175). In that touch runs the shiver of an exchange of power, of pure power without metaphysics, without ethics, without morality: an aesthetic power previsioned in the *pietà* and completed in the accidental touch of their hands over the body of the girl. Honor, whose essence seems to escape Martin, does not escape the reader. She remains distanced, mysterious, unknowable, but in the most accessible, the most common way of all. She has been (though with some difficulty) thoroughly classified—Oxford don, anthropologist, *pietà*, incestuous sister, Medusa—and the last two categories, which infringe upon civilized taboo and primitive myth, while they seem to be the most transgressive of all classifications, are actually the least dangerous, the most completely integrated into Martin's structure and his reader's through our parallel researches in the library stacks. Honor is, in addition, Martin's mother, and as his mother exists only to give him life: "No women, then, if I have read [Nietzsche] correctly," says Derrida. No women, "with the notable exception of the mother, of course. But this makes up part of the system, for the mother is the faceless, unfigurable figure of a *figurante*. . . . She survives—on the condition of remaining in the background."[17] Honor, in the final analysis, is as cunningly shaped for the role chosen for her by men as is Martin's well-mannered, well-connected wife, Antonia, and as heedless in falling into her scripted part as Dorothea Brooke and Jane Eyre.

If Iris Murdoch, rather than giving us the story of the comic entanglements of "free love" through the eyes of the obsessed amateur historian, had chosen as her spokeswoman the curiously submissive, motherly (but childless) Antonia who seems trapped by her vague connections to the glittering Bloomsbury world, the reader might expect to find a memoir not dissimilar to the one given us by

Doris Lessing. Unlike the mysterious Honor, Antonia is too easily categorizable; even her mysteries—her love affairs with her psychiatrist and with her brother-in-law—are resoundingly banal. Antonia's role as the beautiful (not overly) and intelligent (not excessively) wife and hostess to a brilliant (self-styled) professional man undergoes no alteration. She is the archetypal woman, an adornment to the drawing room.

In Lessing's novel, drawing-room manners and literary connections are niceties of social organization that gradually come to have less and less meaning. Yet the survivor, who is both a survivor of "the end" and a survivor of the old ways of life, does not have the courage or the decisiveness to step outside the role decreed for women according to the mores of the disappearing societal structure. She is, nevertheless, aware of the intolerable constrictions of her role as housewife and mother; she merely does not possess the fortitude to break down the small coherences and face the chaos she observes through her window. Instead, the narrator, childless like Antonia, gives birth to an idea; a dream of a still more coherent household elsewhere:

> And so—we would have to move. Yes, we would have to go. Not quite yet. But it would soon be necessary, and we knew it . . . and all this time my ordinary life was the foreground . . . of a mystery that was taking place, had been going on for a long time, "someplace else." . . . That wall had become to me—but how can I put it? I was going to say, an obsession. (M, p. 11)

Curious: the project the narrator sets for herself from the opening pages of the book—"we would have to move"—is an action constantly deferred throughout the text as the author remains a passive observer to the dramatic changes occurring around her. It is an action deferred because of the mysterious other life "developing there so close to me, hidden from me"; a movement into the unknown that the writer postpones indefinitely in favor of the slow coming to consciousness of this other unknown life. This slow development, like a mental pregnancy, falls "precisely into the category of under-

standing we describe in the word 'realize,' with its connotation of a
gradual opening into comprehension" (M, p. 7). It is a dawning realization and a process of making real, a process that the narrator
describes in terms of the incubation of an egg. The narrator is aware
and waiting, expectant, as the slow passage of time reaches its necessary conclusion: the chick's biological clock tells it "the precise
and accurate time it needs to get itself out of the dark prison—it is
as if a weight distributes itself, as when a child shifts position in the
womb" (M, p. 12). Then, suddenly, like a chick that pushes its way
out of the wall/prison of its egg, like the child that pushes its way
out of the womb, like Alice who slides through the looking glass,
the narrator pushes her way through the narrow constrictions of
her small apartment into a spacious mansion. But unlike the chick,
unlike the newborn baby, and unlike Alice, the narrator is constrained to return again and again to the tiny apartment/eggshell/
womb. She is constrained by the most primary of all society's in-
junctions—duty:

> I could not help thinking that to have a child with me, just as
> the wall was beginning to open itself up, would be a nuisance,
> and in fact she and her animal were very much in the way. . . . I
> longed simply to walk through the wall and never come back.
> But this would be irresponsible; it would mean turning my
> back on my responsibilities. (M, p. 24)

The narrator's resentment at being trapped by the child is reduplicated in a feeling of entrapment in certain regions of the formerly
spacious, free wall world. Clear air, illimitable space, endless time,
gives way, suddenly, to the restrictions of the "personal": "But to
enter the 'personal' was to enter a prison . . . where the air was tight
and limited, and above all where time was a strict unalterable law
and long—oh, my God, it went on, and on and on, minute by decreed minute, with no escape" (M, p. 42). This slow wearing away
of time in the "personal" compares with the slow wearing away of
time in the cramped apartment after the arrival of Emily. Its temporal restrictiveness contrasts with the pregnant time of an unfulfilled possibility before the wall opens, when the narrator is still

contemplating a possible move from the city and when her state of watchfulness is eventually rewarded by the vista of vast, endless rooms to clean.

While the narrator is aware of her own entrapment, of the closing of her own possibilities with the arrival of Emily and the attendant duties that the mother of a growing daughter must fulfill, she is also aware of the sufferings of the child, a girl-woman who soon comes to the realization of her own stifling entrapment. The narrator constructs an early life for Emily in the horrors of the "personal," a life of unrelieved white on white of a nursery, "an interminable plain of white [where] an infant lay buried and unable to free its arms" (M, p. 138). It is only the little girl who suffers in this stifling white room; her baby brother is placid when surrounded by the same repressive atmosphere: "The windows were closed. . . . the little boy lay silent, his mouth open, but . . . the girl was tossing and struggling to get out, to get out, to get out" (M, p. 91). The boy, a perfect child, rests quietly, but the girl, even asleep, is already uncomfortably aware of the restrictions, the responsibilities, the closed windows and doors.

The infant girl squirms, the child rebels, but the young adolescent seems to accept the responsibilities that society has thrust upon her. When she arrives at the narrator's apartment she is already conditioned, at least outwardly; she is "a child, presenting herself as one" (M, p. 29). Even her adolescent rebellion against her housewife-foster mother's conventions takes the form of that which she has rejected. Emily has found a dress that she adapts to her needs and her moods: young girl's dress, bride's dress, nightdress, evening gown. The older woman stands by helplessly and full of fear, then she realizes that this creation is the "archetype of a girl's dress—or, rather, this composite of archetypes" (M, p. 58). This dress is "her first self-portrait" (M, p. 57), and Emily "had found the materials for her dreams in the rubbish heaps of our old civilisation . . . but [they were] such old images, so indestructible, so *irrelevant*" (M, p. 58). Indestructible and irrelevant: these two words express the paradox of Emily's plight; in a civilization that has been utterly destroyed, the old archetypes of female behavior are absolute, the old responsibilities remain, the old images and old roles are passed on from one generation to the next. Young girl's dress, bride's dress, nightdress, evening gown: Emily is all in pieces. She is a child, a wife, a mistress, a man's companion.

The woman's role is to be for a man; it is a role that Emily consciously and willingly picks up when she becomes one of Gerald's women, a part of his harem. Before a mirror in her schoolgirl's room, "the sort of mirror one associated with a film set or a smart dress shop or the theater" stood a young woman, poised and considering. There, drawing another self-portrait, acting another role, "was Emily, a girl presented or parcelled up as a young woman." Fourteen-year-old Emily is suddenly perverted into a thing, into a man's dream of the sensual, manipulable doll-woman. She has clothed—or unclothed—herself in an evening gown. It was a shocking dress, says the narrator, shocking because it had been tolerated, even more shocking because it was once "coveted by women, admired by women in innumerable mirrors," shocking "because of what [it] made of the woman" (M, p. 187). Emily's many parts come down to this one piece of cloth, this one role, "dolled up" as a plaything for a male, practicing the traditional labor of women— the responsibility, and hence, the discipline, of making herself aesthetically pleasing to men. She becomes the archetype of man's dreams of womanly beauty, womanly accessibility, a thing to be used, even as Emily innocently considers using the dress to gain her own ends. The mother, however, sees beyond the vulgar attractiveness of this dress; this "scarlet horror" starts Emily on the first steps of her preordained path of conversion from a movie queen into a Medusa queen: "It was a dress of blatant vulgarity. It was also, in a perverted way, non-sexual, for all its advertisement of the body, and embodied the fantasies of a certain kind of man who, dressing a woman thus, made her a doll, ridiculous, both provocative and helpless; disarmed her, made her something to hate, to pity, to fear—a grotesque" (M, p. 187). Lessing condenses the transformation within the compactness of a single sentence; from provocative helplessness to a fearful grotesque, the dress spun from man's dreams and woman's compliance results in the manufacture of a monster. The perversity begun with a considering look in front of a mirror ends with the decapitation in the mirror of Athena's shield; the sensual object becomes a nonsexual doll, a statue of man's aesthetic ideals. "And," says the narrator, "that was the last time I saw

Emily there in what I have called the 'personal'. . . . That horrible
mirror-scene, with its implications of perversity, was the end" (M,
p. 189). The end, that is, another definition of the undefined, anticipated "it."

Emily the infant is already being prepared for this passive role in
a man's dreams by the torture she undergoes at the hands of her
father in a bedtime ritual that the mother observes with solid, blank
indifference:

> He was "tickling" the child. This was a "game," the bedtime
> "game," a ritual. The elder child was being played with, was
> being made tired, was being given her allowance of attention,
> before being put to bed, and it was a service by the father to
> the mother, who could not cope with the demands of her day,
> the demands of Emily. . . . [The little girl] was hot and sweat-
> ing, and her body was contorting and twisting to escape the
> man's great hands. . . , to escape the great cruel face that bent
> so close over her with its look of private satisfaction. The room
> seemed filled with a hot anguish, the fear of being held tight
> there, the need for being held and tortured, since this was how
> she pleased her captors. . . . helpless, being explored and laid
> bare by this man. (M, p. 88)

Thus is the woman taught her role, thus is she trained in submis-
siveness to a man, thus is she instructed that her function is dutiful
martyrdom to a man's pleasure, that her pleasure is to be the masochistic twistings and turnings, the proddings and pressures as she is
forced into a bridal gown, the nightdress, a scarlet evening gown,
always passive, always laid bare. The child Emily cannot speak to
stop the torture; she can only shriek, "No, no, no, no"; the woman
Emily, like her foster mother the narrator, cannot speak of her wants
or of her desire to be set free. She has no power to speak; it is taken
away from her by the cruel torturing hands of the father-lover. Neither are there words for Emily's conception or for any child's conception; although her birth is recorded in the passage through the
wall, her anguished infancy and childhood occur in the enclosure of
the "personal," her growth from girl to woman is transcribed in the

stifling narrow confines of the apartment with its closed window to the future and wall open onto the past.

The child passes almost without transition from the screaming helplessness of a girl being tortured by her father to the weeping of an adult; the intolerable tears of a woman who weeps "as if the earth were bleeding" for her lost hopes, her self lost in endless self-portraits. Yet in the anguish of a woman's tears, there are still the remnants of the child's helpless anguish: "Yes, in spite of myself, every word I put down is on the edge of farce; somewhere there is a yell of laughter—just as there is when a woman cries in precisely that way. For in life there is often a yell of laughter, which is every bit as intolerable as the tears" (M, p. 171). Emily weeping a woman's tears is also weeping out of a child's anguish, is shrieking in the grip of hot, sweaty hands that tickle her unmercifully.

By the end of the novel, the infant is aged beyond time, weary beyond human weariness. She has suffered love like a dread illness, has endured its ravages, and knows it to be the deadliest of all the traps of a dead civilization. What Barbara Bellow Watson writes of Anna in *The Golden Notebook* is true of Emily as well: "She has had a rigorous training in disenchantment."[18] All of these changes have taken place and nothing has changed; for good or ill, Emily is still linked to her mother's rooms and to her mother's dreams.

From the beginning, what Emily fears in her adoptive mother is the mirror image of her concluding self-portrait: "Emily saw some dry, controlled, distant old person. I frightened her, representing to her that unimaginable thing, old age." The narrator also recognizes the young girl: "But for my part, she, her condition, was as close to me as my memories" (M, p. 47). In her fear, Emily rejects her mother's civilization, her airless rooms, and takes to the life of the streets. Yet, short months or years later, Emily is discovered on a pile of furs in her own tightly closed rooms, and the circuit of duplication is complete. The narrator nurtures Emily; Emily, as Gerald's woman responsible for a household of foster children of her own, returns the favor and provides food to her foster mother. Emily's children return in a murderous attack on the narrator, an attack motivated not out of spite, but out of long acquaintanceship, even "friendship."

The narrator, less objective about her apartment personality, recognizes the terrible mother in her Edwardian counterpart beyond the wall. This "cart-horse woman," this "tall, solid, confident woman" is indifferent to Emily, is deaf to her pleas for attention, lavishes all her love and attention on the male child. Still, this woman too is trapped: "No one else was there, for her. . . . She was trapped, but did not know why she felt this, for her marriage and her children were what she personally had wanted and aimed for—what society had chosen for her" (M, p. 70). What society had chosen, what she had chosen; trapped because she does not recognize the coercion. She is trapped by the same hard, cruel hands that hold her daughter. Thus it is that when the narrator, searching the labyrinth of rooms in the "personal" for the source of infant Emily's cry, finds the woman she has become:

> I never found Emily. But I did find . . . The thing is, what I did find was inevitable. . . . Who else could it possibly be but Emily's mother, the large cart-horse woman, her tormentor, the world's image? It was not Emily I took up in my arms, and whose weeping I tried to shush. Up went the little arms, desperate for comfort, but they would be one day those great arms that had never been taught tenderness. (M, p. 151)

The child needing comfort is the woman with no comfort to give. The child, whose need for nurture is bound to the strict, arbitrary laws of an invented necessity, is the desperate, trapped woman without words to express her confusion. With their twin cries, infant and woman are numbing echoes of each other, sound mirrors that reflect their parallel needs. The room (or rooms) and the woman (or women) become part of a cycle, or a single entity, entrapped by civilization's requirements, enclosed in the room/womb/shell from which there is no escape except "the end." And for that end to occur it is necessary to transcend the cycle of infant, child, woman in a dream that is also beyond words, in a semimystic vision of an unnamable "she" who leads Emily, Gerald, and the children beyond the claustrophobia of the rooms and the agoraphobia that women learn as part of their necessary training in submission.

Is the narrator mad? Could the novel be the working through of a bout of schizophrenia? The question is irrelevant. Sanity would seem to be a part of the "slave ethics" described by Nietzsche in *The Genealogy of Morals*, and like other slave ethics—goodness, meekness, pity, kindness, humility, patience—it undergoes a transvaluation in the work of the survivor. Emily is trapped as a small child by the stifling hands of custom, by what has been accepted as healthy, right, and good. She, her mother, and her foster mother are all similarly trapped by the stifling restrictions of man's definition of sanity, by man's needs and wants. When Jane, Emily's only girl friend, leaves Emily's foster mother to join a women's tribe and disappears from the area, Emily abandons the confines of Gerald's house where she was constantly giving her strength and energy to the children and to the boy-man with no hope of return. Emily returns to the small apartment of her foster mother, to the long days of listless quietude, until Gerald comes to her with his renewed demands:

> He was all appeal; Emily all listlessness and distance. The situation was comic enough. Emily, a woman, was sitting there expressing with every bit of her the dry You want me back, you need me—look at you, a suitor, practically on your knees, but when you have me you don't value me; you take me for granted. . . . He stuck it out. So did she. . . . Is there any need to describe what happened? Emily smiled at last, dryly, and for herself . . .; she roused herself in response to the appeal which he had no idea he was making, the real one. . . . Then she went off with him. (M, pp. 173–74)

The words of her lover lead Emily back into the world of the man's needs for order, control, sanity. But this time Emily goes with her eyes open, ironically, with no illusions. She answers Gerald's unspoken appeal, the one his body speaks when his flow of words, his strategy of exhortation and appeal has no effect. And what does Gerald say with his silent body? Anna in *The Golden Notebook* tells us as she sits, will-less, confronted by the force of Saul Green's personality: "I, I, I, I, I, he shouted, but everything disconnected, a vague spattering boastfulness, and I felt as if I were being spattered by machine-gun bullets" (GN, p. 580). Or later, she realizes that "he was not listening, except to his own words, I I I, the words spattering against the walls and ricocheting everywhere, I I I, the naked ego" (GN, p. 629). In Gerald's appeal, Emily recognizes the same I I I that men use as a weapon against women, as a means of maintaining sanity in a chaotic existence. Emily smiles, wiser now, but she goes because against the I I I, because of the I I I she loves Gerald. But now she knows that love to be a trap.

The Memoirs of a Survivor is a war novel, telling of the battlegrounds of richocheting I's like machine-gun bullets. Yet it is not simply, not merely, the story of a war between the sexes. It is also the story of the helpless war within the self: "Inside it was all chaos: the feeling one is taken over by, at the times in one's life when everything is in change, movement, destruction—or reconstruction, but that is not always evident at the time—a feeling of helplessness, as if one were being whirled about in a dust-devil or a centrifuge" (M, p. 81). The destructiveness comes not only from the stifling demands of men, from their machine-gun egos, but also from the chaos of a female trying to free herself of the constraints of self-portraiture. Thus, the narrator describes not only the relationship between the infant Emily and her mother, between the girl Emily and herself, but also the underlying identity of the three (or four) women in their relationships with men. Of the "One who went ahead showing them the way out of this collapsed little world" (M, p. 217), the narrator cannot speak, nor can she describe that other order of world into which they enter. This world of chaos, of collapsing civilizations, of age-old male demands that change only in outward form with the passage of time, is the only possible theme of the *Memoirs*. And in that world the narrator cannot escape; she can only achieve the ironic twist of self-consciousness that marks her as an old, old woman. She is a large, terrifying maternal witch because men have made her one, and she is a frightened agoraphobic, trapped in her narrow rooms because the Authority seems to demand it. She cannot control even these limited surroundings and veers off into what men might call madness, what Doris Lessing calls "a wordless statement" (GN, p. xiv), a human history that is not man's history, not the official history, but the private memoirs of a life restricted to a woman's rooms, a woman's egg/womb, a woman's consciousness.

In *Les Guérillères* battle is waged more openly, and the women apparently do not make "wordless statements." They speak, speak repeatedly, intensely, violently. These women combat the machine-like staccato of man's speech with arms of their own: "They say, let those who call for a new language first learn violence. They say, let those who want to change the world first seize all the rifles. They say that they are starting from zero" (p. 85). Their language does not repeat the language of authority with its outworn forms. Instead, "they say everything must begin over again. . . . They say that the sun is about to rise" (p. 66). And the sun rises among the clashing of arms, for the sun goddess, their mother, is also the goddess of war. Their weapons, their mirrors, confront the I I I of men and turn the ego bullets back on their enemies. Then the women press forward their own attack, countering the scattered forces of I with the collective voice of they. Their role, unlike that of men, is not to impose names, but to speak the varied and contradictory myths of experience. They do not need recorded histories to tell them the truth; truth is the story that each woman remembers, retells, invents. Truth is knowledge shared and utilized, not knowledge stored in books (not even in feminaries) or in libraries.

Truth is not even, in this violently antimale society where women laugh as they conduct war against men and torture them to death, an exclusively female truth. Thus Sophie Ménade, the storyteller, devoted, as her name implies, to the goddess of wisdom and to Dionysus, retells, retools, the myth of Eden and the story of Orpheus, into a solar myth that is also the story of a Medusa transfigured, a Medusa who goes from beautiful to glorious, a Medusa that is indeed a queen:

> Sophie Ménade's tale has to do with an orchard planted with trees of every colour. A naked woman walks therein. Her beautiful body is black and shining. Her hair consists of slender mobile snakes which produce music at her every movement. . . . Orpheus, the favourite snake of the woman who walks in the garden, keeps advising her to eat the fruit of the tree in the center of the garden. The woman tastes the fruit of each tree asking Orpheus the snake how to recognize that which is good . . . the answer is given that, as soon as she has eaten the fruit . . . she will grow, . . . her forehead will touch the stars. And he Orpheus and the hundred thousand snakes of her head-

dress will extend from one side of her face to the other, they will afford her a brilliant crown, her eyes will become pale as moons, she will acquire knowledge. (p. 52)

The snake in the Garden of Eden, who tempts Eve into sin and death, becomes Orpheus, a god's son, whose powers of musical expression allow him to raise the dead, and whose courage is such that he dares venture into Hades to reclaim his wife, Eurydice, dead from a snakebite inflicted as she fled from the importunities of her husband's half-brother, the beekeeper, the librarian, the inventor of bookkeeping. This Orphic snake, furthermore, is only one of a hundred thousand voices, all of them subordinate to the voice of the woman whose headdress they form and whose mastery they acknowledge. The queen or goddess with the poisonous, beautiful (male) head of writhing snakes is unfeminine by masculine standards of femininity; she is too powerful, too wise, too deadly for their comfort. Yet the Medusa does not terrify the women; they are pleased by the story, if awed by her beauty and wisdom. The deadly snakes offer no menace—the women in *Les Guérillères* frequently raise them to their lips and kiss them, and the musical snake, Orpheus, has a name that begins with the magical letter that symbolizes woman, the letter O, the same letter that is the content of the Siren's song.

Nevertheless, despite her celebratory reevaluation of the Medusa myth, neither Sophie Ménade nor Wittig can put in words the nature of the knowledge acquired by the queenly woman in the garden: "Sophie Ménade says that the woman of the orchard will have a clear understanding of the solar myth that all the texts have deliberately obscured" (p. 52). The women besiege the storyteller with questions; they remain unanswered. Why is the solar myth obscured, and why "deliberately"? These are questions which cannot be answered, which the women eventually abandon for dance.

The unresolved mystery remains as an example of the unsolved enigmas that fill the book, enigmas that teach the reader more of what she does not want to know than of the valuable knowledge still to be acquired. Wittig educates us in the erasure of former ways of saying and doing. It is curious that her fierce, aggressive, singing, positive women are described so often in the negative, leaving the reader confused between a plenum of woman-lore and a blankness of woman-speech. Their myths, ultimately, cannot be told at all:

> *They do not say* that vulvas with their elliptical shape are to be compared to suns, planets, innumerable galaxies. *They do not say* that gyratory movements are like vulvas. *They do not say* that the vulva is the primal form which describes the world in all its extent, in all its movement. *They do not* in their discourses create conventional figures derived from these symbols. (p. 61, my emphases)

In linguistic constructions, "the women *do not* employ hyperboles metaphors, they *do not* proceed sequentially or by gradation" (p. 66). Their social organization is similarly described by what it is not: "They say that *they do not want* to become prisoners of their own ideology. They say that *they did not garner and develop* the symbols that were necessary to them at an earlier period to demonstrate their strength" (p. 57, all emphases mine). Wittig, in telling us what the women are not and do not do, provides us, not with a model for a new society and a new speech, but with a summary of all the rejected forms that the women *say* they have transcended. In the obsessive cataloguing, in the teaching of the blankness of the new ways, Wittig and her guérillères also provide an even stronger education into the ways of the library. Instead of a new knowledge that cannot be spoken, the women are reminded of the old knowledge that they are striving to destroy. By means of indirection, these natural women receive a rigorous training in the old ways of society. Thus, although these women say and say, singly and collectively, what they say is as much a distortion and a masquerade of male sayings as the final poem in the text is a distortion and a masquerade of a poem by Mallarmé. Their speech, so apparently full, becomes a simulacrum of the male speech they combat in their long wars. Significantly, the text cannot continue once the war is over for, like the survivor in Lessing's book, the women must now pass into a new world altogether. The old world, the world of *Les Guérillères*, is a world of opposition, a world maintained in tension by the pressures of war. The women's ideology of pure negativity must necessarily collapse when the war is over and the victory won. Unfortunately, in what they do not say, the women give no indication that the new order will not be a female-dominated replication of the defeated male word; a reversal and not a transvaluation. The most vexing question remains unanswered: are Wittig's forceful, violent women able to unlearn the lessons of authority, of power and knowledge institutionalized in what it is permissible to say? Or have they/will they become victims of their own realized potential?

In order to avoid subversion by that which they fought to subvert (the return of the repressed as evidenced in their negative program), their deadly violence must be channeled into a new, unspoken project of cultural innovation. The hypostatization of desire in a polymorphous female sexuality is, perhaps, essential in the first stages of the revolution, but to focus the impulse in negativity will eventually be counterproductive, leading, as it must, to a new, disguised theology, a new history, an ideology not dissimilar from the former law of the fathers. It is a dilemma difficult to avoid, for these guérillères, like the other women examined here, are children of the book. Along with the men who inhabit the libraries, the women too suckle at the breasts of a distanced, dehumanized wisdom.

Even more strict correspondences could be made. Like Peter Kien, who destroys the library he loves and himself as well in a frenzy of misdirected passion, Puttermesser, whose golem self destroys her mother's law in a love frenzy that cannot achieve procreation, is herself destroyed with the disintegration of that golem self. Wittig, like Borges, is a cataloguer of all the flotsam and jetsam of human civilization; that her catalogues are sex-conscious and couched in the negative when they refer to the projects of man, is only a minor, and ultimately, insignificant variation on the theme. And if Sartre's Roquentin sees his refuge become uncannily organic by the invasion of vegetation into the realm of the library, so too the narrator of *The Memoirs of a Survivor* is drawn, almost against her will, through the constricting walls of the apartment, through the intolerable "white" as her mind follows the "suggestions of trees and a garden" (M, p. 11) into the equally intolerable white of the nursery presided over by the hard-bosomed nurse and the indifferent carthorse mother. Finally, Murdoch's characterization of the mysterious anthropologist in *A Severed Head* is not dissimilar in general outline from Madame Curie, the potent woman, the scientist, the destroyer used by Williams as his ideal of feminine fission/fusion.

Perhaps the most interesting correspondence of all, however, lies in the fact that for all these authors, male and female alike, the figure of the woman of power is uncannily similar. The woman as prostitute or the woman as Sophia; these are attributes relatively easy to describe, easy to distance and dismiss. It is the woman who escapes this double negation, the woman who is affirmative in her self, the Medusa mother with her terrible destructive, equally terrible procreative powers, who exercises the strongest and the most sustained hold on our attention. For unlike the other two loved and dreaded women, the Medusa possesses not only the power to give life, but also the power to destroy it through a petrification that copies man's name-giving powers. Moreover, the Medusa is inhuman, unassimilable to civilized society, while at the same time she is inextricably bound up in the most intimate workings of the necessarily private functions of society and the individual. Thus it is that the librarian, who is and dreads the castrated and castrating women, cannot establish a relation of identity with the most sincerely loved and dreaded figure of the triad. There is, of course, a considerable distancing factor in even the first two relationships. To say "He was . . . such a . . . woman" imposes not only the obvious distancing of gender difference, but the syntactic distanciation of the ellipsis as well.

For the woman author, the woman librarian, the case is slightly different as the identification with the prostitute and the Sophia figures becomes less forced, more complete. The Medusa, however, is still beyond a woman's knowledge. Lessing distances her through walls of white and refuses to name her at the end of the novel; Murdoch distances her through untrustworthy memoirs written by a bemused male admirer; Wittig confronts her only partially and indirectly in the story told by Sophie Ménade, but leaves the women's questions unanswered. While male librarians strain against the Medusa's femaleness, but try to capture her form-giving possibilities; the female authors suffer from a different kind of tension as they strain against the forms, while at the same time striving with all their hearts to adopt the Medusa face of the uniquely potent woman.

The Medusa, then, is feared and desired for different reasons, but always we return to the same image. Feared and celebrated, used or above human use, valued and denigrated, misunderstood, shunted aside, killed, half-forgotten, the Medusa rises from her monuments to exercise her power.

> "But what are these salutarily-bound books?" He began turning the covers back.
> "I don't want you to read them."
> "Why not?" he said, reading them.
> "Only one person read them. He tried to kill himself, failed, blinded himself, and has now turned into what he tried to kill himself to prevent." (GN, p. 659)

Tommy, boy-man, reading in the books of his mother's woman friend, blinds himself (too late) and is transformed into society's puppet, a stone puppet created from the unshielded gaze into the Medusa's eyes.

"The rest," says Julia Kristeva, "its archaeology and its exhaustion—is nothing but literature."[19] Who can say how these women's texts, inserted into the library against the will of the male librarians, will act upon the catalogue of the whole? And what future archaeologist will uncover the ruins of the Ever-unapproachable become one with its opposite?

CHAPTER 8

Conclusion:
Medusa and the Machine

PERSEUS, SAYS GEOFFREY Hartman in *The Unmediated Vision*, now goes against the Medusa unshielded, his naked eye staring directly into the formless chaos that is also the birthplace of form. The outcome of this encounter is unknown. In one version, the Medusa's power remains unassailable; the hero is turned to stone. His project is completed as his enterprise is monumentalized in a visible product. In the second version, the hero's glance triumphs over the tyranny of the Medusan gaze; chaos is obliterated and Pegasus is released from the bonds of her blood. Yet, in both cases, the formalization of myth provides its own iconographic frame to the episode in the workings of historical remembrance. Medusa victorious is still a Medusa captured in art; Medusa defeated still has the power to formalize experience indirectly through the centering function of Mount Helicon's fountain, beloved of the Muses. The hero, seeing all, misses a crucial element; his vision is limited to the scene before him. He does not observe the inevitable presence of the immortal Muses who overshadow the scene and impress upon both Perseus and the Medusa the monumentalization of their gaze which preserves the icon—in art, in writing—for those who were absent from the time and place of that interchanged glance. They are immortal spectators to a mortal act, powerful deathless sisters of the murdered Gorgon. The presence of the Muses is more nearly absolute because it is invisible to the ostensible principals of the drama. But little can be said of this theoretical absolute, as Louis Marin has noted in another context: "It could well be that the present of the absolute, because it is absolute, is forever opaque to itself and that it is the very essence of the absolute to be incapable of reflecting itself in undistanced immediacy, without becoming relative."[1] The mirrored shield that Perseus carries (or discards) is not the mirror of the unreflecting absolute, but the mirror of art. In his search, Perseus discovers not the original abyss, but the created chaos, a woman, a monster, a reflection of the formalizing presence of the eternal Muses.

To the extent that Perseus' unshielded enterprise is successful, his gaze can also be interpreted as Medusan. He reduces the living monster to the stasis of death after a battle that begins with the first transfixing wound of his gaze. Perseus, an upright heroic figure, bringer of the truth and of law and of order, looks upon the ambiguous sexuality of the monster with horror and sees in her a remnant of that old chaos that preceded man's domination over the earth. He sees her, and knows she must be destroyed. His victory, in some sense, represents the victory of the thinking man's Apollonian formalism of visual and spatial metaphorics over the Dionysian relativism that touches the extremes of madness, of undifferentiation, and of destruction. The Medusa, poor Gorgon, contradicts his single truth; she offends his sight, and he kills her. Her power to turn men to stone is abstracted from her concrete presence; she too is subjected in death to man's impulse to exert a perfect control and reduce others to his system-building mania. Her power is co-opted in the service of the system. All sight is henceforth Medusan, all writing is monumentalizing, all nonformalist impulse is eroded by inertia:

> The truth is that there comes a time
> When we can mourn no more over music
> That is so much motionless sound.
>
> There comes a time when the waltz
> Is no longer a mode of desire, a mode

Of revealing desire and is empty of shadows

. . . .

[There are] voices crying without knowing for what,

Except to be happy, without knowing how,
Imposing forms they cannot describe
Requiring order beyond their speech.

Too many waltzes have ended. Yet the shapes
For which the voices cry, these, too, may be
Modes of desire, modes of revealing desire.[2]

The voices Stevens evokes cry out for form, demand form and create it out of their very need for the permanencies of space and time that are given them in the measures of a dance. Mankind cannot tolerate too much freedom—in its frenzy for order, the mob demands a reestablishment of the "motionless sound," the silent and frozen world of penetrating gaze and monumental gesture. They demand the death that only the Muses (or their earthly simulacrum, the Perseus-Medusa) can provide. Says Foucault: "It is death that fixes the stone that we can touch, the return of time, the fine, innocent earth beneath the grass of the words. In a space articulated by language, it reveals the profusion of bodies and their simple order."[3] Time, space, individuality are obliterated in the memorials of death, which are perpetual and eternally present. In the library, the arch-memorial to abstracted death, the word or the image is not made flesh again, but is subsumed in a magical architecture of signs that is also, as Stevens has it, a "mode of revealing desire."

Death, says Foucault, is the mediating factor between desire (madness) and silence on the one hand, and reason and language on the other. For Jacques Derrida, the balance would need to be supplemented by "an *economy* escaping this system of metaphysical oppositions." "This economy," he continues, "would not be an energetics of pure, shapeless force. The differences examined *simultaneously* would be differences of site and differences of force."[4] The inscribed monuments raised to the dead are the concrete emblems of this economy of death, and at the same time, its critical appreciation. The library is full, not of bodies, but of memorials to these bodies, memories preserved in perpetuity to retain (regain) the presentness and presence of the past. They are memorials rooted in the earth of the "profusion of bodies and their simple order," but they are not of the earth. The memorials reign over the dead, yet their inscriptions and their concrete presence keep the visitor at a distance. The visitor is also a critic, gazing upon a face that is no face, trying to establish a relationship with the absent body. It is, in fact, another version of the gaze of the Medusa, which cannot be reciprocated without fatal consequences.

Reciprocation occurs on another level. The critic gazes upon the work (the monument), discovers value in the involutions of its form, surrounds the representation of its inscription with an accommodation to the current values, and enters it into the reciprocal transactions of literary commerce. The process is remorseless, and remorselessly logical, as the site of the text gives way before the economy of that force which reevaluates it. In the exchanges of literary commerce the stone becomes a grindstone—or an industrial age machine:

> There is a—let us say—a machine. It evolved itself (I am severely scientific) out of a chaos of scraps of iron and behold!—it knits. I am horrified at the horrible work and stand appalled. I feel it ought to embroider—but it goes on knitting. . . . And the most withering thought is that the infamous thing has made itself; made itself without thought, without conscience, without foresight, without eyes, without heart. It is a tragic accident—and it has happened. You can't interfere with it. The last drop of bitterness is in the suspicion that you can't even smash it. In virtue of that truth one and immortal which lurks in the force that made it spring into existence it is what it is—and it is indestructible!
>
> It knits us in and it knits us out. It has knitted time, space, pain, death, corruption, despair and all the illusions—and nothing matters. I'll admit however that to look at the remorseless process is sometimes amusing.[5]

The economic processes not only resist the insertion of bodies into the machine; in the development of critical capitalism the machinery of production becomes ever more alienated. It is blind, thoughtless, self-evolved. Even the Medusa's freezing gaze can provide no surcease from the voracious machine. There is no end to its productivity: no end and no exit, only the inexorable knitting, the piling up of one book on top of another in the library. Says Foucault: "We are doomed historically to history, to the patient construction of discourses about discourses, and to the task of hearing what has already been said." To comment upon these commentaries is to give the knitting machine new fuel: "to comment is to admit by definition an excess of the signified over the signifier . . . but to comment also presupposes that this unspoken element slumbers within speech." Conrad says that the knitting machine is eternal and indestructible; Foucault says much the same about commentary: "By opening up the possibility of commentary, this double plethora dooms us to an endless task that nothing can limit."[6] Yet, critics persist in their knitting, in their pursuit of "that truth one and immortal," of that force, of the Word, of the secret, silent Revelation.

If such are the exigencies of the critical task, wherein lies the general threat of the library? Surely such recondite searches would be harmless? Conrad suggests one reason: "It knits us in and it knits us out"; it imposes form on the multitudes and it disentangles the forms, alternately repressing and foresaking us, leaving us crying for the shapes of revealing desire. What is this knitting machine, this monument, this library if not a home, a sepulcher, and the representation and site of an absolute force? It is dangerous to experience, and it is "sometimes amusing" to look upon.

The Medusa and the machine; two monumentalizing forces. The first is emblematic of the atemporal realm of myth and inspiration by the Muses, the second is representative of the insertion of self into a blind knitting up of history. Both the Greek tale and Conrad's machine are purified, the first by myth, the second by the abstracting power of imagination, into iconographic representations. The Medusa and the machine serve as useful points of entry into the library (the machine) and the books (Medusan language). Thus, the library is preeminently a historical form; like the machine it constantly and heartlessly knits in new elements. Its syntax (the order of its collections) is determined by historical usage, by the circumstances that rule the deployment of language at any given moment. The structure that governs it is inorganic, artificial, wholly rationalized; the library, like the machine, presses "time, space, pain, death, corruption, despair and all the illusions" into a visible architecture, a specific construction.

The Medusan monumentalization operates more clearly on the level of the individual work. Where the library's presence is physical, the Medusa's habitual mode of operation is covert and metaphysical. The words of the work become fused in the pure Word, the structured object before us. The book, once transfixed by the Medusa's gaze, has no history. Or rather, as Derrida finds, "This history of the work is not only its *past*, . . . but is also the impossibility of its ever being *present*. . . . This is why, as we will verify, there is no *space* of the work."[7] The book is a presence without ever being present; it is a monumental form that in some sense stands outside history, an object that refuses spatial definition. To attempt a recuperation of words from the Word, the monster must be slain; the books and the construction that houses them must be burned. Thus, the contrast between the two forms of monumentalization—physical and metaphysical—is resolved in a single act: the burning of the library/books.

The existence of such incendiary passions and their recurrence indicate that the library is not so impenetrable as it may at first seem. If, on the one hand, the library/books can be seen as a transcendental structure that serves as an emblem of the formalization of history and of individual life, it is, on the other hand, a peculiarly inept structure. The monument has innumerable cracks and crevices; its theoretical perfection is marred by the myriad actual defects in structure (library) and execution (books). These institutional imperfections create opportunities for the exertion of a counterforce in the interstices of form, for the increased ardor that propels others into the exercise of power.

The issue is at least partially a political one. Through the structuring impetus of the library and the book, history and language are constituted in an official, absolute form. To read a book or read in the library's formal structures is to come into contact with the essence of this political impetus. Memory is formalized in narrative representations. And with the formalization of memory, so too is the individual thrust into the Medusan orbit of a categorical identity, into the machine's infernal, remorseless knitting.

The monumental structure can be counteracted with fire—the agent of continual change—and with what Williams calls "green writing," that is, impermanent writing that refuses a monumental form:

> And the scribes and Pharisees brought unto him a woman taken in adultery; and when they had set her in the midst, they say unto him, Master, this woman was taken in adultery, in the very act. Now Moses in the law commanded us, that such should be stoned: but what sayest thou? This they said, tempting him, that they might accuse him. But Jesus stooped down, and with *his* finger wrote on the ground, *as though he heard them not.* (John 8: 3–6)

In his explication of this passage, Tony Tanner notes a shift in force and a crumbling of form when the monolithic power of the law is confronted with a changing form outside its experience. The Pharisees, "invoke Mosaic law, but Christ's response completely alters the terms and premises of the debate, for he *refuses to answer* and starts to *write* on the ground. Thus silence and writing introduce a gap in the monolithic generalities of the Mosaic law."[8] Christ ignores the structures that are set up to entrap him and obliterates their pertinence to the individual case at hand by addressing the question obliquely, with silence and with a written message that cannot be formalized because its content is unrevealed. The interrogation of the lawgivers, meant to reveal the criminality of their proposed victim by the force of their spoken words, is turned back on them and annulled by Christ's silence, by the unspoken presence of the truth ("I am the way, the truth, and the life" [John 14: 6]) in their midst, by his act of shifting the mode of discourse from the written revelations of law to an unrevealed writing, by scratching tiny excavations in the sand.

The eschewal of speech is a doubly effective weapon; not only does it transfer the context of the discourse to a different plane, the refusal to speak also serves as a reminder of the imperfections inherent in any speech in a post-Babel world. Not only is the law suspect, but also the very language of its inscription that is, by definition, only an imperfect copy of the law given Moses by God, a semblance of that originary principle, subject to the vagaries of a language become dispersed and opaque. The inscription of the law does not do justice to the immense clarity of incarnate Truth, and no combination of discourses could reproduce the density and impact of that moment of silence. Christ remained silent, and he wrote in the sand. But Christ's writing is a formal act, a visible sign of his silence, a distinction that published writings cannot maintain. They are thrust willy-nilly into the orders of the archive and the timeless presence of the books. The law (of language, of the library) is applied rigorously to lesser beings, submitting expression to the regularizing force of the collective. In contemporary practice, silent challenges to the law are remanded to the limiting condition of madness. Still, the option of rebellion can be exercised to a certain degree even from within the system.

Hayden White says of Foucault that he "writes 'history' in order to destroy it, as a discipline, as a mode of consciousness, and as a mode of social existence."[9] In effect, then, Foucault conducts forays against the very archive that he envisions in much the same manner as Conrad's indestructible machine. But since the written sign is not yet divine, it cannot encompass that perfect destruction achieved by Jesus Christ in his confrontation with the scribes and the Pharisees. To destroy, it is also necessary to open oneself to destruction:

> To write is not only to know that the Book does not exist and that forever there are books, against which the meaning of a world not conceived of by an absolute object is shattered, before it has even become a unique meaning. . . . To write is not only to know that through writing, through the extremities of style, the best will not necessarily transpire, as Leibnitz thought it did in divine creation. . . . It is also to be incapable of making meaning absolutely precede writing: it is thus to lower meaning while simultaneously elevating inscription. The eternal fraternity of theological optimism and of pessimism: nothing is more reassuring, but nothing is more despairing, more destructive of our books than the Leibnizian Book.[10]

The destruction is never total, just as the construction is never unflawed. Roland Barthes describes the confrontation between the original, creative writer and the library as an arduous chipping away at a personal language in order to release it from "the slime of primary languages afforded him by the world, history, his existence." And he adds, "the whole task of art is to *unexpress* the expressible."[11] The exactitude and precision of language required of an authentic artist predestine him to rebellion against outmoded forms, and while the scandalous behavior of the artist eventually self-destructs in the general conflagration, the optimism and the despair are not invalidated: the nest must be burned before the Phoenix can arise from the ashes. The author sacrifices his freedom and his life in the performance of this duty.

The blindness of the machine in its unthinking pursuit of absolute truth finds its counterpart in the petrifying gaze of the Medusa, which is ineffective only against the unseeing eye of the blind man who cannot be made a monumental product of the act of vision. The song of despair is perfected in the turning away from light, in the rejection of the hypostatizing illumination of truth, in the concealment of self. Valéry provides the rationalist's interrogation into the metaphysics of enforced blindness: "What is to be thought of this custom: Piercing the eyes of a bird so that it may sing better. Explain and develop (3 pages)."[12] The blinded bird is no longer subject to the restrictions of the Medusan gaze; it has advanced an infinitesimal degree toward the inexorability of the blind machine. As with birds, so too with men:

> Men are to be fashioned to the needs of the time, that they may soon take their place in the machine. They must work in the factory of the "common good" before they are ripe; for this would be a luxury that would draw away a deal of power from the "labor market." Some birds are blinded that they may sing better; I do not think men sing today better than their grandfathers, though I am sure they are blinded early. But light, too clear, too sudden and dazzling, is the infamous means used to blind them.[13]

The bird or the man is blinded, and it becomes invisible; it is converted into pure song. Says Derrida: "In this heliocentric metaphysics, force, ceding its place to *eidos* (i.e., the form which is visible for the metaphorical eye) has already been separated from itself in acoustics."[14] The blind bird sings; it becomes voice. The man, blinded by light, becomes the work he habitually performs. Christ, however, is the all-seeing; his presence is the concrete presence of truth in the midst of the darkness of error. The bird's darkness makes it invisible; Christ's light-filled presence instigates the search for truth in the act of gazing upon his face: "The meaning of becoming and of force, by virtue of their pure, intrinsic characteristics, is the repose of the beginning and the end, the peacefulness of a spectacle, horizon or face."[15] Christ brings sight to the blind, brings the light of truth to the darkness of existence, brings clarity and transparency of meaning by virtue of his presence. He would restore to the bird its eyes and its mediocrity. He represents, thus, the unachievable goal of every librarian.

In actual and fictional libraries the presence of the librarian does not possess such a force to heal and bring light to the deepest reaches of darkness. Indeed, as Sartre has shown, light and dark intermingle and corrupt each other. In Roquentin's dream sodomization of the author Maurice Barrès, the spectacle is anything but peaceful, as the heliocentric face that turns to the light is replaced by the dark face of the buttocks; the seeing eye of the head exchanges places with the blind eye of the anus. Furthermore, the gaze of the dreamer is anything but passive. The librarian embarks upon a strategy of domination: the eyes and the face are eliminated in the headless soldier, the unseeing eye that remains is violated. The violent superimposition of one part of the anatomy upon the other follows a mechanics of power in which the claims of reason and light are constantly undercut and supplemented by the encroachments of unreason and darkness.

The game is a very serious one indeed, and all the more serious because it is, in Borges's words, symmetrical, arbitrary, and tedious. To this list might be added the category of invisibility, since the game is invisible to the casual gaze, not because its workings cannot be seen, but because they are so often ignored. Derrida, who would consider the library and the librarian as arch-representatives of the Apollonian impulse, speaks of the opening up of all such structures by willed Dionysian blindness that turns away from history to passion. For Dionysus has penetrated the indifferent wall of invisibility: "Dionysus is worked by difference. He sees and lets himself be seen. And tears out (his eyes). For all eternity, he has had a relationship to his exterior, to visible form, to structure, as he does to his death. This is how he appears (to himself)."[16] He recognizes the exterior mode of historical reality, but goes beyond the arbitrary stopping point of fixed form by blinding himself to outward show and directing meaning inward, rejecting representative history (and the library) for poetic history, for myth, for the Dionysian song of the blinded bird.

The denouement—"he sees . . . and tears out (his eyes)"—is repeated in many of these fictional accounts of librarians and responds to an experience that is primarily visual, that of sight and insight. In the beatitude of a Dionysian vision, says Henri Birault, "necessity is reconciled with chance, eternity with the instant, being with becoming—but all that outside of time, its lengths, its progress, its moments, its mediations."[17] To break the Apollonian structures, it is necessary to confront them directly and then go beyond to a new beatific vision. It is at this point that the machinery of the library will be abandoned or destroyed; it is at this turning point that the librarians must choose between the comfortable, rational mode of existence of the library, or enter into the uncertainties of a Dionysian discourse, rejecting history for what Joseph Campbell calls the "no-place, no-time, no-when, no-where of mythological consciousness, which is here and now."[18] Such a transformation entails the abandonment of the superfluity of presence in the library space for the absence ("worked by difference") of a mythological nonspace, a transition that is spurred by the recognition of the emptiness of the monumentalized books and the plentitude of the Dionysian nothing. Superficial similarity and difference are revealed as pure difference—or pure undifferentiability.

In the larger context, however, the exercise of or refusal to accept the Dionysian option is still inexorably grounded in and bound to the structures of the library. The text can parody that structure, awaken the reader to its invisible web of control, but cannot (as text) escape incorporation into the monument. The "being" of the authorial text cannot be withdrawn into chance or becoming; only certain concealed workings of the machine or of the Medusa can be disclosed in the author's willed blindness (as in Williams's reference to "green writing") to the more powerful enticements of the library. Such books underline the lack of innocence in the library space and in the textual displacements of that space into a secondary, written level. Neither is the text innocent. Though it may deny history, the presence of the text is a historical fact, orienting the reader and the author, taking a specific position, and fixing the results of the investigation. The author may submit a Dionysian thesis, but the text masks a desire to *be*, to avoid death and the Dionysian abyss. Language, because it has both historical and poetic components, licenses such an ambiguity of motive, but also forces the recognition that the poetic moment is necessarily ironic, that myth is only accessible in parody. This is not to say that the realm of the superrational, the library, can only be approached rationally. Roland Barthes, at the beginning of *The Pleasure of the Text*, indicates an alternative:

> Imagine someone . . . who abolishes within himself all barriers, all classes, all exclusions, not by syncretism but by simple discard of that old specter: *logical contradiction*; who mixes every language, even those said to be incompatible; who silently accepts every charge of illogicality, of incongruity; who remains passive in the face of Socratic irony . . . and legal terrorism. . . . Now this anti-hero exists: he is the reader of the text at the moment he takes his pleasure. Thus the Biblical myth is reversed, the confusion of tongues is no longer a punishment, the subject gains access to bliss by the cohabitation of languages *working side by side*: the text of pleasure is a sanctioned Babel.[19]

The abolition of all barriers is, however, a theoretically conceived rather than a practically conceivable reality. The bliss Barthes hypothesizes as the consequence of such abolitions is a mental construct that is only partially reflected in actual experience. Geoffrey Hartman, in a sentence taken out of context, comes closer to a more realistic projection of desires onto the text. He says, "Art, like Romance, teaches us to interrupt."[20] To interrupt bliss, to interrupt

coitus, to experience a mitigated pleasure mingled with frustration—
a necessary measure if we are to prevent, as we are constrained to
do, word from being made flesh once again. Lukács makes this
point very clearly: "This interruption is not an end, because it does
not come from within, and yet it is the most profound ending because a conclusion from within would have been impossible."[21] All
reading is tinged by this unavoidable perversity.

The gaze of the author, though reified in the internal and external
libraries, nevertheless plays a legitimate and necessary role in that it
is aware of both the source of illumination and the object it is looking at. The text recognizes the regulations of the gaze; of the frozen
Medusan sexuality, of the interrupted bliss of reading. It conducts a
voyage through the chaotic orders of the labyrinthine library. As
Nietzsche has it, "A labyrinthian man does not look for truth, he
forever seeks only his Ariadne."[22] Everyone is lost in the midst of
the excessive structure, the guide (blinded bird) equally with the
guided. The librarian's text is meant to elucidate the structure, not
to raise false hopes of melting the frozen gaze or of discovering the
key to the unfathomable machine. Structure abuts structure but
does not demolish it. Not surprisingly, the light of partial knowledge remits the reader/author/librarian to a vaguely recalled mythical fire:

> Hölderlin's Empedocles, reaching, by voluntary steps, the very
> edge of Etna, is the death of the last mediator between mortals
> and Olympus, the end of the infinite on earth, the flame return-
> ing to its native fire, leaving as its sole remaining trace that
> which had precisely to be abolished by his death: the beautiful,
> enclosed form of individuality; after Empedocles, the world is
> placed under the sign of finitude, in that irreconcilable, inter-
> mediate state in which reigns the Law, the harsh law of limit;
> the destiny of individuality will be to appear always in the ob-
> jectivity that manifests and conceals it.[23]

The flames that consume Empedocles are repeated in the flames of
unrequited desire, in the flames of the passionate frustration of unachievable bliss, and in the flames of constant change that reduce

structure to pure ash. Fires are set in the memory of these other, divine fires, in the recognition that earthly fires caress, but do not consume, the products of human imagination. It provokes but little surprise that again and again the librarian futilely endeavors to set fire to Alexandria.

NOTES

Preface

1. Michel Foucault, *Language, Counter-memory, Practice: Selected Essays and Interviews*, p. 67.
2. Harold Bloom, *Kabbalah and Criticism* (New York: Seabury Press, 1975), p. 96.
3. Ihab Hassan, *The Right Promethean Fire* (Urbana: Univ. of Illinois Press, 1980), pp. 169–70.

1 Founding the Library

1. George Steiner, *After Babel: Aspects of Language and Translation*, p. 3.
2. Friedrich Nietzsche, *The Birth of Tragedy* in *The Birth of Tragedy and the Genealogy of Morals*, p. 137.
3. Frank Kermode, *The Sense of an Ending: Studies in the Theory of Fiction* (New York: Oxford Univ. Press, 1967), p. 41.
4. Werner Heisenberg, "The Representation of Nature in Contemporary Physics," in *The Discontinuous Universe*, ed. Sallie Sears and Georgianna Lord (New York: Basic Books, 1972), p. 128.
5. Ibid., p. 127.
6. Ibid., p. 128.
7. Kenneth Burke, "Definition of Man," in Sears and Lord, eds., *Discontinuous Universe*, p. 384.
8. Ibid., p. 384.
9. Michel Foucault, *The Archaeology of Knowledge and The Discourse on Language*, p. 7.
10. Wallace Stevens, *The Collected Poems*, pp. 466, 468.

11. James Joyce, *Finnegans Wake*, pp. 185–86.

12. Samuel Beckett, *How It Is*, p. 70.

13. Roland Barthes, *S/Z An Essay*, trans. Richard Miller (New York: Hill and Wang, 1974), p. 10.

14. John Updike, "The Author as Librarian, *New Yorker* 41 (October 30, 1965), pp. 244–45.

15. Michel Foucault, *The Order of Things: An Archaeology of the Human Sciences*, pp. xviii–xix.

16. Roland Barthes, *Critical Essays*, p. xix.

17. Eugene Ionesco, *The Lesson*, in *Four Plays*, trans. Donald M. Allen (New York: Grove Press, 1958), p. 76.

18. Stéphane Mallarmé, *Selected Prose Poems, Essays, and Letters*, trans. Bradford Cook (Baltimore, Md.: Johns Hopkins Univ. Press, 1956), p. 38.

19. Roland Barthes, *The Pleasure of the Text*, trans. Richard Miller (New York: Hill and Wang, 1973), p. 4.

20. Foucault, *Order*, p. 317.

21. Ibid.

22. Mallarmé, *Selected Prose Poems, Essays, and Letters*, p. 48.

23. Fray Luis de Granada, quoted in *European Literature and the Latin Middle Ages*, by Ernst Robert Curtius, trans. Willard R. Trask (Princeton, N.J.: Princeton Univ. Press, 1953), p. 320: "letras quebradas e iluminadas."

24. Foucault, *Archaeology*, p. 129.

25. Ibid., p. 130.

26. André Malraux, *The Walnut Trees of Altenburg*, trans. A. W. Fielding (London: John Lehmann, 1942), p. 90.

27. Marthe Robert, *The Old and the New: From "Don Quixote" to Kafka*, p. 66.

28. Friedrich Nietzsche, *The Use and Abuse of History*, 1957, p. 18.

29. Ibid., p. 69.

30. *The Odyssey of Homer*, trans. Richmond Lattimore (New York: Harper and Row, 1967), p. 136.

31. Mallarmé, quoted in Gérard Genette, *Figures* (Paris: Seuil, 1966), p. 126: "Le monde existe pour aboutir à un Livre."

32. Foucault, quoted in *Rizoma* by Gilles Deleuze and Felix Guattari (Mexico City: Premia Editora, 1978), p. 39.

33. Referred to by Huberto Batis in "La ciencia, la poesía y la tarea de educar la sensibilidad," *Communidad CONACYT*, 8, no. 124–25 (1981), p. 31.

34. Gérard Genette, "La littérature selon Borges," *L'Herne* (1964), p. 326: "une nouvelle idée du livre et de son *usage*."

35. This may be, incidentally, the thrust of Philippe Sollers's insistence on the verbal qualities of his own texts which must be read aloud if they are to be read at all.

36. Hugh Kenner, *The Stoic Comedians* (Berkeley: Univ. of California Press, 1962), p. 31.

37. Geoffrey H. Hartman, *Saving the Text: Literature/Derrida/Philosophy*, p. 120.

38. Edmund Wilson, *Axel's Castle: A Study in the Imaginative Literature of 1870–1930* (New York: Charles Scribner's Sons, 1969), p. 265.

39. Philippe Auguste Villiers de l'Isle-Adam, *Axel*, trans. June Guicharnaud (Englewood Cliffs, N.J.: Prentice-Hall, 1970), p. 16. Further references will be contained within the text.

40. Vladimir Nabokov, *Pale Fire*, p. 204.

41. Jacques Derrida, *Writing and Difference*, p. 62.

42. W. B. Yeats, "Crazy Jane Talks with the Bishop," in *Collected Poems* (New York: Macmillan, 1956), p. 255.

43. Foucault, *Order*, p. 328.

44. Jean-Paul Sartre, *Nausea*, p. 28.

45. Ibid., p. 28.

46. Maurice Blanchot, *Le livre á venir*, quoted in Emir Rodríguez Monegal, "Borges y Nouvelle Critique," *Revista Iberoamericana* 38 (1972), p. 369: ". . . l'experience de la littérature est peut-être fondamentalement proche des paradoxes et des sophismes de ce que Hegel, pour l'écarter, appelait le mauvais infini."

47. Michel Foucault, *Language, Counter-memory, Practice: Selected Essays and Interviews*, p. 109.

48. Nietzsche, *History*, p. 28.

49. Sigmund Freud, *Beyond the Pleasure Principle*, p. 22.

50. Heisenberg, "Representation of Nature," p. 134.

51. Maurice Merleau-Ponty, *Phenomenology of Perception*, trans. Colin Smith (London: Routledge and Kegan Paul, 1962), pp. 410–11.

52. Kenner, *Stoic Comedians*, pp. 73–74.

53. Hartman, *Saving the Text*, pp. xxi–xxii.

54. Geoffrey Hartman, *Criticism in the Wilderness: The Study of Literature Today* (New Haven, Conn.: Yale Univ. Press, 1980), pp. 26–27.

55. Nietzsche, *History*, p. 69.

56. P. W. Bridgman, "The Instrumentally Extended World," in Sears and Lord, eds., *Discontinuous Universe*, pp. 141–42.

57. Ionesco, *The Lesson*, p. 76.

58. Frances A. Yates, *Giordano Bruno and the Hermetic Tradition* (Chicago: Univ. of Chicago Press, 1964), pp. 166–67. Yates quotes Anthony a Wood, *The History and Antiquities of the University of Oxford*, ed. J. Gutch, vol. 3, pt. 1 (*Annals*), p. 107.

59. Sigmund Freud, *Sexuality and the Psychology of Love*, p. 27.

60. Sigmund Freud, *Civilization and Its Discontents*, pp. 26–27.

61. Ibid., p. 26.

62. Ibid., p. 28.

63. Sigmund Freud, "The Uncanny," in *Studies in Parapsychology*, ed. Philip Rieff (New York: Collier Books, 1963), p. 29.

64. Stéphane Mallarmé, "L'Angoisse," in *Ouevres complètes*, ed. Henri Mondor and G. Jean-Audry (Paris: Gallimard, 1956), p. 69:

> Elle, défunte nue en le miroir, encor
> Que, dans l'oublie fermé par le cadre, se fixe
> De scintillations sitôt le septuor.

65. Freud, "The Uncanny," p. 47.

66. W. B. Yeats, *A Vision* quoted in "Yeats's Romanticism," by Allen Tate in *Yeats: A Collection of Critical Essays*, ed. John Unterecker (Englewood Cliffs, N.J.: Prentice-Hall, 1963), p. 157.

67. Robert Browning, "'Childe Roland to the Dark Tower Came,'" in *The Major Victorian Poets: Tennyson, Browning, Arnold*, ed. William E. Buckler (Boston: Houghton Mifflin, 1973), p. 283.

68. Ibid., p. 289.

69. Foucault, *Order*, p. 317.

70. Jorge Luis Borges, "A New Refutation of Time," in *Labyrinths: Selected Stories and Other Writings*, p. 226.

71. Nietzsche, *Tragedy*, p. 112.

72. Friedrich Nietzsche, *The Gay Science*, p. 333.

73. Nietzsche, *Tragedy*, p. 112.

74. Foucault, *Language*, p. 37.

75. Jacques Derrida, "White Mythology," quoted in "Who Rules Metaphor" by Dominick LaCapra, *Diacritics* 10, no. 4 (1980), p. 27.

76. Friedrich Nietzsche, *Beyond Good and Evil: Prelude to a Philosophy of the Future*, p. 161.

77. Nietzsche, *Tragedy*, p. 145.

78. Paul de Man, *Allegories of Reading: Figural Language in Rousseau, Nietzsche, Rilke, and Proust* (New Haven, Conn.: Yale Univ. Press, 1979), p. 10.

2. Librarians and Madness

1. Michel Foucault, *Madness and Civilization: A History of Insanity in the Age of Reason*, p. 18.

2. Ibid., pp. 18–19.

3. Ibid., p. 25.

4. Michel Foucault, *The Archaeology of Knowledge*, p. 215. As Melvin Friedman has pointed out, Foucault is in error when he refers to this Beckettian voice as that of Molloy. These words are spoken by the Unnamable at the end of his novel. In his translation of "L'Ordre du Discours," Rupert Sawyer has chosen to follow Foucault's French text rather than the English translation of the novel made by Patrick Bowles in collaboration with Beckett. (Cf. *L'innommable* [Paris: Editions de Minuit, 1953], p. 261: "il faut continuer, je ne peux pas continuer, . . . il faut dire des mots, tant qu'il y en a, il faut les dire, jusqu'à ce qu'ils me trouvent, jusqu'à ce qu'ils me disent, étrange peine, étrange faute, il faut continuer, c'est peut-être déjà fait, ils m'ont peut-être déjà dit.")

5. Foucault, *Madness*, p. 34.

6. Georg Lukács, *Soul and Form*, p. 8.

7. Foucault, *Archaeology*, p. 7.

8. Werner Hamacher, "The Reader's Supper: A Piece of Hegel," pp. 62–63.

9. Jacques Derrida, "Le Puits et le pyramide," in *Marges* (Paris: Editions de Minuit, 1972), p. 88. Quoted in Eugenio Donato, "Topographies of Memory," *Substance* 21 (1978), p. 39.

10. Jacques Derrida, "Cogito and the History of Madness," in *Writing and Difference*, trans. Alan Bass (Chicago: Univ. of Chicago Press, 1978), p. 36.

11. Ibid., pp. 34–35.

12. Octavio Paz, *Los hijos del limo* (Barcelona: Editorial Seix Barral, 1974), p. 109. "Ironía y analogía son irreconciliables. La primera es la hija del tiempo lineal, sucesivo e irrepetible; la segunda es la manifestación del tiempo cíclico: el futuro está en el pasado y ambos en el presente. La analogía se inserta en el tiempo del mito, y más: es su fundamento; la ironía pertenece al tiempo histórico, es la consecuencia (y la conciencia) de la historia."

13. Jean-Paul Sartre, *The Words*, trans. Bernard Frechtman (New York: George Braziller, 1964), p. 251.

14. Ibid., p. 199.

15. Derrida, "Cogito and the History of Madness," p. 46.

16. Michel Foucault, *The Order of Things: An Archaeology of the Human Sciences*, p. 326.

17. Foucault, *Madness*, pp. 20–21.

18. Foucault, *Order*, p. 46.

19. Marthe Robert, *The Old and the New: From "Don Quixote" to Kafka*, pp. 114–15.

20. Robert Alter, *Partial Magic: The Novel as a Self-Conscious Genre* (Berkeley: Univ. of California Press, 1975), p. 11.

21. Foucault, *Madness*, pp. 288–89.

22. Vladimir Nabokov, *Pale Fire*, p. 55. Further references will be contained within the text.

23. Samuel Beckett, *How It Is*, p. 42.

24. Flann O'Brien, *At Swim-Two-Birds*, p. 33. Further references will be contained within the text.

25. Alter, *Partial Magic*, p. 196.

26. Robert, *Old and the New*, p. 21. The reference to Kafka comes from *Wedding Preparations in the Country*.

27. Foucault, *Madness*, pp. 31–32.

28. James Joyce, *Ulysses*, p. 186.

29. Foucault, *Order*, p. 59.

30. Ibid., p. 46.

31. Ibid., p. 56.

32. Ibid., p. 49.

33. Robert, *Old and the New*, p. 104.

34. Miguel de Cervantes Saavedra, *Don Quixote of La Mancha*, p. 83. Further references will be contained within the text.

35. William Carlos Williams, *Paterson*, p. 95.

36. Vladimir Nabokov, Afterword to *Lolita* (New York: Berkley Publishing Corp., 1955), p. 286.

37. Sigmund Freud, *Sexuality and the Psychology of Love*, p. 168.

38. Foucault, *Order*, p. 48.

39. Michel Foucault, *Language, Counter-memory, Practice: Selected Essays and Interviews*, p. 67.

40. Vladimir Nabokov, *Speak Memory*, quoted in Alter, p. 184.

41. Quoted in Miles Orvell, "Entirely Fictitious: The Fiction of Flann O'Brien," *The Journal of Irish Literature* 3, no. 1, (1974), p. 94.

42. Jorge Luis Borges, "Partial Enchantments of the *Quixote*," in *Other Inquisitions*, p. 46.

3. The Self and the Catalogue

1. Trevor Winkfield, "(A)N(ECD)OTES" to "How I Wrote Certain of My Books," by Raymond Roussel (New York: Sun, 1977), p. 33.

2. Michel Foucault, *Language, Counter-memory, Practice: Selected Essays and Interviews*, p. 56.

3. Jorge Luis Borges, *Labyrinths: Selected Stories and Other Writings*, p. 213. Henceforth cited in the text as L.

4. Jonathan Swift, *Gulliver's Travels* (New York: The Modern Library, 1958), p. 146.

5. Jorge Luis Borges, *Other Inquisitions*, p. 57. Henceforth cited in the text as OI.

6. Piétro Citati, "L'imparfait bibliothécaire," *L'Herne* (1964), p. 274: "Celui qui voudrait écrire un livre nouveau devrait posséder une force d'imagination assez immense pour lui faire oublier l'existence de la Bibliothèque; mais Borges n'a pas d'imagination."

7. Anatole France, *The Crime of Sylvestre Bonnard*, p. 100. Further references will be contained within the text.

8. Mary Kinzie, "Recursive Prose," *TriQuarterly* no. 25 (Fall 1972), p. 48.

9. Jorge Luis Borges, *The Book of Sand*, p. 119. Henceforth cited in the text as BS.

10. George Herbert, "The Collar," in *The English Poems of George Herbert*, ed. C. A. Patrides (London: J. M. Dent and Sons, 1974), pp. 161–62.

11. Michel Foucault, *The Order of Things: An Archaeology of the Human Sciences* (New York: Random House, 1970), p. 387.

12. The word rendered as "convenient" is "cómodo" in the original Spanish text, a word that more adequately conveys the sense of uncanny discomfort felt in the presence of the monstrous book.

13. Foucault, *Order*, p. xviii.

14. Jorge Luis Borges, "To Leopoldo Lugones," *TriQuarterly* no. 25 (Fall, 1972), p. 186.

15. Maurice-Jean Lefebve, "Qui a écrit Borges," *L'Herne*, 1964, p. 226. "Supposons les volumes rangés de la manière suivante: d'abord tous les ouvrages dont la première lettre est A, puis tous ceux dont la première lettre est B, etc. Dans le groupe A, ceux dont la deuxième lettre est A, puis ceux dont la deuxième lettre est B. Et ainsi de suite. On voit aussitôt qu'un catalogue devrait mentionner, pour décrire et situer un ouvrage quelconque, *toutes* les lettres de cet ouvrage. Autrement dit, le catalogue de Babel doit reproduire, pour designer chaque volume, le volume entier. Le catalogue est donc une seconde bibliothèque identique à la première et contenue en elle. Ce qui est impossible par hypothèse, si tous les ouvrages sont distincts. La conclusion est qu'un monde fini et total ne peut contenir son image."

16. Kinzie, "Recursive Prose," pp. 49–50.

17. Nestor Ibarra, "From *Borges et Borges*: the final dialogues," *TriQuarterly* no. 25 (Fall, 1972), p. 98.

18. Jorge Luis Borges, *Ficciones*, p. 17. "'Yo reivindico para esa obra,' le oí decir, 'los rasgos esenciales de todo juego: la simetría, las leyes arbitrarias, el tedio.'"

19. Michel Butor, "La critique et l'invention," *Critique* (December 1967), p. 984. "La bibliothèque nous donne le monde, mais elle nous donne un monde faux; de temps en temps des fissures se produisent, la réalité se révolte contre les livres, par l'intermédiare des paroles ou de certains livres, un extérieur nous fait signe et nous donne le sentiment d'être enfermés; la bibliothèque devient donjon."

20. Jorge Luis Borges, *Evaristo Carriego*, quoted in Ronald Christ, "Borges justified: Notes and Texts Toward Stations of a Theme," *TriQuarterly* no. 25 (Fall 1972), p. 63.

21. Jorge Luis Borges, *El hacedor*, p. 72. "Yo que me figuraba el Paraíso / Bajo la especie de una biblioteca."

22. Borges, *Hacedor*, p. 84.

> Infinitos los veo, elementales
> Ejecutores de un antiguo pacto
> Multiplicar el mundo como el acto
> Generativo, insomnes y fatales.

23. Carter Wheelock, *The Mythmaker: A Study of Motif and Symbol in the Short Stories of Jorge Luis Borges* (Austin: Univ. of Texas Press, 1969), p. 8.

24. Tzvetan Todorov, *The Fantastic: A Structural Approach to a Literary Genre*, trans. Richard Howard (Ithaca, N.Y.: Cornell Univ. Press, 1973), p. 175.

25. Gérard Genette, "La littérature selon Borges," *L'Herne*, 1964, p. 327. "La littérature selon Borges n'est pas un sens tout fait, une révélation que nous avons á subir: c'est une réserve de formes qui attendent leur sens, c'est *l'imminence d'une révélation qui ne se produit pas.*"

26. Borges, *Hacedor*, pp. 155–56. "Un hombre se propone la tarea de dibujar el mundo. . . . Poco antes de morir, descubre que ese paciente laberinto de líneas traza la imagen de su cara."

27. Virgil, *The Aeneid*, trans. Rolfe Humphries (New York: Charles Scribner's Sons, 1951), pp. 19–20.

28. Kinzie, "Recursive Prose," p. 51.

4. The Refuge Turns Noxious

1. Edward Said, *Beginnings: Intention and Method* (New York: Basic Books, 1975), p. 302.

2. Ezra Pound, *The Cantos* (New York: New Directions, 1972), p. 8.

3. Jean-Paul Sartre, *Nausea*, trans. Lloyd Alexander (New York: New Directions, 1964), p. 40. Further references will be contained within the text.

4. Samuel Beckett, *Krapp's Last Tape* in *Krapp's Last Tape and Other Dramatic Pieces*, p. 24. Further references will be contained within the text.

5. Samuel Beckett, *Proust* (New York: Grove Press, 1957), pp. 2, 6.

6. Juan Goytisolo, *Count Julian*, p. 2. Further references will be contained within the text. The Spanish edition also referred to is: *Reivindicación del Conde don Julian* (Mexico City: Editorial Joaquín Mortiz, 1970).

7. Julio Ortega, "Entrevista con Juan Goytisolo," in *Juan Goytisolo*, by G. Sobejano, et al. (Madrid: Editorial Fundamentos, 1975), p. 126; "una obra cerrada, circular, totalizante que no deja, o aspira no dejar, ningún cabo suelto y obliga al lector a volver a cada paso sobre una serie de elementos que aparentemente habían cumplido ya su misión de información."

8. Ronald Hayman, *Samuel Beckett*, p. 74.

9. T. S. Eliot, "Baudelaire," in *Selected Prose*, ed. Frank Kermode (New York: Harcourt Brace Jovanovich, 1975), pp. 234–35.

10. Philippe Auguste Villiers de l'Isle-Adam, *Axel*, trans. June Guicharnaud (Englewood Cliffs, N.J.: Prentice-Hall, 1970), p. 48.

11. Edith Kern, *Existential Thought and Fictional Technique* (New Haven, Conn.: Yale Univ. Press, 1970), pp. 94–95. Kern says in a footnote: "Golffing's version is here too far removed from the original so I have given my own more literal translation based on *Die Geburt Tragödie* (Stuttgart: Alfred Kroner Verlag, 1945), p. 82."

12. Jacques Ehrmann, "Radical," in "Selections from Texts II," *Yale French Studies* no. 58 (1979), pp. 36–37.

13. It is pertinent to note that the enemy of the historico-mythic Don Julian was punished for his ravishment of Don Julian's daughter by having his penis devoured by a snake, and he died as a serpent penetrated his body. Cf. Genaro J. Pérez, *The Formalist Elements in the Novels of Juan Goytisolo* (Potomac, Md.: José Porrúa Turantes, North American Division, 1979), p. 140.

14. Maurice Barrès would seem to stand for Sartre (and Roquentin) in the same relation as the fictional Don Alvaro stands to Goytisolo's Count Julian. An author and a fervent supporter of General Boulanger, Maurice Barrès (1862–1923) was, like Don Alvaro, a fierce patriot and a strong believer in the moral and cultural value of close contact with the native soil. As P. E. Charvet indicates (*A Literary History of France*, vol. 5 [London: Ernst Benn, 1967], p. 127), "Historical fact, fiction and characters, all are made to subserve Barrès's main purpose, the communication of a moral message." This reduction of literature to sermonizing would be equally distasteful to Roquentin and Julian.

15. Fredric Jameson, *Sartre: The Origins of a Style*, p. 35.

16. Ibid., p. 36.

17. Ibid., p. 36.

18. Juan Goytisolo, *Juan the Landless*, trans. Helen R. Lane (New York: Viking Press, 1977), pp. 11, 13.

5. Burning the Books

1. Gaston Bachelard, *The Psychoanalysis of Fire*, p. 7.

2. Hayden White, *Metahistory: The Historical Imagination in Nineteenth-Century Europe* (Baltimore, Md.: Johns Hopkins Univ. Press, 1975), p. 363.

3. Harold Bloom, *Agon: Towards a Theory of Revisionism* (New York: Oxford Univ. Press, 1982), p. 67.

4. Michel Foucault, *Language, Counter-memory, Practice: Selected Essays and Interviews*, p. 160.

5. Norman O. Brown, *Closing Time* (New York: Random House, 1973), p. 44.

6. Mikhail Bakhtin, *Rabelais and His World*, trans. Hélène Iswolsky (Cambridge, Mass.: MIT Press, 1968), p. 9.

7. Foucault, *Language*, p. 160.

8. Bakhtin, *Rabelais*, p. 39.

9. Foucault, *Language*, p. 161.

10. Ibid., p. 160.

11. Michel Foucault, *The Order of Things*, p. 340.

12. Sigmund Freud, *Beyond the Pleasure Principle*, p. 9.

13. Harold Bloom, *Kabbalah and Criticism* (New York: Seabury Press, 1975), p. 89.

14. Foucault, *Order*, p. 10.

15. Samuel Beckett, *How It Is*, p. 9.

16. José Ortega y Gasset, *The Dehumanization of Art and Other Essays on Art, Culture, and Literature* (Princeton, N.J.: Princeton Univ. Press, 1968), p. 10.

17. Foucault, *Language*, p. 55.

18. Gustav Gusdorf, *Traité de metaphysique* (Paris: A. Colin, 1966), p. 228; "le miroir est-il absent des cultures primitives. . . . L'historien américain Mumford prétend que la vogue de l'autobiographie comme genre littéraire date du moment où l'on a appris a fabriquer des bons miroirs."

19. Roland Barthes, *Roland Barthes*, trans. Richard Howard (New York: Hill and Wang, 1977), p. 72.

20. Ramón López Velarde, "La última odalisca," in *Poesías completas y el minutero*, quoted in *El signo y el garabato* by Octavio Paz (Mexico City: Joaquín Mortiz, 1973), p. 203.

Voluptuosa melancolía:
en tu talle mórbido enrosca
el Placer su caligrafía
y le Muerte su garabato.

21. Jean-Paul Sartre, *Nausea*, p. 56.

22. Ibid., p. 33.

23. Johann Wolfgang Goethe, *Faust: Part One*, trans. Philip Wayne (Middlesex, England: Penguin Books, 1949), p. 70.

24. William Carlos Williams, *Paterson*, p. 100. Further references will be contained within the text.

25. Quoted in "Borges Justified: Notes and Texts toward Stations of a Theme" by Ronald Christ, *TriQuarterly* no. 25 (Fall 1972), p. 72.

26. Foucault, *Language*, p. 67.

27. Monroe K. Spears, *Dionysus and the City* (New York: Oxford Univ. Press, 1970), p. 30.

28. Jacques Derrida, *Writing and Difference*, p. 54.

29. Wallace Stevens, *The Collected Poems*, p. 57.

30. George Steiner, "The Gift of Tongues," review of *Auto-da-Fé*, by Elias Canetti, *New Yorker*, May 19, 1980, p. 155.

31. Elias Canetti, "The First Book: *Auto-da-Fé*," in *The Conscience of Words*, trans. Joachim Neugroschel, pp. 205—6.

32. William Carlos Williams, *The Great American Novel*, p. 50.

33. Foucault, *Language*, p. 47.

34. William Blake, "Jerusalem," in *Complete Writings*, ed. Geoffrey Keynes (New York: Oxford Univ. Press, 1972), p. 621.

35. Ralph Waldo Emerson, *Selections*, ed. Stephen E. Whicher (Boston: Houghton Mifflin, 1957), pp. 185—86.

36. Elias Canetti, *Auto-da-Fé*, p. 57. Further references will be contained within the text.

37. Foucault, *Language*, p. 67.

38. William Carlos Williams, "Of Medicine and Poetry," in *American Poetic Theory*, ed. George Perkins (New York: Holt, Rinehart and Winston, 1972), p. 256.

39. Helen Vendler, *Part of Nature, Part of Us: Modern American Poets* (Cambridge, Mass.: Harvard Univ. Press, 1980), p. 155.

40. J. K. Huysmans, *Against the Grain* (New York: Dover Publications, 1969), pp. 151—52.

41. Roland Barthes, *Critical Essays*, p. 126.

42. Goethe, *Faust*, p. 98.

43. Bachelard, *Psychoanalysis of Fire*, p. 7.

44. Brown, *Closing Time*, p. 23.

45. Richard A. Macksey, "'A Certainty of Music': Williams' Changes," in *William Carlos Williams: A Collection of Critical Essays*, p. 135.

46. Giambattista Vico, *The New Science*, pp. 72—73.

47. Joseph N. Riddel, *The Inverted Bell: Modernism and the Counterpoetics of William Carlos Williams*, p. 122.

48. Canetti, *Conscience*, p. 204.

49. Ibid.

50. Raymond Williams, "A Note on *Auto-da-Fé*," *New Left Review* 25 (1962), p. 106.

51. Bachelard, *Psychoanalysis of Fire*, pp. 13–14.

52. Sigmund Freud, *The Interpretation of Dreams*, p. 120.

53. Ibid., p. 194.

54. Emerson, *Selections*, p. 358.

55. Richard Shiff, "Art and Life: A Metaphoric Relationship," in *On Metaphor*, ed. Sheldon Sacks (Chicago: Univ. of Chicago Press, 1979), p. 107.

56. Liu Wu-Chi, *A Short History of Confucian Philosophy* (Middlesex, England: Penguin Books, 1955), p. 116.

57. Ernst Cassirer, *The Phenomenology of Knowledge*, vol. 3, *The Philosophy of Symbolic Forms*, p. 277.

58. Riddel, *Inverted Bell*, p. 248.

59. Emerson, *Selections*, p. 230.

60. Ibid.

61. James Joyce, *Finnegans Wake*, p. 378.

62. Riddel, *Inverted Bell*, p. 229.

63. Gabriêle D'Annunzio, *Il fuoco*, quoted in Bachelard, p. 56.

64. Jacques Derrida, Discussion of "Structure, Sign, and Play in the Discourse of the Human Sciences," in *The Structuralist Controversy*, eds. Richard Macksey and Eugenio Donato (Baltimore, Md.: Johns Hopkins Univ. Press, 1972), p. 271.

65. Stevens, "An Ordinary Evening in New Haven," in *Poems*, pp. 478–79.

66. Bachelard, *Psychoanalysis of Fire*, p. 19.

67. Williams, *Novel*, p. 60.

68. Friedrich Nietzsche, "A Critical Backward Glance" to *The Birth of Tragedy*, in *The Birth of Tragedy and the Genealogy of Morals*, trans. Francis Golffing (New York: Doubleday, 1956), p. 10.

69. Sigmund Freud, "The Uncanny," in *Studies in Parapsychology*, p. 36.

70. Derrida, *Structuralist Controversy*, p. 271.

6. Women in the Library

1. Gaston Bachelard, *The Psychoanalysis of Fire*, p. 13.

2. Sigmund Freud, *Civilization and Its Discontents*, p. 37.

3. Bachelard, *Psychoanalysis of Fire*, p. 53.

4. Freud, *Civilization*, p. 37.

5. Roland Barthes, *The Pleasure of the Text*, p. 35.

6. Ibid., p. 17.

7. William Carlos Williams, *Paterson*, p. 126. Further references will be contained within the text.

8. Sigmund Freud, *Beyond the Pleasure Principle*, p. 48.

9. Michel Foucault, *Language, Counter-memory, Practice: Selected Essays and Interviews*, pp. 50–51.

10. Jacques Lacan, "The Insistence of the Letter in the Unconscious," *Yale French Studies*, no. 36/37 (1966), p. 135.

11. Jacques Lacan, *The Language of the Self: The Function of Language in Psychoanalysis*, p. 59.

12. Ibid., p. 60.

13. Anthony Wilden, translator's notes to Lacan, *Language*, pp. 143–44.

14. Giambattista Vico, *The New Science*, p. 347.

15. Gabriel García Márquez, *Cien años de soledad* (Barcelona: Círculo de lec-

tores, 1967), p. 45. "Ésta es la vaca, hay que ordeñarla todas las mañanas para que produzca leche y a la leche hay que hervirla para mezclarla con el café y hacer café con leche."

16. Ibid., p. 46. ". . . repasar todas las mañanas, y desde el principio hasta el fin, la totalidad de los conocimientos adquiridos en la vida."

17. Françoise Gaillard, "An Unspeakable (Hi)story," *Yale French Studies*, no. 59 (1980), p. 150.

18. Lacan, *Language*, p. 13.

19. Lacan, *Language*, p. 21.

20. Anthony Wilden, *System and Structure: Essays in Communication* (New York: Barnes and Noble, 1972), p. 23.

21. Quoted by Anthony Wilden, "Lacan and the Discourse of the Other," in Lacan, *Language*, p. 269.

22. Friedrich Nietzsche, *The Gay Science*, pp. 122, 124.

23. Friedrich Nietzsche, *The Birth of Tragedy* in *The Birth of Tragedy and the Genealogy of Morals*, p. 10.

24. Jacques Derrida, "The Question of Style," in *The New Nietzsche: Contemporary Styles of Interpretation*, ed. David B. Allison (New York: Dell, 1977), pp. 185–86, 188.

25. Miguel de Cervantes Saavedra, *Don Quixote of La Mancha*, pp. 313–14. Further references will be contained within the text.

26. Marthe Robert, *The Old and the New: From "Don Quixote" to Kafka*, p. 147.

27. Anatole France, *The Crime of Sylvestre Bonnard*, p. 113. Further references will be contained within the text.

28. See for example ibid., p. 93: "I would that I could have a son who might be able to see you when I shall see you no more. How I should love him! Ah! such a son would—what am I saying?"

29. Geoffrey H. Hartman, *Saving the Text: Literature/Derrida/Philosophy*, p. 108.

30. Ibid., p. 110.

31. Samuel Beckett, *Krapp's Last Tape*, in *Krapp's Last Tape and Other Dramatic Pieces*, p. 25. Further references will be contained within the text.

32. John Fletcher and John Spurling, *Beckett: A Study of His Plays*, p. 89.

33. Eugene Webb, *The Plays of Samuel Beckett* (Seattle: Univ. of Washington Press, 1972), p. 73.

34. Elias Canetti, *Auto-da-Fé*, pp. 46–48. Further references will be contained within the text.

35. Elias Canetti, *The Tongue Set Free: Remembrance of a European Childhood*, trans. Joachim Neugroschel (New York: Seabury Press, 1979), p. 67.

36. In German: "Sein Kopf war ja FEUERrot."

37. Bachelard, *Psychoanalysis of Fire*, p. 30.

38. Jean-Paul Sartre, *Nausea*, p. 96. Further references will be contained within the text.

39. Sigmund Freud, *Sexuality and the Psychology of Love*, (New York: Macmillan, 1963), p. 168.

40. Ibid., p. 167.

41. Serge Doubrovsky, "'The Nine of Hearts': Fragment of a Psycho-Reading of *La Nausée*," p. 413.

42. Ibid., p. 418.

43. Ibid., p. 417.
44. Freud, *Sexuality*, p. 108.
45. Ibid., p. 119.
46. Ibid., p. 127.
47. Ibid., p. 126.
48. Ibid., p. 69.
49. Jacques Derrida, "Economimesis," pp. 23–25.
50. Ibid., p. 22.
51. Ibid., p. 25.
52. Ibid., p. 21.
53. Werner Hamacher, "The Reader's Supper: A Piece of Hegel," p. 67.
54. Freud, *Sexuality*, p. 212.
55. Nietzsche, *Tragedy*, p. 26.
56. Norman O. Brown, *Love's Body* (New York: Vintage Books, 1966), p. 124.
57. Ibid., p. 66.
58. Ibid., p. 125.
59. Jean-Paul Sartre, *The Words*, trans. Bernard Frechtman (New York: George Braziller, 1964), p. 96.
60. Friedrich Nietzsche, *The Use and Abuse of History*, trans. Adrian Collins (New York: Liberal Arts Press, 1957), pp. 48–49.
61. Freud, *Sexuality*, pp. 212–13.
62. Nietzsche, *Tragedy*, p. 102.
63. Stendhal, *The Red and the Black*, p. 30. Further references will be contained within the text.
64. Freud, *Sexuality*, p. 212.
65. Cf. ibid., p. 191.
66. William Carlos Williams, *The Great American Novel*, p. 17.
67. Quoted in *The Inverted Bell* by Joseph N. Riddel, p. 95.
68. H. J. Rose, *A Handbook of Greek Mythology* (New York: E. P. Dutton, 1959), p. 30.
69. Quoted in Hartman, p. 113.
70. Derrida, "Question of Style," p. 180.
71. Williams, *Novel*, p. 21.
72. Ibid., p. 21.
73. Robert Creeley, "A Character for Love," in *William Carlos Williams: A Collection of Critical Essays*, ed. J. Hillis Miller, Twentieth-century Views (Englewood Cliffs, N.J.: Prentice-Hall, 1966), p. 160.
74. Erich Neumann, *The Great Mother: An Analysis of the Archetype*, trans. Ralph Manheim (New York: Pantheon Books, 1955), p. 310.
75. Harold Bloom, *The Anxiety of Influence: A Theory of Poetry* (New York: Oxford Univ. Press, 1973), pp. 26, 37.
76. Octavio Paz, *Los signos en rotación y otros ensayos* (Madrid: Alianza Editorial, 1971), p. 77. "El excremento es *otro* falo, *otro* sol. Asimismo, es el sol podrido, como el oro es luz congelada. . . . Guardar oro es atesorar vida (sol) y retener el excremento."
77. William Carlos Williams, "Notes from a Talk on Poetry," *Poetry* 14 (1919), pp. 211–26, quoted in Jerome Mazzaro, *William Carlos Williams: The Later Poems* (Ithaca, N.Y.: Cornell Univ. Press, 1973), p. 12.
78. Geoffrey H. Hartman, *The Unmediated Vision: An Interpretation of Wordsworth, Hopkins, Rilke, and Valéry*, p. 156.

7. Women of the Book

1. Friedrich Nietzsche, *The Use and Abuse of History*, p. 32.
2. Jean-Paul Sartre, *The Words*, trans. Bernard Frechtman (New York: George Braziller, 1964), p. 194.
3. Ibid., p. 166.
4. Antonin Artaud, "L'Art et la mort," in *Oeuvres complètes*, vol. I (Paris: Gallimard, 1970), p. 173: "Ce flux, cette nausée, ces lanières, c'est dan *ceci* que commence le Feu. Le feu de langues. Le feu tissé en torsades de langues, dans le miroitemente de la terre qui s'ouvre comme un ventre en gésine, aux entrailles de miel et de sucre. De toute sa blessure obscène il bâille ce ventre mou, mais le feu bâille pardessus en langues tordues et ardentes. . . . La terre est mère sous la glace du feu."
5. Sandra M. Gilbert and Susan Gubar, *The Madwoman in the Attic* (New Haven, Conn.: Yale Univ. Press, 1979), pp. 498–99.
6. Charlotte Brontë, *Jane Eyre*, p. 91. Further references will be contained within the text.
7. George Eliot, *Middlemarch: A Study of Provincial Life*, p. 21. Further references will be contained within the text.
8. Gilbert and Gubar, *Madwoman in the Attic*, p. 361.
9. Doris Lessing, *The Memoirs of a Survivor*, p. 5. Henceforth referred to in the text as M.
10. Doris Lessing, *The Golden Notebook*, p. 525. Henceforth referred to in the text as GN.
11. Iris Murdoch, *A Severed Head*, p. 11. Further references will be contained within the text.
12. Cynthia Ozick, *Levitation: Five Fictions*, p. 34. Further references will be contained within the text.
13. Samuel Beckett, *Murphy* (New York: Grove Press, 1938), p. 103.
14. Monique Wittig, *Les Guérillères*, p. 89. Further references will be contained within the text.
15. Marcelle Thiébaux ("A Mythology for Women: Monique Wittig's *Les Guérillères*," *13th Moon* 4, no. 1 [1978]) and Laura Durand ("Heroic Feminism as Art," *Novel* 8 [1974]) have both discussed Wittig's use of the first two lines of Mallarmé's poem: "Le vierge, le vivace et le bel aujourd'hui / va-t-il nous déchirer avec un coup d'aile ivre, / ce lac dur . . ." in terms of Wittig's reversal of the male myth. I see the reference to the Master as Wittig's ironic recognition of the constraints of the library that imprisons the guérillères beyond denial or attempts at destruction.
16. Iris Murdoch, *Sartre: Romantic Rationalist* (London: Bowes and Bowes, 1953), p. 62.
17. Jacques Derrida, "All Ears: Nietzsche's Otobiography," trans. Avital Ronell, *Yale French Studies* no. 63 (1982), p. 250.
18. Barbara Bellow Watson, "Leaving the Safety of Myth: Doris Lessing's *The Golden Notebook*," in Robert K. Morris, ed., *Old Lines, New Frontiers: Essays on the Contemporary British Novel 1960–1970* (Cranbury, N.J.: Associated Univ. Presses, 1976), p. 31.
19. Julia Kristeva, *Pouvoirs de l'horreur* (Paris: Seuil, 1980), p. 240, quoted in Alice Jardine, "Introduction to Julia Kristeva's 'Women's Time'," *Signs* 7 (1981), p. 12.

Conclusion: Medusa and the Machine

1. Louis Marin, "The Inscription of the King's Memory: On the Metallic History of Louis XIV," *Yale French Studies*, no. 59 (1980), p. 20.

2. Wallace Stevens, "Sad Strains of a Gay Waltz," in *Collected Poems* (New York: Alfred A. Knopf, 1978), pp. 121–22.

3. Michel Foucault, *The Birth of the Clinic: An Archaeology of Medical Perception*, p. 197.

4. Jacques Derrida, "Force and Signification," in *Writing and Difference*, trans. Alan Bass (Chicago: Univ. of Chicago Press, 1978), pp. 19–20.

5. Joseph Conrad, *Letters to R. B. Cunninghame Graham*, Dec. 20, 1897, pp. 56–57.

6. Foucault, *Birth of the Clinic*, p. xvi.

7. Derrida, "Force and Signification," p. 14.

8. Tony Tanner, *Adultery in the Novel: Contract and Transgression* (Baltimore, Md.: Johns Hopkins Univ. Press, 1979), p. 21.

9. Hayden White, "Foucault Decoded," quoted in Allan Megill, "Foucault, Structuralism, and the Ends of History," *Journal of Modern History* 51 (1979), p. 456.

10. Derrida, "Force and Signification," p. 10.

11. Roland Barthes, *Critical Essays*, p. xvii.

12. Paul Valéry, *Lettres à quelques-uns* (Paris: La Nouvelle Revue Française, 1952), "à P. Louys," May 15, 1916, p. 114. Quoted in Geoffrey Hartman, *The Unmediated Vision* (New York: Harcourt, Brace and World, 1966), p. 129.

13. Friedrich Nietzsche, *The Use and Abuse of History*, trans. Adrian Collins (New York: Liberal Arts Press, 1957), pp. 44–45.

14. Derrida, "Force and Signification," p. 27.

15. Ibid., p. 26.

16. Ibid., p. 29.

17. Henri Birault, "Beatitude in Nietzsche," in *The New Nietzsche: Contemporary Styles of Interpretation*, ed. David B. Allison (New York: Dell, 1977), p. 230.

18. Joseph Campbell, *The Masks of God: Primitive Mythology* (New York: Viking Press, 1959), p. 170.

19. Roland Barthes, *The Pleasure of the Text*, pp. 3–4.

20. Geoffrey Hartman, "The Interpreter: A Self-Analysis," *New Literary History* 4 (1973), p. 221.

21. Georg Lukács, *Soul and Form*, p. 14.

22. Friedrich Nietzsche, "Letter to J. Burckhardt, 4 Jan. 1889," quoted in Paul Valadier, "Dionysus versus the Crucified," in Allison, *The New Nietzsche*, p. 251.

23. Foucault, *Birth of the Clinic*, p. 198.

SELECTED BIBLIOGRAPHY

Allison, David B., ed. *The New Nietzsche: Contemporary Styles of Interpretation.* New York: Dell Publishing Co., 1977.

Bachelard, Gaston. *The Psychoanalysis of Fire.* Translated by Alan C. M. Ross. Boston: Beacon Press, 1964.

Barthes, Roland. *Critical Essays.* Translated by Richard Howard. Evanston, Ill.: Northwestern Univ. Press, 1972.

————. *The Pleasure of the Text.* Translated by Richard Miller. New York: Hill and Wang, 1973.

Beckett, Samuel. *How It Is.* New York: Grove Press, 1964.

————. *Krapp's Last Tape.* In *Krapp's Last Tape and Other Dramatic Pieces.* New York: Grove Press, 1960.

Borges, Jorge Luis. *The Book of Sand.* Translated by Norman Thomas Di Giovanni. New York: E. P. Dutton, 1975.

————. *Ficciones.* Buenos Aires: Emece Editores, 1956.

————. *El hacedor.* Buenos Aires: Emece Editores, 1960.

————. *Labyrinths: Selected Stories and Other Writings.* Edited by Donald A. Yates and James E. Irby. New York: New Directions, 1962.

————. *Other Inquisitions.* Translated by Ruth L. C. Simms. Austin: Univ. of Texas Press, 1964.

Brontë, Charlotte. *Jane Eyre.* New York: Washington Square Press, 1953.

Canetti, Elias. *Auto-da-Fé.* Translated by C. V. Wedgwood. New York: Seabury Press, 1979.

————. *The Conscience of Words.* Translated by Joachim Neugroschel. New York: Seabury Press, 1979.

Cassirer, Ernst. *The Phenomenology of Knowledge.* vol. 3. *The Philosophy of Symbolic Forms.* Translated by Ralph Manheim. New Haven, Conn.: Yale Univ. Press, 1957.

Cervantes Saavedra, Miguel de. *Don Quixote of La Mancha.* Translated by Walter Starkie. New York: New American Library, 1964.

Conrad, Joseph. *Letters to R. B. Cunninghame Graham*. Edited by C. T. Watts. London: Cambridge Univ. Press, 1969.

Derrida, Jacques. "Economimesis." *Diacritics* 11, no. 2 (Summer, 1981), pp. 3–25.

———. *Writing and Difference*. Translated by Alan Bass. Chicago: Univ. of Chicago Press, 1978.

Doubrovsky, Serge. "'The Nine of Hearts': Fragment of a Psycho-Reading of *La Nausée*." *Boundary* 5 (1977), pp. 411–20.

Eliot, George. *Middlemarch: A Study of Provincial Life*. New York: Collier, 1962.

Fletcher, John and John Spurling. *Beckett: A Study of His Plays*. London: Methuen, 1978.

Foucault, Michel. *The Archaeology of Knowledge and The Discourse on Language*. Translated by A. M. Sheridan Smith. New York: Harper and Row, 1972.

———. *The Birth of the Clinic: An Archaeology of Medical Perception*. Translated by A. M. Sheridan Smith. New York: Random House (Vintage Books), 1975.

———. *Language, Counter-memory, Practice: Selected Essays and Interviews*. Translated by Donald F. Bouchard and Sherry Simon. Ithaca, N.Y.: Cornell Univ. Press, 1977.

———. *Madness and Civilization: A History of Insanity in the Age of Reason*. Translated by Richard Howard. New York: Random House, 1965.

———. *The Order of Things: An Archaeology of the Human Sciences*. New York: Random House (Vintage Books), 1970.

France, Anatole. *The Crime of Sylvestre Bonnard*. Translated by Lafcadio Hearn. New York: Dodd-Mead, 1918.

Freud, Sigmund. *Beyond the Pleasure Principle*. Translated and edited by James Strachey. New York: W. W. Norton, 1961.

———. *Civilization and Its Discontents*. Translated and edited by James Strachey. New York: W. W. Norton, 1961.

———. *The Interpretation of Dreams*. Translated by James Strachey. New York: Avon Books, 1965.

———. *Sexuality and the Psychology of Love*. Edited by Philip Rieff. New York: Macmillan, 1963.

———. *Studies in Parapsychology*. Edited by Philip Rieff. New York: Collier Books, 1963.

Goytisolo, Juan. *Count Julian*. Translated by Helen R. Lane. New York: Viking Press, 1974.

Hamacher, Werner. "The Reader's Supper: A Piece of Hegel." *Diacritics* 11, no. 2 (Summer 1981), pp. 52–67.

Hartman, Geoffrey H. *Saving the Text: Literature/Derrida/Philosophy*. Baltimore, Md.: Johns Hopkins Univ. Press, 1981.

———. *The Unmediated Vision: An Interpretation of Wordsworth, Hopkins, Rilke, and Valéry*. 2nd ed. New York: Harcourt, Brace, and World, 1966.

Hayman, Ronald. *Samuel Beckett*. New York: Frederick Ungar, 1973.

Jameson, Fredric. *Sartre: The Origins of a Style*. New Haven, Conn.: Yale Univ. Press, 1962.

Joyce, James. *Finnegans Wake*. New York: Penguin Books, 1967.

Lacan, Jacques. *The Language of the Self: The Function of Language in Psychoanalysis*. Translated by Anthony Wilden. New York: Dell Publishing Company, 1968.

Lessing, Doris. *The Golden Notebook*. New York: Bantam Books, 1962.

———. *The Memoirs of a Survivor*. New York: Bantam Books, 1975.

Lukács, Georg. *Soul and Form*. Translated by Anna Bostock. London: Merlin Press, 1971.

Miller, J. Hillis, ed. *William Carlos Williams: A Collection of Critical Essays*. Englewood Cliffs, N.J.: Prentice-Hall, 1966.

Murdoch, Iris. *A Severed Head*. Middlesex, England: Penguin Books, 1961.

Nabokov, Vladimir. *Pale Fire*. New York: G. P. Putnam's Sons, 1962.

Newman, Charles and Mary Kinzie, eds. *Prose for Borges*. TriQuarterly, no. 25 (Fall 1972).

Nietzsche, Friedrich. *Beyond Good and Evil: Prelude to a Philosophy of the Future*. Translated by Walter Kaufmann. New York: Random House, 1966.

————. *The Birth of Tragedy*. In *The Birth of Tragedy and The Genealogy of Morals*. Translated by Francis Golffing. New York: Doubleday, 1956.

————. *The Gay Science*. Translated by Walter Kaufmann. New York: Random House, 1974.

O'Brien, Flann (Brian O'Nolan). *At Swim-Two-Birds*. New York: New American Library, 1966.

Ozick, Cynthia. *Levitation: Five Fictions*. New York: Alfred A. Knopf, 1982.

Riddel, Joseph N. *The Inverted Bell: Modernism and the Counter-poetics of William Carlos Williams*. Baton Rouge, La.: Louisiana State Univ. Press, 1974.

Robert, Marthe. *The Old and the New: From "Don Quixote" to Kafka*. Translated by Carol Cosman. Berkeley: Univ. of California Press, 1977.

Roux, Dominique, et al., eds. *Jorge Luis Borges*. L'Herne (1964).

Sartre, Jean-Paul. *Nausea*. Translated by Lloyd Alexander. New York: New Directions, 1964.

Sobejano, G., et al. *Juan Goytisolo*. Madrid: Editorial Fundamentos, 1975.

Stendhal (Henri Beyle). *The Red and the Black*. Translated by Lloyd C. Parks. New York: New American Library, 1970.

Stevens, Wallace. *The Collected Poems*. New York: Alfred A. Knopf, 1978.

Vico, Giambattista. *The New Science*. Translated by Thomas Goddard Bergin and Max Harold Fisch. Ithaca, N.Y.: Cornell Univ. Press, 1970.

Villiers de l'Isle-Adam, Philippe Auguste. *Axel*. Translated by June Guicharnaud. Englewood Cliffs, N.J.: Prentice-Hall, 1970.

Williams, William Carlos. *The Great American Novel*, n.p.: Norwood Editions, 1978.

————. *Paterson*. New York: New Directions, 1963.

Wittig, Monique. *Les Guérillères*. Translated by David Le Vay. New York: Avon Books, 1969.

Index

The support given this book by the University of Tulsa Faculty Research Program is gratefully acknowledged.